Rick Steves' ®
PORTUGAL
2006

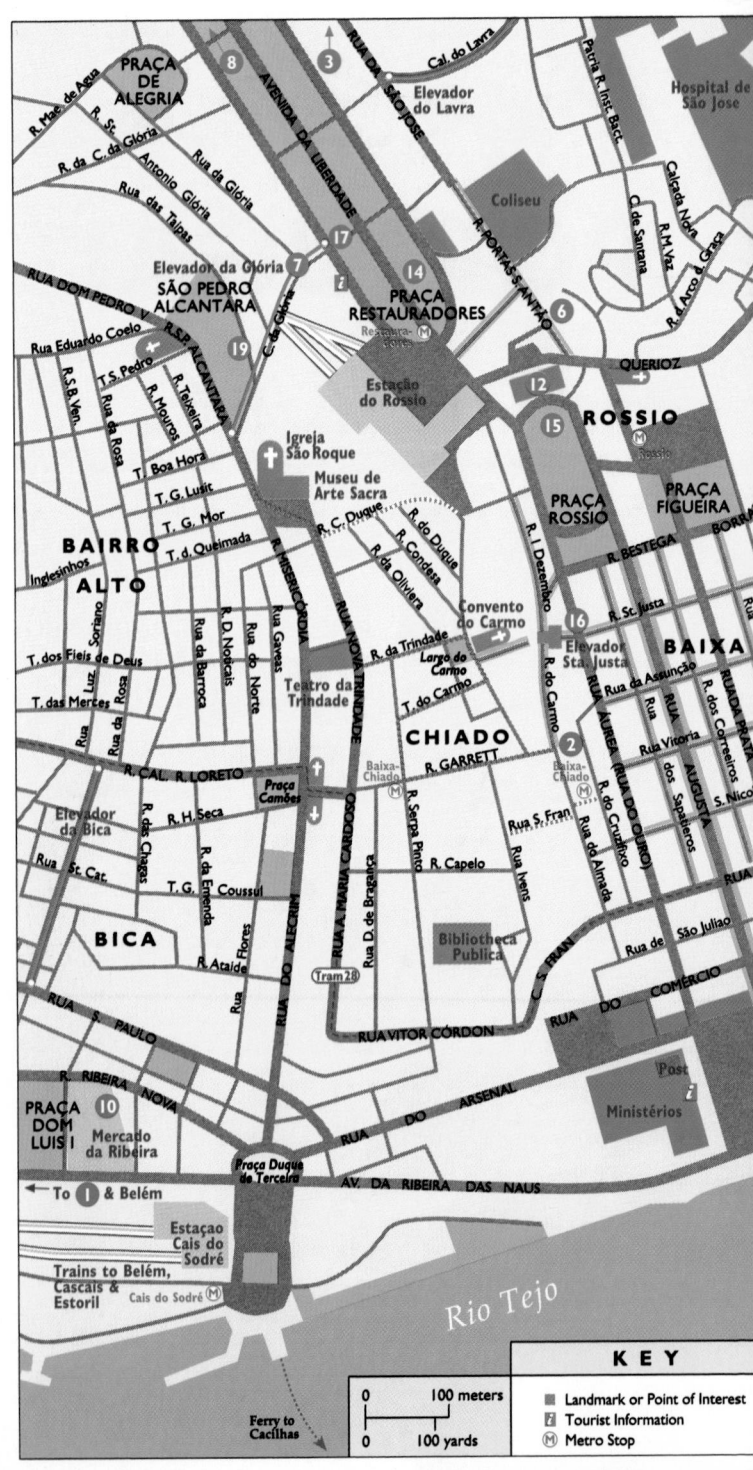

PRAÇA DE ALEGRIA

R. Mãe de Agua

R. Sc.

R. da C. da Glória

Antonio Glória

Rua das Talpas

Rua da Glória

AVENIDA DA LIBERDADE

Cal. do Lavra

RUA DE SÃO JOSÉ

Elevador do Lavra

Hospital de São Jose

Patria R. Inst. Bact.

Calçada Nova

R. M. Vaz

C. da Santana

R. d. Arco d. Graça

Coliseu

RUA PORTAS SANTÃO

Elevador da Glória

SÃO PEDRO ALCANTARA

Rua Eduardo Coelho

R.S.P. ALCANTARA

T.S. Pedro

R.S.B. Ven.

R. Teixeira

R. da Rosa

R. Mouros

R. da Rosa

Igreja São Roque

Museu de Arte Sacra

BAIRRO ALTO

T. Boa Hora

T. G. Lusit

T. G. Mor

T. d. Queimada

Inglesinhos

Vitoriano

T. dos Fieis de Deus

T. das Mertes

Rua da Rosa

R. D. Noronha

Rua da Barroca

Rua do Norte

Rua Gávea

R. C. Duque

R. do Duque

R. Condesa

R. da Oliveira

Convento do Carmo

R. da Trindade

Largo do Carmo

T. do Carmo

Teatro da Trindade

CHIADO

PRAÇA RESTAURADORES

Restaura-dores

Estação do Rossio

17

7

14

19

QUERIOZ

ROSSIO

Rossio

12

15

6

PRAÇA ROSSIO

PRAÇA FIGUEIRA

R. I. Dezembro

R. BESTEGA

BORRA

R. St. Justa

Elevador Sta. Justa

BAIXA

Rua da Assunção

RUA DA PRATA

Rua da Assunção

RUA DOS

RUA AUREA (RUA DO OURO)

RUA AUGUSTA

dos Sapateiros

R. dos Correeiros

Rua Vitoria

S. Nicol.

RUA

16

R. do Carmo

2

R. GARRETT

Baixa-Chiado

Baixa-Chiado

R. Serpa Pinto

R. Capelo

Rua S. Fran

Rua do Crucifixo

R. do Almada

Rua Ivens

BAIRRO ALTO

R. CAL. R. LORETO

Praça Camões

R. D. A. Seca

R. das Chagas

T. G. Emenda

Coussul

R. Ataide

RUA DA VARA CARDOSO

RUA NOVA TRINDADE

R. D. Flores

RUA DO ALECRIM

Tram 28

Rua D. de Bragança

Elevador da Bica

Rua St. Cat.

BICA

Biblioteca Publica

Rua de São Juliao

RUA DO COMERCIO

Post

Ministérios

RUA S. PAULO

R. RIBEIRA NOVA

PRAÇA DOM LUIS I

10

Mercado da Ribeira

To 1 & Belém

C. S. FRAN

RUA VITOR CORDON

RUA DO ARSENAL

Praça Duque de Terceira

AV. DA RIBEIRA DAS NAUS

Estação Cais do Sodré

Trains to Belém, Cascais & Estoril

Cais do Sodré

Ferry to Cacilhas

Rio Tejo

To 1 & Belém

KEY

0 — 100 meters	■ Landmark or Point of Interest
0 — 100 yards	*i* Tourist Information
	Ⓜ Metro Stop

Map labels (streets and places):

RUA DAMASCENO MONTEIRO

C. do Monte

R.D. OLIARIAS

RUA DOS LAGARES

RUA SENHORA GLORIA

Rua do Benformoso

R. do Terreirinho

LARGO DE GRAÇA

Largo da Graça

Convento
N. S. da Graça

T. da Pereira

RUA D. R. ROSALINA

DE PALMA

R. DOS CAVALEIROS

Rua de Mouraria

RUAV. DO OPERARIO

Liceu
Gil Vicente

Martin
Moniz

R.I. do Outeiro

Rua M. P. de Lima

P. de Coleginho

Tram 28

C. DE SANTO ANDRE

C. DE GRAÇA

R. DAS OLIVAS

TELHEIRO DE SÃO VICENTE

COSTA DO CASTELO

Museu da
Marioneta

M. S. VICENTE
de Fora

Rua das Farinhas

Castelo de
São Jorge

B. Lage

4

R.D. S.AVOMOTE

18

ALFAMA

R.S.O. do Castelo

R. Escolas Gerais

R. Escobas Gerais

C.M. Tancos

21

i

R.C. da Ferra

L. do C. Mor

11

Largo Portas do Sol

Rua da Madeira

R.M.S. ANTONIO L. LOIOS

R. Saudade

R.S. TIAGO

20

Largo Santa Luzia

R.S. Miguel

RUA DE SÃO MAMEDE

R.P. Negras

R.D. LIMOEIRO

R.N. Araujo

R.S. Pedro

TERREIRO TRIGO

To
Santa Apolónia
& Oriente
Train Stations,
Tile Museum &
Parque das Nações

Cruzes da Sé

Tram 28

Largo
Chafariz
de Dentro

9

R. Judiaria

R.D.

S. Ant.

5

Sé

R.S.J. da Praça

R. BACALHOEIROS

R. Padaria

R.D. CAIS D. SANTARÉM

Doca do Terreiro do Trigo

ONCEIÇÃO

RUA DA ALFÂNDEGA

INFANTE

DOM HENRIQUE

13

Ministérios

Doca da Marina

N

PRAÇA
DO
COMÉRCIO

Terreiro
do Paço

Estação Fluvial
Terreiro do Paço

River
Cruises

▦ Pedestrian-Friendly Area
▦ Popular Shopping Area
••••••• Walking Tour

LISBON SIGHTS

1. To Ancient Art Museum
2. Armazéns do Chiado Mall
3. To Bullring
4. Castelo São Jorge
5. Cathedral (Sé)
6. "Eating Lane"
7. Elevador da Glória Funicular
8. To Gulbenkian Museum & Sete Rios Station
9. House of Fado
10. Produce Market
11. Santo Silva Decorative Arts Museum

12. National Theater
13. Praça do Comércio
14. Praça dos Restauradores
15. Praça Rossio
16. Elevador de Santa Justa
17. Start of Bairro Alto and Chiado Stroll
18. Start of Alfama Stroll

Viewpoints:

19. Miradouro de São Pedro Alcantara
20. Miradouro de Santa Luzia
21. Miradouro São Jorge

Rick Steves' ®

PORTUGAL

2006

AVALON
TRAVEL

CONTENTS

INTRODUCTION   1

    Planning 3
    Resources 6
    Practicalities. 10
    Money 12
    Transportation 15
    Communicating 21
    Sleeping 24
    Eating. 28
    Traveling as a Temporary Local 31
    Back Door Travel Philosophy 33

PORTUGAL   35

Lisbon 38

Sintra 101

The Algarve 113
    Salema 115
    Cape Sagres 125
    Lagos 129
    Tavira 134

Évora 141

Nazaré and Nearby 157
    Nazaré 157
    Batalha. 166
    Fátima 172
    Alcobaça 174
    Óbidos 177

Coimbra. 184

Porto 207

Douro Valley. 237
    Peso da Régua. 247
    Pinhão 251

APPENDIX   255

Portuguese Capsule History **255**
Festivals and Public Holidays **257**
Let's Talk Telephones **259**
European Calling Chart **260**
Numbers and Stumblers **262**
Metric Conversion **262**
Climate Chart. **263**
Hotel Reservation Form. **264**
Portuguese Survival Phrases **265**

INDEX   267

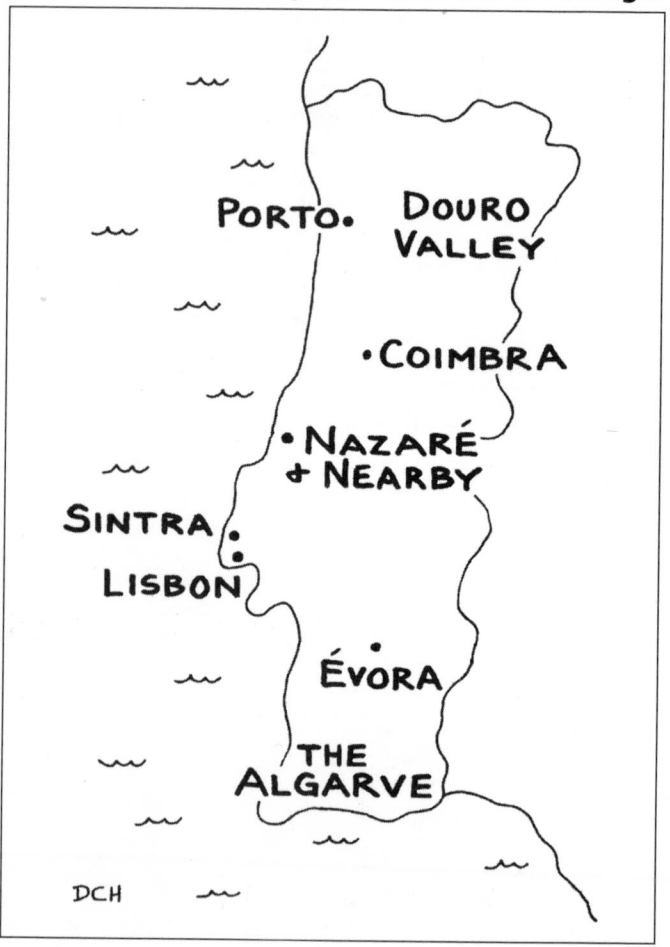

INTRODUCTION

Tucked into a far corner of the Continent, Portugal is Western Europe's least-touristed country. Its relative isolation preserves a traditional culture of widows in black and fishermen mending nets. Along with the old, you'll find the modern, culturally-rich capital of Lisbon, and resort towns that rival Spain's, but feel more authentic. If your idea of travel includes friendly locals (who speak no English), exotic architecture, windswept castles, and fresh seafood with chilled wine on a beach at sunset...you've chosen the right destination.

Because of its recent economic boom, Portugal is no longer Europe's bargain basement for travelers. But compared to the tourist-mobbed destinations of northern Europe, it's very affordable.

This book gives you all the information and opinions necessary to wring the maximum value out of your limited time and money. If you're planning a month or less in Portugal, this lean and mean little book is all you need.

Experiencing Portugal's culture, people, and natural wonders economically and hassle-free has been my goal for three decades of traveling, tour-guiding, and writing. With this book, I pass on to you the lessons I've learned, updated for 2006.

Rick Steves' Portugal is a tour guide in your pocket, with a balanced, comfortable mix of big cities and cozy towns. It covers the predictable biggies and stirs in a healthy dose of "Back Door" intimacy. You'll eat barnacles with green wine, recharge your solar cells in an Algarve fishing village, and wax nostalgic over bluesy fado singing. I've been selective, including only the most memorable sights and experiences. Rather than listing a string of mediocre Algarve beach towns, I focus on the top stops: Salema and Tavira.

The best is, of course, only my opinion. But after spending half my adult life researching Europe, I've developed a sixth sense for what travelers enjoy.

This Information Is Accurate and Up-to-Date

This book is updated every year. Most guidebook publishers can only afford an update once every two or three years (and even then, it's often by e-mail or fax). Since this book is selective, covering only the places that make the best two weeks or so in Portugal, it's easy for me to update it in person each summer. The telephone numbers and hours of sights listed in this book are accurate as of mid-2005. Even with annual updates, things change. Still, if you're traveling with the current edition of this book, I guarantee you're using the most up-to-date information available in print (for the very latest, see www.ricksteves.com/update). Also at our Web site, you'll find a valuable list of reports and experiences—good and bad—from fellow travelers who have used this book (www.ricksteves.com/feedback).

Use this year's edition. People who try to save a few bucks by traveling with an old book are not smart. They learn the seriousness of their mistake...in Portugal. Your trip costs about $10 per waking hour. Your time is valuable. This guidebook saves lots of time.

About This Book

This book is organized by destination. Each destination is a mini-vacation on its own, filled with exciting sights and homey, affordable places to stay. In the following chapters, you'll find:

Planning Your Time, a suggested schedule with thoughts on how best to use your limited time.

Orientation, including tourist information, city transportation, and an easy-to-read map designed to make the text clear and your arrival smooth.

Self-Guided Walks to take you through interesting neighborhoods, with a personal tour guide in hand.

Sights with ratings: ▲▲▲—Don't miss; ▲▲—Try hard to see; ▲—Worthwhile if you can make it; No rating—Worth knowing about.

Sleeping and **Eating,** with addresses and phone numbers of my favorite good-value hotels and restaurants.

Transportation Connections to nearby destinations by train, bus, or car.

The **appendix** is a traveler's tool kit, with telephone tips, a climate chart, a list of festivals, a brief look at Portuguese history, and a selection of key survival phrases.

Browse through this book, choose your favorite destinations, and link them up. Then have a great trip! You'll travel like a temporary local, getting the absolute most out of every mile, minute, and euro. As you travel the route I know and love, I'm happy you'll be meeting some of my favorite Portuguese people.

PLANNING

Trip Costs

Five components make up your trip cost: airfare, surface transportation, room and board, sightseeing/entertainment, and shopping/miscellany.

Airfare: Don't try to sort through the mess. Find and use a good travel agent. A basic round-trip U.S.-to-Lisbon flight should cost $700 to $1,300, depending on where you fly from and when (cheapest in winter). If you're adding Spain to your trip, consider saving time and money by flying "open jaw" (into one city and out of another; e.g., into Lisbon and out of Barcelona).

Surface Transportation: For a two-week whirlwind trip linking all of my recommended destinations, allow $150 per person for second-class trains and buses or $500 per person (based on 2 people sharing) for a two-week car rental, gas, and insurance. Car rental is cheapest to arrange from the U.S.

While train passes (generally designed to be purchased in your home country *before* arriving in Europe) are a convenience, they're a waste of money for a Portugal-only trip. It's cheaper to simply buy bus and train tickets as you go (see "Transportation," page 15).

Room and Board: You can thrive in Portugal on $80 a day for room and board. A $80-a-day budget allows $10 for lunch, $5 for snacks, $15 for dinner, and $50 for lodging (based on 2 people splitting the cost of a $100 double room that includes breakfast; note that hotels outside of Lisbon are often cheaper than $100 a day). If you have more money, I've listed great ways to spend it. And students and tightwads can get by on $30 a day ($15 per bed, $15 for meals and snacks).

Sightseeing and Entertainment: Allow $3 to $5 per major sight (museums, churches), $2 for minor ones (climbing towers), and about $30 for splurge experiences (fado concerts, bullfights). An overall average of $10 a day works for most. Don't skimp here. After all, this category is the driving force behind your trip—you came to sightsee, enjoy, and experience Portugal.

Shopping and Miscellany: Figure $1 per coffee, beer, ice-cream cone, and postcard. Shopping can vary in cost from nearly nothing to a small fortune. Good budget travelers find that this category has little to do with assembling a trip full of lifelong and wonderful memories.

Portugal's Two-Week Best Trip By Car

Day	Plan	Sleep in
1	Arrive in Lisbon	Lisbon
2	Lisbon	Lisbon
3	Sintra side-trip by train, pick up car and drive to Salema in evening	Salema
4	Salema	Salema
5	Salema, side-trip to Cape Sagres	Salema
6	To Tavira via Lagos	Tavira
7	To Évora	Évora
8	To Nazaré via Óbidos	Nazaré
9	Nazaré	Nazaré
10	Near Nazaré (Alcobaça, Batalha, and Fátima), continue to Coimbra	Coimbra
11	Coimbra	Coimbra
12	To Douro Valley	Douro Valley
13	Douro Valley, end in Porto (could drop car)	Porto
14	Porto	Porto
15	Fly out of Porto; or drive or train back to Lisbon; or drive north to Santiago, Spain	

Try to avoid being in Lisbon (or Porto) on a Monday, when many sights are closed (including Lisbon's Gulbenkian Museum and Monastery of Jerónimos, and Sintra's Pena Palace). If you like big cities, Lisbon is worth an extra day. But if you're a beach-lover, leave Lisbon early and drive to Salema.

If, after touring Portugal, you're continuing to the Spanish destinations of Salamanca or Madrid, it's better to visit Porto and the Douro Valley before Coimbra.

While this itinerary is designed to be done by car, it can be done by train and bus. Stay three nights in Lisbon and catch a bus to Salema on the morning of Day 4. Consider skipping Tavira unless you're a beach connoisseur. From the Algarve, take the bus to Évora (via Lagos) and spend a day and night, then take a bus to Nazaré (there's no direct service, so you have to go via

Sightseeing Priorities

Depending on the length of your trip, here are my recommended priorities:

3 days:	Lisbon, Sintra
6 days, add:	The Algarve (Salema and Tavira)
9 days, add:	Évora, Nazaré
11 days, add:	Sights near Nazaré, Coimbra
14 days, add:	Porto, Douro Valley

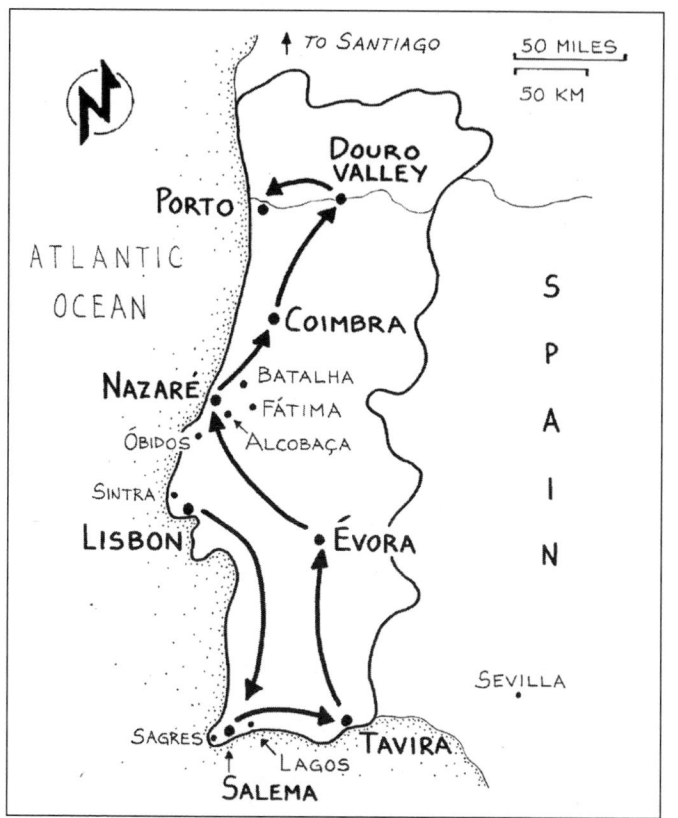

Lisbon). See the sights near Nazaré by bus, using Nazaré as your home base. Take the train to Coimbra. Catch the bus or train to Porto and, using Porto as a home base, see the Douro Valley on a combination boat/train tour (or, with extra time, spend the night).

When to Go

In peak season, May through September, sightseeing attractions are wide open. While it's not nearly as hot in Portugal as it is in Spain (except in the Alentejo region), an air-conditioned room is worth the splurge in summer.

Spring and fall offer the best combination of good weather, light crowds, long days, and plenty of tourist and cultural activities. In the off-season, roughly October through April, expect shorter hours, more lunchtime breaks, and fewer activities. Be sure to confirm your sightseeing plans locally, especially when traveling off-season. For weather specifics, see the climate chart in the appendix.

Travel Smart

Your trip to Portugal is like a complex play—easier to follow and really appreciate on a second viewing. While no one does the same trip twice to gain that advantage, reading this book in its entirety before your trip accomplishes much the same thing.

Design an itinerary that enables you to hit museums and festivals on the right days. As you read this book, note that Monday is a problem day, when many museums are closed. Sundays have the same pros and cons as they do for travelers in the U.S. Sightseeing attractions are generally open, shops and banks are closed, and public-transportation options are fewer. City traffic is light. Rowdy evenings are rare on Sundays. Saturdays are virtually weekdays with earlier closing hours (though transportation connections can be less frequent than on Mon–Fri).

Plan ahead for banking, laundry, post-office chores, and picnics. Maximize rootedness by minimizing one-night stands. Mix intense and relaxed periods. Every trip (and every traveler) needs at least a few slack days. Pace yourself. Assume you will return.

Reread this book as you travel and visit local tourist information offices. Upon arrival in a new town, lay the groundwork for a smooth departure; write down the schedule for the train or bus you'll take when you depart. Buy a phone card (or mobile phone) and use it for reservations and reconfirmations. Use taxis in the big cities, bring along a water bottle, and linger in the shade.

Connect with the culture. Set up your own quest for the best cod dish, cloister, fado bar, custard tart, or whatever. Enjoy the friendliness of the local people. Ask questions. Most locals are eager to point you in their idea of the right direction. Keep a notepad in your pocket for organizing your thoughts. Those who expect to travel smart, do.

RESOURCES

Tourist Information Offices

In the U.S.

The national tourist office in the U.S. is a wealth of information. Before your trip, get the free general information packet and request any specific information you want, such as city maps and schedules of upcoming festivals.

Portuguese National Tourist Office: 590 5th Ave., 4th floor, New York, NY 10036, tel. 800/PORTUGAL or 212/354-4403, fax 212/764-6137, www.visitportugal.com, tourism@portugal.org. Maps, regional information, golf courses, and beach resorts.

In Portugal

Your best first stop in a new city is the tourist information office (abbreviated as **TI** in this book). Get a city map and advice on public transportation (including bus and train schedules), special events, and recommendations for nightlife. Some TIs have information on the entire country. When you visit a TI, try to pick up maps for towns you'll be visiting later in your trip.

While the TI has listings of all lodgings and is eager to book you a room, use its room-finding service only as a last resort (bloated prices, fees, no opinions, and they take a cut from your host). You'll get a far better value by using the listings in this book and booking direct.

Rick Steves' Guidebooks, Public Television Show, and Radio Show

Rick Steves' Europe Through the Back Door gives you budget-travel skills, such as minimizing jet lag, packing light, planning your itinerary, traveling by car or train, finding rooms, changing money, avoiding rip-offs, buying a mobile phone, hurdling the language barrier, staying healthy, taking great photographs, using a bidet, and much more. The book also includes chapters on 38 of my favorite "Back Doors," including two on Portugal.

Country Guides: These annually updated books offer you the latest on the top sights and destinations, with tips on how to make your trip efficient and fun. Here are the titles:

Rick Steves' Best of Europe	*Rick Steves' Great Britain*
Rick Steves' Best of	*Rick Steves' Ireland*
Eastern Europe	*Rick Steves' Italy*
Rick Steves' England (new in 2006)	*Rick Steves' Portugal*
Rick Steves' France	*Rick Steves' Scandinavia*
Rick Steves' Germany	*Rick Steves' Spain*
& Austria	*Rick Steves' Switzerland*

City and Regional Guides: Updated every year, these focus on Europe's most compelling destinations. Along with specifics on sights, restaurants, hotels, and nightlife, you'll get self-guided, illustrated tours of the outstanding museums and most characteristic neighborhoods.

Rick Steves' Amsterdam,	*Rick Steves' Prague*
Bruges & Brussels	*& the Czech Republic*
Rick Steves' Florence	*Rick Steves' Provence*
& Tuscany	*& the French Riviera*
Rick Steves' London	*Rick Steves' Rome*
Rick Steves' Paris	*Rick Steves' Venice*

Rick Steves' Phrase Books: In Portugal, a phrase book is as fun as it is necessary. This practical and budget-oriented series covers Portuguese, Spanish, Italian, French, German, and French/Italian/German. You'll be able make hotel reservations over the phone, chat with your cabbie, and bargain at street markets.

And More Books: *Rick Steves' Europe 101: History and Art for the Traveler* (with Gene Openshaw) gives you the story of Europe's people, history, and art. Written for smart people who were sleeping in their history and art classes before they knew they were going to Europe, *101* helps Europe's sights come alive.

Rick Steves' Easy Access Europe, geared for travelers with limited mobility, covers London, Paris, Bruges, Amsterdam, and the Rhine River.

Rick Steves' Postcards from Europe, my autobiographical book, packs 25 years of travel anecdotes and insights into the ultimate 2,000-mile European adventure.

My latest book, *Rick Steves' European Christmas*, covers the joys, history, and quirky traditions of the holiday season in seven European countries.

Public Television Show: My series, *Rick Steves' Europe*, keeps churning out shows. Several of the nearly 100 shows feature sights covered in this book.

Radio Show: My new weekly radio show, which combines call-in questions (à la *Car Talk*) and interviews with travel experts, airs on public radio stations. For a schedule of upcoming topics, an archive of past programs, and details on how to call in, see www.ricksteves.com/radio.

Other Guidebooks

Especially if you'll be traveling beyond my recommended destinations, you may want some supplemental information. When you consider the improvement it will make in your $3,000 vacation, $30 for extra maps and books is money well spent. Particularly for several people traveling by car, the extra weight and expense are negligible. One budget tip can save the price of an extra guidebook.

Lonely Planet's *Portugal* is thorough, well-researched, and packed with good maps and hotel recommendations for various budgets. The similar *Rough Guide to Portugal* and *Rough Guide to Lisbon* are hip and insightful, written by British researchers. Neither of these is updated annually—use them only with a one- or two-year-old copyright. The highly-opinionated *Let's Go: Spain & Portugal*, researched every year by Harvard students, is great for students and vagabonds. If you're a low-budget train traveler interested in hosteling and the youth and nightlife scene (which I have basically ignored), get *Let's Go: Spain & Portugal*. Older travelers enjoy Frommer's *Portugal* guide, even though it, like the Fodor's guide, ignores alternatives that enable travelers to save money by dirtying their fingers in the local culture. The popular, skinny *Michelin Green Guide: Portugal* is excellent, especially if you're driving. The green guides are known for their city and sightseeing maps, dry but concise and helpful information on all major sights, and good cultural and historical background. English editions are sold in Portugal. The encyclopedic *Blue Guide Portugal* is as dry as the sands of the Algarve, but just right for scholarly types.

The colorful, popular Eyewitness series has editions covering Portugal, Lisbon, and the Algarve. They're fun for their great, easy-to-grasp graphics and photos, 3-D cutaways of buildings, aerial-view maps of historic neighborhoods, and cultural background. But the Eyewitness written content is relatively skimpy, and the books weigh a ton. I simply borrow them for a minute from other travelers at certain sights to make sure I'm aware of that place's highlights. The *Time Out* travel guide provides good, detailed coverage of Lisbon, particularly on arts and entertainment.

Portuguese history is mentioned (but not thoroughly covered) in various guidebooks, such as Cadogan, Eyewitness, and the Michelin Green Guide.

Recommended Reading

To get the feel of Portugal while still in the States, consider reading some of these books:

Non-Fiction: *Portugal: A Companion History* (Jose Hermano Saraiva); *The History of Portugal* (James Anderson); *The Portuguese Empire, 1415–1808* (A. J. R. Russell-Wood); *Over the Edge of the World: Magellan's Terrifying Circumnavigation of the Globe* (Laurence Bergreen); *Unknown Seas: How Vasco Da Gama Opened The East* (Ronald Watkins); *Prince Henry the Navigator: A Life* (Peter Russell); *Food of Portugal* (Jean Anderson); Lonely Planet's *World Food Portugal* (Lynelle Scott-Aitken and Clara De Vitorino).

Fiction: *Baltasar and Blimunda* and *Blindness* (both by José Saramago, who won the 1998 Noble Prize for Literature); *Pereira Declares: A Testimony* and *Requiem: A Hallucination* (both by Antonio Tabucchi); *The Last Kabbalist of Lisbon* (Richard Zimler); *The Lusíads* (Luís Vaz de Camões); and *Distant Music* (Lee Langley).

Maps

The black-and-white maps in this book, designed and drawn by Dave Hoerlein, are concise and simple. Dave, who is well-traveled in Portugal, designed the maps to help you get oriented and find places listed in the text quickly and painlessly. His maps also point out the local tourist information office, where you can pick up free

Begin Your Trip at www.ricksteves.com

At www.ricksteves.com you'll find a wealth of **free information** on destinations covered in this book, including fresh European travel and tour news every month and helpful "Graffiti Wall" tips from thousands of fellow travelers.

While you're there, the **online Travel Store** is a great place to save money on travel bags and accessories designed by Rick Steves to help you travel smarter and lighter, plus a wide selection of guidebooks, planning maps, and DVDs.

Traveling through Europe by rail is a breeze, but choosing the right railpass for your trip—amidst hundreds of options—can drive you nutty. At www.ricksteves.com, you'll find **Rick Steves' Annual Guide to European Railpasses**—your best way to convert chaos into pure travel energy. Buy your railpass from Rick, and you'll get a bunch of free extras to boot.

Travel agents will tell you about mainstream tours of Europe, but they won't tell you about **Rick Steves' tours.** Rick Steves' Europe Through the Back Door travel company offers more than two dozen itineraries and 300 departures reaching the best destinations in this book...and beyond. You'll enjoy the services of a great guide, a fun bunch of travel partners (with group sizes in the twenties), and plenty of room to spread out in a big, comfy bus. You'll find trips to fit every vacation size, from week-long city getaways to longer cross-country adventures. For details, visit www.ricksteves.com or call 425/771-8303 ext 217.

in-depth maps (some hotels have them too). Better maps are sold at newsstands—take a look before you buy to make sure it has the level of detail you want.

Drivers should invest in a good 1:400,000 map—such as Michelin's *Spain & Portugal Tourist and Motoring Atlas* or *Portugal Map*—and learn the key to maximize the sightseeing value. Good regional driving maps are available throughout Portugal. Train travelers can do fine with a simple rail map (such as the one that comes with a train pass) and city maps from TIs.

PRACTICALITIES

Red Tape: You currently need a passport, but no visa and no shots, to travel in Portugal.

Time: In Portugal, and in this book, you'll be using the 24-hour clock. After 12:00 noon, keep going—13:00, 14:00, and so on. For anything over 12, subtract 12 and add p.m. (14:00 is 2:00 p.m.).

Though Portugal and Spain are neighbors, Portugal sets

its clock one hour earlier than Spain and most of continental Europe. (This is always true, even during daylight saving time.) Portugal's time zone is the same as Great Britain's: five hours ahead of the U.S.' East Coast and eight hours ahead of the West Coast.

Business Hours: Many businesses take an afternoon break (about 13:00–15:00). When it's 100 degrees in the shade, you'll understand why. Small shops are usually open on Saturday only in the morning and are closed all day Sunday. The biggest museums stay open all day. Smaller ones often close for lunch.

Discounts: Don't expect youth or senior discounts on sights in Portugal. Discounts are generally available only to people who are members of the European Union and "reciprocating countries," meaning countries that offer discounts to European youths and seniors. The U.S. isn't big on giving price breaks to Europeans.

Metric: Get used to metric. A liter is about a quart, four to a gallon. A kilometer is six-tenths of a mile. I convert kilometers to miles by cutting them in half and adding back 10 percent of the original (120 km: 60 + 12 = 72 miles, 300 km: 150 + 30 = 180 miles).

Watt's Up? If you're bringing electrical gear, you'll need a two-prong adapter plug (sold cheap at travel stores in the U.S.) and a converter. Travel appliances often have convenient, built-in converters; look for a voltage switch marked 120V (U.S.) and 240V (Europe).

News: Portugal's main English-language newspaper is the colorful *Portugal News* (www.the-news.net). Americans keep in touch with the *International Herald Tribune* (published almost daily via satellite). Every Tuesday, the European editions of *Time* and *Newsweek* hit the stands with articles of particular interest to European travelers. Sports addicts can get their fix from *USA Today*. Good Web sites include www.portugalpost.com and http://news.bbc.co.uk.

Theft Alert: Thieves target tourists throughout Portugal, especially in Lisbon. While hotel rooms are generally safe, thieves snatch purses, pick pockets, and break into cars. Be on guard, use a money belt, and treat any disturbance around you as a smoke screen for theft. Don't believe any "police officers" looking for counterfeit bills. When traveling by train, keep your backpack in sight. For tips for drivers, see page 21).

Language Barrier: Portugal can surprise English-speaking travelers with one of the biggest language barriers in Western Europe.

Portuguese is difficult to learn and pronounce. If you're having trouble communicating in Portuguese, try English, French, and Spanish, in that order (because some locals give Spanish-speakers the cold shoulder). The Portuguese do, however, speak more English than their Spanish neighbors, since English is required in school. (Their American movies are also subtitled, while the Spanish get their Hollywood flicks dubbed.)

Locals visibly brighten when you know and use some key Portuguese words (see "Portuguese Survival Phrases" in the appendix). Travel with a phrase book, particularly if you want to interact with local people. You'll find that doors open quicker and with more smiles when you can speak a few words of the language.

Considering how fun it is to eat local dishes, the food phrase list in this book is particularly helpful (see "Typical Portuguese Foods," page 29). Use it and you'll eat much better than the average tourist.

MONEY

Exchange Rates

I list prices in euros throughout this book. Portugal uses the euro currency.

---

1 euro (€) = about $1.20

Just like the dollar, the euro is broken down into 100 cents. You'll find coins ranging from 1 cent to 2 euros, and bills from 5 euros to 500 euros. To roughly convert prices in euros to dollars, add 20 percent to Portuguese prices: €20 is about $24, €45 is about $55, and so on.

While the euro is the only official currency in Portugal, you might still see and hear locals quoting prices in the old currency, the *escudo,* especially in supermarkets and hotels. If you see a price in the thousands for an ordinary item, it's likely in *escudos.*

Banking

Bring plastic (ATM, credit, or debit cards) along with several hundred dollars in hard cash as an emergency backup. Traveler's checks are a waste of time and money.

Portugal has readily available, easy-to-use, 24-hour ATMs with English instructions. I've traveled painlessly throughout Portugal with my VISA debit card. Before you go, verify with your bank that your card will work, inquire about fees (can be up to $5 per transaction), and alert them that you'll be making withdrawals in Europe; otherwise, the bank may not approve transactions if it perceives unusual spending patterns. Bring an extra copy of your card (or another of your cards) just in case one gets demagnetized or gobbled up by a machine. In Portugal, all ATMs are marked by a white sign with blue lettering that says MB, or *Multibanco.*

Damage Control for Lost or Stolen Cards

If you lose your credit, debit, or ATM card, you can stop people from using your card by reporting the loss immediately to the respective global customer-assistance centers. Call these 24-hour U.S. numbers collect: Visa (tel. 410/581-9994), MasterCard (tel. 636/722-7111), and American Express (tel. 336/393-1111).

Have, at a minimum, the following information ready: the name of the financial institution that issued you the card, along with the type of card (classic, platinum, or whatever). Ideally, plan ahead and pack photocopies of your cards—front and back—to expedite their replacement. Providing the following information will allow for a quicker cancellation of your missing card: full card number, whether you are the primary or secondary cardholder, the cardholder's name exactly as printed on the card, billing address, home phone number, circumstances of the loss or theft, and identification verification (your birth date, your mother's maiden name, or your Social Security number—memorize this, don't carry a copy). If you are the secondary cardholder, you'll also need to provide the primary cardholder's identification-verification details. You can generally receive a temporary card within two or three business days in Europe.

If you promptly report your card lost or stolen, you typically won't be responsible for any unauthorized transactions on your account, although many banks charge a liability fee of $50.

Visa and MasterCard are more commonly accepted than American Express. Just like at home, credit or debit cards work easily at larger hotels, restaurants, and shops, but smaller businesses prefer payment in local currency. If you have lots of large bills, break them at a bank, especially if you like shopping at mom-and-pop places; they rarely have huge amounts of change.

Banks are generally open Monday through Friday from 8:30 to 15:00. They charge outrageous, unregulated commissions for cashing a traveler's check (about $9). Shop around. Sometimes the hole-in-the-wall exchange offices offer better deals than the bank. Look for the rare American Express office. Better yet, use a cash machine.

Use a money belt (a pouch with a strap that you buckle around your waist like a belt and wear under your clothes). Thieves target tourists. A money belt provides peace of mind, allowing you to carry lots of cash more safely.

Don't be petty about withdrawing money. You don't need to waste time every few days tracking down a cash machine. Change a week's worth of money, get big bills, stuff them in your money belt, and travel!

VAT Refunds and Customs Regulations

VAT Refunds for Shoppers: Wrapped into the purchase price of your souvenirs is a Value Added Tax (VAT) that's generally about 19 percent. If you make a purchase of more than €60 in Portugal at a store that participates in the VAT refund scheme, you're entitled to get most of that tax back. Personally, I've never felt that VAT refunds are worth the hassle, but if you do, here's the scoop.

If you're lucky, the merchant will subtract the tax when you make your purchase (this is much more likely to occur if the store ships the goods to your home). Otherwise, here's what you'll need to do:

Get the paperwork. Have the merchant completely fill out the necessary refund document, called a "cheque." You'll have to present your passport at the store.

Have your cheque(s) stamped at the border or airport at your last stop in the European Union by the customs agent who deals with VAT refunds. It's best to keep your purchases in your carry-on for viewing, but if they're too large or dangerous (such as knives) to carry on, then track down the proper customs agent to inspect them before you check your bag. You're not supposed to use your purchased goods before you leave. If you show up at customs wearing your hand-knit Portuguese sweater, officials might look the other way—or deny you a refund.

To collect your refund, you'll need to return your stamped documents to the retailer or its representative. Many merchants work with a service, such as Cashback or Premier Tax Free, which have offices at major airports, ports, or border crossings. These services, which extract a 4 percent fee, can refund your money immediately in your currency of choice or credit your card (within 2 billing cycles). If you have to deal directly with the retailer, mail the store your stamped documents, and then wait. It could take months.

Customs Regulations: You can take home $800 in souvenirs per person duty-free. The next $1,000 is taxed at a flat 3 percent. After that, you pay the individual item's duty rate. You can also bring in duty-free a liter of alcohol (slightly more than a standard-sized bottle of wine), a carton of cigarettes, and up to 100 cigars. As for food, anything in cans or sealed jars is acceptable. Don't bring back dried meats, cheeses, or fresh fruits and veggies. To check customs rules and duty rates, visit www.customs.gov.

TRANSPORTATION

By Car or Train?

Cars are best for three or more traveling together (especially families with small kids), those packing heavy, and those scouring the countryside. Trains and buses are best for solo travelers, blitz tourists, and city-to-city travelers.

Overview of Trains and Buses

Portugal straggles behind the rest of Europe in train service, but offers excellent bus transportation. Off the main Lisbon–Porto–Coimbra train lines, buses are usually a better bet. In cases where buses and trains serve the same destination, the bus is often more efficient, offering more frequent connections and sometimes a more central station.

The best public-transportation option is to mix bus and train travel. Always verify bus or train schedules before your departure. Never leave a station without your next day's schedule options in hand. To ask for a schedule at an information window, say, *"Horario para _____–_____* (fill in names of cities), *faz favor."* (The local TI will sometimes have schedules available for you to take or copy.) To study train schedules in advance, see www.cp.pt (for domestic routes) or Germany's handy all-Europe web site http://bahn.hafas .de/bin/query.exe/en, for international connections.

Departures and arrivals are *partidas* and *chegadas,* respectively. These key Portuguese "fine-print" words may also come in handy in your travels: Both *as* and *aos* mean "on"; *de* means "from," as in "from this date to that date"; *só* means "only," as in "only effective on..."; *não* means "not"; and *feriado* means "holiday." On schedules, exceptions are noted, like in this typical qualifier: *"Não se efectua aos sábados, domingos, e feriados oficiais"* ("Not effective on Saturdays, Sundays, and official holidays").

Trains (Comboios)

Portugal has a mix of slow milk-run trains and an occasional Expresso. On Portuguese train schedules, *diario* means "daily" and *mudança de comboio* means "change trains."

Because you'll use a mix of trains and buses on your trip, a Portuguese Flexipass is generally not a good value. If you're traveling beyond Portugal, the Iberic Flexipass (which includes Spain) or Eurail Selectpass can make sense, but use the pass wisely, only for your long train trips. These passes are sold outside of Europe only. For specifics, see the railpass chart on page 16, contact your travel agent, or see my Guide to European Railpasses at www .ricksteves.com/rail. Even if you have a railpass, use buses when

Railpasses

Prices listed are for 2005. My free Rick Steves' Guide to European Railpasses has the latest prices and details (and easy online ordering) at www.ricksteves.com/rail.

Saverpass prices are per person for 2 or more people traveling together. Kids 4-11 pay half adult or saver fare on all rail-only passes. Youth prices are only for those under 26.

SPAIN FLEXIPASS

	1st Class	2nd Class
Any 3 days in 2 months	$225	$175
Extra rail days (max. 7)	35	30

SPAIN-PORTUGAL FLEXIPASS

	1st Class Individual	1st Class Saverpass
Any 3 days in 2 months	$259	$229
Extra rail days (max 7)	35	30

Covers Spain and Portugal. Saverpass prices are per person based on two or more traveling together. Kids 4-11 half of individual or saver fare, under 4 free.

PORTUGUESE FLEXIPASS

1st class: Any 4 days out of 15 for $130. Kids 4-11 half fare, under 4 free. Not valid on Hotel Train to Madrid.

Iberia:

Map shows approximate point-to-point one-way 2nd class rail fares in $US. 1st class costs 50% more. Add up fares for your itinerary to see whether a railpass will save you money. Dashed lines are buses.

SPAIN RAIL & DRIVE PASS

Any 3 rail days and 2 car days in 2 months.

	1st Class	Extra car day
Economy car	$249	$39
Compact car	269	49
Intermediate car	279	59
Compact automatic	299	80

Prices are per person for 2 traveling together. Solo travelers pay $50-$75 extra. 3rd and 4th persons sharing car buy only the railpass. Extra rail days (2 max) cost $39. To order Rail & Drive passes, call Rail Europe at 800/438-7245.

FRANCE–SPAIN PASS

	1st Class Individual	1st Class Saver	2nd Class Individual	2nd Class Saver	2nd Class Youth
Any 4 days in 2 months	$309	$269	$269	$239	$199
Extra rail days (max 6)	34	30	30	26	23

EURAIL SELECTPASS

This pass covers travel in three adjacent countries.

	1st Class Selectpass	1st Class Saverpass	2nd Class Youthpass
5 days in 2 months	$370	$316	$241
6 days in 2 months	410	348	267
8 days in 2 months	488	414	317
10 days in 2 months	564	480	367

Please go to www.ricksteves.com/rail for four- and five-country options.

they're more convenient and direct than the trains.

Overnight Trains: If you'll be going to Madrid, book ahead for the overnight train to ensure you get a berth and/or seat. It's a pricey Hotel Train called the "Lusitania" (prices listed on page 16; railpass accepted if you pay extra sleeper fee). No cheaper rail option exists between these two capital cities. You can save money by taking a bus (€40, Intercentro Lines), or save time by taking a plane (average fare for a Madrid–Lisbon flight is €220).

Buses (Autocarros)

Portugal has a number of different bus companies, sometimes running buses to the same destinations and using the same transfer points. If you have to transfer, make sure to look for a bus with the same name/logo as the company you bought the ticket from. The largest national company is Rede Expressos (www.rede-expressos .pt). You can pre-plan bus trips between cities online, but you should always confirm the schedule in person.

A few buses are entirely non-smoking; others are non-smoking only in the front. When you buy your ticket for a long-distance bus (4 hours or more), ask for non-smoking *(não fumador)*. It's usually futile, since passengers ignore the signs, but it's a statement.

If the bus station is not central, ask at the tourist information office about travel agencies near your hotel that sell bus tickets. Don't leave a bus station to explore a city without checking your departure options and buying a ticket in advance if necessary (and possible). Bus service on holidays, Saturdays, and especially Sundays can be dismal.

You can (and most likely will be required to) stow your luggage under the bus. For longer rides, give some thought to which side of the bus will get the most sun, and sit on the opposite side. Even if a bus is air-conditioned and has curtains, direct sunlight can still heat up your seat.

Drivers and station personnel rarely speak English. Buses usually lack WCs but stop every two hours or so for a break (usually 15 min, but can be up to 30). Ask the driver, "How many minutes here?" *("Quántos minutos aqui?")* so you know if you have time to get out. Bus stations have WCs (rarely with toilet paper) and cafés offering quick and cheap food.

Your ride will likely come with a soundtrack: taped music (usually American pop), a radio, or sometimes videos. If you prefer silence, bring earplugs.

Bus schedules in Portugal are clearly posted at each major station. *Directo* is "direct." *Ruta* buses are slower because they make many stops en route. Posted schedules list most, but not all, destinations. If your intended destination isn't listed, check at the ticket/information window for the most complete

Portugal's Public Transportation

SANTIAGO
LUGO
TO SAN SEBASTIÁN
VIGO
OURENSE
GUILLAREI
VALENÇA
BRAGA
PINHÃO
POCINHO
TO SALAMANCA
PORTO
REGUA
GUARDA
PAMPIL-HOSA
TO SALAMANCA
FIG. DO FOZ
VILA FORMOSA
COIMBRA
VALADO
NAZARÉ
ÓBIDOS
MARVÃO
CÁCERES
TO MADRID
SINTRA
ENTRON.
CASCAIS
LISBON
ÉVORA
MÉRIDA
FUNCHEIRA
BEJA
TO MADRID
SAGRES
TUNES
SALEMA
AVE
SEVILLA
LAGOS
FARO
TAVIRA
AYA.
VILA REAL
DCH

— RAIL LINES
--- BUS
AVE AVE HIGH SPEED RAIL-SPAIN
···· BOAT
o BORDER TOWNS

schedule information. For long trips, your ticket might include an assigned seat.

Taxis (Táxis)

Most taxis are reliable and cheap. Drivers generally respond kindly to the request, "How much is it to ____, more or less?" ("Quanto é para ____, mais ou menos?") Rounding the fare up to the nearest large coin (maximum of 10 percent) is adequate for a tip. City rides cost $4 to $8. Keep a map in your hand so the cabbie knows (or thinks) you know where you're going. Big cities have plenty of taxis. In many cases, couples can travel by cab for little more than two bus or subway tickets.

Car Rental

Research car rentals before you go. It's cheaper to arrange car rentals from the U.S., either with your travel agent or directly with the companies. You'll want a weekly rate with unlimited mileage. I normally rent the smallest, least expensive model. Figure about $500 a week, including gas and insurance. For three weeks or longer, it's cheaper to lease; you'll save money on taxes and insurance. Comparison shop through your agent. Remember, you can turn in your car at any office on any day (normally

with credit for early turn-in or extra charge for extension). Also remember that rental offices usually close from midday Saturday until Monday.

For peace of mind, I spring for the Collision Damage Waiver insurance (CDW, about $15–25 per day), which limits my financial responsibility in case of an accident. Unfortunately, CDW now has a high deductible hovering around $1,000–1,500. When you pick up your car, many car-rental companies will try to sell you "super CDW" at an additional cost of $7–15 per day to lower the deductible to zero.

Some credit cards offer CDW-type coverage for no charge to their customers. Quiz your credit-card company on the worst-case scenario. You have to choose between the coverages offered by your car-rental company and your credit-card company. This means that if you go with the credit-card coverage, you'll have to decline the CDW offered by the car-rental company. In this situation, some car-rental companies put a hold on your credit card for the amount of the full deductible (which can equal the value of the car). This is bad news if your credit limit is low—particularly if you plan on using that card for other purchases during your trip.

Another alternative is buying CDW insurance from Travel Guard for $9 a day (U.S. tel. 800/826-4919, www.travelguard .com). It's valid throughout Europe, but some car-rental companies refuse to honor it, especially in Italy and the Republic of Ireland. Oddly, residents of some states (including Washington) are not allowed to buy this coverage.

Driving in Portugal: Distance and Time

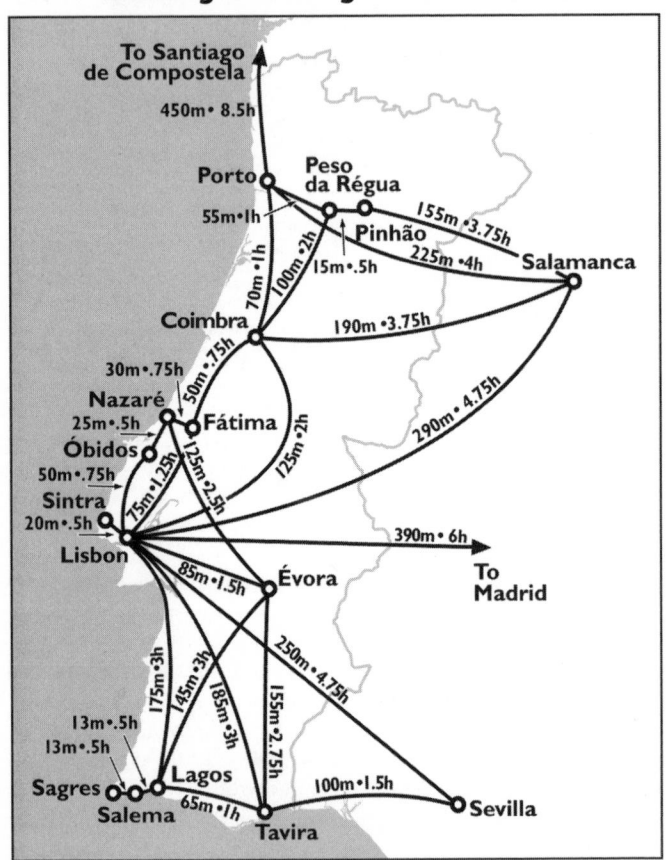

To Santiago de Compostela
450m • 8.5h

Porto
Peso da Régua
55m•1h
Pinhão
100m •2h
70m •1h
15m•.5h
155m •3.75h
225m •4h
Salamanca

Coimbra
190m •3.75h
290m • 4.75h

30m•.75h
50m•.75h
Nazaré
25m•.5h
Fátima
125m•2h
Óbidos
50m•.75h
Sintra
75m•1.25h
125m•2.5h
20m•.5h
Lisbon
85m•1.5h
Évora
390m • 6h
To Madrid

175m•3h
145m•3h
185m•3h
155m•2.75h
250m • 4.75h

13m•.5h
13m•.5h
Sagres
Lagos
65m•1h
Salema
Tavira
100m•1.5h
Sevilla

In sum, buying CDW—and the supplemental insurance to buy down the deductible, if you choose—is the easiest but priciest option. Using the coverage that comes with your credit card is cheaper, but can involve more hassle. If you're taking a short trip, an easy solution is to buy Travel Guard's very affordable CDW. For longer trips, leasing is the best way to go.

Driving

Drivers in Portugal encounter sparse traffic and generally good roads. While the International Driver's License is officially required (cheap and easy to obtain from the nearest AAA office; bring 2 photos and $10), I drive in Portugal with only my U.S. driver's license. (The Portuguese version of AAA is the Automóvel Clube de Portugal.)

You can pick up a Michelin map in the U.S. or buy one of

the good, inexpensive maps available throughout Portugal. Freeways come with tolls (about $5/hr), but save huge amounts of time. Always pick up a ticket as you enter a toll freeway, and then pick up tickets at each opportunity along the way (or risk a fine). Don't use the no-stop-necessary speed lane (labeled *Reservada a Aderentes,* reserved for locals with a monthly pass), or you'll pay for a trip across the country in order to exit—a lesson I learned the expensive way. On freeways, navigate by direction *(norte, oeste, sul, este).* Also, since road numbers can be confusing and inconsistent, navigate by city names.

Portugal, statistically one of Europe's most dangerous places to drive, has lots of ambulances on the road. Drive defensively. If you're involved in an accident, expect a monumental head-ache—you will be blamed. Seat belts are required by law. Expect to be stopped for a routine check by the police (be sure your car-insurance form is up-to-date). Small towns come with speed traps and corruption. Tickets, especially for foreigners, are issued and paid for on the spot. Insist on a receipt so the money is less likely to end up in the cop's pocket.

Gas and diesel prices are controlled and the same every-where—around $5 a gallon for gas *(gasolina)*, less for diesel *(diesel).*

Choose parking places carefully. Ask your hotelier for advice. In cities, you can park safely but expensively in guarded lots. Parking areas in cities generally have a large white "P" on a blue background. Don't assume it's free—check around for meters or ticketing machines. Keep your valuables in your hotel room, or, if you're between destinations, covered in your trunk. Leave noth-ing worth stealing in the car, especially overnight. If your car's a hatchback, take the trunk cover off at night so thieves can look in without breaking in. Try to make your car look locally owned by hiding the "tourist-owned" rental-company decals and putting a local newspaper in your front or back window.

COMMUNICATING

Telephones
Smart travelers learn the phone system and use it daily to reserve or reconfirm rooms, get tourist information, or phone home.

Types of Phones
You'll encounter various kinds of phones in your European travels.

Portuguese **pay phones** are easy to find but refuse to be rushed. After you insert your card into the phone, dial slowly and deliberately. To make a new call, push the square R button. The phone doesn't beep to remind you that you've left the card in, so don't forget to remove it when you're done.

Hotel room phones are fairly cheap for local calls, but pricey for international calls, unless you use an international phone card (see below).

American mobile phones work in Europe if they're GSM-enabled, tri-band (or quad-band), and on a calling plan that includes international calls. With a T-Mobile phone, you can roam using your home number, and pay $1–2 per minute for making or receiving calls.

Some travelers buy a **European mobile phone** in Europe. For about $125, you can get a phone that will work in most countries once you pick up the necessary chip (about $30) per country. Or you can buy a cheaper, "locked" phone that only works in the country where you purchased it (about $100, includes $20 worth of calls). If you're interested, stop by any European shop that sells mobile phones; you'll see prominent store window displays. You aren't required to (and shouldn't) buy a monthly contract—buy prepaid calling time instead (as you use it up, buy additional minutes at newsstands or mobile-phone shops). If you're on a budget, skip mobile phones and use international phone cards instead.

Paying for Calls

You can spend a fortune making phone calls in Europe...but why would you? Here's the skinny on different ways to pay, including the best deals.

Portuguese Phone Cards: These come in two types—official phone cards that you insert into a pay phone, and international phone cards that can be used from virtually any phone. Either type of phone card works only in Portugal.

An **insertable phone card,** called a *cartão telefónico,* is used to make calls from a pay phone. You can buy these cards at post offices and many newsstand kiosks. To use an insertable card, simply slide it into the slot on the phone, wait for a dial tone and digital readout to show how much value remains on your card, and dial your local, long-distance, or international call. The cost of the call is automatically deducted from your card. These cards are best for making calls within Portugal.

An **international phone card,** called a *cartão telefónico com código pessoal,* is a better deal for overseas calls. Unlike the official phone cards, an international phone card is *not* inserted into the phone. Instead, you dial the toll-free number listed on the card, reaching an automated operator. When prompted, you dial in a scratch-to-reveal code number, also written on the card. Then dial your number. You can use the cards to make local and domestic long-distance calls as well. Since they're not insertable, you can use them from any phone—including the one in your hotel room (if your phone is set on pulse, switch it to tone). You can buy an international phone card at most kiosks and newsstands, but the best selection is usually at hole-in-the-wall shops catering to immigrants, who are the leading experts on calling home cheaply. These cards, made by numerous (sometimes fly-by-night) companies, offer good rates but don't consistently work well. Try to confirm that the card can be used for calls to America (the salesclerk may not know), and buy a lower-denomination card in case the card is defective.

Dialing direct from your hotel room without using an international phone card is usually quite expensive for international calls, but it is convenient. I always ask first how much I'll be charged. Keep in mind that you have to pay for local and occasionally even toll-free calls.

Receiving calls in your hotel room is often the cheapest way to keep in touch with the folks back home—especially if your family has an inexpensive way to call you (either a good deal on their long-distance plan, or a prepaid calling card with good rates to Europe). Give them a list of your hotels' phone numbers before you go. As you travel, send your family an e-mail or make a quick payphone call to set up a time for them to call you, and then wait for the ring.

Metered phones are sometimes available in bigger post offices. You can talk all you want, then pay the bill when you leave—but be sure you know the rates before you have a lengthy conversation.

U.S. Calling Cards (such as the ones offered by AT&T, MCI, or Sprint) are the worst option. You'll nearly always save a lot of money by paying for your call in any of the other ways described above.

How to Dial

Calling from the U.S. to Portugal, or vice versa, is simple—once you break the code. The European calling chart on page 260 will walk you through it. Remember that Portugal time is five/eight hours ahead of the East/West Coasts of the U.S.

Dialing within Portugal: Portugal has a direct-dial phone system (no area codes). To call anywhere within Portugal, just dial the number. For example, one of my recommended Lisbon hotels is 213-219-030. To call it from a Lisbon train station, just dial 213-219-030. If you call it from Salema, it's the same: 213-219-030. All phone numbers in Portugal are nine digits.

Dialing International Calls: When calling internationally, dial the international access code (00 if you're calling from Europe, 011 from the U.S. or Canada), the country code of the country you're calling (351 for Portugal; see appendix for list of other countries), and the local number. So, to call the Lisbon hotel from the U.S., dial 011 (the U.S. international access code), 351

(Portugal's country code), then 213-219-030. To call my office in Edmonds, Washington, from Portugal, I dial 00 (Europe's international access code), 1 (the U.S. country code), 425 (Edmonds' area code), and 771-8303.

E-mail and Mail

E-mail: Cybercafés and little hole-in-the-wall Internet-access shops (offering a few computers, no food, and cheap prices) are popular in most cities. E-mail use among Portuguese hoteliers is increasing. I've listed e-mail addresses when possible. Some family-run pensions can become overwhelmed by the volume of e-mail they receive, so be patient if you don't get an immediate response.

Wireless Internet access (Wi-Fi) is becoming more common throughout Portugal. (Spain and Portugal are locked in a technology rivalry to see who can catch up with the rest of Europe the fastest—tech-savvy tourists benefit.) If you travel with a Wi-Fi-enabled laptop and know where to look, you'll find hundreds of spots to get online (see the latest list at www.ptwifi.pt).

Mail: To arrange for mail delivery, reserve a few hotels along your route in advance and give their addresses to friends. Allow 10 days for a letter to arrive. E-mailing and phoning are so easy that I've dispensed with mail stops.

SLEEPING

Portugal offers some of the best accommodation values in Western Europe. Most places are government-regulated, with posted prices. While prices are low, street noise can be high. Always ask to see your room first. Check the price posted on the door, consider potential night-noise problems, ask for another room, or bargain down the price. You can request *com vista* (with a view) or *tranquilo* (quiet). In most cases, the view comes with street noise. Breakfast will frequently be included in your hotel room cost; double-check before accepting a room. Most of the year, prices are soft.

In the interest of smart use of your time, I favor hotels (and restaurants) handy to your sightseeing activities. Rather than list hotels scattered throughout a city, I describe my favorite couple of neighborhoods and recommend the best accommodations values in each, from $10 bunks to $270 suites.

All rooms have sinks with hot and cold water. Rooms with private bathrooms are often bigger and renovated, while the cheaper rooms without bathrooms often will be dingier and/or on the top floor. Any room without a bathroom has access to a bathroom on the corridor. Towels aren't routinely replaced every day, so drip-dry and conserve.

Sleep Code

To help you easily sort through these listings, I've divided the rooms into three categories based on the price for a standard double room with bath:

$$$ Higher Priced
$$ Moderately Priced
$ Lower Priced

To pack maximum information into minimal space, I use this code to describe accommodations in this book. Prices listed are per room, not per person. When there is a range of prices in one category, that means the price fluctuates with the season; these seasons are usually posted at the hotel desk. Especially in resort areas, prices go way up in July and August. Hotel breakfasts are often included in Portugal.

S = Single room (or price for one person in a double).
D = Double or twin. Double beds are usually big enough for nonromantic couples.
T = Triple (often a double bed with a single bed moved in).
Q = Quad (an extra child's bed is usually cheaper).
b = Private bathroom with toilet and shower or tub.
s = Private shower or tub only (the toilet is down the hall).

According to this code, a couple staying at a "Db-€90" hotel would pay a total of €90 (about $110) for a double room with a private bathroom. You can assume a hotel takes credit cards unless you see "cash only" in the listing. The hotel staff speaks basic English unless otherwise noted.

Types of Accommodations

Hotels: Don't judge hotels by their bleak and dirty entryways. Landlords, stuck with rent control, often stand firmly in the way of hardworking hoteliers who'd like to brighten up their buildings.

Any regulated place will have a complaint book *(livro de reclamações)* checked by authorities. A request for this book will generally prompt the hotelier to solve your problem to keep you from writing a complaint.

Hotels are officially prohibited from using central heat before November 1 and after April 1 (unless it's unusually cold); prepare for cool evenings if you travel in spring and fall. Summer can be extremely hot. Consider air-conditioning, fans, and noise (since you'll want your window open), and don't be shy about asking for ice at the fancier hotels. Many rooms come with mini-refrigerators (if it's noisy at night, unplug it).

Most hotel rooms with air-conditioners come with control sticks (like a TV remote, sometimes requires a deposit) that generally have the same symbols and features: fan icon (click to toggle through wind-power from light to gale); louver icon (choose steady air flow or waves); snowflake and sunshine icons (heat or cold, depending on season); clock ("O" setting: run X hours before turning off; "I" setting: wait X hours to start); and the temperature control ($20°$ or $21°$ Celsius is comfortable).

Historic Inns: Portugal has luxurious, government-sponsored historic inns. These *pousadas* are often renovated castles, palaces, or monasteries, many with great views and stately atmospheres. While full of Old World character, they often are run in a very sterile, bureaucratic way. These are pricey (doubles $110–260), but can be a good deal for younger people (30 and under) and seniors (60 and over), who often get discounted rates; for details, bonus packages, and family deals, see www.pousadas.pt.

Rooms in Private Homes: You'll find rooms in private homes, typically in touristy areas where locals decide to open up a spare room and make a little money on the side. These rooms are usually as private as hotel rooms, often with separate entries. Especially in resort towns, the rooms might be in small, apartment-type buildings. Ask for a *quarto*. They're cheap ($25–45 for a double without breakfast) and usually a good experience.

Hostels and Campgrounds: Portugal has plenty of youth hostels and campgrounds, but considering the great bargains on other accommodations, I don't think they're worth the trouble and don't cover them in this book. Instead, I prefer simple family-run hotels (*pensões* and *residencials*); they're easy to find, inexpensive, and, when chosen properly, a fun part of the Portuguese cultural experience. If you're on a starvation budget or just prefer camping or hosteling, plenty of information is available in backpacker guidebooks (see "Resources," page 6), through the national tourist office, and at local tourist information offices.

Making Reservations

Even though Easter, July, and August are often crowded, you can travel at any time of year without reservations. But given the high stakes and the quality of the gems I've found for this book, I'd recommend calling ahead for rooms. You can reserve long in advance from home or grab rooms a few days to a week in advance as you travel.

If you prefer the flexibility of traveling without reservations, you'll have greater success of snaring the best rooms if you arrive early in the day. When you anticipate crowds, call hotels between 9:00 and 10:00 on the day you plan to arrive, when the hotel clerk knows who'll be checking out and just which rooms will be available. Risk-takers on a tight budget can save pocketfuls of euros by traveling with no reservations and taking advantage of the discounted prices hotels offer when it's clear they'll have empty rooms that day. A few of the hotels I recommend offer discounted prices if you have this book; mention it—and claim the discount—when you call to reserve.

I've taken great pains to list telephone numbers with long-distance instructions (see "Telephones," page 21; also see the appendix). Use the telephone and convenient telephone cards. Most hotels listed are accustomed to English-only speakers. (If you have difficulty, ask the fluent receptionist at your current hotel to call for you.) A hotel receptionist will usually trust you and hold a room until 16:00 without a deposit, though some will ask for a credit-card number.

If you know where you want to stay each day (and you don't need or want flexibility), reserve your rooms from the U.S. in advance. To book from home, e-mail, phone, or fax your request. Phone and fax costs are reasonable, e-mail is a steal (and preferred by most hotels), and simple English is usually fine. To fax, use the handy form in the appendix (online at www.ricksteves.com /reservation). If you don't get an answer to your fax request, consider that a "no." (Many little places get 20 faxes a day after they're full, and they can't afford to respond.)

A two-night stay in August would be "2 nights, 16/8/06 to 18/8/06." (Europeans write the date in this order—day/month/year—and hotel jargon uses your day of departure.)

If you receive a response from the hotel stating its rates and room availability, it's not a confirmation. You must confirm that you indeed want a room at the given rate. One night's deposit is generally required. Your credit-card number will usually be accepted as the deposit. Be sure to fax your card number (rather than e-mail it) to keep it private, safer, and out of cyberspace. You can pay with your card or cash when you arrive; if you don't show up, your card will be billed for one night. To make things easier on yourself and the hotel, be sure you really intend to stay at the hotel on the dates you requested. These family-run businesses lose money if they turn away customers while holding a room for someone who doesn't show up. Understandably, some hotels bill no-shows for one night. *If you must cancel, do so well in advance.* Long distance is cheap and easy from public phone booths. Don't let these people down—I promised you'd call and cancel if for some reason you won't show up.

Reconfirm your reservations a few days in advance for safety, and let them know about what time you'll arrive. Don't needlessly confirm rooms through the tourist office or Web services; they'll take a commission of up to 20 percent. On the small chance that a hotel loses track of your reservation, bring along their faxed confirmation or a hard copy of their e-mailed confirmation.

EATING

The Portuguese meal schedule is slightly later than in the U.S. Lunch *(almoço)* is the big meal, served between noon and 14:00,

while supper *(jantar)* is from about 19:30–21:30. You'll eat well in mom-and-pop restaurants for €8.

Eat seafood in Portugal. Fish soup *(sopa de peixe)* and shellfish soup *(sopa de mariscos)* are worth seeking out. *Caldo verde* is a popular vegetable soup. *Frango assado* is roast chicken; ask for *piri-piri* sauce if you like it hot and spicy. *Porco á Alentejana* is an interesting combination of pork and clams. Potatoes and greens are popular side dishes. Carbs never went out of style in Portugal—it's common to get both potatoes *and* rice with a meal. As in Spain, garlic and olive oil are big.

Meia dose means half-portion (which is enough for one person), while *prato do dia* is the daily special. If appetizers (olives and bread, a veritable mini-buffet of tasty temptations) are brought to your table before you order, they are not free. If you don't want them, push them off to the side. Most mom-and-pop restauranteurs will figure the bill in front of you, so everyone agrees on the final amount to be paid.

For a quick snack, remember that cafés are usually cheaper than bars. Sandwiches *(sandes)* are everywhere. The Portuguese breakfast *(pequeno almoço)* is just coffee and a sweet roll, but due to the large expat English community, a full British "fry" is available in most touristy areas. A standard, wonderful local pastry is the custard tart, *pastel de nata* (called *pastel de Belém* in Lisbon's fancy suburb of the same name).

When you want the bill, say, *"A conta, faz favor."*

Portuguese Drinks

For its size, Portugal is a major wine producer—145 million gallons in 2000. And Portuguese wines are cheap, decent, and distinctively fruity.

Vinho verde (VEEN-yoo VAIR-day) is light, refreshing, almost always white, and slightly fizzy. This "green wine" is actually golden in color, but "green" (young) in age—picked, made,

Typical Portuguese Foods

bacalhau	dried and salted cod, served a reputed 365 different ways. It's arguably the national dish, but is definitely an acquired taste.
frango assado	roast chicken, commonly served with *piri-piri* hot sauce
Porco á Alentejana	pork cubes covered with clams, Portugal's unique contribution to world cuisine
sardinhas grelhadas	fresh sardines, grilled or barbecued

Soups and Stews (Sopas)

caldo verde	"green" soup of kale greens and potato puree
cataplana	seafood and potatoes cooked in a copper clamshell dish
caldeirada de peixe	like *cataplana,* but cooked in a casserole
sopa de mariscos	thick seafood soup
feijoada	pork and beans
arroz de mariscos	rice and mixed seafood stew (the "Portuguese paella")
sopa á Alentejana	garlic soup with a poached egg and bread crumbs dropped in

Snacks

prego	steak sandwich
tosta mista	grilled ham and cheese sandwich
batatas fritas	potato chips

Desserts

You'll find various concoctions made from egg yolk and sugar, such as *barrigas de freiras* (nuns' tummies) and *papos de anjo* (angels' breasts).

pudim	flan
arroz doce	rice pudding with cinnamon
salame de chocolate	cookies and chocolate pressed together to look like salami
queque	muffin

Tips on Tipping

Tipping in Portugal isn't as automatic and generous as it is in the U.S., but for special service, tips are appreciated, if not expected. As in the U.S., the proper amount depends on your resources, tipping philosophy, and the circumstance, but some general guidelines apply.

Restaurants: In most restaurants, service is included—your menu typically will indicate this by noting *serviço incluido*. Still, if you like to tip and you're pleased with the service, it's customary to leave up to 5 percent. If service is not included (*serviço não incluido*), tip up to 10 percent. Leave the tip on the table. It's best to tip in cash, even if you pay with your credit card. Otherwise, the tip may never reach your server.

Taxis: To tip the cabbie, round up. For a typical ride, round up to the next euro on the fare (to pay a €13 fare, give €14); for a long ride, to the nearest €5 (for a €37 fare, give €40). If the cabbie hauls your bags and zips you to the airport to help you catch your flight, you might want to toss in a little more. But if you feel like you're being driven in circles or otherwise ripped off, skip the tip.

Services: Tour guides at public sites sometimes hold out their hands for tips after they give their spiel. If I've already paid for the tour, I don't tip extra, though some tourists do give a euro or two, particularly for a job well done. I don't tip at hotels, but if you do, give the porter a euro for carrying bags and leave a couple of euros in your room at the end of your stay for the maid if the room was kept clean. In general, if someone in the service industry does a super job for you, a tip of a couple of euros is appropriate...but not required.

When in doubt, ask. If you're not sure whether (or how much) to tip for a service, ask your hotelier or the TI; they'll fill you in on how it's done on their turf.

and drunk within a year. The grapes, from the northern Minho region, are low-sugar and high-acid. After the initial fermentation, wine-makers introduce a second fermentation, whose by-product is carbon dioxide—the light fizz. They're somewhat bitter alone but great with meals, especially seafood. The best are from Monaco Amarante and Aveleda, but the one on every menu is the perfectly acceptable Casal Garcia. If you like white *vinho verde*, you might enjoy the harder-to-find red version. It's dark in color, like a cabernet, but still fizzy and light in flavor, like a rosé—a unique combination.

The Dão region also produces fine red wines, mostly from the Mondego Valley between Coimbra, Guarda, and Viseu. They should sit for a year or two in the bottle before drinking. The

Alentejo region (look for bottles labeled "Borba") is known for its quality red. Madeira, from the Madeira Islands, is fortified and blended (as is port), and usually served as a sweet dessert wine. The grapes are grown in volcanic soil. The English and George Washington both liked it ("Have some Madeira, m'dear"), though today's version is drier and less syrupy. A Madeira called *Sercial* is served chilled (like sherry) with almonds. If you find yourself drowning in choices, simply try a glass of the house wine *(vinho da casa)*. And if you like port wine, what better place to sample it than its birthplace, Port-ugal? (For a crash course on port wine, see page 226.) *Reserva* on the label means it's the best-quality port (and the most expensive). All bottles of port should have a *selo de garantia* (a seal of guarantee) issued by the Port Wine Institute.

Beer *(cerveja)* is also popular—for a small draft beer, ask for *uma imperial.* Freshly squeezed orange juice *(sumo de laranja)*, mineral water *(água mineral)*, and soft drinks are widely available. When ordering water, fizzy or not, you will always be asked, *"Fresco o natural?"* *Fresco* is chilled, and *natural* is room temperature. Coffee lovers enjoy a *bica,* the very aromatic shot of espresso so popular in Portugal.

These words will help quench your thirst:

água com/sem gás	water with/without bubbles
água torneira	tap water
meia de leite	coffee with warm milk
galão	1/4 coffee, 3/4 warm milk served in a tall glass
carioca	espresso diluted with hot water (like American coffee)
chá	tea
vinho tinto	red wine
vinho branco	white wine
cerveja	beer
imperial	small draft beer
aguardente	firewater distilled from grape seeds, stems, and skins, with a kick like a mule
ginjinha	cherry liqueur, served at special bars in Lisbon and Óbidos

TRAVELING AS A TEMPORARY LOCAL

We travel all the way to Europe to enjoy differences—to become temporary locals. You'll experience frustrations. Certain truths that we find "God-given" or "self-evident," such as cold beer, ice in drinks, bottomless cups of coffee, hot showers, and bigger being better, are suddenly not so true. One of the benefits of travel is

Send Me a Postcard, Drop Me a Line

If you enjoy a successful trip with the help of this book and would like to share your discoveries, please fill out the survey at www.ricksteves.com/feedback. I personally read and value all feedback.

the eye-opening realization that there are logical, civil, and even better alternatives. A willingness to go local ensures that you'll enjoy a full dose of Portuguese hospitality.

If there is a negative aspect to the image Europeans have of Americans, it is that we are big, aggressive, impolite, rich, loud, and a bit naive. Americans tend to be noisy in public places, such as restaurants and trains. Our raised voices can demolish Europe's reserved and elegant ambience. Talk softly.

While Europeans look bemusedly at some of our Yankee excesses—and worriedly at others—they nearly always afford us individual travelers all the warmth we deserve.

Judging from all the happy postcards I receive from travelers who have used this book, it's safe to assume you'll enjoy a great, affordable vacation—with the finesse of an independent, experienced traveler.

BACK DOOR TRAVEL PHILOSOPHY
From *Rick Steves' Europe Through the Back Door*

Travel is intensified living—maximum thrills per minute and one of the last great sources of legal adventure. Travel is freedom. It's recess, and we need it.

Experiencing the real Europe requires catching it by surprise, going casual..."Through the Back Door."

Affording travel is a matter of priorities. (Make do with the old car.) You can travel—simply, safely, and comfortably—anywhere in Europe for $100 a day plus transportation costs. In many ways, spending more money only builds a thicker wall between you and what you came to see. Europe is a cultural carnival, and, time after time, you'll find that its best acts are free and the best seats are the cheap ones.

A tight budget forces you to travel close to the ground, meeting and communicating with the people, not relying on service with a purchased smile. Never sacrifice sleep, nutrition, safety, or cleanliness in the name of budget. Simply enjoy the local-style alternatives to expensive hotels and restaurants.

Extroverts have more fun. If your trip is low on magic moments, kick yourself and make things happen. If you don't enjoy a place, maybe you don't know enough about it. Seek the truth. Recognize tourist traps. Give a culture the benefit of your open mind. See things as different but not better or worse. Any culture has much to share.

Of course, travel, like the world, is a series of hills and valleys. Be fanatically positive and militantly optimistic. If something's not to your liking, change your liking. Travel is addictive. It can make you a happier American as well as a citizen of the world. Our Earth is home to six billion equally important people. It's humbling to travel and find that people don't envy Americans. They like us, but, with all due respect, they wouldn't trade passports.

Globe-trotting destroys ethnocentricity. It helps you understand and appreciate different cultures. Regrettably, there are forces in our society that want you dumbed down for their convenience. Don't let it happen. Thoughtful travel engages you with the world—more important than ever these days. Travel changes people. It broadens perspectives and teaches new ways to measure quality of life. Many travelers toss aside their hometown blinders. Their prized souvenirs are the strands of different cultures they decide to knit into their own character. The world is a cultural yarn shop. And Back Door travelers are weaving the ultimate tapestry. Come on, join in!

PORTUGAL

Portugal is underrated. The country seems somewhere just beyond Europe and the pace of life is noticeably slower than in Spain. Prices are cheaper. While the unification of Europe is bringing sweeping changes, the traditional economy is based on fishing, cork, wine, and textiles.

Portugal isn't touristy—even its coastal towns lack glitzy attractions. The beach and the sea are enough, as they have been for centuries, the source of Portugal's seafaring wealth long ago and the draw for tourists today.

The locals, not jaded by tourists, will meet you with warmth—especially if you learn at least a few words of Portuguese instead of launching into Spanish (see "Portuguese Survival Phrases" in the appendix).

Over the centuries, Portugal and Spain have had a love-hate, on-again, off-again relationship, but they have almost always remained separate, each with their own distinct language and culture. The Portuguese seem humbler and friendlier than the Spanish. In Spain, if you ever feel you can't do anything right, you'll find it's just the opposite in Portugal—you can't do anything wrong. Portugal is also more ethnically diverse than Spain, as it's inhabited by many people from its former colonies in Brazil, Africa, and Asia. The Portuguese continue to feel a special affinity to their Brazilian cousins.

Portugal bucked the Moors before Spain did, establishing its present-day borders 800 years ago. A couple of centuries later, the Age of Discovery (1500–1700) made Portugal one of the world's richest nations.

Prince Henry the Navigator, Bartolomeu Dias, and Vasco da Gama traveled to Africa seeking—and finding—a trade route to India. Portuguese-born Ferdinand Magellan, sailing for Spain, was the first to circumnavigate the globe.

Portugal Almanac

Offical Name: It's República Portuguesa, but locals just say "Portugal."

Population: 10.5 million people. Most Portuguese are Roman Catholic (95 percent), with indigenous Mediterranean roots; there are a few black Africans from former colonies (less than 1 percent) and some East Europeans.

Latitude and Longitude: 39°N and 8°W (similar latitude to Washington, D.C., or San Francisco).

Area: 35,000 square miles, which includes the Azores and Madeira, two island groups in the Atlantic which (distantly) guard the Straits of Gibraltar.

Geography: Portugal is rectangular, 325 miles long and 125 miles wide. (Indiana is a little shorter and wider.) The half of the country north of Lisbon is more mountainous, cool, and rainy. The south consists of rolling plains, hot and dry. Portugal has 350 miles of coastline.

Rivers: The major rivers, most notably the Tejo (or Tagus) River (600 miles long, spilling into the Atlantic at Lisbon) and the Douro (100 miles, running through wine country, ending at Porto), run east-west from Spain.

Best Skiing: Serra Estrela, at 6,500 feet, is the highest point on the mainland, but Portugal's highest peak is Mt. Pico (7,713 ft.) in the Azores.

Biggest Cities: Lisbon (the capital, 560,000 in core, with 2.6 million in greater Lisbon), Porto (265,000 in core, with 1.2 million total), and Coimbra (150,000 in core, and 435,000 in greater metropolitan area).

A naval superpower for a century, Portugal established colonies in Brazil and throughout Africa. The gold that flowed into the country led to an explosion of the arts back home. (Now named the Manueline period—after King Manuel I—its finest architecture is in Lisbon, represented by Belém's tower and monastery.) But no country can corner the market on trade for long, and as with Spain, Portugal underwent a long decline.

Portugal endured the repressive regime of António de Oliveira Salazar and his successor Marcello Caetano from 1932–1974—the longest dictatorship in Western European history. Salazar pumped money into fighting wars to hang on to the last of the country's African colonies. When Portuguese military officers staged a coup in 1974, the locals were on their side. Portugal lost its colonies, but the Portuguese—and their former colonies—won their freedom.

Economy: The Gross Domestic Product is $185 billion (same as Indiana). The GDP per capita is $18,000 (Indiana's is $35,000). Some major money-makers for Portugal are fish (canned sardines), cork, budget clothes and shoes, port wine, and tourism. A quarter of Portugal's foreign trade is with Spain. Though still 30 percent poorer than Europe's leaders, Portugal has improved considerably since joining the European Union in 1986 (then called the European Community), thanks to EU subsidies. One in 10 Portuguese still works in agriculture, 60 percent work in service jobs, and 30 percent in industry.

Government: The Prime Minister—currently the center-left Socialist, Jose Socrates—is the chief executive, assuming power as the head of the leading vote-getting party in legislative elections. The President (Jorge Sampao) commands the military and calls for new elections. There are 230 legislators, elected to four-year terms, making up the single-house Assembly. Regionally, Portugal is divided into 20 districts (Lisbon, Coimbra, Porto, etc.).

Flag: The flag is two-fifths green and three-fifths red, united by the Portuguese coat of arms—a shield atop a navigator's armillary sphere.

Soccer: The three most popular teams are Sporting Lisbon, Benfica (also from Lisbon), and FC Porto.

Senhor Average: The average Portuguese is 38 years old and will live 77 years. One in three Portuguese use the Internet, one in three live near either Lisbon or Porto, and slightly less than two in three own a car.

The poorest European Union country in Western Europe, Portugal has worked hard to meet EU standards...and has enjoyed heavy EU investment. Today Portugal is a success story, with huge improvements in its infrastructure and a relatively strong economy. Although prices have started to rise, Portugal is still prime territory for budget travelers.

LISBON

(Lisboa)

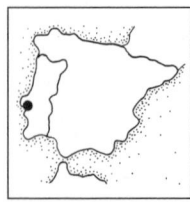

Lisbon is a ramshackle but charming mix of now and then. Vintage trolleys shiver up and down its hills, bird-stained statues mark grand squares, taxis rattle and screech through cobbled lanes, and well-worn people sip coffee in Art Nouveau cafés. It's a city of faded ironwork balconies, multicolored tiles, and mosaic sidewalks, of bougainvillea and red-tiled roofs with antique TV antennas. Men in suits and billed caps offer to "plastify" your documents, and Africans in traditional garb sell gemstones from handkerchiefs spread on sidewalks.

Lisbon, Portugal's capital, is the country's banking and manufacturing center. A port city on the yawning mouth of the Tejo River, Lisbon welcomes large ships to its waters and state-of-the-art dry docks. "Lisboa" (as locals call their city) comes from the Phoenician "Alis Ubbo," or "calm port."

While Lisbon's history goes back to the Romans and Moors, its glory days were in the 15th and 16th centuries, when explorers such as Vasco da Gama opened new trade routes around Africa to India, making Lisbon one of Europe's richest cities. Portugal's "Age of Discovery" fueled rapid economic growth, which sparked the flamboyant art boom called the Manueline period—named after King Manuel I (r. 1495–1521). In the 17th and 18th centuries, the gold, diamonds, and sugarcane of Brazil (one of Portugal's colonies) made Lisbon even wealthier.

Then, on All Saints' Day in 1755, while most of the population was in church, a tremendous earthquake hit the city. Candles quivered as far away as Ireland. Two-thirds of Lisbon was leveled. Fires started by the many church candles raged through the

Lisbon Overview

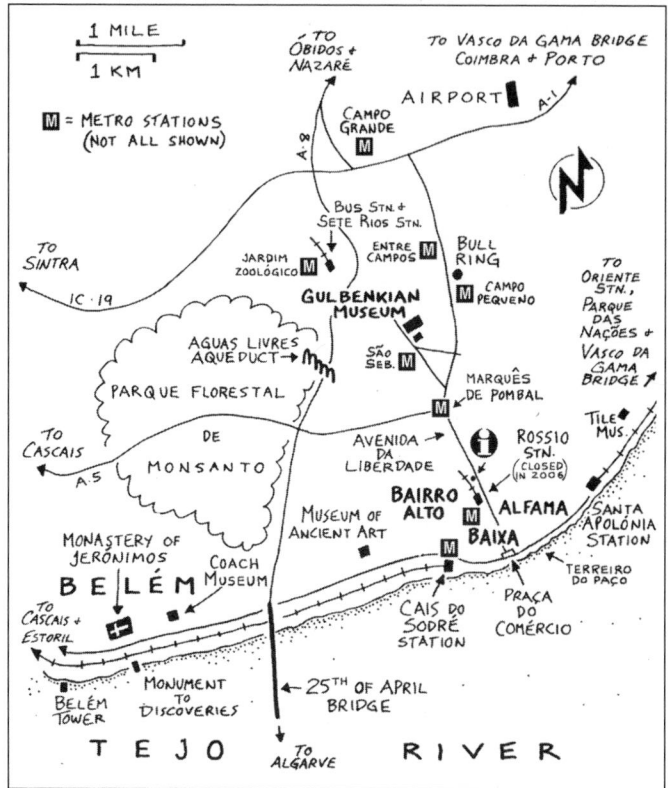

city, and a huge tidal wave blasted the waterfront. Of Lisbon's 270,000 people, 30,000 were killed.

Under the energetic and eventually dictatorial leadership of Prime Minister Marquês de Pombal—who had the new city planned within a month of the quake—downtown Lisbon was rebuilt on a progressive grid plan, with broad boulevards and square squares. Remnants of Lisbon's pre-earthquake charm survive in Belém, the Alfama, and the Bairro Alto district. The bulk of your sightseeing will likely be in these neighborhoods.

As the Paris of the Portuguese-speaking world, Lisbon (pop. 560,000) is the Old World capital for some 100 million people whose origins stretch from Europe to Brazil to Africa to China. Immigrants from former colonies such as Mozambique and Angola have added diversity and flavor to the city, making it as likely that you'll hear African music as Portuguese fado these days.

But Lisbon's heritage survives. The city—with newly restored downtown squares and a hearty financial boost from the European

Central Lisbon

Union—seems better organized, cleaner, and more prosperous and people-friendly than ever. With its elegant outdoor cafés, exciting art, stunning vistas, entertaining museums, a salty sailors' quarter, and a hill-capping castle, Lisbon is a world-class city.

Planning Your Time

For a two-week tour of Portugal, Lisbon is worth three days, including a day for a side-trip to Sintra. If you have an extra day, Lisbon has plenty to offer. Remember, many top sights are closed on Monday, particularly in Belém. Sintra's Pena Palace is also closed Monday.

Day 1: See Lisbon's three downtown neighborhoods. Start by touring Castle São Jorge at the top of the Alfama, and survey the city from its viewpoint. Hike down to another fine viewpoint (Largo das Portas do Sol), then descend into the Alfama. Explore. Back in the Baixa ("lower city"), have lunch on or near Rua Augusta and walk to the funicular near Praça dos Restauradores.

Pronunciation Guide to Lisbon

Lisboa	leezh-BOH-ah
Rossio (main square)	roh-SEE-oo
Baixa (lower city)	BYE-shah
Alfama (hilly neighborhood)	al-FAH-mah
Bairro Alto (high town)	BYE-roh AHL-toh
Chiado (part of Bairro Alto)	shee-AH-doo
Belém (suburb with sights)	bay-LEHM
Tejo River	TAY-zhoo
praça (plaza)	PRAH-sah
rua (road)	ROO-ah

Kick off the described walk through the Bairro Alto with a ride up the funicular. Joyride on a trolley. Art lovers can then take a taxi or the Metro to the Gulbenkian Museum. Consider dinner at a fado show in the Bairro Alto or the Alfama.

Day 2: Trolley to Belém and tour the monastery, tower, and Coach Museum. Have lunch in Belém. Tour the Museum of Ancient Art, and spend the rest of your afternoon browsing through the Rossio, Bairro Alto, and Alfama neighborhoods.

Day 3: Side-trip to Sintra to tour the Pena Palace and explore the ruined Moorish castle. (If you only have 2 days for Lisbon, it's possible, but really rushed, to substitute Sintra for the ancient art museum on the 2nd afternoon.)

ORIENTATION

Downtown Lisbon is a valley flanked by two hills, along the banks of the Tejo River. At the heart sits the main square, **Rossio,** in the center of the valley (with Praça dos Restauradores and Praça da Figueira nearby). The **Baixa,** or lower city, stretches from Rossio to the waterfront. It's a flat, pleasant shopping area of grid-patterned streets and the pedestrian-only Rua Augusta. The **Alfama,** the hill to the east, is a colorful tangle of medieval streets, topped by Castle São Jorge. The **Bairro Alto** ("high town"), the hill to the west, has characteristic old lanes on the top and high-fashion stores along Rua Garrett (in the neighborhood called the Chiado).

From Rossio, the **modern city** stretches north (sloping uphill) along wide Avenida da Liberdade and beyond (way beyond), where you find the airport, bullring, Edward VII Park, and breezy botanical gardens. The suburb of **Belém,** home to several Age of Discovery sights, is three miles west of the city, along the waterfront.

Greater Lisbon has roughly two million people and some frightening sprawl, but for the visitor, the city can be a delightful small-town series of parks, boulevards, and squares. Focus on the three characteristic neighborhoods that line the downtown harborfront: the Baixa, the Bairro Alto, and the Alfama.

Tourist Information

Lisbon has several tourist offices, and additional information kiosks sprout around town late each spring. The main TIs are at: **Palacio Foz** at the bottom of Praça dos Restauradores (daily 9:00–20:00, overworked and tired staff, tel. 213-463-314; TI for rest of Portugal in same office, tel. 218-494-323 or 213-463-658), **"Ask Me Lisbon" center** (Praça do Comércio, daily 9:00–20:00, Internet access, tel. 210-312-810), **airport** (daily 7:00–24:00, tel. 218-450-660), **Santa Apolónia train station** (kiosk open Tue–Sat 8:00–13:00, closed Sun–Mon, far end by the lockers), and **Belém** (kiosk open Tue–Sat 10:00–13:00 & 14:00–18:00, closed Mon, in front of monastery, tel. 213-658-435).

For a handy city map, pick up a Gray Line or Cityrama tour brochure or a free copy of the Lisbon city map (with helpful inset of town center) at a TI. To help make sense of the many public transportation options, ask for the in-depth *Public Transport Guide,* which shows bus, Metro, and trolley lines in amazing detail. And while you're at it, take some free publications, such as the semimonthly *Follow Me Lisboa* (cultural listings) and the biannual *ConVida* (shopping, culture, and dining). For the most up-to-date lowdown on current exhibits, hip new bars and restaurants, and a concert schedule, you can't beat the in-Portuguese-only *Agenda LX* (if you see a picture of something you like, ask your hotelier to translate—then go someplace most tourists miss). If you want a LisboaCard (see below), buy it at a TI. Two good Web sites are www.atl-turismolisboa.pt and www.portugalinsite.pt.

LisboaCard: This card covers all public transportation (including the Metro) and free entrance to many museums (plus Sintra sights and transport). It also offers discounts on additional museums, city tours, and the Aero-Bus airport bus. You can buy this only at Lisbon's TIs (including the airport TI), not at participating sights. If you plan to museum-hop, the card is a good value, particularly for a day in Belém (covers your transportation and most sightseeing), but don't get the card for Sunday, when many sights are free until 14:00, or for Monday, when most sights are closed (24-hour card-€13.50, 48-hour-€23, 72-hour-€28; includes excellent explanatory guidebook). You choose the start date and time. While Lisbon's Shopping and Restaurant Cards are needlessly complicated, the LisboaCard is straightforward and can save a frugal and busy sightseer 5 to 100 percent on many top attractions (over €25 if you visit all my listed sights).

Arrival in Lisbon

By Train: Lisbon has four primary train stations—Santa Apolónia (to Spain and most points north), Rossio (closed for most of 2006—see below; for Sintra, Óbidos, and Nazaré), Oriente (for the Algarve and Évora), and Cais do Sodré (for Cascais and Estoril). If leaving Lisbon by train, see if your train requires a reservation (look for a boxed R in the timetable). For specifics on journeys, see "Transportation Connections," page 99.

Santa Apolónia Station covers international trains and nearly all of Portugal (except the south). It's just east of the Alfama. It has ATMs, a TI (by the lockers), and good bus connections to the town center. Buses #9 and #39 go to Praça dos Restauradores, #46 and #90 continue up Avenida da Liberdade. (As you exit the station, these bus stops are to your left and run alongside the station.)

A taxi from Santa Apolónia to any recommended hotel costs roughly €5. All of Santa Apolónia Station's northbound departures stop at the **Oriente Station** (built for the World's Fair, Metro: Oriente). Trains from Évora and Lagos also arrive at Oriente Station, crossing the 25th of April Bridge and dropping you in Lisbon proper.

Rossio Station will be closed for most of 2006 due to the construction of a massive tunnel under the Marquês de Pombal roundabout. To get to Sintra, Óbidos, or Nazaré, you must depart from the **Sete Rios** train station, just above the Metro stop Jardim Zoológico and next to the main bus station.

Rossio Station is in the town center (an easy walk from most recommended hotels, ATM near track 5). When Rossio reopens (maybe in fall of 2006), it will again handle trains to Sintra (direct, 4/hr, 35 min) and to Óbidos and Nazaré (both require a transfer at Cacém; the bus is a better option); its all-Portugal ticket office on the ground floor will sell long-distance and international train tickets to virtually everywhere except nearby destinations such as Sintra (Mon–Fri 7:00–20:00, closed Sat–Sun, cash only). You'll be able to buy tickets to Sintra upstairs in the lobby in front of the tracks, either at the ticket office or from the easy-to-use machines (select English, pop in coins—about €2.80 round-trip, TV monitor in lobby lists departure times).

Cais do Sodré Station, on the waterfront (just west of Praça do Comércio, Metro: Cais do Sodré), covers Cascais and Estoril (40 min).

By Bus: Lisbon's efficient bus station is in the modern part of the city, several miles inland from the harbor, next to the Sete

Rios train station. It has ATMs, a leaflet rack of schedules (near entrance/exit), a nifty computer that can display your route, and two information offices—one for buses in Portugal, the other for international routes (on opposite sides of the station, both closed Sun). If you plan to leave Lisbon by bus, you can virtually always buy a ticket just a few minutes before departure, but you can also purchase it up to seven days in advance if you prefer the peace of mind.

To get from the bus station to downtown Lisbon, it's a €7 taxi ride or a short Metro trip on the Blue line (to access Metro system from bus station, walk down and across to Sete Rios train station, then follow signs for Metro: Jardim Zoológico). For national bus info, call 707-223-344. The EVA company handles the south and Rede Nacional de Expressos does the rest.

By Plane: Lisbon's easy-to-manage airport is five miles northeast of downtown, with a 24-hour bank, ATMs, and a TI (see below).

To get downtown, you can take a 20-minute taxi ride (€10 fare if you get metered rate). There is no legitimate "airport fee." Timid travelers buy a €15 voucher at the TI for a fixed price, but smart ones pick up the taxi fairness flier at the TI and show the cabbie the €10 price it lists if he tries to rip them off.

There are also good bus connections into town by public city bus (#44 or #45, €1.20) or the airport bus, Aero-Bus #91. The Aero-Bus runs from the airport to Avenida da Liberdade, Praça dos Restauradores, Rossio, and Praça do Comércio (3/hr, 30 min, daily 7:45–20:45 in either direction, buy ticket on bus, €3). Your ticket is actually a one-day Lisbon transit pass that covers bus, trolley, and funicular rides, but not the Metro. If you fly in on TAP airline, show your boarding pass to get a free lift into town on the Aero-Bus (TAP tel. 707-205-700). For airport info, call 218-413-700.

While you're at the airport, take advantage of the all-Portugal tourist office, in the same place as the Lisbon TI (both open daily 8:00–24:00, tel. 218-493-689 or 218-491-323).

By Car: Notice that in Portugal, you will need cash for tolls (about €5/hr) along most freeways, where credit cards are not accepted. To reach downtown Lisbon, follow signs for *Marquês de Pombal*, then *Rossio*.

Helpful Hints

Theft Alert: Lisbon has piles of people doing illegal business on the street. While it's generally safe, if you're looking for trouble—especially after dark—you may find it. Pickpockets target tourists on the trolleys (especially #12, #15, and #28).

Pedestrian Warning: Sidewalks are narrow, and drivers are daring—cross streets with care. You'll see warnings painted at most crosswalks, alerting pedestrians to "stop to look and to be seen" and graphically showing the consequences of ignoring this advice.

Calendar Concerns: Tuesdays and Saturdays are flea- and food-market days in the Alfama's Campo de Santa Clara. National museums are free on Sunday (all day or until 14:00) and closed all day Monday. The bullring has been closed for renovation; bulls are hoping it won't reopen in 2006. But when it opens again, bullfights will take place most summer Thursdays and Sundays.

Money: ATMs are the way to go—they're all over Lisbon and the rest of Portugal and give out the most euros per dollar. Banks offer fine rates but charge outrageous fees (around €8) to change checks or cash (bank hours are generally Mon–Fri 8:30–15:00, closed Sat–Sun). American Express is outside the city center (Mon–Fri 9:30–13:00 & 14:30–18:30, closed Sat–Sun, in Top Tours office at Avenida Duque de Loule 108, Metro: Rotunda, tel. 213-194-190).

Internet Access: The TI has a list of the latest. The handiest is Portugal Telecom (PT), on the northwest corner of Rossio near Rossio Station (12 stations, daily 8:00–23:00). The "Ask Me Lisbon" center on Praça do Comércio has six computers (€2.50/30 min). Abracadabra Café on Rossio and Western Union on Praça da Figueira have a few Internet terminals. All post offices, many public gathering places (especially malls), and many McDonald's offer Wi-Fi Internet access (see www.ptwifi.pt for current list).

Post Office and Telephones: The post offices *(correios)* on Praça do Comércio (Mon–Fri only) and at Praça dos Restauradores 58 are modern and user-friendly (Mon–Fri 8:00–22:00, Sat–Sun 9:00–18:00). The Portugal Telecom office on Rossio, mentioned above, sells phone cards and has metered phones and card phones (daily 8:00–23:00).

Travel Agency: Agencies line the Avenida da Liberdade. For flights (but not train tickets), Star Turismo is handy and helpful (Mon–Fri 9:30–18:30, closed Sat–Sun, Praça dos Restauradores 14, southwest corner of square, tel. 213-245-240).

Local Guides: The city has no regular walking tours, and the sights do not come with audioguides. A local guide can be a big help. For a private guide, contact the Guides' Union (€85/4 hrs, €140/day, more on weekends, tel. 213-467-170). Claudia da Costa is a hardworking, reliable guide who really knows Lisbon well (mobile 965-560-216, claudiadacosta@hotmail.com). Another good guide is Cristina Quental (mobile 919-922-480, anacristinaquental@hotmail.com).

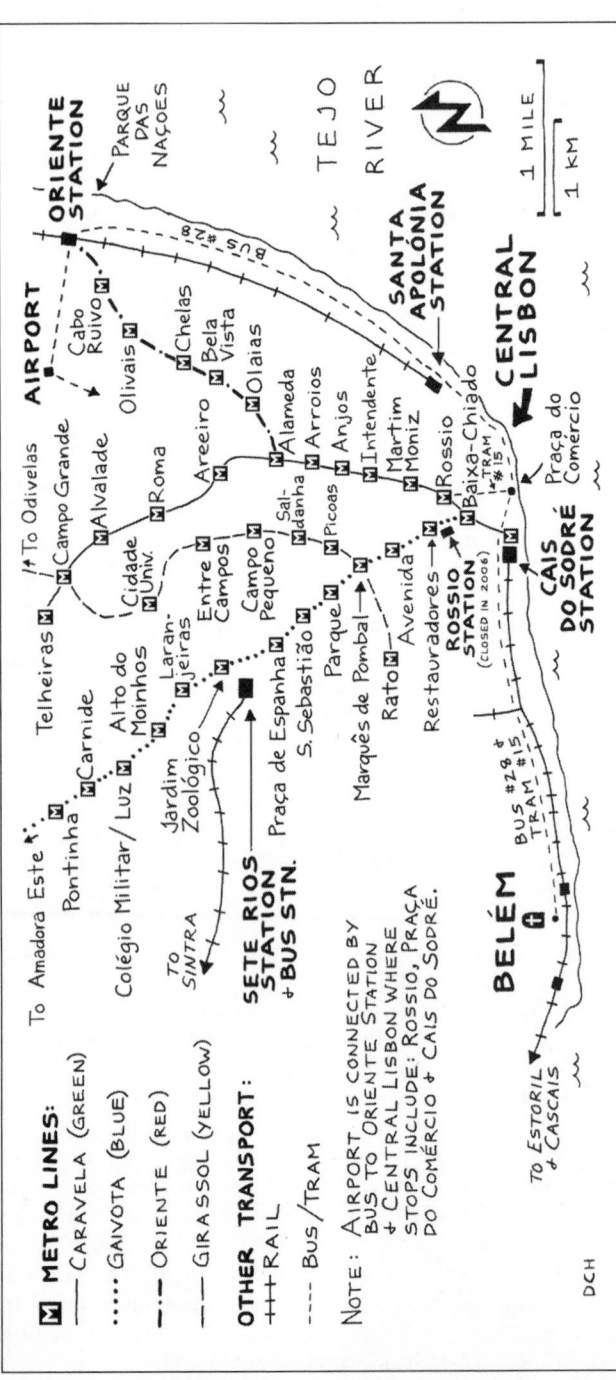

Lisbon's Public Transportation

Getting Around Lisbon

A one-day pass (called "7 Colinas") that covers the Metro, funiculars, trolleys, and buses costs €3.50 (keep card if you want to renew it for €3/day, 5-day card-€12.10; sold at Carris booths on Praça da Figueira, at bullfight ticket kiosk at Praça dos Restauradores, behind Elevador de Santa Justa, and at ticket offices at Metro stations). Note that the LisboaCard (see "Tourist Information," page 42) also covers public transportation and many museums.

By Metro: Lisbon's simple, fast subway stretches northward from Baixa-Chiado in two lines, Green and Blue (with Yellow and Red lines branching off Green and Blue). While not very good for getting you around the historic downtown, it is handy for trips to  or from Rossio (Metro: Rossio or Restauradores), the Gulbenkian Museum (Metro: São Sebastião), the Chiado neighborhood (Metro: Baixa-Chiado), Colombo Mall (Metro: Colégio Militar-Luz), Parque das Nações and the Oriente train station (both at Metro: Oriente), and the long-distance bus station and Sete Rios train station (both at Metro: Jardim Zoológico). Rides cost €0.70 (covered by LisboaCard, or 10-pack for €6.15, or use all-day bus/Metro pass described above). Remember to validate your ticket in the machine and keep it until your trip is over—the ticket is required to exit the sliding doors. Metro stops are marked above ground with a red M. *Saída* means exit. You can find a Metro map at any Metro stop, in the TI's in-depth *Public Transport Guide,* or on the Web at www.metrolisboa.pt.

By Trolleys, Funicular, and Buses: For fun and practical public transport, use the trolleys and the funicular. If you buy your ticket from the driver, one ride costs €1.20 (no transfers). You get two rides for €1.40 if you buy a "BUC-2" ticket from a Carris kiosk (kiosk sites listed above; tickets good for trolley, funicular, or bus). Like San Francisco, Lisbon sees its trolleys as part of its heritage and is keeping a few. Trolleys #12 (circling the Alfama), #28 (a scenic ride across the old town), and #15 (to Belém) are here to stay.

By Taxi: Lisbon is a great taxi town. Cabbies are good-humored and (except for some at the airport) are willing to use their meters. Rides start at €2, and you can go anywhere in the center for around €4. Decals on the window clearly spell out all charges in English. The most typical scam is the cabbie setting his meter at the high-price tariff. The meter should read *Tarifa* 1 (6:00–22:00, including the airport) or *Tarifa* 2 (nights and weekends); if it's *Tarifa* 3, 4, or 5, simply tell him to change it. The meter should not read over about €2 at the start. Cabs are generally easy to hail on the street (green light means available, lit number on the roof indicates they are taken). If you're having a hard time flagging one down, ask a local the location of the nearest taxi stand: *praça de taxi* (PRAH-sah duh taxi). They're all over the town center.

Especially if you're traveling with a companion, Lisbon's cabs are a cheap time-saver. For an average trip, couples save less than a dollar by taking public transport and spend an extra 15 minutes to get there—bad economics. If your time is limited, taxi everywhere.

TOURS

▲▲**Ride a Trolley**—Lisbon's vintage trolleys, most from the 1920s, shake and shiver through the old parts of town, somehow

safely weaving within inches of parked cars, climbing steep hills, and offering sightseers breezy views of the city for about a euro (rubberneck out the window and you die). Just pay the conductor as you board, sit down, and catch the pensioners as they lurch by at each stop.

Trolley #28 is a Rice-A-Roni Lisbon joyride. Stops from west to east include Estrela (the 18th-century, late-Baroque Estrela Basilica and Estrela Park—cozy neighborhood scene with pondside café and a "garden library kiosk"); the top of the Bica funicular (which drops steeply through a rough-and-tumble neighborhood to the riverfront); Chiado's main square (the café and "Latin Quarter"); Baixa (on Rua da Conceição between Augusta and Prata); the cathedral (Sé); Largo das Portas do Sol (the Alfama viewpoint); Santa Clara Church (flea market on Tue and Sat); and the pleasant and untouristy Graça district (with another excellent viewpoint).

Trolley #15, while not vintage or pickpocket-free, whisks you efficiently from Praça da Figueira to Belém.

Circular Tour on Trolley #12: For a colorful, 20-minute loop around the castle and the Alfama, catch #12 on Praça da Figueira (departs every few minutes from the stop at closest corner of square to castle). The driver can tell you when to get out for the Largo das Portas do Sol viewpoint near the castle (about three-quarters of the way up the hill), or stay on the trolley and you'll be dropped where you started.

Here's what you'll see on your self-guided tour: Leaving Praça da Figueira, you enter Largo de Martim Moniz—named for a

Lisbon's Viewpoints
(*Miradouros* and Belvederes)

The first three are included in the self-guided walking tours:

- Miradouro de São Pedro Alcântara (in Bairro Alto, at top of Elevador da Glória funicular; see "The Bairro Alto and Chiado Stroll," page 51)
- São Jorge Castle (on top of the Alfama; see photo above and "The Alfama Stroll," page 58)
- Miradouro de Largo das Portas do Sol (south slope of Alfama; see "The Alfama Stroll," page 58)
- Elevador de Santa Justa (Baixa)
- Monument to the Discoveries (Belém)
- Belém Tower (Belém)
- Cristo Rei (statue on hillside across the Tejo River)
- Edward VII Park (at north end of Avenida da Liberdade)
- Bica *miradouro* (atop the Bica funicular)

knight who died heroically while using his body as a doorjamb to pry open the castle gate, allowing his Christian Portuguese comrades to get in and capture Lisbon from the Moors in 1147. The big, maroon-colored building capping the hill on the left was a Jesuit monastery until 1769, when the dictatorial Marquês de Pombal booted that pesky order out of Portugal and turned the building into the Hospital São Jose.

Turning right onto Rua de Cavaleiros, you climb through the atmospheric Mouraria neighborhood on a street so narrow that a single trolley track is all that fits. Notice how the colorful mix of neighbors who fill the trolley all seem to know each other. Look up the skinny side streets. Marvel at the creative parking and classic laundry scenes. This is the area given to the Moors after they were driven out of the castle and Alfama. Locals know it as the home of the legendary fado singer Severa.

At the crest of the hill (Largo Rodrigues de Freitas), you can get out to explore, eat at a cheap restaurant (see "Eating," page 94), or follow Rua de Santa Marinha to the Campo de Santa Clara flea market (Tue and Sat).

When you see the river, you're at Largo das Portas do Sol (Gates of the Sun), where you'll see the remains of one of the seven old Moorish gates of Lisbon. Hop out here if you want to visit the Fundação Ricardo do Espírito Santo Silva (formerly Decorative Arts) Museum, enjoy the most scenic cup of coffee in town, explore the Alfama, or tour the castle.

The trolley continues downhill past the fortress-like cathedral (on left) and into the Baixa (grid-planned Pombaline city). After a few blocks, you're back where you started.

Carris City Bus and Tram Tours—Carris Tours offers a confusing array of bus and tram tours giving tired tourists a lazy overview of the city. While uninspiring and not cheap, they're handy and operate daily year-round. They all start and end at Praça do Comércio, with trams on one side and buses (with trolley info booth) on the other.

Bus Tours: The **Tagus Tour** (which loops around west Lisbon) and the **Orient Express** (which loops east) are double-decker, hop-on, hop-off bus tours: You can get off, tour a sight, and catch a later bus. Major stops on the Tejo Tour are the Gulbenkian Museum and Belém sights (runs twice hourly 9:15–20:15 March–Oct, less in winter). The major stops of the Orient Express are Parque das Nações and the Tile Museum (runs hourly 10:30–17:30 March–Oct, less in winter). Both tours include audioguides and cost €14 apiece. For either tour, your ticket functions as a transit pass the rest of the day, covering trolleys, buses, and funiculars (but not the Metro, which is owned by a different company). You can't hop on and hop off between the tours.

Carris' **Discovery Tour** goes to Belém (€17, 90 min, 3/day, live guide). Their **Sintra Tour** makes a swing around the scenic and historic peninsula (an hour free in Sintra, but no Pena castle visit) and all the way out to Cabo da Roca—which is frustrating to reach on your own, even if you have a car (€40, includes Hills Tramcar tour—see below, daily at 14:00, 4.5 hrs, with a live 3-language guide).

Tram Tours: Carris offers four tram tours, including the **Hills Tramcar** tour, which takes you on a 1900s tramcar through the Alfama and the Bairro Alto. Scenic ride...sparse information (€17, 90-min tour with no stops and an audioguide narration most of the time, about 18/day June–Sept, 13/day rest of year). A €30 two-day ticket allows you to take all four 90-minute tours. For more information, stop by their yellow info bus (with an awning, west side of Praça do Comércio, cash only, discount with LisboaCard, tel. 213-613-010).

Tejo River Cruise—Lisboa Desde el Rio runs trips from the Terreiro do Paço dock off Praça do Comércio, cruising to the Vasco da Gama Bridge and Parque das Nações, then east to Belém and back (€20, discount with LisboaCard, 2 hours, April–Sept 2/day at 11:00 and 15:00—confirm time at TI or the kiosk at dock entrance, 4-language narration includes English, drinks and WC on board; hop-on, hop-off option at Parque das Nações and Belém sometimes possible on weekends; tel. 218-820-348).

SELF-GUIDED WALKS

While Lisbon had a famous quake, there's nothing earth-shaking about most of its downtown sights. The charm of Lisbon is the city itself—hilltop views, ramshackle neighborhoods, and slices of urban life. See it on foot.

The "Three Neighborhoods" Walk

You could see Lisbon's three downtown neighborhoods—the Bairro Alto, the Baixa, and the Alfama—in a single three-hour walk, linking together the two walks described below. Start with "The Bairro Alto and Chiado Stroll": From north of Rossio Station, take the Elevador da Glória funicular up to the Bairro Alto and walk downhill to Café A Brasileira and Rua Garrett. From there, you can get to the beginning of "The Alfama Stroll" by catching trolley #28 across the Baixa and up the Alfama. At the Largo das Portas do Sol viewpoint (3rd stop past the Sé Cathedral), walk five minutes uphill to Castle São Jorge, where you can start the Alfama walk back down the hill to the Baixa. (To avoid the walk up to the castle, take bus #37 from Praça da Figueira.)

The Bairro Alto and Chiado Stroll

For a ▲▲ walk, rise above the Baixa on the funicular called "Elevador da Glória" (€1.20, 6/hr, buy ticket from driver), near the obelisk at Praça dos Restauradores. Leaving the funicular on top, turn right (go 100 yards, up a few steps into a park) to enjoy the city view from Miradouro de São Pedro Alcântara (San Pedro Park belvedere). The tile map guides you through the view, stretching from the twin towers of the Cathedral (Sé, far right), to the ramparts of the castle birthplace of Lisbon (right), to the skyscraper towers of the new city in the distance (on far left). The highlights of the park are a bust honoring a 19th-century local journalist (founder of Lisbon's first daily newspaper) and a statue of a charming, barefooted delivery boy. This district is famous for its writers, poets, publishers, and bohemians. (The walk always goes downhill from here.)

Ways to Get from the Baixa up to the Bairro Alto and Chiado

- Ride the Elevador da Glória funicular (a few blocks north of Rossio on Avenida da Liberdade).
- Walk up the stairs from Rossio (due west of the central column).
- Taxi to Miradouro de São Pedro Alcântara.
- Take the Metro to the Baixa-Chiado stop.
- Catch trolley #28 from Rua da Conceição.
- Walk up Rua do Carmo from Rossio to Rua Garrett.
- Take escalators or elevators from the Armazéns mall to Rua Garrett.

The Elevador de Santa Justa takes you oh-so-close to Convento do Carmo and the Chiado...but access is closed to the public.

• *Directly across the street from the Elevador da Glória is the...*

Port Wine Institute: If you're into port (the fortified wine that takes its name from Porto, covered later in this book), you'll find the world's greatest selection at **Solar do Vinho do Porto** (run by the Port Wine Institute, Mon–Sat 11:00–24:00, closed Sun, WCs, Rua São Pedro de Alcântara 45, tel. 213-475-707, www. ivp.pt). The plush, air-conditioned, Old World living room holds leather chairs and cigar smokers (it's not a shorts-and-T-shirt kind of place). On entering, you can order from a selection of over 300 different ports from €1–22 per glass, poured by an English-speaking bartender. (You may want to try only 150 or so, and save the rest for the next night.) Fans of port describe it as "a liquid symphony playing on the palate." Browse through the easy menu. Start white and dry, try spicy and red, then finish mellow and tawny—a *colheita* is particularly good. Appetizers *(aperitivos)* are listed in the menu. The service can be slow and disinterested. To be served without a long wait, go to the bar. For more on port, see page 244.

• *Follow the main street (Rua São Pedro de Alcântara, which turns into Rua Misericordia) downhill a couple of blocks. Throughout this walk, look up and notice the fine old tile work on the buildings. When you reach the small square, Largo Trindade Coelho, on your left you'll see...*

São Roque Church: Step inside, read the English description at the back of the right nave, and then sit on a pew in the middle to take it all in (Mon–Fri 8:30–17:00, Sat–Sun 9:30–17:00). Built in the 16th century, the church of Saint Roque is one of Portugal's first Jesuit churches. The painted wood, false-domed ceiling is perfectly flat. The acoustics here are top-notch, important in a Jesuit church, where the emphasis is on the sermon. Notice all the

The Bairro Alto and Chiado Stroll

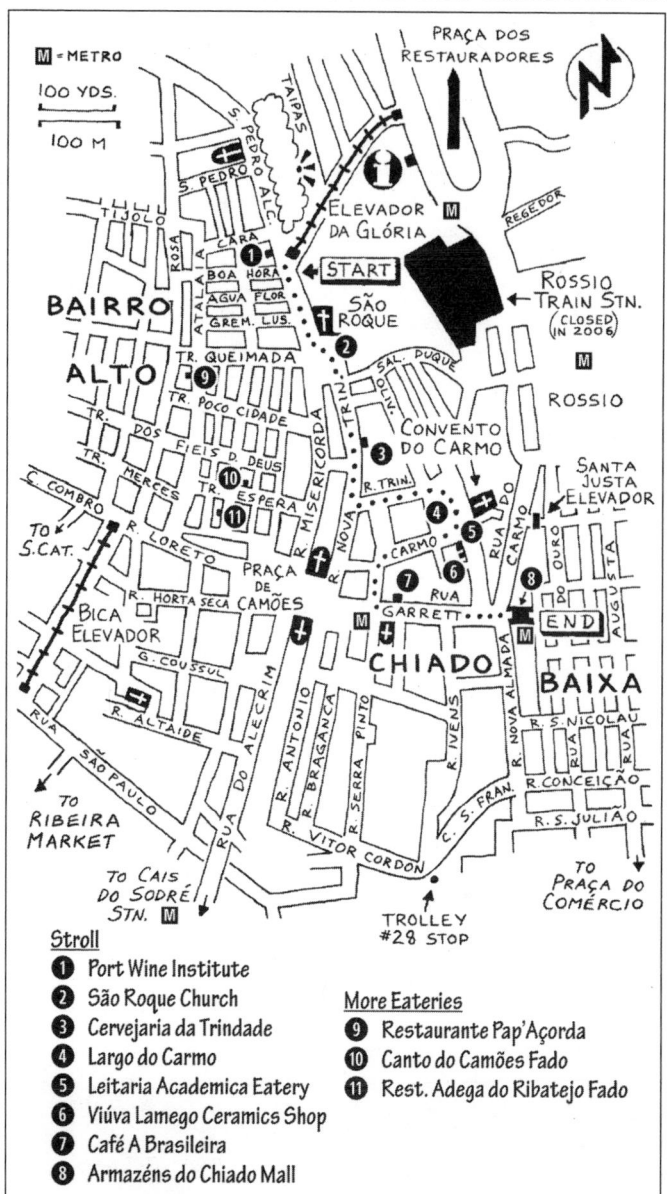

Stroll

1. Port Wine Institute
2. São Roque Church
3. Cervejaria da Trindade
4. Largo do Carmo
5. Leitaria Academica Eatery
6. Viúva Lamego Ceramics Shop
7. Café A Brasileira
8. Armazéns do Chiado Mall

More Eateries

9. Restaurante Pap'Açorda
10. Canto do Camões Fado
11. Rest. Adega do Ribatejo Fado

numbered panels on the floor. These are tombs, nameless because they were for lots of people. They're empty now—the practice was stopped in the 19th century when parishioners didn't want dead plague victims rotting under their feet.

Survey the rich side chapels. The highlight is the Chapel of St. John the Baptist (left of altar, gold and blue lapis lazuli columns). It looks like it came right out of the Vatican. It did. Made in Rome out of the most precious materials, it was the site of one papal Mass; then it was disassembled and shipped to Lisbon. Per square inch, it was probably the most costly chapel ever constructed. Notice the mosaic floor (with the spherical symbol of Portugal) and the three paintings that are actually intricate, beautiful mosaics—a Vatican specialty, designed to avoid damage from candle smoke that would darken paintings. To the right, a glass case of relics is trying to grab your attention. The next chapel to the left features a riot of babies. Individual chapels are explained in the English leaflet available near the door. The São Roque Museum, with some old paintings and church riches, is not as interesting as the church itself (€1.50, Tue–Sun 10:00–17:00, closed Mon).

Back outside in the church square, visit with the poor pigeon-drenched man (a statue to the unknown lottery ticket salesman—there are 2 lottery kiosks on this square, WC nearby), and continue (kitty-corner across the square) downhill along Rua Nova da Trindade. At #20, you can pop into **Cervejaria da Trindade,** the famous "oldest beer hall in Lisbon," for a look at the 19th-century tiles (see "Eating," page 96). Once the refectory (dining hall) of a monastery, it became a brewery after the monks were expelled in 1834. If you're tired of all this history, continue downhill to #16, Lisbon's biggest used bookstore, where you can sell this book.

• *Continue down the hill, where at the next intersection signs point left to the ruined Convento do Carmo. Follow the inside trolley tracks downhill to the next square...*

Largo do Carmo: On this square, the police guard the head-quarters of the National Guard, famous among locals as the last refuge of the fascist dictator Antonio Salazar before the people won their democracy in the Revolution of 1974. It was a peaceful uprising, called the Carnation Revolution because of the flowers placed in the guns of the soldiers as people made it clear it was time for democracy in Portugal. For more information, see page 72.

On Largo do Carmo, check out the ruins of **Convento do Carmo** (€2.50—or cheapskates can do a deep knee-bend at the ticket desk, sneak a peek, and crawl away; Mon–Sat 10:00–18:00, closed Sun). After the church was destroyed by the 1755 earthquake, Marquês de Pombal (see sidebar on page 62) directed that its delicate Gothic arches be left standing—supporting nothing but open sky—as a permanent reminder of that disastrous event.

If you're hungry, consider **Leitaria Academica,** a venerable little working-class eatery with tables spilling onto the breezy square. For €8, you can have one of their traditional specialties (Sr. Raul has an English cheat sheet), a salad, and a beverage.

Just off Largo do Carmo is a well-respected ceramics shop, **Viúva Lamego** (Calçada do Sacramento 29; described on page 85).

• *Leave Largo do Carmo, walking a block uphill on Travessa do Carmo. At the square, take a left on Rua Serpa Pinto, walking downhill to Rua Garrett, where—in the little pedestrian zone 50 yards uphill on the right—you'll find a famous old café across from the Baixa–Chiado Metro stop.*

Rua Garrett and Chiado: On the pedestrian street Rua Garrett, coffee-house junkies enjoy the grand **Café A Brasileira,** reeking of smoke and the 1930s. Drop in for a *bica* (Lisbon slang for an espresso) and a €1 *pastel de nata* custard tart—a local specialty. (WCs are in the basement, down the stairs near the entrance.) This café was the literary and creative soul of Lisbon in the 1920s and 1930s, when the country's avant-garde poets, writers, and painters would hang out here. The statue outside is of the poet Fernando Pessoa, making him a perpetual regular at Café A Brasileira.

> *It isn't enough to open the window*
> *To see the fields and rivers.*
> *It's not enough not to be blind*
> *To see the trees and flowers.*

> —Fernando Pessoa (1888–1935)

At the Baixa-Chiado (shee-AH-doo) Metro stop across the street, a slick series of escalators whisks people effortlessly between Chiado Square and the Baixa. It's a free and fun way to survey a long, long line of Portuguese—but for now, we'll stay in the Chiado neighborhood. (If you'll be coming up for fado in the evening, consider zipping up the escalator to get here—a recommended fado restaurant, Canto do Camões, is roughly 3 blocks away; see "Nightlife," page 87.)

The **Chiado** district is popular for its shopping and theaters. Browse downhill on Rua Garrett and notice its mosaic sidewalks, ironwork balconies, and fine shops. Peek into classy stores, such as the venerable Bertrand bookstore (at #73, English books and a good guidebook selection in Room 5). The street lamps you see are decorated with the symbol of Lisbon: a ship, carrying the remains of St. Vincent, guarded by two ravens.

Lisbon at a Glance

In Lisbon

▲▲▲Gulbenkian Museum Lisbon's best museum, featuring an art collection spanning 2,000 years, from ancient Egyptian to Impressionist to Art Nouveau. **Hours:** Tue–Sun 10:00–18:00, closed Mon.

▲▲Museum of Ancient Art Portuguese paintings from the 15th- and 16th-century glory days. **Hours:** Tue 14:00–18:00, Wed–Sun 10:00–18:00, closed Mon.

▲National Tile Museum Tons of artistic tiles, including a panorama of pre-earthquake Lisbon. **Hours:** Tue 14:00–18:00, Wed–Sun 10:00–18:00, closed Mon.

▲House of Fado and Portuguese Guitar Museum singing the story of Portuguese folk music. **Hours:** Daily 10:00–13:00 & 14:00–17:30.

Port Wine Institute Plush place selling tastes of the world's greatest selection of ports. **Hours:** Mon–Sat 11:00–24:00, closed Sun.

São Roque Church Fine 16th-century Jesuit church with false dome ceiling, chapel made of precious stones, and a less-interesting museum. **Hours:** Mon–Fri 8:30–17:00, Sat–Sun 9:30–17:00.

São Jorge Castle Eighth-century bastion, first built by the Moors, with kingly views at the highest point in town. **Hours:** Daily March–Oct 9:00–21:00, Nov–Feb 9:00–18:00.

Fundação Ricardo do Espírito Santo Silva Museum (formerly Decorative Arts Museum) A stroll through aristocratic households richly decorated in 16th- to 19th-century styles. **Hours:** Mon–Sat 10:00–17:00, closed Sun.

• *Rua Garrett ends abruptly downhill at the entrance of the big vertical mall...*

Armazéns do Chiado: This grand, six-floor shopping center connects Lisbon's lower and upper towns with a world of ways to spend money (lively food circus on 6th floor—see "Eating," page 98). It fills an old building gutted by a tragic 1988 fire (daily 10:00–22:00, eateries 10:00–23:00).

Elevador de Santa Justa A 150-foot-tall iron elevator offering a glittering city vista. **Hours:** Daily 7:00–22:45.

Cathedral (Sé) From the outside, an impressive Romanesque fortress of God; inside, not much. **Hours:** Tue–Sat 9:00–19:00, Sun–Mon 9:00–17:00.

In Belém
Note that all of these sights are closed on Monday.

▲▲▲**Monastery of Jerónimos** King Manuel's giant 16th-century, white-limestone church and monastery, with remarkable cloisters and the explorer Vasco da Gama's tomb. **Hours:** May–Sept Tue–Sun 10:00–18:30, Oct–April 10:00–17:00, closed Mon and during Sun Mass.

▲▲**Coach Museum** Dozens of carriages, from simple to opulent, displaying the evolution of coaches from 1600 on. **Hours:** Tue–Sun 10:00–17:30, closed Mon.

▲**Monument to the Discoveries** Giant riverside monument honoring the explorers who brought Portugal great power and riches centuries ago. **Hours:** Tue–Sun 9:00–18:00, closed Mon.

▲**Belém Tower** Consummate Manueline building with a worthwhile view up 120 steps. **Hours:** May–Sept Tue–Sun 10:00–18:30, Oct–April 10:00–17:00, closed Mon.

Folk Art Museum A sneak preview of the folk art you'll see throughout the rest of Portugal. **Hours:** Tue–Sun 10:00–12:30 & 14:00–17:00, closed Mon.

Maritime Museum A salty selection of exhibits on the ships and navigational tools of the Age of Discovery. **Hours:** April–Sept Tue–Sun 10:00–18:00, Oct–March Tue–Sun 10:00–17:00, closed Mon.

To end this walk, you have several options: Catch the subway (Baixa-Chiado stop is at Café A Brasileira) to your next destination; catch trolley #28 to the Alfama to connect with the next walk (stop is 100 yards away on Rua Antonio Maria Cardoso); walk down Rua do Carmo to reach Rossio (facing the mall entrance, it's the road to your left); or enter the Armazéns mall. To get from the mall to the Baixa—the lower city—take the elevator (press 0) or the escalators down (you'll pass through the Intersports shop on the lower floors—exit through ground level of store).

The Alfama Stroll

For another ▲▲ walk, explore the Alfama, the colorful sailors' quarter that dates back to the age of Visigoth occupation (6th–8th centuries A.D.). This was a bustling district during the Moorish period, and eventually became the home of Lisbon's fishermen and mariners (and of the poet Luis de Camões, who wrote, "our lips meet easily, high across the narrow street"). The Alfama's tangled street plan is one of the few features of Lisbon to survive the 1755 earthquake. It helps make the neighborhood a cobbled playground of Old World color. It's best to visit during the busy mid-morning market (Tue and Sat 8:00–15:00, on Campo de Santa Clara) or in the cooler hours in the late afternoon or early evening, when the streets teem with locals.

• *Start your walk at the highest point in town, São Jorge Castle. Get to the castle gate by taxi (€3) or by bus #37 from Praça da Figueira. (Trolleys #28 and #12 go to Largo Santa Luzia and Largo das Portas do Sol respectively, a few blocks below.)*

São Jorge Castle Gate: Just inside the castle gate (on left) is a little statue of George, named for England's patron saint in the 14th century. A sensitive guy, the king dedicated the castle to Saint George (São Jorge; pronounced "sow zhorzh") to please his homesick English queen (castle entry-€3, 30 percent discount with LisboaCard, daily March–Oct 9:00–21:00, Nov–Feb 9:00–18:00, last entry 30 min before closing, free guided tours at 10:30, 11:30, 14:30, and 16:00—reserve at ticket office).

• *Pick up your ticket and then follow the cobbles uphill past the first lanes of old Lisbon to the...*

View Terrace (Miradouro de São Jorge): Enjoy the grand view. The Tejo River is one of five main rivers in Portugal, all of

which come from Spain. While Portugal and Spain generally have very good relations, the major sore point is the control of all this water. From here, you have a good view of the 25th of April Bridge, which leads to the Cristo Rei statue (described on page 73). Under the bridge, you can barely see the Monument to the Discoveries and the Belém Tower on a clear day.

Stroll inland along the **ramparts** for a more extensive view of Pombal's Lisbon (the square and grid streets leading up to the big

The Alfama Stroll

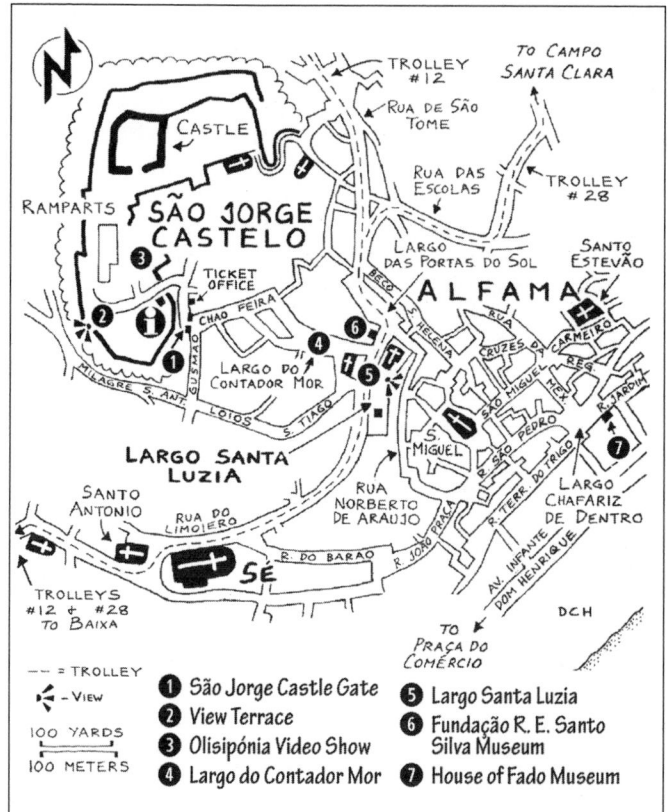

Legend:
- --- = TROLLEY
- = VIEW
- 100 YARDS
- 100 METERS

❶ São Jorge Castle Gate
❷ View Terrace
❸ Olisipónia Video Show
❹ Largo do Contador Mor
❺ Largo Santa Luzia
❻ Fundação R. E. Santo Silva Museum
❼ House of Fado Museum

Edward VII Park on the far right). Find places you know (such as the Elevador de Santa Justa, the Eiffel-style elevator in front of the ruined convent). Before the restaurant (after walking under the 2nd arch), take a right and then a left to enter the actual inner castle (free and empty, offering only a chance to climb up for more views, sometimes exhibitions are housed here, daily 9:00–21:00).

The **castle** was first built by the Moors in the eighth century. After Portugal's King Afonso Henriques (whose statue stands on the view terrace) beat the Moors in the 12th century, the castle began its four-century-long stint as a royal residence. In the 16th century, the king moved and the castle fell into ruins. What you see today was mostly rebuilt by the dictator Salazar in the 1960s (for more on Salazar, see page 71).

• *Heading back out, you'll pass...*

Olisipónia: This high-tech, syrupy, English-language multi-media presentation, called Olisipónia after Lisbon's Roman name, offers two sweeping video overviews of the city's history. The video presentation at the Monument to the Discoveries in Belém is much better, but as a place to cool off from the Lisbon heat, Olisipónia gets two thumbs up.

Leave the castle. Across the ramp from the castle entrance/exit is the recommended restaurant Arco do Castelo (see "Eating," page 94). Facing the restaurant, go left, take your first right, and follow the striped lane downhill through **Largo do Contador Mor.** This small square contains the recommended restaurants A Tasquinha and Comidas de Santiago.

• *From there, pass another restaurant, Farol de Santa Luzia, to reach a superb Alfama viewpoint at...*

Largo Santa Luzia: From this square (a stop for trolleys #12 and #28), admire the panoramic view from the small terrace, Miradouro de Santa Luzia, where old-timers play cards amid lots of tiles. Find the wall of 18th-century tiles that shows Praça do Comércio before the earthquake. The 16th-century Royal Palace (on the left of tile work) was completely destroyed in the quake. For an even better city view, hike around the church to the Largo das Portas do Sol catwalk. This is the place for the most scenic cup of coffee in town—at the Cerca Moura's café terrace (across the street from main café, daily 11:00–22:00, Largo das Portas do Sol 4).

• *Next door to Cerca Moura's main café on the square, you'll find the...*

Fundação Ricardo do Espírito Santo Silva Museum: This offers a unique (but nearly meaningless, with its lack of decent English descriptions) stroll through aristocratic households richly decorated in 16th- to 19th-century styles (€5, 20 percent discount with LisboaCard, Mon–Sat 10:00–17:00, closed Sun, Largo das Portas do Sol 2, tel. 218-814-600, www.fress.pt).

• *From here, it's downhill all the way.*

Descending the Alfama: From Largo das Portas do Sol (near Cerca Moura's bar), go down the stairs (Rua Norberto de Araújo, between the church and the catwalk) into the Alfama. The old wall once marked the end of Moorish Lisbon. As soon as the stairs end, turn left...and down more stairs.

Explore downhill from here until you end up on Rua de São Pedro, a main drag a few blocks below. The Alfama's urban-jungle roads are squeezed into tangled, confusing alleys—the labyrinthine street plan was designed to frustrate invaders trying to get up to the castle. What was defensive then is atmospheric now. Bent houses comfort each other in their romantic shabbiness, and the air drips with laundry and the smell of clams. Get lost. Poke aimlessly, peek through windows, buy a fish. Locals hang plastic water bags from windows to try to keep away the flies. Favorite saints decorate doors protecting families. St. Peter, protector of fishermen, is big in the Alfama. Churches are generally closed, since they share a roving priest. The rash of scaffolding you'll see throughout the Alfama is a sign of the local scramble to renovate and gentrify Old Lisbon with European Union funds before they run out soon.

The neighborhood here is historically tightly knit—families routinely sit down to communal dinners in the streets. Feuds, friendships, and gossip are all intense. Even today, when a woman loses her husband, she typically wears black for the rest of her life. If a widow goes back to colors, neighbors question her respect and love for her dead husband. The neighborhood hosts Lisbon's most popular outdoor party to St. Anthony on June 13. Imagine tables set up everywhere, bands playing, colorful plastic flowers strung across the squares, and all the grilled sardines *(sardinhas grelhadas)* you can eat.

If you see carpets hanging out to dry, it means a laundry is nearby. Because few homes have their own, every neighborhood has a public laundry and bathroom. In the early morning hours, the streets are traditionally busy with locals in pajamas, heading for the public baths. Today, young people are choosing to live elsewhere, lured by modern conveniences unavailable here.

• *Rua de São Pedro, the fish market and liveliest street around, leads left downhill to the square called Largo do Chafariz de Dentro and the...*

House of Fado and Portuguese Guitar: Rated ▲, this museum tells the story of fado in English—push the buttons in each room for music. Don't miss Coimbra's male students' voices singing fado. Finish with a rest in a simulated fado bar, where you can watch old Alfama videos and hear the Billie Holidays of Portugal (30-min cycle includes crazy Portuguese bullfighting scenes). As you leave the fake fado bar, notice—on the wall by the door—the lyrics that were censored by the dictator Salazar (€2.50, 30 percent discount with LisboaCard, daily 10:00–13:00 & 14:00–17:30, Largo do Chafariz de Dentro, tel. 218-823-470). Two blocks uphill from this square is the recommended fado restaurant A Baiuca (see "Nightlife," page 88).

• *To get back downtown from the fado museum, you can walk a block to the main waterfront drag (facing museum, go left around it) where Avenida Infante Dom Henrique leads back to Praça do Comércio downtown (a 10-min walk, plenty of taxis, buses #9 and #39 go to Praça dos Restauradores, #46 and #90 continue up Avenida de Liberdade).*

Pombal's Lisbon

In 1750, lazy King José I (r. 1750–1777) turned the government over to a minor noble, the Marquês de Pombal (1699–1782). Talented, ambitious, and handsome, Pombal was praised as a modern reformer, but reviled for his ruthless tactics. Having learned modern ways as the ambassador to Britain, he battled Church repression and promoted the democratic ideals of the Enlightenment, but enforced his policies with arrest and torture. He expelled the Jesuits to keep them from monopolizing the education system, put the bishop of Coimbra in prison, and broke relations with the Pope. When the earthquake of 1755 leveled the city, within a month Pombal had kicked off major rebuilding in much of today's historic downtown—featuring a grid plan for the world's first quake-proof buildings. In 1777, the king died and the controversial Pombal was dismissed.

SIGHTS

Historic Downtown: The Baixa

Lisbon's sights, listed below, start at the top of the Baixa neighborhood and continue downhill to the riverfront.

The Baixa is the flat valley between two hills, sloping gently from Rossio to the water. After the disastrous 1755 earthquake, the neighborhood was rebuilt on a grid street plan, with many streets named for the crafts and shops historically found there. Its pedestrian streets, inviting cafés, bustling shops, and elegant old storefronts give the district a cer-

tain magnetism. I find myself doing laps in a people-watching stupor. Its delightful ambience for strolling reminds me of Barcelona's Ramblas.

The highlight of mosaic-decorated Rua Augusta is its grand arch, which stands near the river, framing the equestrian statue of King José I.

Notice the uniform and utilitarian Pombaline architecture—its decoration is limited to wrought iron and tiles. In the years after the earthquake, Lisbon had to rebuild quickly, on a slim budget, and with a new focus on designing practical buildings that could withstand future quakes.

Praça dos Restauradores—The monumental square is at the top end of the Baixa and the lower end of Avenida da Liberdade

The Lisbon Earthquake of 1755

At 9:40 in the morning on November 1, All Saints' Day, an earthquake of 8.9 magnitude rumbled through the city, punctuated by three main jolts. Its arrival came midway through Mass. Ten minutes later, thousands lay dead under rubble.

Along the waterfront, shaken survivors scrambled aboard boats to sail to safety. They were met by a 20-foot wall of water, the first of three tsunamis rushing up the Tejo River. The ravaging water capsized ships, swept people off the docks, crested over the seawall, and crashed 800 feet inland.

After the quake, fires from overturned furnaces and candles ignited the city. They raged for five days, ravaging the downtown from the Bairro Alto across Rossio to the castle atop the Alfama.

Of Lisbon's 270,000 citizens, some 30,000 perished. Besides leveling the city, the quake shook Portugal's moral underpinnings. Had God punished Lisbon for the Inquisition killings they sanctioned on nearby Praça do Comércio?

(listed below). Its centerpiece, an obelisk, celebrates the restoration of Portuguese independence from Spain in 1640. (In 1580, the Portuguese king died without a direct heir. The closest heir was Philip II of Spain—yuck. He became Philip I of Portugal, ushering in an unhappy 60 years during which 3 Spanish Philips ruled Portugal.)

On the square is the neo-Manueline-style Rossio Station, Lisbon's oldest hotel (the recommended Hotel Avenida Palace, built to greet those arriving by train, see page 90), the Art Deco facade of the Eden Theater from the 1920s, a TI, a green ABEP kiosk (selling tickets for concerts, movies, and sports events) at the southern end, the Elevador da Glória funicular that climbs to the Bairro Alto, and a Metro station. A block to the east is Lisbon's "eating lane" (Rua

das Portas de Santo Antão), lined with restaurants.

Rossio—Lisbon's historic center, Rossio is still the city's bustling cultural heart. It's home to the colonnaded National Theater, a McDonald's, and street vendors who can shine your shoes, laminate your documents, and sell you cheap watches, chestnuts, and lottery tickets. The column in the square's center honors Pedro IV— King of Portugal and Emperor of Brazil (many maps refer to the square as "Praça Dom Pedro IV").

From Rossio, the pedestrian-only Rua Augusta slopes down-hill through the Baixa to the waterfront. As you face the water, the Alfama is to your left and the Bairro Alto to your right. Pop into Pastelaria Suiça (on the east side of the square) and look out the other side onto adjoining Praça da Figueira, congested with buses, subways, taxis, trolleys, and pigeons leaving in all directions.

To the northeast of the square is the "eating lane," and at its mouth is the small square...

Largo de São Domingos—This square is busy with immigrants from Portugal's former African colonies. In the shadow of the Church of São Domingos, they hang out, trade news from home, strategize on how to gain legal residency, and sample various food products from their native lands. Lisbon's most classic *ginjinha* bar faces this square.

Liquid Sightseeing—*Ginjinha* (zheen-ZHEEN-yah) is a favorite Lisbon drink. The sweet liquor is made from the sour cherry–like *ginja* berry, sugar, and schnapps. It's sold for €1 a shot in funky old

shops throughout town. Buy it with or without berries (*com elas* or *sem elas*—that's "with them" or "without them") and *gelada* (if you want it poured from a chilled bottle—very nice). In Portugal, when people are impressed by the taste of something, they say, "*Sabe melhor que nem ginjas*" ("It tastes even better than *ginja*"). The old-est *ginjinha* joint in town is a colorful hole-in-the-wall at Largo de São Domingos 8 (just off northeast corner of Rossio, across from entrance of "eating lane"). Another *ginjinha* bar is nearby on the "eating lane" itself, Rua das Portas de Santo Antão, next to #59 (just down the street from the recommended Casa do Alentejo restaurant).

Church of São Domingos—It's forgettable from the outside (100 feet left of *ginjinha* stand, free, daily 7:30–19:00). But the evoca-tive inside—rebuilt from the ruins left by the tragic 1755 earth-quake—reminds visitors of that horrible All Saints' Day Sunday,

when most of the city was at Mass and the earth rolled. Heavy stone churches like this collapsed on their congregations.

Elevador de Santa Justa—In 1902, a student of Gustav Eiffel built this 150-foot-tall iron eleva-tor to connect the lower city with the high town. While you can no

longer enter the Bairro Alto from the skyway at the top, you can still ride the elevator for a fine city view and a cup of coffee (€1.20, daily 7:00–22:45). A Carris ticket booth on the back (uphill side) of the elevator sells "BUC-2" tickets for €1.40, which will get you two rides for nearly the price of one.

Praça do Comércio ("Trade Square")—At this riverfront square bordering the Baixa, ships used to dock and sell their goods. Nicknamed "Palace Square" by locals, it was the site of Portugal's royal palace for 200 pre-earthquake years. Government ministries ring the square these days. It's the

departure point for city bus and tram tours and the boat across the Tejo River. The area opposite the harbor was conceived as a residential neighborhood for the upper class, but they chose the suburbs, and it's been pretty dead for the last century. The statue is of King José I, the man who put Pombal to work rebuilding the city. The big arch is Pombal's attempt to restore Lisbon's Parisian-style grandeur.

Cathedral (Sé)—The cathedral, just a few blocks east of Praça do Comércio, is not much on the inside, but its fortress-like exterior is a textbook example of a stark and powerful Romanesque fortress of God. Twin castle-like towers solidly frame an impressive rose window. Started in 1150, after the Christians retook Lisbon from the Islamic Moors, and built on the site of a mosque, its crenellated towers made a powerful statement: The *Reconquista* was here to stay.

The church is built on the site of the baptism of St. Anthony—another favorite saint of Portugal (locals appeal to him for help in finding a parking spot or a true love, and generally for lost objects). Also, some of St. Vincent is buried here—legend has it that in the 12th century, his remains were brought to Lisbon on a ship guarded by two sacred black ravens, the symbol of the city.

The **cloisters** (€1 entry) are peaceful and an archaeological work in progress—they're now uncovering Roman ruins. The humble **treasury** is worthwhile only if you want to support the church and climb some stairs (€2.50, free with LisboaCard, Tue–Sat 9:00–19:00, Sun–Mon 9:00–17:00, on Largo da Sé, several blocks east of Baixa, take Rua da Conceição east, which turns into Rua de Santo António da Sé).

Greater Lisbon

Avenida da Liberdade—This tree-lined grand boulevard, running north from Rossio, connects the old town near the river (where most of the sightseeing action is) with the newer upper town. Before the great earthquake, this was a royal promenade. After 1755, it was the grand boulevard of Pombal's new Lisbon—originally limited to the aristocracy. The present street, built in the 1880s and inspired by Paris' Champs-Élysées, is lined with banks, airline offices, nondescript office buildings...and eight noisy lanes of traffic. The grand "rotunda"—as the roundabout formally known as Marquês de Pombal is called—tops off the Avenida da Liberdade with a commanding statue of Pombal. Allegorical symbols of his impressive accomplishments decorate the statue. (A single-minded dictator can do a lot in 27 years.) Beyond that lies the fine Edward VII Park. From the Rotunda (Metro: Marquês de Pombal), it's an enjoyable 20-minute downhill walk along the mile-long avenue to the old city (the Baixa). The black-and-white cobbled sidewalks are a Lisbon tradition.

▲▲▲Gulbenkian Museum—This is the best of Lisbon's 40 museums. Calouste Gulbenkian (1869–1955), an Armenian oil tycoon, gave Portugal his art collection (or "harem," as he called it). His gift was an act of gratitude for the hospitable asylum granted him during World War II (he lived in Lisbon from 1942 until he died in 1955). The Portuguese consider Gulbenkian—whose billion-dollar estate is still a growing and vital arts foundation promoting culture in Portugal—an inspirational model of how to be thoughtfully wealthy. (He made a habit of "tithing for art," spending 10 percent of his income on things of beauty.) The foundation often hosts classical music concerts in the museum's auditoriums.

Gulbenkian's collection, spanning 5,000 years and housed in a classy modern building, offers the most purely enjoyable museum experience in Iberia—it's both educational and just plain beautiful. The museum is cool, uncrowded, gorgeously lit, and easy to grasp, displaying only a few select and exquisite works from each epoch. Walk through five millennia of human history, appreciating our ancestors by seeing objects they treasured.

From the entrance lobby, there are two wings, covering roughly pre-1500 and post-1500. Following the museum's layout, you'll see...

Egypt (2,500–500 B.C.): Ancient Egyptians, believing that life really began after death, carved statues to preserve the memory of the deceased, whether it be a prince (Statue of the Courtier Bes, 664–610 B.C., with an inscription calling him "the king's friend") or a likeness of the family pet. The cat statue nurses her kittens atop a coffin that once held the cat's mummy, preserved for the afterlife. Egyptians honored cats—even giving them gold earrings like the statue's. They believed cats helped the goddess Bastet keep watch over the household. Now, 2,500 years later, we remember the Egyptians for these sturdy, dignified statues, built for eternity.

Gulbenkian Museum

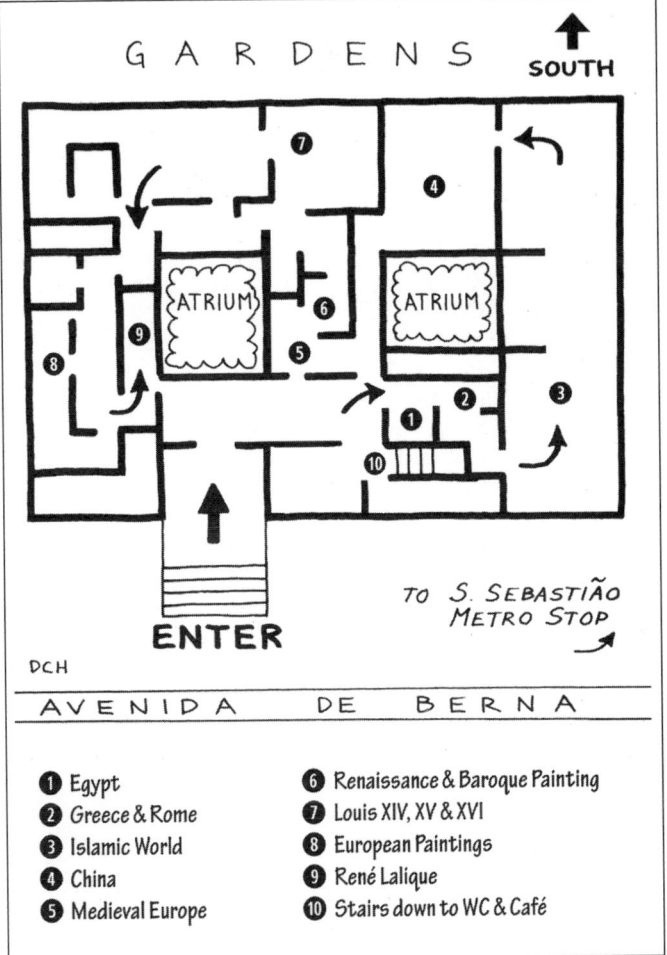

1. Egypt
2. Greece & Rome
3. Islamic World
4. China
5. Medieval Europe
6. Renaissance & Baroque Painting
7. Louis XIV, XV & XVI
8. European Paintings
9. René Lalique
10. Stairs down to WC & Café

Greece and Rome (500 B.C.–A.D. 500): The black-and-red Greek vase (calyx-crater), decorated with scenes of half-human satyrs chasing human women, reminds us of the rational Greeks' struggle to overcome their barbarian, animal-like urges and to invent civilization. Alexander the Great (r. 336–323 B.C., seen on a coin) used war to spread Greek culture throughout the Mediterranean, creating a cultural empire that would soon be taken over by Roman emperors (seen on medallions). Journey even further back in time to the very roots of civilization—Mesopotamia (modern Iraq), where writing was invented. Five thousand years ago, the cylinder seals were used to roll an impression in sealing wax or clay.

Islamic World (700–1500): The Muslims who lived in Portugal—as far from Mecca as you could get back then—might have decorated their homes with furnishings from all over the Islamic world. Imagine a Moorish sultan, dressed in a shirt from Syria, sitting on a carpet from Persia in a courtyard with Moroccan tiles. By a bubbling fountain, he puffs on a hookah.

Islam is not all Taliban extremists, and the culture of Moorish Iberia (711–1492) was among Europe's most sophisticated after the Fall of Rome. The intricate patterns on the glass lanterns are not only beautiful...they're actually quotes (in Arabic) from the Koran, such as "Allah is the light of the world, shining like a flame in a glass lamp, as bright as a star."

China (1368–1644): For almost 300 years, the Ming dynasty ruled China, having reclaimed the country from Genghis Khan and his sons. When Portuguese traders reached the Orient, they brought back blue-and-white ceramics such as these. They became all the rage, inspiring the creation of both Portuguese azulejo tiles and Dutch Delftware.

In the other wing, look for the art of...

Medieval Europe (500–1500): While China was thriving and inventing, Europe was stuck in a thousand-year medieval funk. Europeans from the "Age of Faith" channeled their spirituality into objects of Christian devotion. A priest on a business trip could pack a portable altarpiece in his backpack, travel to a remote village that had no church, and deliver a sermon carved in ivory. In monasteries, the monks with the best penmanship laboriously copied books (illuminated manuscripts) and illustrated them with scenes from the text—and wacky doodles in the margins. These books were virtual time capsules, preserving the knowledge of Greece and Rome until it could emerge again, a thousand years later, in the Renaissance.

Renaissance and Baroque Painting (1500–1700): Around 1500, a cultural revolution was taking place—the birth of humanism. Painters saw God in the faces of ordinary people, whether in Domenico Ghirlandaio's fresh-faced maiden, Frans Hals' wrinkled old woman, or Rembrandt's portrait of an old man, whose crease-lined hands tell the story of his life.

Louis XIV, XV, XVI (1700–1800): After the Italian-born Renaissance, Europe's focus shifted northward to the luxurious court of France, where a new secular culture was blossoming. In one tapestry, love is in the air (see cupids flying overhead) as Venus frolics in a landscaped garden. Powder-wigged nobles in their palaces enjoyed the luxury of viewing art like this pagan scene, while relaxing in chairs like the kind you see here. This furniture, once actually owned by French kings (and Marie Antoinette and Madame de Pompadour), is a royal home show. Anything heavy, ornate, and gilded (or that includes curved legs and animal-clawed feet) is from the time of Louis XIV. The Louis XV style is lighter and daintier, with Oriental motifs, while furniture from the Louis XVI era is stripped-down, straight-legged, tapered, and more modern.

European Paintings (1700–2000): Europe ruled the world, and art became increasingly refined. Young British aristocrats (Thomas Gainsborough portrait) traveled Europe on the Grand Tour to see great sights like Venice (Guardi landscape). Follow the progression in styles from stormy Romanticism (J. M. W. Turner's tumultuous shipwreck) to Pre-Raphaelite dreamscapes (Mirror of Venus) to Realism's breath-of-fresh-air simplicity (Manet's bubble-blower) to the glinting, shimmering Impressionism of Monet... Renoir...and the Englishman John Singer Sargent.

Finish your walk with the sumptuous Art Nouveau glasswork and jewelry of French designer René Lalique (1860–1945). Fragile beauty like this, from the elegant turn-of-the-century belle époque, was about to be shattered by the tumultuous 20th century. The work of Lalique—just another of Gulbenkian's circle of friends—is a fitting finale to a museum that features both history and beauty.

Cost, Hours, Location: €3, free Sun, 20 percent discount with LisboaCard, Tue–Sun 10:00–18:00, closed Mon, pleasant gardens, good air-con cafeteria, Berna 45, tel. 217-823-000, www .museu.gulbenkian.pt. To get here from downtown, hop a cab (€4) or take the Metro from Restauradores to São Sebastião, exit the station at Avenida de Aguiar, and walk downhill, past a row of gorgeous Art Deco buildings on your left. Before reaching the roundabout, you'll see a sign pointing right to the *fundação*—walk straight to the museum entrance. From here, Belém is a quick €6 taxi ride away.

▲▲**Museum of Ancient Art (Museu Nacional de Arte Antiga)**— This is Portugal's finest museum for paintings from its glory days, the 15th and 16th centuries. (Most of these works were gathered from Lisbon's abbeys and convents after their dissolution in 1834.) You'll also find a rich collection of furniture, as well as art by renowned European masters such as Hieronymus Bosch, Jan van Eyck, and Raphael—all in a grand palace. Here are some highlights:

Third Floor—Portuguese Paintings: The *Adoration of St. Vincent* is a many-paneled altarpiece by the late-15th-century master Nuno Gonçalves. A gang of 60 real people—everyone from royalty to sailors and beggars—surrounds Lisbon's patron saint.

Second Floor—Japanese Screen and Jewels: Find the enchanting Namban screen painting (Namban means "barbarians from the south"). It shows the Portuguese from a 16th-century

Japanese perspective—with long noses and great skill at climbing rigging like acrobats. The Portuguese, the first Europeans to make contact with Japan, gave the Japanese guns, Catholicism (Nagasaki was founded by Portuguese Jesuits), and the word for "thank you" (ever notice how similar the Japanese word *arigato* is to the Portuguese *obrigado*?).

On the same floor, in a free-standing glass case, is the Monstrance of Belém, made for Manuel I from the first gold brought back by Vasco da Gama. Squint at the fine enamel creatures filling a tide pool on the base, the 12 apostles gathered around the glass case for the Communion wafer (the fancy top pops off), and the white dove hanging like a mobile under the all-powerful God bidding us all peace on earth. There is another impressive monstrance nearby, as well as more jewels and fine porcelain on the rest of this floor.

First Floor—European Paintings: Look for Bosch's *Temptations of St. Anthony* (a 3-paneled altarpiece fantasy, c. 1500, in room 57) and Albrecht Dürer's *St. Jerome* (just opposite).

Cost, Hours, Location: €3, free until 14:00 on Sun, free with LisboaCard, Tue 14:00–18:00, Wed–Sun 10:00–18:00, closed Mon. It's located about a mile west of Praça do Comércio (from Praça da Figueira, take trolley #15 to Cais Rocha, cross street and walk up a lot of steps; or take bus #49 or #60 to Rua das Janeles Verdes 9). Tel. 213-912-800. The museum has a good cafeteria with seating in a shaded garden overlooking the river.

▲**National Tile Museum (Museu Nacional do Azulejo)**—Filling the Convento da Madre de Deus, the museum features piles of tiles,

which, as you've probably noticed, are an art form in Portugal. They've tried to showcase the tiles as they would have originally appeared (note the diamond-shaped staircase tiles). While the presentation is low-tech, the church is sumptuous, and the tile panorama of pre-earthquake Lisbon (upstairs) is fascinating (€3, free until 14:00 on Sun, free with LisboaCard, Tue 14:00–18:00, Wed–Sun 10:00–18:00, closed Mon; museum is about a mile east of Praça do Comércio, 10 min on bus #105 from Praça da Figueira or #105 and #104 from Praça do Comércio, Rua da Madre de Deus 4, tel. 218-100-340).

Parque das Nações—Lisbon celebrated the 500th anniversary of Vasco da Gama's voyage to India by hosting Expo '98. The theme was "The Ocean and the Seas," emphasizing the global importance of healthy, clean waters. The riverside fairgrounds are east of the Santa Apolónia train station, in an area revitalized with luxury

Antonio Salazar

Q: What do you get when you cross a lawyer, an economist, and a dictator?

A: Antonio Salazar, who was all three—a dictator who ruled Portugal through harsh laws and a strict budget that hurt the poor.

Shortly after a 1926 military coup "saved" Portugal's floundering democracy from itself, General Oscar Carmona appointed Antonio de Oliveira Salazar (1889–1970) as finance minister. As a former professor of economics and law at the University of Coimbra, Salazar balanced the budget *and* the interests of the country's often-warring factions. His skill and his reputation as a clean-living, fair-minded patriot earned him a promotion. In 1932, he became prime minister, and he set about creating his New State *(Estado Novo)*.

For nearly four decades, Salazar ruled a stable but isolated nation based on harmony between the traditional power blocs of the ruling class—the military, big business, large landowners, and the Catholic Church. This Christian fascism, backed by the military and secret police, was ratified repeatedly in elections by the country's voters—the richest 20 percent of the populace.

As a person, Salazar was respected, but not loved. The son of a farm manager, he originally studied to be a priest before going on to become a scholar and writer. He never married. Quiet, low-key, and unassuming, he attended church regularly and lived a non-materialistic existence. But when faced with opposition, he was ruthless, and his secret police became an object of fear and hatred.

Salazar steered Portugal through the turmoil of Spain's Civil War (1936–1939), remaining officially neutral while secretly supporting Franco's fascists. He detested Nazi Germany's "pagan" leaders, but respected Mussolini for reconciling with the pope. In World War II, Portugal was officially neutral, but often friendly with longtime ally Britain. After the war, they benefited greatly from the United States' Marshall Plan for economic recovery, and the country joined NATO in 1949.

Salazar's regime was undone by two factors: the liberal 1960s and the unpopular, draining wars Portugal fought abroad to try to keep its colonial empire intact. When Salazar died in 1970, the military-backed regime that followed became increasingly less credible, leading to the liberating events of the Carnation Revolution in 1974.

The Carnation Revolution

On April 25, 1974, several prominent members of the military reluctantly sided with a growing popular movement to oust the government. They withdrew their support from the military-backed regime that had ruled Portugal under Antonio Salazar for five decades. Only five people died that April day in a well-planned, relatively bloodless coup. Citizens spilled into the streets to cheer and put flowers in soldiers' rifle barrels, giving the event its name—the Carnation Revolution. Suddenly, people were free to speak aloud what they formerly could only whisper in private.

In the Revolution's aftermath, the country struggled to get the hang of modern democracy. Their economy suffered as overseas colonies fell to nationalist uprisings, flooding the country with some 800,000 emigrants. In 1976, the Portuguese adopted a constitution that separated church and state. These changes helped to break down the almost medieval class system and establish parliamentary law.

Mario Soares, a former enemy of the Salazar regime, became the new prime minister, ruling through much of the next two decades as a stabilizing presence. Today, Portugal is a strong example of democratic government.

condos, crowd-pleasing terraces, and restaurants. Ride the Metro to the last stop on the Red line (Oriente—meaning east end of town), walk to the water, turn right, and join the riverside promenade. You can rent a bike by the hour, go up the Vasco da Gama tower (€3, daily 10:00–18:00, tel. 218-969-869), or visit Europe's biggest aquarium, the Oceanário, which simulates four different oceanic underwater and shoreline environments (€10, 40 percent discount with LisboaCard, daily 10:00–18:00, last entry 17:15). Popular café/bars—such as Bar de Palha—line the waterfront just south of the tower. This area is fully open on Monday (when many Lisbon museums are not) and most vibrant on Sunday afternoons.

Vasco da Gama Bridge—Europe's second-longest bridge was opened in 1998 to connect the Expo grounds with the south side of the Tejo and to alleviate the traffic jams on Lisbon's only other bridge over the river, the 25th of April Bridge. Built low to the water, its towers and cables are meant to suggest the sails of a caravel ship.

▲**25th of April Bridge (25 de Abril)**—At 1.5 miles (3,280 feet between the towers), this is one of the longest suspension bridges in the world. The foundations are sunk 260 feet into the riverbed, making it the world's deepest bridge. It was built in 1966 by the same company that did its San Francisco cousin (but notice the lower deck for train tracks). Originally named for the dictator

Salazar (see sidebar), the bridge was renamed for the date of Portugal's 1974 revolution and liberation. For a generation, locals have showed their political colors by choosing what name to use. While conservatives still called it the Salazar Bridge, liberals refer to it as the "25th of April" Bridge.

Cristo Rei (Christ of Majesty) —A huge, 330-foot concrete statue of Christ (à la Rio de Janeiro) overlooks Lisbon from across the Tejo River, stretching its arms wide to symbolically bless the city (or dive into the river). It was built in 1959 as thanks to God, funded by locals grateful that Portugal stayed out of World War II. While the statue was designed to be seen from a distance, an elevator takes visitors to the top for a panoramic view (€3, daily 9:30–18:15). From left to right, see Belém, the 25th of April Bridge, downtown Lisbon (the green Alfama hilltop with the castle), and the long Vasco da Gama Bridge.

To get to Christo Rei, catch the ferry from downtown Lisbon (6/hr, from Praça do Comércio) to Cacilhas, then take a bus marked *Cristo Rei* (4/hr, from ferry dock). Because of bridge tolls, taxis to or from the site are expensive. For drivers, the most efficient visit is a quick stop on your way to or from the Algarve.

Belém District

Three miles from downtown Lisbon, the Belém District is a stately pincushion of important sights from Portugal's Golden Age, when Vasco da Gama and company turned the country into Europe's richest power. Belém was the send-off point for voyages in the Age of Discovery. Sailors would stay and pray here before embarking. The tower welcomed them home. The grand buildings of Belém survived the great 1755 earthquake, so this is the best place to experience the grandeur of pre-earthquake Lisbon. After the earthquake, safety-conscious (and rattled) royalty chose to live here—in wooden rather than stone buildings. The modern-day president of Portugal calls Belém home (you could, too—the recommended Hotel da Torre is listed in "Sleeping," page 94).

To celebrate the 300th anniversary of independence from Spain, a grand exhibition was held here in 1940, resulting in the fine parks, fountains, and monuments.

Virtually all of Belém's museums are covered by the LisboaCard (except for the Maritime Museum, which offers a discount) and closed on Monday.

Getting to Belém: You'll get here quickest by taxi (€7 from downtown), or slower and cheaper by trolley #15 (30 min, catch at Praça da Figueira or Praça do Comércio) or by bus #28 (just east of Praça do Comércio opposite Terreiro do Paço boat station). In Belém, the first stop is the Coach Museum; the second is the monastery. Even if you miss the first subtle stop (named Belém),

Belém

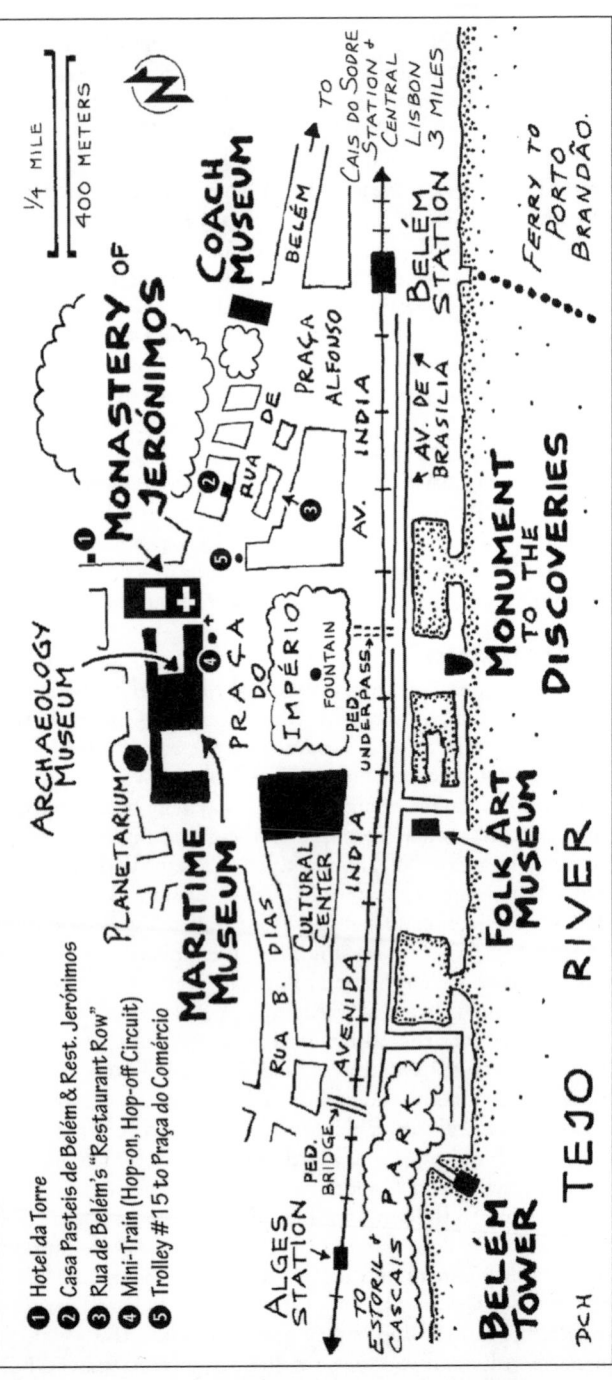

1 Hotel da Torre
2 Casa Pastéis de Belém & Rest. Jerónimos
3 Rua de Belém's "Restaurant Row"
4 Mini-Train (Hop-on, Hop-off Circuit)
5 Trolley #15 to Praça do Comércio

you can't miss the second stop at the massive monastery.

Consider doing Belém in this order: the Coach Museum, pastry and coffee break, Monastery of Jerónimos, Maritime Museum (if interested) and/or lunch at its cafeteria (public access, museum admission not required), Monument to the Discoveries, and Belém Tower. If arriving by taxi, start at Belém Tower, the farthest point. Belém also has a cultural center, a children's museum, and a planetarium—not priorities for a quick visit.

When you're through, hop on trolley #15 to return to Praça da Figueira or Praça do Comércio. Bus #28 takes you to downtown Lisbon and continues to Parque das Nações.

Tourist Information: The little TI kiosk (Tue–Sat 10:00–13:00 & 14:00–18:00, tel. 213-658-455) is directly across the street from the entrance to the monastery. A little red-and-white **Mini-Train** does a handy 45-minute hop-on, hop-off circuit of the Belém sights—which can feel far-flung if you're tired—departing nearly every hour from the monastery entrance (€3, discount with LisboaCard, includes audioguide, daily year-round at 10:00, 11:00, 12:00, 14:00, 15:00, 16:00, and 17:00, June–Sept also 18:00 and 19:00; exact pickup times listed at each stop; you can get off to explore a sight and catch the next mini-train).

Eating in Belém: You'll find snack bars at Belém Tower, a cafeteria at the Maritime Museum, and fun little restaurants along Rua de Belém, between the Coach Museum and the monastery. I like the busy little **Restaurante Jerónimos,** where Carlos treats his customers well and serves fine €7 meals (closed Sat, Rua de Belém 74, next to pastry place listed below). Many more fine places are in the restaurant row behind the McDonald's that faces the park.

The **Casa Pasteis de Belém** café is the birthplace of the wonderful custard tart that's called *pastel de nata* throughout Portugal but here is dubbed *pastel de Belém*. Since 1837, locals have come to this café to get them warm out of the oven (daily 8:00–24:00, Rua de Belém 88). Sit down. Enjoy one with a *café com leite.* Sprinkle on the cinnamon and powdered sugar. If the café is packed, you'll save time and money ordering at the bar.

Ferry Across the Tejo to Porto Brandão: For a delightfully untouristy little adventure, consider having lunch across the river in Porto Brandão. The ferry terminal is immediately in front of the Coach Museum (€0.75 each way, 8-min cruise, departing Belém :30 past every hour and the top of each rush hour until 23:00; for a memorable Tejo experience, tall men can use the urinal while sticking their head out the porthole). Boats continue to Trafaria before returning to Belém via Porto Brandão. Upon arrival, confirm return times carefully.

Porto Brandão is a tiny (and dead) three-street town whose harborfront square has several good fish restaurants. I liked

Manueline Architecture
(c. 1480–1580)

Portugal's unique style (from its peak of power under King Manuel I, the Fortunate, r. 1495–1521) reflects the wealth of the times and the many cultural influences of the Age of Discovery. The purpose is decorative, not structural. Whether the building uses pointed Gothic or round Renaissance arches, it can be embellished with elaborate Manueline carved stonework, particularly around windows and doors.

Manueline aesthetic is ornate, elaborate, and intertwined, often featuring symbols from a family's coat of arms (shields with castles, crosses, lions, banners, and crowns) or motifs from the sea (rope-like columns or borders, knots, shells, coral, anchors, and nets). Manuel's personal symbol, the armillary sphere, was a globe of the earth surrounded by movable rings of stars. (Sailors used it to calculate their location on earth in relation to the heavens.)

Architecture students will recognize elements from Gothic's elaborate tracery, the abstract designs of Moorish culture, Spain's intricate Plateresque style, and the elongated excesses of Italian Mannerism.

Restaurante O Parafuso (€9 cod meals, Tue–Sun 12:00–16:00 & 19:00–23:00, closed Mon, reserve for Fri and Sat eves, tel. 212-954-431). Their *bacalhau a lagareiro* is for garlic lovers. The *cataplana* (a traditional fish and veggie stew) and seafood fondue meals are made for two but stuff three (€20/person).

▲▲**Coach Museum (Museu dos Coches)**—In 1905, the last Queen of Portugal saw that cars would soon obliterate horse-drawn carriages as a form of transportation. She decided to use the palace's riding-school building to preserve her fine collection of royal coaches. It's impressive, with more than 70 dazzling carriages (described in English) lining the elegant old riding room. Look for coach #1 (from around 1600). This crude and simple coach was once used by Philip II, King of Spain and Portugal, to shuttle between Madrid and Lisbon. Notice that this coach has no driver's seat—its drivers would actually ride the horses. (You'll have to trust me on this, but if you lift up the cushion, you'll find a potty hole—also handy for road sickness. Imagine how slow and rough the ride would be with bad roads and a crude, leather-strap suspension.)

Study the evolution of suspension from the first coach, or "Kotze," made in the 15th century in a Hungarian town of that name. Trace the improvement of coaches through the next century, noticing how the decoration increases, as does the comfort.

The Portuguese coat of arms indicates this carriage is part of the royal fleet. The ornamentation includes a folk festival of exotic faces from Portugal's distant colonies.

The lumbering "Ocean Coach," as ornate as it is long, stands shining in the center. At the stern, gold figures symbolize the Atlantic and Indian Oceans holding hands, reminding all who view it of Portugal's mastery of the sea.

The second room shows sedan chairs and the development of carriages as a common means of transport. They got lighter and faster, culminating in a sporty, horse-drawn Lisbon taxi.

Cost, Hours, Location: €3, free Sun until 14:00, free with LisboaCard, Tue–Sun 10:00–17:30, closed Mon, tel. 213-610-850. A taxi stand is across the street. The Coach Museum is on Rua de Belém, along with the monastery, the guarded entry to Portugal's presidential palace, some fine pre-earthquake buildings, and a famous pastry shop—an obligatory stop (Casa Pasteis de Belém café, mentioned above).

▲▲▲**Monastery of Jerónimos**—King Manuel (who ruled from 1495) erected this giant white-limestone church and mon-

astery—stretching 300 yards along the Lisbon waterfront—as a "thank you" for the discoveries made by early Portuguese explorers. It was financed in part with "pepper money," a 5 per-cent tax on spices brought back from India. Manuel built it on the site of a humble sailors' chapel where they would spend their last night in prayer before embarking on their frightening voyages. What is the style of Manuel's church? Manueline.

Here's a tour, starting outside the monastery:

❶ **South Portal:** The fancy south portal, facing the street, is textbook Manueline. Henry the Navigator stands between the doors with the king's patron saint, St. Jerome (above on the left, with the lion). Henry (Manuel's uncle) built the original sailors' chapel on this site. This door is only used when Mass lets out or for Saturday weddings.

❷ **Church Entrance:** As you approach the ticket booth, the church entrance (free) is on your right and the cloisters (€4.50, free Sun until 14:00, free with LisboaCard) are straight ahead (hours for both: May–Sept Tue–Sun 10:00–18:30, Oct–April 10:00–17:00, closed Mon and during Sun Mass, last entry 30 min before closing). Flanking the church door are kneeling statues of King Manuel I, the Fortunate (left of door), and his wife, Mary (right).

Monastery of Jerónimos

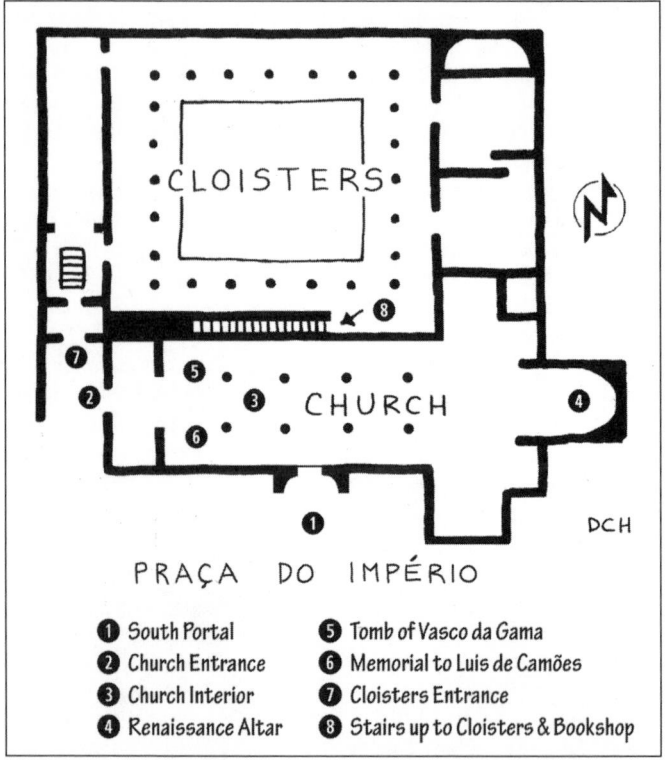

Monastery of Jerónimos

CLOISTERS

CHURCH

PRAÇA DO IMPÉRIO

❶ South Portal
❷ Church Entrance
❸ Church Interior
❹ Renaissance Altar
❺ Tomb of Vasco da Gama
❻ Memorial to Luis de Camões
❼ Cloisters Entrance
❽ Stairs up to Cloisters & Bookshop

DCH

❸ **Church Interior:** The Manueline style is on the cusp of the Renaissance. Unlike earlier medieval churches, the space is more open. Slender palm-tree-like columns don't break the interior space (as Gothic columns do), and the ceiling is all one height. Motifs from the sea hide in the decor. You'll see rope-like arches, ships, and monsters that evoke the mystery of undiscovered lands. Artichokes—eaten for their vitamin C, to fight scurvy—remind us of the hardships sailors faced at sea. Exotic new animals (another aspect of the Age of Discovery) peer out of the capitals. It is, after all, the sea that brought Portugal 16th-century wealth and power, making this art possible.

❹ **Renaissance Altar:** Nearly everything survived the 1755 earthquake, except for the stained glass (replacement glass is from 1940). In the main altar, elephants—who dethroned lions as the most powerful and kingly beasts—support two kings and two queens (King Manuel I is front-left). Walk back on the side with the seven wooden confessional doors (on your right). Notice the ornamental carving around the second one: a festival of faces from newly discovered corners of the world. Ahead of you (near the entry, under a ceiling which is a veritable *Boy Scout's Handbook* of rope and knots) is the tomb of Vasco da Gama.

❺ Tomb of Vasco da Gama: The night of July 7, 1497, Vasco da Gama (1460–1524) prayed for a safe voyage in the small chapel that stood here before the current church was built. The next day, he set sail from Belém with four ships (see the caravel carved in the middle of the tomb's side) and 150 men. He was armed with state-of-the-art maps and sailing technology, such as the carved armillary sphere, a globe surrounded by rings of stars to help sailors track their location on Earth. (Some say its diagonal slash is symbolic of the unwritten pact and ambition of Spain and Portugal to split the world evenly, but it actually represents the path of the planets as they move across the heavens.)

Da Gama's mission? To confirm what earlier navigators had hypothesized—that the ocean recently discovered when Bartolomeu Dias rounded Africa was the same one seen by overland travelers to India. Hopefully, he'd find a direct sea route to the vast, untapped wealth of Asia. The three symbols on the tomb show the source of the money (the cross symbolizing the Knights Templar, the soldier monks who funded these voyages), the method (the caravel ship), and the result (Portugal's domination of the globe).

By Christmas, da Gama rounded the Cape of Good Hope. After battling hostile Arabs in Mozambique, he hired an Arab guide to pilot the ships to India, arriving in Calicut (from which we get the word "calico") in May 1498. He traded for spices, networked with the locals for future outposts, battled belligerent chiefs, and then headed back home. Da Gama and his crew arrived home to Lisbon in September 1499 (after 2 years and 2 months on the seas), and were greeted with all-out Vasco-mania. The few spices he'd returned with (many were lost in transit) were worth a staggering fortune. Portugal's golden age was launched.

King Manuel dubbed da Gama "Admiral of the Sea of India" and sent him out again, this time to subdue the Indian locals with his sword, establish more trade outposts, and again return home to wealth and honor. Da Gama died on Christmas Eve, 1524, in India. His memory lives on due to the adoration of two men: Manuel, who built this large church, and Luis de Camões (honored on the other side of the church), who turned da Gama's history-making voyage into an epic poem.

❻ Memorial to Luis de Camões: Camões (kah-MOISH, 1524/5–1580) is Portugal's Shakespeare and Casanova rolled into one, an adventurer and writer whose heroic poems glorifying the nation's sailing exploits live on today. It was Camões who described Portugal as the place "where land ends and the sea begins."

After college at Coimbra, Camões was banished from the court (1546) for flirting with the noble lady Dona Caterina. He lost an eye soldiering in Morocco, served jail time for brawling with a bureaucrat, and then caught a ship to India and China, surviving a shipwreck on the way. While serving as a colonial administrator in India, he plugged away at the epic poem that would become his masterpiece. Returning to Portugal, he published *Os Lusiadas* (*The Lusiads*, 1572), winning minor recognition and a small pension.

The long poem describes Vasco da Gama's first voyage to India in heroic terms, on the scale of Homer's *Odyssey*. *The Lusiadas* begins:

> *"Arms and the heroes, from Lisbon's shore,*
> *sailed through seas never dared before,*
> *with awesome courage, forging their way*
> *to the glorious kingdoms of the rising day."*

The poem goes on to recite many events in Portuguese history, from the time of the "Lusiadas" (the original pre-Roman natives) onward. Even today, Camões' words are quoted by modern Portuguese politicians in search of a heroic sound bite. And Portugal's national holiday, June 10, is known as Camões Day, remembering the day in 1580 when the great poet died. The stone monument here—with literary rather than maritime motifs—is a memorial (his actual burial spot is unknown).

❼ **Cloisters:** Leave the church (turn right, buy a €4.50 ticket) and enter the cloisters. These newly-restored cloisters are the architectural highlight of Belém. The lacy arcade is Manueline; the simpler frieze above the top floor is Renaissance. Study the carvings, especially the gargoyles—find a monkey, a kitten, and a cricket. The small fountain (where the monks washed up before meals) marks the entrance to the refectory, or dining hall—today a concert hall lined with fine old tiles.

Upstairs (❽), you'll find a bookshop and better views of the church and the cloisters (women's WC upstairs, men's downstairs).

The sheer size of this religious complex is a testament to the religious motivation that—along with money—propelled the Age of Discovery. Monks often accompanied the sailor/pirates on their trading/pillaging trips, hoping to convert the heathen locals to Christianity. Many expeditions were financed by the Knights Templar, a brotherhood of soldier monks from the time of the crusades. (The monks who inhabited these cloisters were Hieronymites.)

It was a time of extreme Christian faith. King Manuel, who did so much to promote exploration, was also the man who expelled all Jews from the country. (In 1497, the Church agreed

---

Caravels

These easily maneuverable trading ships were fast, small (80 feet), and light (100 tons), with few guns and three triangular-shaped sails (called lateen-rigged sails) that could pivot quickly to catch the wind. They were ideal for sailing along coastlines. Many ocean-going caravels, such as the one pictured on Vasco da Gama's memorial at the Monastery of Jerónimos, were also rigged with a square foresail to make them more stable. Columbus' *Niña* and *Pinta* were re-rigged caravels.

---

to allow him to marry a Spanish princess on the condition that he deport the Jews.) Francis Xavier, a Spanish Jesuit, did much of his missionary work traveling in Asia in the service of Portugal.

Maritime Museum (Museu de Marinha)—If you're interested in the ships and navigational tools of Portugal's Age of Discovery, this museum, which fills the east wing of the monastery, has good English descriptions and is worth a look. Sailors love it (€3, free Sun 10:00–13:00, 25 percent discount with LisboaCard, April–Sept Tue–Sun 10:00–18:00, off-season Tue–Sun 10:00–17:00, closed Mon; facing the planetarium from the square, a decent cafeteria—open to the public—is to your left and the museum entrance is to your right).

▲Monument to the Discoveries (Padrão dos Descobrimentos)—In 1960, the city honored the 500th anniversary of the death of Prince Henry the Navigator by building this giant riverside monument (see photo on page 83; reached from the monastery via a pedestrian tunnel under the busy boulevard). The elevator inside takes you up to a tingly view (€2, Tue–Sun 9:00–18:00, closed Mon, tel. 213-031-950).

Inside the monument, you can see the **Lisbon Experience,** a 30-minute video shown in a comfortable theater at the top of each hour. This relaxing, well-done sweep through the story of the city is a fun review and leaves you feeling good about Lisbon (€3.50, Tue–Sun 10:00–16:00, closed Mon, in English, a shorter €2 15-min version plays at :40 past the hour).

Walk around the huge monument. The 170-foot concrete structure shows that exploring the world was a team effort. The men who braved the unknown stand on the pointed, raised prow of a caravel about to be launched into the Tejo River.

Leading the charge is Prince Henry the Navigator (for more about him, see page 128 in Algarve chapter), holding a model of a caravel and a map, followed by kneeling kings and soldiers who Christianized foreign lands with the sword. Behind Henry (on the

Portugal Explores the Sea

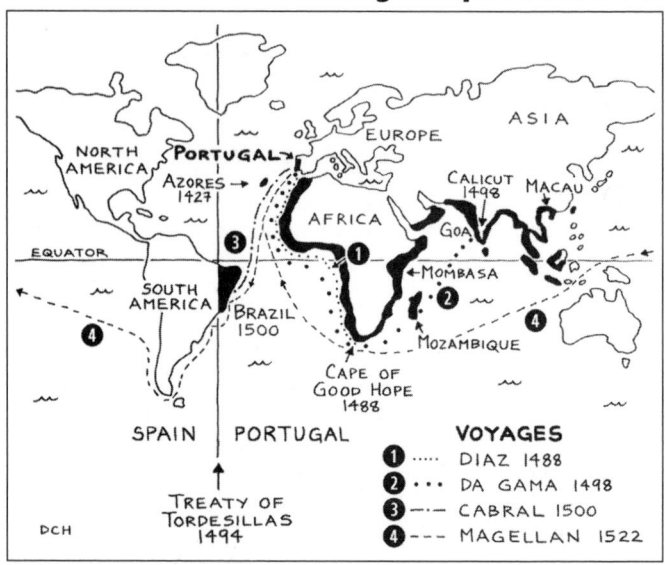

west side), find the men who financed the voyages (King Manuel I, holding an armillary sphere, his personal symbol), those who glorified it in poems and paintings (like Luis de Camões, holding a poem), and, at the very end, the womenfolk left behind to pine away, humming fado.

On the east side, Vasco da Gama keeps an eye on the horizon and his hand on his sword. Magellan holds a circle, representing the round earth his ship circumnavigated, while in front of him, Pedro Cabral puts his hand to his heart, thankful to have (perhaps accidentally) discovered Brazil. Various monks, navigators with maps, and crusaders with flags complete the crew. Near the back, a stone cross on a box juts up, ready to be planted in heathen soil.

In the **marble map in the pavement** (a gift from South Africa) in front of the Monument to the Discoveries, follow Portugal's explorers as they inched out into monster-infested waters at the edge of the world.

From their tiny, isolated nation in Europe, the Portuguese first headed south to the coast of Morocco, conquering the Muslims of Ceuta in God's name (1415) and gaining strategic control of the mouth of the Mediterranean. They braved the open Atlantic to the west and southwest, stumbling on the Madeiras (1420), which Prince Henry planted with vineyards, and the remote Azore Islands (1427).

Meanwhile, they slowly moved southward, hugging the African coast, each voyage building on the knowledge from

The Age of Discovery

In 1560, you could sail from Lisbon to China without ever losing sight of Portuguese-claimed land. The riches of the world poured into the tiny nation—spices from India and Java (black pepper, cinnamon, and curry powder); ivory, diamonds, and slaves from Africa (sold to New World plantations); sugarcane, gold, and (later) diamonds from Brazil; and, from everywhere, knowledge of new plants, animals, and customs. How did tiny Portugal pull this off?

First, its people were motivated by greed, hoping to break the Venetian monopoly on Eastern luxury goods (the price of pepper was jacked up 1,000 percent by the time it reached European dinner tables). They also were driven by a crusading Christian spirit, a love of science, and a spirit of adventure. An entire 15th-century generation was obsessed with finding the legendary kingdom of the fabulously wealthy Christian named "Prester John," supposedly located in either India or Africa. (The legend may be based on an historical figure from around 1120 who visited the pope in Rome as "patriarch of India.")

Portugal also had certain natural advantages. Its Atlantic location led to a strong maritime tradition. A unified nation-state (one of Europe's first) financed and coordinated expeditions. And a core of technology-savvy men used and developed their expansive knowledge of navigational devices, astronomy, maps, shipbuilding, and languages.

previous expeditions. They cleared the biggest psychological hump when Gil Eanes sailed around Cape Bojador (Western Sahara, 1434)—the border of the known world—and into the equatorial seas where sea monsters lurked, no winds blew, and ships would be incinerated in the hot sun. Eanes survived, returning home with 200 Africans in chains, the first of what would become a lucrative commodity. Two generations later, Bartolomeu Dias rounded the southern tip of Africa (1488), discovering the sea route to Asia that Vasco da Gama (1498) and others would exploit to colonize India, Indonesia, Japan, and China (Macao in 1557, on the south coast).

In 1500, Pedro Cabral (along with Diaz and 1,200 men), took a wi-i-i-ide right turn on the way down Africa, hoping to avoid windless seas, and landed (perhaps accidentally) on the tip of Brazil. Brazil proved to be an agricultural goldmine of sugar plantations worked by African slaves.

In 1520, the Portuguese Ferdinand Magellan, employed by Spain, sailed west with five ships and 270 men, broke for R&R in Rio, continued through the Straits of Magellan (tip of South America), named the Pacific Ocean, and suffered through mutinies, scurvy, and dinners of sawdust and ship rats before touching land in Guam. Magellan was killed in battle in the Philippines, but one remaining ship continued west, arriving back in Europe, having circumnavigated the globe after 30 months at sea.

By 1560, Portugal's global empire had peaked. Tiny-but-filthy-rich Portugal claimed (though they didn't actually occupy) the entire coastline of Africa, Arabia, India, the Philippines, and south China—a continuous stretch from Lisbon to Macao—plus Brazil. The Treaty of Tordesillas (1494) with Spain divvied up the colonial world between the two nations, split at 45 degrees west longitude (bisecting South America—and explaining why Brazil speaks Portuguese and the rest of the continent speaks Spanish) and 135 degrees east longitude (bisecting the Philippines and Australia).

But all of the wealth was wasted on Portugal's ruling class, who neglected to reinvest it in the future. Easy money ruined the traditional economy and stunted industry, hurting the middle class and the poor. Over the next four centuries, one by one, Portugal's colonies were lost to other European nations or to local revolutions. Today, only the (largely autonomous) islands of the Azores and Madeiras remain from the once-global empire.

▲Belém Tower—Perhaps the purest Manueline building in Portugal (built 1515–1520), this white tower protected Lisbon's harbor. Today, it symbolizes the voyages that made Lisbon powerful, with carved stone representing ropes, Manuel's coat of arms, armillary spheres, and shields with the cross of Manuel's military, called the Order of the Cross. This was the last sight sailors saw as they left and the first as they  returned, loaded with gold, spices, and social diseases. When the tower was built, the river went nearly to the walls of the monastery and the tower was mid-river. Its interior is pretty bare, but the views of the bridge, river, and Cristo Rei statue are worth the 120 steps (€3, free Sun until 14:00, free with LisboaCard, May–Sept Tue–Sun 10:00–18:30, Oct–April Tue–Sun 10:00–17:00, closed Mon, exhibitions sometimes held here, tel. 213-620-034). The float-plane on the grassy lawn is a monument to the first flight across the South Atlantic (Portugal to Brazil) in 1922. The original plane (which beat Charles Lindbergh's *Spirit of Saint Louis* across the Atlantic by 5 years) is in Belém's Maritime Museum.

If you're choosing between towers, the Monument to the Discoveries is probably the better choice, because it offers a better view of the monastery. Both towers are interesting to see from the outside, whether or not you go up.

Folk Art Museum (Museu de Arte Popular)—This museum takes you through Portugal's folk art one province at a time, providing a sneak preview of what you'll see throughout the country (€1.50, free Sun until 14:00, free with LisboaCard, Tue–Sun 10:00–12:30 & 14:00–17:00, closed Mon, between the Monument and the Tower on Avenida de Brasília—but it's not the white restaurant in the middle of the pond).

SHOPPING

Viúva Lamego—Portugal has been producing some of the world's finest ceramics, including the famous azulejo tiles, ever since the Spanish Moors introduced the craft in the early 16th century. The tradition continues on at Viúva Lamego, the oldest and most respected ceramics maker, which recently opened a branch in this central location. In business since 1849, their tiles can be seen decorating most of Lisbon's Metro stations. Drop by for a peek at an art form that's now required study for every university art student in Portugal (Mon–Fri 10:00–19:00, Sat 10:00–14:00, closed Sun, Calçada do Sacramento 29, just off Largo do Carmo in Chiado, tel. 213-469-692, Isabel speaks English).

Produce Market—The market closest to downtown is Mercado da Ribeira (Mon–Sat 6:00–14:00, closed for produce on Sun but open for a coin collectors' market, Metro: Cais do Sodré). If you can't make it to the market, any local grocery store should have a large variety of fresh produce and picnic fare.

Flea Markets—On Tuesday and Saturday, the Feira da Ladra flea market attracts bargain hunters to Campo de Santa Clara in the Alfama (best in morning). A Sunday market—with coins, books, antiques, and more—is at Parque das Nações (10:00–18:00, in garden Garcia da Horta, Metro: Oriente) and another coin market jingles at Mercado da Ribeira, listed above, on Cais do Sodré (Sun 9:00–13:00).

Colombo Shopping Mall—While downtown Lisbon offers decaying but still-elegant department stores, a shopping center in Chiado (described below), classy specialty shops, and a teeming flea market, nothing is as impressive as the enormous Centro Colombo, the largest shopping center in Spain and Portugal. More than 400 shops—including FNAC's biggest department store, 10 cinemas, 60 restaurants, and a health club—sit atop Europe's biggest underground parking lot and under a vast, entertaining play center. There's plenty to amuse children here, and the place offers a fine look at work-a-day Lisbon (daily 10:00–24:00, pick up a map at info desk, Metro: Colégio Militar-Luz takes you right there, tel. 217-113-636).

Armazéns do Chiado—This grand six-floor shopping center connects Lisbon's lower and upper towns with a world of ways to spend money (part of the Chiado walk described above, lively food circus on 6th floor—see "Eating," page 98). The FNAC department store is known for its helpful, English-speaking staff. It hides behind an old facade. Here's how to find the mall: If you approach from Chiado, take Rua Garrett, which dead-ends at the main entrance. If coming from the Baixa, head up Rua Assunção toward the mall, where you'll find three subtle entrances on Rua do Crucifixo—through the Intersports store (take their escalators up into the mall), at #113, or at #89 (where small, simple doorways lead to elevators). The mall is open daily 10:00–22:00 (eateries 10:00–23:00).

El Corte Inglés—The Spanish mega-department store has arrived in Lisbon with a huge store at the top of Edward VII Park. Inside, there's an enormous supermarket, a food court, and even a cinema (Mon–Sat 10:00–22:00, closed Sun, Av. Antonio Augusto de Aquair 31, Metro: São Sebastião, near Gulbenkian Museum, tel. 213-711-700).

NIGHTLIFE

Nightlife in the Baixa seems to be little more than loitering prostitutes and litter stirred by the wind. Head up instead to the Bairro Alto for fado halls, bars, and the Jardim do São Pedro viewpoint, a pleasant place to hang out. Nearby Rua Diario de Noticias is lined with busy bars and fun crowds spilling onto the street.

The trendy hot spot for young locals is the dock district under the 25th of April Bridge. The Docas (DOH-kash) is a 400-yard-long strip of warehouses turned into pricey restaurants and discos (particularly Doca de Alcântara and Doca de Santo Amaro). Popular places include Hawaii, Salsa Latina, Havana, and Friday's (catch a taxi or trolley #15 from Praça da Figueira to the stop Avenida Infante Santo, take overpass, then a 10-min walk toward bridge; or bus #14 from Praça da Figueira, ask driver for *"Parada Docas"*). If you're returning late, night bus #201 starts at 1:00 and runs every 30 minutes to Cais do Sodré, where you can connect with night bus #205 or #207 to Rossio.

You can hear classical music by national and city companies at the Gulbenkian Museum and the Cultural Center of Belém. Traditional Portuguese theater plays in the National Theater on Rossio and in theaters along Rua das Portas de Santo Antão (the "eating lane," see page 97) stretching north from Rossio. Buy tickets to all arts and sports events at the green ABEP kiosk on Praça dos Restauradores.

For popular music, these days you're more likely to find rock, jazz, Brazilian, and African music than traditional fado. The monthly *Agenda LX* (free at TI, €0.50 at newsstands) provides a complete listing of music, arts, and entertainment in Portuguese only.

▲▲**Fado**—Fado is the folk music of Lisbon's back streets. Since the mid-1800s, it's been the Lisbon blues—mournfully beautiful and haunting ballads about lost sailors, broken hearts, and bittersweet romance. While generally sad, fado can also be jaunty... but in a nostalgic way.

Fado has become one of Lisbon's favorite late-night tourist traps, but it's easy to find a funky bar—without the high prices and tour groups—that still feels very local. Both the Alfama and the Bairro Alto have small, informal fado restaurants. In the Bairro Alto, wander around Rua Diario de Noticias and neighboring streets. In the Alfama, head uphill from the House of Fado museum. Go either for a late dinner (after 21:00) or an even later evening of drinks and music. Homemade "fado tonight" *(fado esta noite)* signs in Portuguese are good news, but even a restaurant filled with tourists can come with good food and fine fado. Prices for a fado performance vary greatly. Many have a steep cover charge, while others just bring out a late-night menu (with prices double those at lunch) and expect you to buy a meal. Any place recommended by a hotel has a bloated price for the kickback.

Fado in Bairro Alto: Run by friendly, English-speaking Gabriel, **Canto do Camões** is easy to reserve and a fine value, with good music, tasty food, and an honest business style. If you reserve a few days in advance, Gabriel can prepare a special regional Portuguese meal for you (open at 20:00, music from 21:00 until around 1:00 in the morning, €22-or-more meal required, after 22:00 €11 minimum for 2 drinks—if seats are available, call ahead to reserve; from Rua Misericordia, go 2.5 blocks west on Travessa da Espera, Travessa da Espera 38; tel. 213-465-464, www.geocities.com/cantodocamoes, canto.do.camoes@clix.pt). The small room feels like a tiny stage show with 15 or 20 diners, mostly tourists, enjoying classic fado (a series of singers accompanied by 2 guitarists). Relax, spend some time, and close your eyes, or make eye contact with the singer. Let the music and wine collaborate.

Restaurante Adega do Ribatejo is a dark, homey place crowded with locals who enjoy open-mike fado *(fado vadio)* nightly (except Sun) from around 8:30. This is just around the corner from Gabriel's Canto do Camoes, less touristy (almost anti-touristy), but really an adventure, which offers a fado dinner with the lights

---

Fado

Fado songs reflect Portugal's bittersweet relationship with the sea. Fado means "fate"—how fate deals with Portugal's adventurers...and the women they leave behind. These are songs of both sadness and hope, a bittersweet emotion called *saudade* (longing)—pining for a loved one across the water, hoping for a future reunion, remembering a rosy past or hoping for a better future, yearning for what might have been if fate had not intervened.

The songs are often in a minor key. The singer *(fadista)* is accompanied by a 12-string Portuguese *guitarra* (with a round body like a mandolin) or other stringed instruments unique to Portugal. Many singers crescendo into the first word of the verse, like a moan emerging from deep inside. Though the songs are often sad, the singers rarely overact—they plant themselves firmly and sing stoically in the face of fate.

A verse from a typical fado song goes:

> *"O waves of the salty sea,*
> *where do you get your salt?*
> *From the tears shed by the women in black*
> *on the beaches of Portugal."*

---

off (€15 meals, Mon–Sat from 19:00, closed Sun, Rua Diario de Noticias 23, tel. 213-468-343).

Fado in the Alfama: A tiny, fun-loving restaurant, **A Baiuca** serves up spirited fado with traditional home-cooking. The menu and wine list are straightforward, but the pre-dinner munchies are costly—turn them away. The English-speaking manager, Henrique, welcomes fado enthusiasts who just want a drink (€12 meals, fado Thu–Mon 20:00–24:00; in the heart of the Alfama, just off Rua São Pedro up the hill from House of Fado, at Rua de São Miguel 20, tel. 218-867-284). This intimate place is a neighborhood affair, as grandma dances with a bottle on her head and the cooks gaze out of their steamy hole in the wall to catch the musical action. It's surround sound, as everyone seems to get into the music.

Club de Fado, a big, bustling, touristy place, has good food and fado nightly (€30 dinners, meal service starts at 20:30, music at 21:30, reservations necessary, around corner from cathedral, Rua São João da Praça 94, tel. 218-882-604).

▲▲▲**Portuguese Bullfight**—If you always felt sorry for the bull, this is Toro's Revenge—in a Portuguese bullfight, the matador is brutalized along with the bull. (Note that Lisbon's bullring may still be closed for renovation.)

In Act I, the horseman *(cavaleiro)* skillfully plants four

ribboned barbs in the bull's back while trying to avoid the leather-padded horns. The horses are the short, stocky Lusitano breed, with excellent balance. In Act II, a colorfully clad eight-man suicide squad (called *forca-dos*) enters the ring and lines up single file facing the bull. With testosterone sloshing

everywhere, the leader taunts the bull—slapping his knees and yelling, *touro!*—then braces himself for a collision that can be heard all the way up in the cheap seats. As he hangs onto the bull's head, his buddies pile on, trying to wrestle the bull to a standstill. Finally, one guy hangs on to *o touro*'s tail and "water-skis" behind him. (In Act III, the *ambulância* arrives.)

Unlike the Spanish *corrida de toros,* the bull is not killed in front of the crowd at the Portuguese *tourada*...but it is killed later. (Some brave bulls with only superficial wounds are spared to fight another day.) Spanish aficionados insist that Portuguese fights are actually more cruel, since they humiliate the bull, rather than fight him as a fellow warrior.

If Lisbon's bullring is still closed for renovation, you can see a bullfight in nearby Cascais or on the Algarve (Easter–Oct, fliers at TI and in hotels). Fights are generally held on Thursday at 22:00 and Sunday on afternoons mid-June through September (tickets €10–50). The ring is small, so there are no bad seats. To sit nearly at ringside, try the cheapest *bancada* seats, on the generally half-empty and unmonitored main floor (Metro: Campo Pequeno).

Important note: Half the fights are simply Spanish-type *cor-ridas* without the killing. For the real slam-bam Portuguese-style fight, confirm that there will be *grupo de forcados* (literally, "bull grabbers"). Tickets are nearly always available at the door (no sur-charge, tel. 217-932-143 to confirm). For a 10 percent surcharge, you can buy them at the green ABEP kiosk (also sells concert and movie tickets) at the southern end of Praça dos Restauradores.

Movies—In Lisbon, unlike in Spain, most films are in the origi-nal language with subtitles. (That's one reason the Portuguese speak better English than the Spanish.) Many of Lisbon's theaters are classy, complete with assigned seats, ushers (tip €0.50), and intermissions. Check the newspaper to see what's playing, or drop by the ABEP kiosk at Praça dos Restauradores, where a list of all the movies playing in town is taped to a side window (on the left). São Jorge Theater (midway up Avenida de Liberdade) is a grand old Art Deco movie palace.

Sleep Code

(€1 = about $1.20, country code: 351)
S = Single, **D** = Double/Twin, **T** = Triple, **Q** = Quad, **b** = bathroom, **s** = shower only. Unless otherwise noted, credit cards are accepted, English is spoken, and breakfast is included.

To help you easily sort through these listings, I've divided the rooms into three categories, based on the price for a standard double room with bath during high season:

$$$ **Higher Priced**—Most rooms €115 or more.
 $$ **Moderately Priced**—Most rooms between
                                            €60–115.
  $ **Lower Priced**—Most rooms €60 or less.

SLEEPING

With a few exceptions, cheaper hotels downtown feel tired and well-worn. Singles cost nearly the same as doubles. Addresses such as 26-3 stand for building #26, third floor (which is the 4th floor in American terms). For hotel locations, see the map on page 92.

Be sure to book in advance if you'll be in Lisbon during its festival—Festas de Lisboa—the last three weeks of June, when parades, street parties, concerts, and fireworks draw crowds to the city. Conventions can clog Lisbon at any time.

In the Center
Central as can be, the Baixa district bustles with lots of shops, traffic, people, street musicians, pedestrian areas, and urban intensity.

On Rossio
$$$ The elegant, central **Hotel Métropole** keeps its 1920s style throughout its 36 rooms. It's a bit overpriced, but you're paying for the prime location. The quieter back rooms are smaller, but cost the same unless you ask for a break (Sb-€150, Db-€170, extra bed-€45, includes breakfast buffet, air-con, elevator, Rossio 30, tel. 213-219-030, fax 213-469-166, www.almeidahotels.com, metropole@almeidahotels.com). These are rack rates—prices drop by a third in slow times (ask when you reserve).

On Praça dos Restauradores
$$$ **Hotel Avenida Palace,** the most characteristic five-star splurge in town, was built with the Rossio Station in 1892 to greet big-shot travelers. Back then, trains were new, and Rossio was the only station in town. The lounges are sumptuous, dripping with

chandeliers, and the 82 rooms mix elegance with 21st-century comforts (Sb-€175, Db-€205, 20 percent less July–Aug, more expensive suites available, reserve on Internet for substantial discounts, includes breakfast, air-con, elevator, laundry service, free parking, hotel's sign is on square but entrance is at Rua 1 de Dezembro 123, tel. 213-218-100, fax 213-422-884, www.hotel-avenida -palace.pt, reservas@hotel-avenida-palace.pt).

$$ Orion Eden Apartment Hotel rents 134 slick and contemporary compact apartments (with small kitchens) and has a rooftop

swimming pool and terrace with commanding city, castle, and river views. The building used to be a 1930s cinema, hence the Art Deco architecture and the slightly pie-shaped rooms. Perfectly located at the Rossio end of Avenida da Liberdade, this is a clean, quiet pool of modernity amid the ramshackle charm of Lisbon. It's also an intriguing option for groups or families of four (Db studio-€89, 2-bedroom apartment with bed-and-sofa combo that can sleep 4 people-€129, breakfast-€5, parking-€14/day, taxes included, air-con, elevator, Praça dos Restauradores 24, tel. 213-216-600, fax 213-216-666, www.viphotels.com, res.eden@viphotels.com).

Near Praça da Figueira

$$ Hotel Lisboa Tejo (LEEZH-boah TAY-zhoo) is an oasis, with 58 comfy, ocean-blue rooms with hardwood floors (Sb-€100, Db-€110, includes air-con, crowded buffet breakfast, Internet access, laundry service, elevator; from southeast corner of Praça da Figueira, walk 1 block down Rua dos Condes de Monsanto and turn left, Condes de Monsanto 2; tel. 218-866-182, fax 218-865-163, www.evidenciahoteis.com, hotellisboatejo@videnciagrupo.com).

Near Rossio

$$ Pensão Residencial Gerês rents 20 bright, basic, cozy rooms with older plumbing. The pension lacks the dingy smokiness that pervades Lisbon's cheaper hotels (S-€45–50, Sb-€55–60, Db-€65–75, Tb-€85–100, 10 percent discount in summer 2006 with cash and this book, no breakfast, Internet access, uphill a block off northeast corner of Rossio, Calçada do Garcia 6, tel. 218-810-497, fax 218-882-006, www.pensaogeres.com, info@pensaogeres.com, Nogueira family speaks some English).

$ Residencial Florescente rents 72 rooms on the "eating lane," a thriving pedestrian street a block off Praça dos Restauradores (see page 97). It's an Old World slumber mill with narrow halls and

Central Hotels and Restaurants

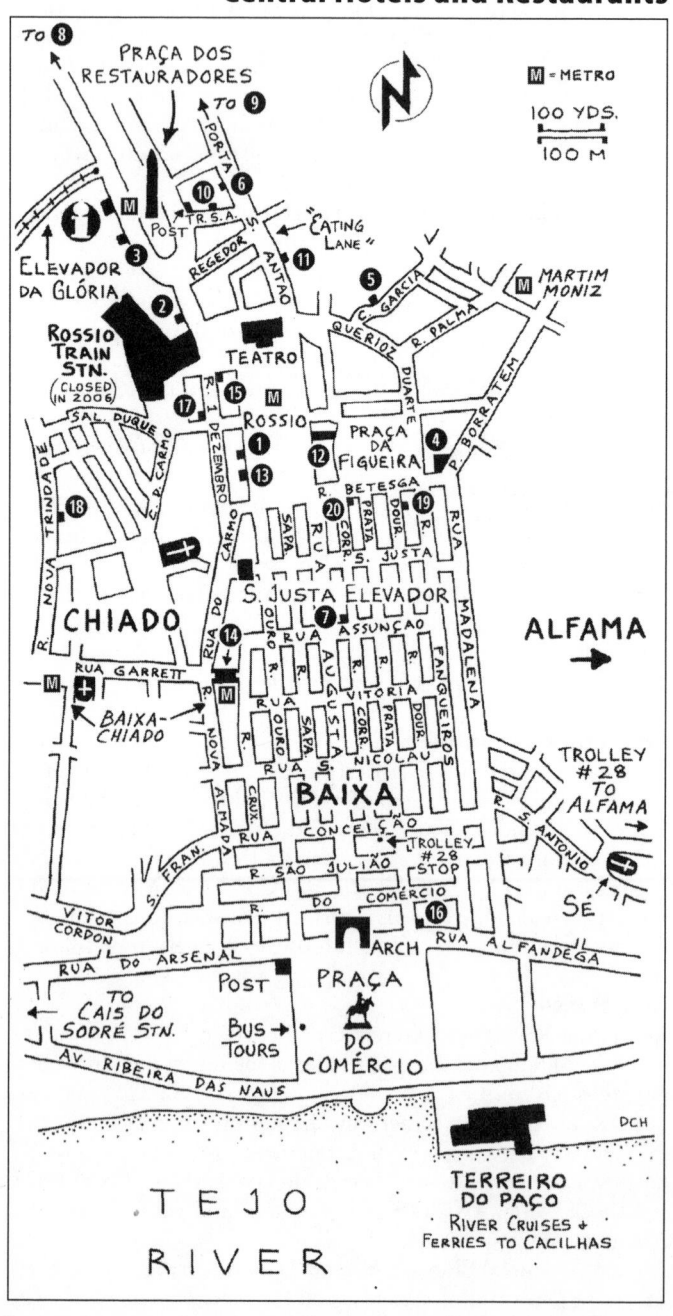

1	Hotel Métropole	**11**	Casa do Alentejo
2	Hotel Avenida Palace	**12**	Pastelaria Suiça
3	Orion Eden Apt. Hotel	**13**	Restaurante Pic-Nic
4	Hotel Lisboa Tejo	**14**	Armazéns do Chiado Mall
5	Pensão Residencial Gerês	**15**	Restaurant Beira-Gare
6	Residencial Florescente	**16**	Martinho da Arcada
7	Albergaria Residencial Insulana	**17**	Pingo Doce Supermarket
8	To Avenida da Liberdade Hotels, Ibis Hotels & Cervejaria Ribadouro	**18**	Cervejaria da Trindade
9	To Rest. Solar dos Presuntos	**19**	Restaurante Gandhi Palace
10	Bonjardim, Rei dos Frangos & Rest. Machado	**20**	Confeitaria Nacional

clean rooms (Sb-€40, Db-€50, Db twin-€60, Tb-€70, includes breakfast, air-con, Rua Portas de Santo Antão 99, tel. 213-426-609, fax 213-427-733, www.residencialflorescente.com).

$ **Albergaria Residencial Insulana,** on a pedestrian street, has 32 quiet, airy rooms and a professional, friendly staff (big Sb-€50, Db-€55, extra bed-€15, includes breakfast, elevator, air-con, Rua da Assuncão 52, tel. 213-423-131, fax 213-428-924, www.insulana.cjb.net, insulana@netc.pt, Fernando speaks English).

Along Avenida da Liberdade

These listings are a 10-minute walk or short Metro ride from the center. The following two places, jointly owned, offer a deal in July and August: free entrance to Lisbon's museums for guests who stay at least three nights.

$$$ **Hotel Lisboa Plaza,** a large, plush, four-star gem, mixes traditional style with bright-pastel classiness. With 106 rooms, it offers snappy and polite service, all the amenities, and a free glass of port with this book (Sb-€146–165, Db-€156–185, Tb-€183–227, the higher prices apply March–June and Sept–Oct, larger "superior" rooms cost 25 percent more, buffet breakfast-€14, air-con, laundry service, 2 non-smoking and 1 non-allergic floor, parking-€9/day, well located on a quiet street off busy Avenida da Liberdade, a block from Metro: Avenida; from Metro, walk downhill and turn right to Travessa do Salitre 7; tel. 213-218-218, fax 213-471-630, www.heritage.pt, plaza.hotels@heritage.pt).

$$$ **Hotel Britania** maintains a 1940s Art Deco feel throughout its 30 spacious rooms, offering a clean and professional haven on a tranquil street one block off Avenida da Liberdade. Run by the Lisboa Plaza folks (above), it offers the same four-star standards for the same prices (air-con, elevator, laundry service, non-smoking floor, free street parking or €9/day in next-door garage, Metro: Avenida; from Metro stop, walk uphill on boulevard, turn right on Rua Manuel de Jesus Coelho and take first left; Rua Rodrigues

Sampaio 17; tel. 213-155-016, fax 213-155-021, www.heritage.pt, britania.hotel@heritage.pt).

$ Residencia Roma, a hardworking little place, rents 40 simple but comfy rooms. It's tucked away on a side street, 50 yards off the big Avenida da Liberdade (Sb-€45–60, Db-€50–70, Tb-€90–105, 25 percent more in Aug, air-con, no elevator, Travessa da Glória 22, tel. 213-460-558, fax 213-460-557, www.residenciaroma.com, res.roma@cyclopnet.pt, Christina speaks English).

$ Pensão Residencial 13 da Sorte, like Residencia Roma, rents 25 basic rooms on a sleepy side street just off Avenida da Liberdade (big Sb-€35, Db-€45–50, Tb-€60, no breakfast, air-con, elevator, tile floors, Rua do Salitre 13, tel. 213-539-746, tel. & fax 213-531-851).

Away from the Center

$$ *In Belém:* For modern comforts on the edge of town, consider **Hotel da Torre,** which rents 59 rooms next to the monastery. After remodeling, they should be open by early 2006 (Sb-€77, Db-€92, extra bed-€15–18, includes breakfast, air-con, elevator, double-paned windows, Rua dos Jerónimos 8, tel. 213-616-940, fax 213-616-946, www.maisturismo.pt/htorre, hoteldatorre.belem@mail.telepac.pt).

$$ *Hotel Ibis:* Three Ibis hotels offer no-stress rooms, no-character rooms for a good price in soulless areas away from the center—but with handy Metro stations nearby. Each has non-smoking floors, air-conditioning, and €4 breakfasts feel (www.ibishotel.com). **Ibis Liberdade** has the best location (Sb or Db-€64, 2 blocks uphill from Avenida da Liberdade's Hotel Tivoli, Metro: Avenida, Barata Salgueiro 53, tel. 213-300-630, fax 213-300-631). The others are **Ibis Saldanha** (Sb/Db-€59, 2-min walk from Metro: Saldanha, Avenida Casal Ribeiro 23, tel. 213-191-690, fax 213-191-699) and **Ibis Jose Malhoa** (Sb or Db-€57, next to Metro: Praça de Espanha, Avenida Jose Malhoa, tel. 217-235-700, fax 217-235-701).

EATING

Ideally, one dinner of your stay in Lisbon should be accompanied by a fado performance. Several good options for this musical dinner are listed under "Nightlife," page 86.

Between the Castle and the Alfama Viewpoint

(These are listed in order from the castle to the viewpoint.)

Arco do Castelo, an eight-table Indo-Portuguese restaurant, dishes up delicious fish and shrimp curries (how spicy is up to you) from Goa, a former Portuguese colony in India. Top off your €10

Alfama Restaurants

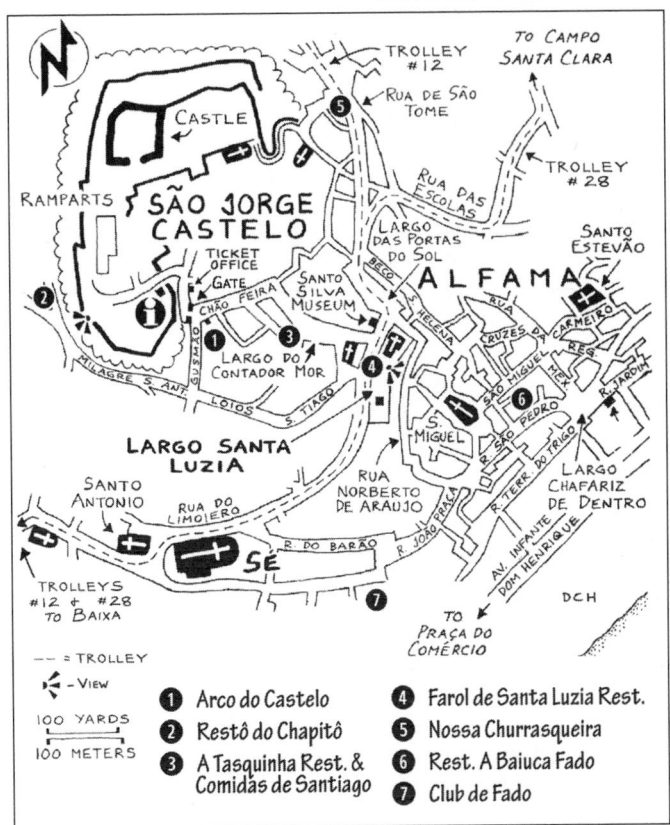

- **①** Arco do Castelo
- **②** Restô do Chapitô
- **③** A Tasquinha Rest. & Comidas de Santiago
- **④** Farol de Santa Luzia Rest.
- **⑤** Nossa Churrasqueira
- **⑥** Rest. A Baiuca Fado
- **⑦** Club de Fado

meal with a shot of the Goan firewater, *feni*, made from cashews (Mon–Sat 12:30–24:00, closed Sun, just across from ramp leading into castle, Rua do Chão da Feira 25, tel. 218-876-598).

The hip **Restô do Chapitô** offers superb views of the river, whether you relax upstairs amid the tasteful and warm decor, in the woody, pub-like downstairs, or on the welcoming, bohemian patio. Dinner from the rotating international menu costs €20 or €25—less for appetizers (Tue–Fri 19:30–24:00, Sat–Sun 12:00–2:00, closed Mon, free jazz after 23:00, cash only; from below the castle—at Arco do Castelo restaurant—go right on Rua do Chaoda Feira 50 yards downhill, take first right to Costa de Castelo 7; tel. 218-867-334).

Largo do Contador Mor—a wispy, cobbled square a block above the Miradouro de Santa Luzia viewpoint and a block below the castle—has two eateries. **A Tasquinha Restaurante,** at the top of the square, is touristy with marginal service, but has atmospheric outdoor seating and serves fine €8 plates of grilled sardines, called *sardinhas assadas* (Tue–Thu 12:00–19:00, closed Wed, Largo do Contador Mor 5). Eat healthy at **Comidas de Santiago,** an inexpensive little salad bar with refreshing summer gazpacho. The self-serve option at the buffet bar is cheaper and faster—the €6.50 *saladas diversas* lets you fill a big plate with salads and meats (understand your bill, daily 12:00–17:00, Largo do Contador Mor 21, tel. 218-875-805).

For a quality seafood feast, consider dining high in the Alfama at the **Farol de Santa Luzia** restaurant (€16 fixed-price *menu turistico*, Mon–Sat 12:00–23:00, closed Sun, Largo Santa Luzia 5, across from Santa Luzia viewpoint terrace, no sign but a window full of decals, tel. 218-863-884).

To mix in some adventure with your sardines, walk past Portas do Sol and follow the trolley tracks along Rua de São Tomé to a square called Largo Rodrigues Freitas. There you'll find **Nossa Churrasqueira** busy serving chicken, sardines, and cod on rickety tables to finger-lickin' locals with meager budgets (chicken with vegetables-€8, sardines-€5.50, Tue–Sun 12:00–22:00, closed Mon; if riding trolley #12, it's at the first stop over the big hill). This neighborhood, a gritty chunk of pre-earthquake Lisbon, is full of interesting eateries. Brighten a few dark bars. Have an aperitif, taste the *branco seco* (local dry white wine). Make a friend, pet a chicken, ponder the graffiti, and pick at the humanity ground between the cobbles.

In Bairro Alto

Lisbon's "high town" has plenty of small, fun, and cheap places. The bright and touristy **Cervejaria da Trindade,** a Portuguese-style beer hall, is full of historic tiles, seafood, and tourists. It's overpriced and in all the guidebooks, but people enjoy the bright and boisterous atmosphere (€15 meals, confirm prices, daily 12:00–24:00, liveliest 20:00–22:00, closed holidays, air-con, courtyard, a block down from São Roque at Rua Nova da Trindade 20C, tel. 213-423-506). They have five Portuguese beers on tap—Sagres is the standard lager. Sagres Preta is a good dark beer. Bohemia is sweet and has more alcohol. Light meals and snacks are served at the bar and in the front.

Restaurante Pap'Açorda, buried deep in the Bairro Alto, is a trendy and mod favorite serving "organic cuisine of aristocratic farm families" from a menu filled with seasonal daily specials. When you step in, you know you've found the right place. The chef, Jose Miranda, runs his restaurant with attitude. Reservations are required for the evening seatings at 20:00 and 22:00 (€25 dinners, lunch from 12:30, closed Sun–Mon, Rua da Atalaia 57, tel. 213-464-811).

You'll find many less-touristed restaurants deeper in the Bairro Alto on the other (west) side of Rua Misericordia. See "Fado" under "Nightlife," page 87, for the best option.

In and Near Rossio

Rua das Portas de Santo Antão is Lisbon's "eating lane"—a galaxy of eateries with excellent seafood (off the northeast corner of Rossio). While the waiters are pushy and it's all very touristy, the lane is still lively with happy eaters and enjoyable to browse. This is a fine spot to down a beer, snack on some snails, and watch the people go by.

The small side street, Travessa de Santo Antão, is famous for three restaurants—**Bonjardim, Rei dos Frangos,** and **Restaurante Machado**—that crank out tasty, roasted chicken (paint on some spicy African *piri-piri* sauce) and fries, for eating inside or streetside.

Casa do Alentejo, specializing in Alentejo cuisine, fills an old second-floor ballroom. The Moorish-looking building is a cultural and social center for people from the traditionalist southern province of Portugal (see jokes in Évora chapter, page 143) living in Lisbon (2-course special of the day–€11, daily 12:00–15:00 & 19:00–22:00, slip into closed-looking building at Rua das Portas de Santo Antão 58 and climb stairs to the right, tel. 213-469-231). While the food is hearty and simple (like the Alentejanos), the ambience is fabulous. It's a good place to try pork with clams or the eggy-almond dessert *encharcada*, both regional specialties. For a full-bodied Alentejo red wine, go with the Borba or simply try the house red.

Restaurante Solar dos Presuntos keeps the theater crowd happily fed with meat and seafood specialties. Its upstairs is subdued, while the downstairs, with a colorful, open kitchen, is touristy and rowdy (€15–20 meals, at the far end of the "eating lane" at Rua das Portas de Santo Antão 150, tel. 213-424-253).

Restaurante Gandhi Palace, a downtown Indian eatery with a friendly staff and non-stop Bollywood movies on the TV, is a local favorite for an inexpensive lunch under €10. Eat in the Pombaline building or ask for it to go *(para fora)* and picnic at a viewpoint...with thoughts of Vasco da Gama's India-bound voyage (daily 11:30–15:00 & 18:00–24:00, follow your nose just off Praça da Figueira to Rua dos Douradores 214, tel. 218-873-839).

Pastelaria Suiça (SWEE-sah) is a bright, modern, air-conditioned place popular with locals (in spite of its surly waitstaff) because it's elegant but affordable and free of riff-raff. They serve more than pastry—try the light meals, sandwiches, salads, and fruit cups (daily 7:00–21:00, inexpensive at the bar, reasonable at inside tables, expensive at outside tables overlooking Rossio or

Praça da Figueira, located directly between the two squares with entrances on each). Across the Rossio, **Restaurante Pic-Nic** is a slightly low-brow, bustling diner, good for breakfast or a light meal and people-watching on the sidewalk.

Confeitaria Nacional has been proudly satisfying sweet tooths for over 175 years—they were once praised by Portuguese royalty. Stop in for a tasty pastry downstairs or enjoy Old World sophistication in the dining room upstairs. You'll find the classy setting—with white tablecloths, sparkling chandeliers, and great street-scene views—affordable at lunch, when traditional menus are around €10 (Mon–Sat 8:00–22:00, closed Sun, on Praça da Figueira 18 just opposite Carris ticket booth).

Armazéns do Chiado shopping center has a sixth-floor food circus with few tourists in sight, offering a huge selection of fun eateries from traditional Portuguese to Chinese (daily about 12:00–23:00, between the low and high towns, between Rua Garrett and Rua da Assuncão; from the low town, find the inconspicuous elevator at Rua do Crucifixo 89 or 113, next to the Baixa-Chiado Metro entrance). Some of the mall's eateries are actual restaurants (that get quiet from about 15:00–18:00); others are smaller fast-food counters that share a common eating area and serve all day. Here are several to consider: **Chimarrão,** a Brazilian place with a Brazilian staff (no English spoken), offers an impressive self-serve salad-and-meat buffet (€12 per big plate, adults can get the €6 kids' plate if preferred); they also have desserts and tropical juices and fruits (€2.50 or €4.50, not part of other buffet). This is where healthy eaters assemble the plate of their dreams—by far the best vegetarian and fruit-filled place I found. Study the exotic juice sheet on the table. Stick with the buffet, since table service doubles the price. (Pick up a plate by the door, raid the meat counter and the salad bar, order drinks at your table, and pay as you leave.) On the same floor, you'll find **Loja das Sopas,** which offers hearty soups with €6 menus (find a table in the food circus nearby), plus **Café de Roma** and a branch of **A Brasileira,** with a wide assortment of fancy coffee drinks. A lot of these places have castle views.

For cod and vegetables prepared faster than a Big Mac and served with more energy than a soccer team, stand or sit at **Restaurant Beira-Gare,** a greasy-spoon diner with a pork sandwich *(bifana no pão)* house specialty. The soup-and-sandwich deal is only €3 (Mon–Sat 6:00–24:00, closed Sun, in front of Rossio Station at the end of Rua 1 de Dezembro).

Martinho da Arcada, poet Fernando Pessoa's old haunt, is a fine option on Praça do Comércio. Founded in 1782, it still enjoys a good reputation, with red-vested waiters serving tasty, traditional cuisine (€20 meals, Mon–Sat 12:00–15:30 & 19:00–22:00, closed Sun, Praça do Comércio 8 at the Rua da Prata corner, tel. 218-879-259).

Rua 1 de Dezembro, located in the Rossio area, is lined with competitive and very cheap restaurants. It's lively for lunch, but dead at dinner. Walk the street and determine the prevailing menu of the day. The chain of little **Ca das Sandes** sandwich shops, found here and scattered about town, offer healthy sandwiches (that you design Subway-style), salads, and usually outdoor seating (daily 9:00–20:00). **Pingo Doce** is a fine supermarket one block south of Rossio Station (daily 8:30–21:00, kitty-corner from a Ca das Sandes shop, on Rua 1 de Dezembro and Calçada do Carmo).

Up Avenida da Liberdade: **Cervejaria Ribadouro** is a popular splurge with locals because of its quality meat and shellfish (€15 meals, daily 12:00–24:00, Avenida da Liberdade 155, at intersection with Rua do Salitre, Metro: Avenida, tel. 213-549-411). Note that seafood prices are listed by the kilogram; the waiter will help you determine the cost of a portion. To limit the cost, actually write down the number of grams you want. For a fun, quick meal or snack anytime, order 100 grams (about a quarter of a pound—good for one person) of *percebes*—barnacles—at the bar with a small beer and *pão torrado con manteiga* (toasted bread with butter).

TRANSPORTATION CONNECTIONS

From Lisbon by Train to: Madrid (1/day, overnight 22:01–8:40; first class-€72, second class-€54; ticket and bed: €76 in quad, €93 in double, €133 in single; discount with railpass—for example, about €19.50 for a bed in quad, €39 in double, €77 in single; cash only; train departs from Santa Apolónia Station), **Paris** (1/day, 16:01–13:40, 21.5 hrs, departs Santa Apolónia), **Évora** (2–4/day, 2.5–3.5 hrs, departs Oriente, transfer in Casa Branca; bus is direct and faster at 2 hrs), **Lagos** (4/day, 4 hrs, departs Oriente, transfer in Tunes), **Faro** (same service as for Lagos, 4/day, 3.5 hrs, departs Oriente), **Coimbra** (17/day, 2–2.5 hrs, departs Santa Apolónia), **Nazaré Valado** (1/day, 2.5–3.5 hrs, departs Santa Apolónia, transfer in Caldas da Rainha), **Óbidos** (8/day, 2.25 hrs, transfer in Cacém), **Porto** (hrly, 4 hrs, departs Santa Apolónia), **Sintra** (round-trip-€2.80, 4/hr, 35 min, departs Sete Rios). For train info, call tel. 808-208-208. Note: Any train leaving from Santa Apolónia also leaves from the Oriente station a few minutes later (which has Metro access from downtown).

To Salema: Both the bus and train take about five hours from Lisbon to Lagos (see Lagos connections above and below). Trains from Lisbon to the Algarve leave from the Oriente Station on the Lisboa-Faro line. At Tunes, there is a transfer to a local train that takes you as far as Lagos. From here, it's either a bus or €18 taxi ride to Salema (see page 116 for details).

From Lisbon by Bus to: Coimbra (11/day, 2.5 hrs, €9.50), **Nazaré** (7/day, 2 hrs, €7.30), **Fátima** (21/day, 1.5 hrs, €8), **Alcobaça** (6/day, 2 hrs, €7.80), **Óbidos** (5/day, 75 min), **Évora** (18/day, 2 hrs, €9.80), **Lagos** (10/day, 5 hrs, €14.50, easier than train, must book ahead, get details at TI), **Madrid** (2/day, 9.5–10 hrs, 9:30–19:00 or 20:30–6:30, €40, Intercentro Lines), **Sevilla** (21:45–6:00 daily, 9:30–18:00 daily, may be less off-season, €36 one-way, buy ticket at station, reservations not necessary, Eurolines, www.eurolines.es). All buses leave from Lisbon's bus station (Metro: Jardim Zoológico, tel. 707-223-344).

Flying: You can generally buy a plane ticket to Madrid on short notice for about €220, depending on the time of the year (usually 5 flights/day). Flying one-way on a round trip is a little cheaper.

Driving in Lisbon

Driving in Lisbon is big-city crazy. If you're starting your trip in Lisbon, don't rent a car until you're on your way out.

If you enter Lisbon from the north, a series of boulevards takes you into the center. Navigate by following signs to Centro, Avenida da República, Marquês de Pombal, Avenida da Liberdade, Praça dos Restauradores, Rossio, and Praça do Comércio. If coming from the east over the Vasco da Gama Bridge and heading for the airport, take the first exit after the bridge.

If you're turning in your car upon arrival in Lisbon, consider driving to the airport (rental-car turn-in clearly signposted, no extra expense to drop it here, very helpful TI open late) and riding a sweat-free taxi for €10 to your hotel. Or consider hiring a taxi (cheap) and following it to your hotel.

There are many safe underground pay parking lots (follow the blue *P* signs), but they get more expensive by the hour and can cost €40 per day (at the most central Praça dos Restauradores).

SINTRA

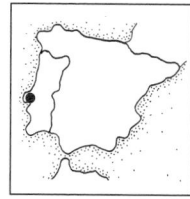

For centuries, Portugal's aristocracy considered Sintra the natural escape from Lisbon. Now tourists do, too. On a day trip to Sintra, you can climb through the Versailles of Portugal, the Pena Palace, and romp along the ruined ramparts of a deserted Moorish castle on a neighboring hilltop.

Sintra is a mix of natural and man-made beauty: fantasy castles set amid exotic tropical plants, lush green valleys, and craggy hilltops with hazy views of the Atlantic and Lisbon. For centuries, Sintra—just 15 miles northwest of Lisbon—was the summer escape of Portugal's kings. Those with money and a desire to be close to royalty built their palaces amid luxuriant gardens in the same neighborhood. Lord Byron called this bundle of royal fancies and aristocratic dreams a "glorious Eden," and though today it's mobbed with tourists, it's still magnificent. Various music festivals in June and July keep it lively and fun.

With extra time, explore the rugged and picturesque westernmost tip of Portugal at Cabo da Roca. You can also mix and mingle with the jet set (or at least press your nose against their windows) at the resort towns of Cascais or Estoril.

Planning Your Time

Note that the Pena Palace and Museum of Modern Art are closed Monday, and the National Palace is closed Wednesday.

By Public Transportation: Getting from Lisbon to Sintra will be a little tricky in 2006. Due to a massive construction project, all train service at Rossio Station (which serviced Sintra) has been shut down. To get to Sintra by train, you must depart from Sete Rios Station (take Metro's Blue line to Jardim Zoológico,

Near Lisbon

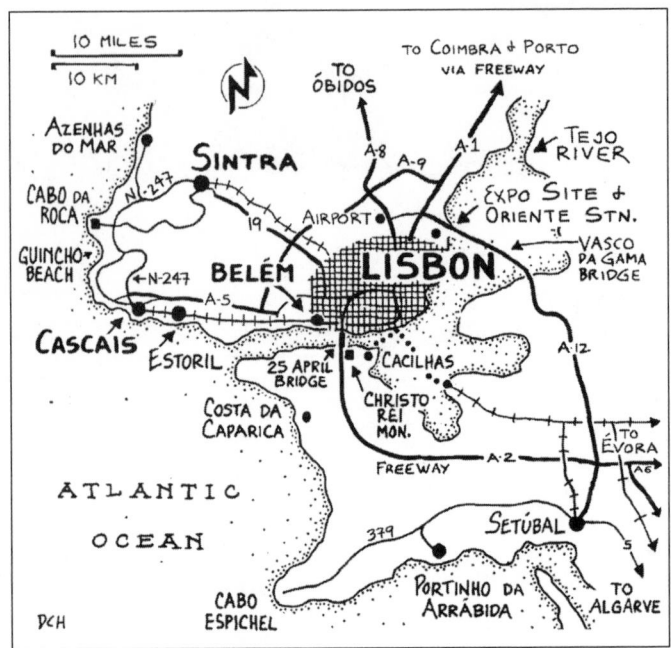

then follow signs for *comboio* up to ground level). At the green CP ticket vending machine, punch "Sintra" and insert your fare (€2.80 round-trip, free with LisboaCard, 4/hr, 35 min). The train departs from platform Linha 2 upstairs (take escalator to left of ticket machines). Be careful: Your train must be marked *Sintra,* as trains to other destinations use the same platform. Try to arrive in Sintra by 9:30, since most major sights open by 10:00. During your ride, take in the views of the aqueduct (on left) and the workaday Lisbon suburbs. On your return, take the Roma-Areeiro train and get off at Sete Rios. (Don't worry if you miss your stop—the last station is on the Metro's Red line.)

If you're bent on seeing everything west of Lisbon (Sintra, Cabo da Roca, Cascais, and Estoril) in a long day, consider a slam-bam swing around the peninsula by bus on Carris' Sintra Tour from Lisbon (€40, 4.5 hrs; see page 50). It is also possible to make a loop trip using public transportation: Buy a one-way train ticket to Sintra from Sete Rios Station in Lisbon, and see the sights in Sintra, but instead of buying a €3.70 ticket on the #434 bus, buy a €8 Day Rover ticket. This bus pass gets you up the hill to Pena Palace and also allows you to catch bus #403 (at the Sintra train station) for a trip out to Cabo da Roca. You can hop off at Cabo da Roca, get a diploma to prove you were there, then catch bus #403 again for the jaunt to Cascais and a seafood dinner on the waterfront. Estoril is a short train ride away on the same line to Lisbon, but seeing both Cascais and Estoril is probably redundant, and Cascais is more appealing. (Bullfight fans could enjoy a bullfight—if scheduled—in either city.) Returning to Lisbon is a snap. Just get a one-way train ticket to Lisbon at the Cascais or Estoril train stations. You'll get off at the last stop on the line (Cais de Sodré Station), a five-minute walk from Praça do Comércio in downtown Lisbon.

By Car: Sintra itself is far easier by train than by car from Lisbon. Consider waiting until after you visit Sintra to pick up your rental car. If you do take a car to Sintra, take the IC-19 freeway out of Lisbon (allow 30 min). When you arrive, follow Sintra *Centro Histórico* signs. Cars are the curse of Sintra—traffic can be terrible and parking difficult. Park your car and use the city bus to get around. If you decide (probably regrettably) to drive to the sights, you'll take a one-way winding loop and be encouraged to park "as soon as you can" or risk having to drive the huge loop again.

It's possible to make a 70-mile circular trip and drive to all the destinations near Lisbon within a day (Lisbon–Belém–Sintra–Cabo da Roca–Cascais–Lisbon), but traffic congestion around Sintra, especially on weekends, can mess up your schedule.

Drivers eager for beach time can leave Lisbon, visit Sintra, and drive directly to the Algarve that evening (4 hrs from Lisbon). To get to the Algarve from Sintra/Cascais, get on the freeway heading for Lisbon and exit at the Sul Ponte A2 sign, which takes you over the 25th of April Bridge and south on A2.

ORIENTATION

Though small, hilly Sintra is gravitationally challenged, and its three main sights—National Palace, Pena Palace, and Moorish

castle—are farther apart than they appear on the tourist maps. The town itself sprawls at the foot of a hill, a 10-minute walk (or shorter bus ride) from the train station. The National Palace, with its unmistakable pair of cone-shaped chimneys, is in the center of the town, a block from the TI. But the other two palaces are a steep, long, uphill walk from town.

Sintra

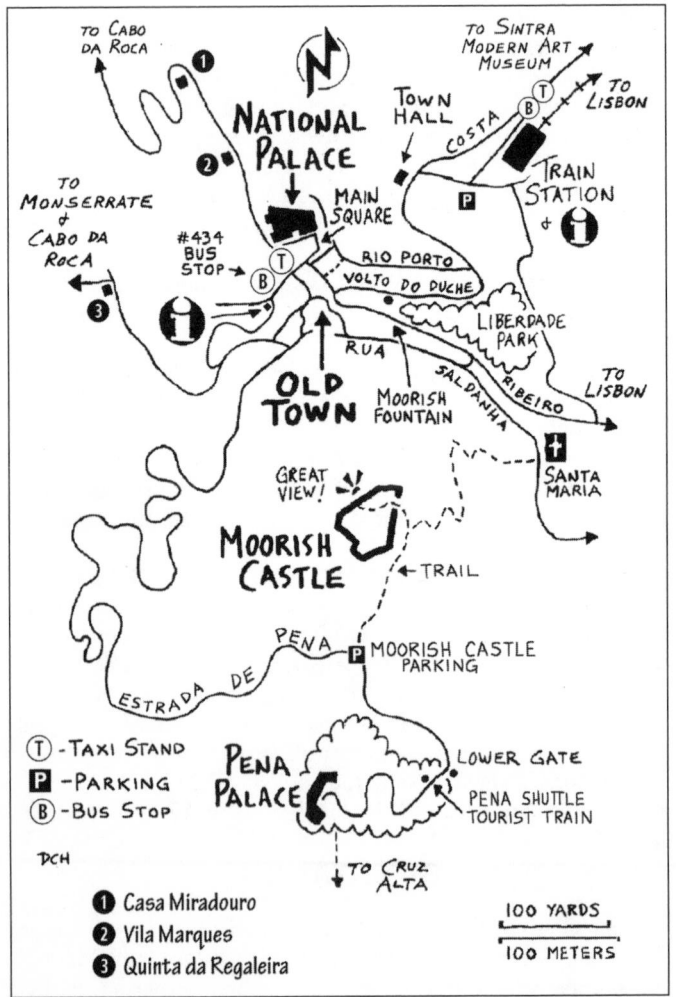

Tourist Information

Sintra has two TIs, a small one in the train station (tel. 219-241-623) and a larger one a block off the main square in the Museu Regional building (both open daily June–Sept 9:00–20:00, Oct–May 9:00–19:00, tel. 219-231-157, both have WCs, www.cm-sintra.pt). Pick up a free map with information on sights, and a schedule for the #434 shuttle bus. The TI can arrange *quartos* (rooms in private homes, Db-€25–60) for overnighters.

LisboaCard: This covers the National Palace and Pena Palace, and gets you a discount on the Moorish castle, Toy Museum, and

Monserrate gardens. If you decide to buy it, purchase it at a Lisbon TI before you visit Sintra because it covers your train ride here (see page 75). Note that the Pena Palace and Museum of Modern Art are free until 14:00 on Sunday (and closed Monday); the National Palace is closed Wednesday.

Arrival in Sintra

By Train: After stopping at the TI in the train station, you can head for the town center on foot (exit station and go left for easy, level 10-min walk) or by bus #434 (exit station to the right, €3.70, valid all day; for more bus info, see "Getting Around Sintra," below). Modern-art lovers can easily visit the Museum of Modern Art before heading into town (exit station to the right).

If you arrive early in Sintra (bus service starts at 10:20), walk into town. Visit the National Palace, then buy a picnic lunch and catch bus #434 up to the Pena Palace (also has café). Enjoy lunch in Pena Gardens, and then tour the palace. Walk down to the Moorish castle ruins and explore. From the castle, take a 30-minute hike down a steep, wooded path into town (get hiking instructions and map at castle entry; fork in path leads down from within the castle grounds). Catch the train back to Lisbon for dinner.

By Car: There's a strip of parking along Volta do Duche, near the town center (€0.50/hr, 2-hour maximum). A small lot is also next to the train station. The most central free parking is on Rio do Porto in the valley just below and northeast of town (after parking, climb the long set of steps to get up to the main square).

Getting Around Sintra

Bus #434 loops together all the important stops: the train station, the town center/TI/National Palace (stop is at TI), the Moorish castle ruins, Pena Palace, and then back to the train station (June–mid-Sept 3/hr, mid-Sept–May 2/hr, €3.70 ticket good for 24 hours, buy from driver; first bus starts at 10:20 from train station, last one leaves station at 18:30, 17:30 in winter, entire circuit takes 30 min). To maximize your time, keep the bus schedule in mind while sightseeing, since there is a 30-minute wait between buses.

To reach the Pena Palace and Moorish castle from the town center or the train station, catch bus #434 or take a taxi. Taxis don't use a meter, but have set fares (e.g., €8 from town center or train station to Pena Palace, confirm with driver). On your way to the Pena Palace, you'll pass by the entrance to the Moorish castle. At the top of the hill, where the bus or taxi drops you off, it's still another 10-minute uphill walk to the Pena Palace entrance (or take green shuttle tram; see below).

From the Pena Palace, it's a 15-minute walk backtracking downhill to the Moorish castle (return to bus-and-taxi stop, then follow signs down road to Moorish castle).

The clip-clop **horse carriages** cost about €30 for 25 minutes (confirm their posted rates). They can take you anywhere; you'll likely see them waiting by the parking lot just in front of the National Palace.

SIGHTS

▲▲**National Palace (Palácio Nacional)**—While the palace dates back to Moorish times, most of what you'll see is from the 15th-century reign of King John (João) I, with later Manueline architectural ornamentation from the 16th century. This oldest surviving royal palace in Portugal is still used for official receptions. Having housed royalty for 500 years until 1910, it's fragrant with history.

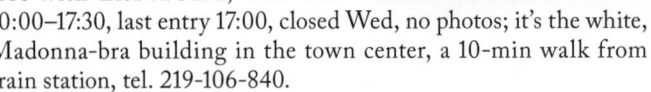

Cost, Hours, Location: (€4, free with LisboaCard, Thu–Tue 10:00–17:30, last entry 17:00, closed Wed, no photos; it's the white, Madonna-bra building in the town center, a 10-min walk from train station, tel. 219-106-840.

➋ **Self-Guided Tour:** The palace is a one-way romp with little information provided. As you tour the place, notice:

Swan Room: This first room is the palace's banquet room. A king's daughter—who loved swans—was married into a royal house in Belgium. The king missed the princess so much that he decorated the ceiling with her favorite animal. These aren't the only creatures in the room, though. Check out the ceramic soup tureens designed in the shape of your favorite barnyard animal.

Courtyard: This was a fortified medieval palace, so rather than fancy gardens outside, it has a stay-awhile courtyard within its protective walls. Notice the unique chimneys. Hans Christian Andersen said they look like two grand bottles of champagne. I disagree. Whatever they look like, they give the kitchen a marvelous open-domed feeling, as you'll see at the end of your tour.

Magpie Room: King John I was caught by his queen kissing a lady-in-waiting. Frustrated by his court—abuzz with gossip—John had this ceiling painted with magpies. But to show what a good-spirited guy he was, around each magpie is the king's slogan—*por bem,* "for good." The 15th-century Moorish tiles are from Spain, brought in before the development of the famous, ubiquitous Portuguese tiles.

King's Bedroom: The king portrayed on the wall where you enter the room is King Sebastian (Dom Sebastião), a gung-ho, medieval-type monarch who went to battle in Africa, chasing the Moors even after they were chased out of Europe. He disappeared at age 24, leaving Portugal in unstable times with only a great uncle as heir. The new king died within two years, and the throne passed to cousin King Philip II of Spain, leading to 60 years of Spanish rule (1580–1640). Note the ebony, silver, and painted copper head-board of the Italian Renaissance bed. The tiles in this room are considered the first Portuguese tiles—from the time of Manuel I. The corn-on-the-cob motif topping the tilework is a reminder of American discoveries. Wander through more rooms, upstairs, and through more rooms to the blue-and-gold...

Stag Room: The most striking room in the palace honors Portugal's loyal nobility. Study the richly decorated ceiling. The king's coat of arms at the top is surrounded by the coats of arms of his children, and below that, the coats of arms of all but one of Portugal's noble families. That family schemed a revolt and received only a blank niche. The Latin phrase circling the room reads, "Honoring all the noble families who've been loyal to the king." The 18th-century tiles hang from the walls like tapestries. Enjoy the view—a garden-like countryside dotted with mansions of nobility who clamored to be near their king, the hill-capping castle, and the wide-open Atlantic. Believe it or not, you're in the westernmost room of the westernmost palace on the European continent.

Kitchen: With all the latest in cooking technology, the palace chef could roast an entire cow on the spit, keep the king's plates warm in the iron dish warmer (with drawers below for the char-coal), and get really dizzy by looking up and spinning around three times. OK, you can go now.

▲▲Pena Palace (Palácio de Pena)—This magical hilltop palace sits high above Sintra, above the Moorish castle ruins. In the 19th century, Portugal had a very romantic prince, German-born Prince Ferdinand. A contem-porary and cousin of Bavaria's "Mad" King Ludwig (of Disneyesque Neuschwanstein Castle fame), Ferdinand was also a cousin of England's Prince Albert (Queen Victoria's  husband). Flamboyant Ferdinand hired a German architect to build a fantasy castle, mixing elements of German and Portuguese style. He ended up with a crazy neo-fortified casserole of Gothic towers, Renaissance domes, Moorish minarets, Manueline carv-ing, Disney playfulness, and an azulejo toilet for his wife.

Cost, Hours, Location: €6 for required gardens/palace combo-ticket, free on Sun until 14:00, free with LisboaCard, Tue–Sun

10:00–18:30, closes at 17:30 off-season, closed Mon, last entry 1 hour before closing, view café, tel. 219-105-340. Purchase your ticket at the small hut opposite the gated entrance. To avoid the 10-minute uphill climb to the palace (and enjoy a lift back down), catch the green shuttle bus just inside the gate at the *paragem* sign (€1.50 round-trip, departures every few minutes in fake vintage Lisbon trolley). If you brought your lunch with you, don't zip up to the palace immediately. Enjoy the picnic-perfect gardens. Your ticket comes with a map showing a circular, 1.5-hour walking route. Wander in, find a spot of shade, and enjoy views fit for a king.

● **Self-Guided Tour:** The palace, built in the mid- to late-1800s, is so well-preserved that it feels as if it's the day after the royal family fled Portugal in 1910 (during a popular revolt making way for today's modern republic). This gives the place a charming intimacy rarely seen in palaces. English descriptions throughout give meaning to the rooms. Here are the highlights.

Entry: After you hop off the green shuttle bus, walk up through the Moorish archway with alligator decor. Get your ticket torn, cross the drawbridge that doesn't draw, and join an onion-domed world of tourists frozen in deep knee-bends with their cameras cocked. Bags and cameras must be checked. Stow your camera in a pocket or give it up (no photos are allowed inside, but you may want your camera for the views). At the base of the stairs, you'll see King Ferdinand, who built this castle from 1840 until 1885, when he died. While German, he was a romantic proponent of his adopted culture and did much to preserve Portugal's architectural and artistic heritage.

Courtyard: Note how the palace was built upon the arcaded ruins of a 16th-century monastery. In spite of its plushness, it retains the coziness of several small rooms gathered in two levels around this cloister.

Queen's Bedroom and Dressing Room: Study the melancholy photos of Queen Amelia, King Charles, and their family in this room. The turn of the 20th century was a rocky time for Portugal's royal family. In 1908, after the queen's husband and eldest son were killed, Amelia fled to France. The palm frond on the headboard of her bed was from her last Palm Sunday Mass in Portugal. Poke around. If you lean far enough, you can see Amelia's toilet. And in the next room, how about that padded velvet bidet?

King's Bedroom: The king enjoyed cutting-edge comforts, including the shower/tub imported from England, and even a telephone to listen to the opera when he felt that the Lisbon commute was too much (you'll see the switchboard later). The bedroom is decorated in classic Romantic style—dark, heavy, and busy with knickknacks.

Queen's View Balcony: On the upper floor, enjoy a sweeping view from Lisbon to the mouth of the Tejo River. Find the Cristo Rei statue and the 25th of April Bridge. The statue on the distant ridge honors the palace's architect. Continue your visit to the fantastically furnished Noble's Room, and then wind through the hallways. You will end at the abundant kitchen; just after, a view café conveniently welcomes us peasants.

▲**Moorish Castle (Castelo dos Mouros)**—Sintra's thousand-year-old Moorish-castle ruins, lost in an enchanted forest and alive with winds of the past, are a castle  lover's dream come true and a great place for a picnic with a panoramic Atlantic view. Though built by the Moors, the castle was taken by Christian forces in 1147. What you'll climb on today, while dramatic, was much restored in the 19th century. To get from Sintra to the ruins, hike two miles, take a taxi, or ride bus #434—see "Getting Around Sintra," above (€3.50, €2 with LisboaCard, daily 9:00–20:00, closes at 19:00 off-season, last entry 1 hour before closing, free flier includes English info and a rough map, tel. 219-107-970).

▲▲**Sintra Museum of Modern Art: The Berardo Collection**—Modern-art lovers rave about this private collection, one of Iberia's best. The collection rotates, with 120 of its 800 pieces shown at any given time. The art (along with temporary exhibits) is presented with thoughtful English descriptions for each section in hopes of giving the novice a better grip on post-WWII art (€3, Tue–Sun 10:00–18:00, free on Sun until 14:00, closed Mon; 500 yards from train station, in Sintra's former casino on Avenida Heliodoro Salgado, exit right from train station and go straight for about 8 min through pedestrian mall into modern town, tel. 219-248-170, www.berardocollection.com).

Quinta da Regaleira—This neo-everything (Manueline/Gothic/Renaissance) 1912 mansion and garden, with mystical and Masonic twists, was designed by an Italian opera-set designer for a wealthy but disgruntled monarchist two years after the royal family was deposed. The two-hour English tour is mostly in the garden (as the palace is quite small) and can be longish unless you're into quirky Masonic esoterica. If you like fantastic caves, bring a flashlight and follow the shaded black lines on the provided maps (€5 to tour on your own, €10 for a guided tour by reservation only, 8 tours/day in summer, 4/day in winter, maximum 30 persons, book by calling 219-106-650, daily 10:00–18:00, a 10-min walk from downtown Sintra, café on site). Ask a local to pronounce "Regaleira" for you.

Toy Museum—Just for fun, you can wander through a collection of several thousand old-time toys, from small soldiers, planes, cars, trucks, and old tricycles to a dolls' attic upstairs. The 20th-century owner João Arbués Moreira started collecting toys when he was 14, and just never quit (€3, €2.10 with LisboaCard, Tue–Sun 10:00–18:00, closed Mon, Rua Visconde de Monserrate, 1 block in front of National Palace, tel. 219-242-171, www.museu-do-brinquedo.pt).

Monserrate—About 2.5 miles outside of Sintra is the wonderful garden of Monserrate. If you like tropical plants and exotic landscaping, a visit is time well spent (€3.50, €2 with LisboaCard, daily 9:00–19:00, last entrance 18:00, shorter hours in winter, no buses run here—allow about €10 for taxi). Some say that the Pena Gardens (below Pena Palace) are just as good as the more famous Monserrate.

SLEEPING AND EATING

Sleeping

$$$ Casa Miradouro is a beautifully restored mansion from 1893. With six spacious, stylish rooms, an elegant lounge, castle and sea views, and a wonderful garden, it's a worthy splurge. The place is graciously run by Frederic, who speaks English with a Swiss accent (Sb-€82–112, Db-€92–125, priciest April–Oct, includes buffet breakfast, closed mid-Jan–mid-Feb, non-smoking rooms, street parking, Rua Soto Major 55; from National Palace, go past Hotel Tivoli Sintra and 400 yards downhill, note that it's a stiff uphill

---

Sleep Code

(€1 = about $1.20, country code: 351)

S = Single, **D** = Double/Twin, **T** = Triple, **Q** = Quad, **b** = bathroom, **s** = shower only. Unless otherwise noted, credit cards are accepted, English is spoken, and breakfast is included.

To help you easily sort through these listings, I've divided the rooms into three categories, based on the price for a standard double room with bath during high season:

$$$ **Higher Priced**—Most rooms €115 or more.

$$ **Moderately Priced**—Most rooms between €60–115.

$ **Lower Priced**—Most rooms €60 or less.

hike to return to center; tel. 219-107-100, fax 219-241-836, www
.casa-miradouro.com, mail@casa-miradouro.com).

$ Vila Marques, another elegant old mansion, is funkier but
filled with pride. It has an eccentric-grandmotherly flair, hardwood
floors, four fine rooms, three suites, and a great garden with birds.
Easy to miss, it's 100 yards downhill from Hotel Tivoli and 200
yards down from the National Palace (S-€35, D-€45, D/twin-
€50, Db suite-€65, Qb-€80, €5 less Oct–May, 1 bath per 2 rooms,
no sinks in rooms, suites and quad on garden lack character of
cheaper rooms actually in mansion, cash only, Rua Soto Mayor 1,
tel. 219-230-027, fax 219-241-155, run by Sra. Maria Marques and
her hardworking maids, Maria and Olga).

Eating

The industrious, tourist-friendly **Restaurant Regional de Sintra**
feeds locals and tourists well (€15 meals, daily 12:00–22:30, ask
the waiter to tell you the legend of the rooster on the napkin; 200
yards from train station at Travessa do Municipio 2, exit train
station left, go downhill to the first square—far right corner, tel.
219-234-444).

The touristy little cobbled lane Rua das Padarias is lined with
charming shops and eateries. For a light café lunch, try **Pastelaria
Vila Velha** (Rua das Padarias 8, tel. 219-230-154).

The venerable **Piriquita** café calls itself an *antiga fabrica de
queijadas*—historic maker of tiny, tasty tarts with a cheesy filling
(at the base of Rua das Padarias). It's a fine place for a sweet and
a coffee. Take a seat to avoid groups who rush in to get pastries to
go, or do battle and grab a half-dozen for €3.60. To avoid crowds,
check out their other shop, **Piriquita Dois,** which has a view terrace (continue uphill and to the right to Rua das Padarias 2).

Bus drivers and tour guides grab a quiet, cheap lunch in the
homey **Café da Villa** (€8 menu, generous portions of homemade-
style soups and salads, open daily, down the road past horse-drawn
carriages at Calçada do Pelourinho 2, tel. 219-241-174).

For a take-out bakery sandwich, stop by **Padarias Reunidas
de Sintra,** across the square from the National Palace. At the
train station, **Pizza Hut's** salad bar is an easy place to get a cheap,
healthy salad for a picnic in Sintra or the ride back to Lisbon.

TRANSPORTATION CONNECTIONS

From Sintra to: Lisbon's Sete Rios Station (4 trains/hr, 35 min,
see Lisbon's "Transportation Connections," page 99, for details),
Cascais (hourly bus #403 also stops at Cabo da Roca, 45–60 min,
bus stop at the Sintra train station).

NEAR SINTRA

Cabo da Roca—Wind-beaten, tourist-infested Cabo da Roca is the westernmost point in Europe, perhaps the inspiration for the Portuguese poet Luis de Camões' line, *"Onde a terra se acaba e o mar começa"* ("Where land ends and the sea begins"). It has a little shop, a café, and a tiny **TI** that sells a "proof of being here" diploma (daily 9:00–20:00). Nearby, on the road to Cascais, you'll pass a good beach for wind, waves, sand, and the chance to be the last person in Europe to see the sun set. For a remote

beach, drive to Praia Adraga (north of Cabo da Roca).

Cascais and Estoril—Before the rise of the Algarve, these towns were the haunt of Portugal's rich and beautiful. Today, they are quietly elegant, with noble old buildings, beachfront promenades, a bullring, a casino, and more fame than they deserve. Cascais is the more enjoyable of the two (depicted in photo); it's not as rich and stuffy and has the cozy touch of a fishing village, great seafood, and

a younger, less pretentious atmosphere (Cascais **TI** at Visconde de Luz 14, Estoril TI at Areada do Parque, shared tel. 214-663-813). Both are a simple day trip from Lisbon (4 trains/hr, 40 min from Lisbon's Cais do Sodré Station).

THE ALGARVE

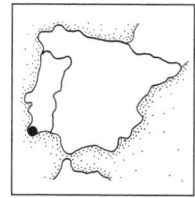

The Algarve was once known as Europe's last undiscovered tourist frontier. But it's well discovered now, and if you go to the places featured in tour brochures, you'll find it much like Spain's Costa del Sol—paved, packed, and pretty stressful. Still, there are a few great beach towns left, mostly on the western tip, and this part of the Algarve is the south coast of any sun worshipper's dreams.

Portugal's warm and dry south coast, stretching for some 100 miles, has beach resorts along the water's edge and rolling green hills dotted with orchards farther inland. The coastline varies from lagoon estuaries in the east (Tavira), to sandy beach resorts in the center (from Faro to Lagos), to rugged cliffs in the west (Sagres).

The Moors (Muslims from North Africa who ruled Portugal for 5 centuries) chose not to live in the rainy north, but rather along the warm, dry south coast, in the land they dubbed Al-Gharb Al-Andalus ("to the west of Andalucía"—the westernmost edge of the huge Islamic world). Today, the Algarve still holds elements introduced by the Muslims—groves of almond and orange trees, and white-domed buildings with pointy chimneys, blue trim, and azulejo tiles.

For some rigorous rest and intensive relaxation, make sunny Salema your Algarve hideaway. In these villages, the tourists and the fishermen sport the same stubble. It's just you, a beach full of garishly painted boats, your wrinkled landlady, and a few

The Algarve

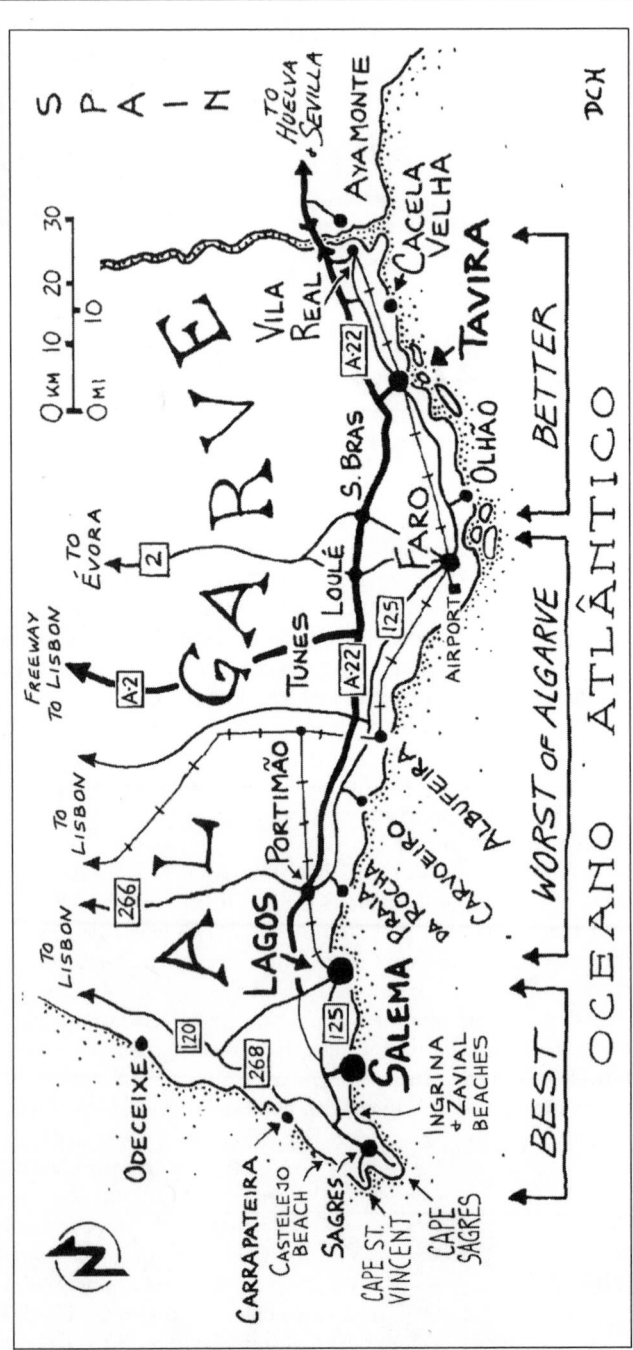

other globetrotting experts in lethargy. Nearby sights include Cape Sagres (Europe's "Land's End" and home of Henry the Navigator's famous navigation school) and the beach-party/jet-ski resort of Lagos. Or you could just work on a tan and see how slow your pulse can get in sleepy Salema. If not now, when? If not you, who?

Planning Your Time

The Algarve is your vacation from your vacation. How much time does it deserve? It depends upon how much time you have, and how much time you need to recharge your solar batteries. On a two-week trip, I'd give it three nights and two days. After a full day of sightseeing in Lisbon (or Sevilla, if you're arriving from Spain), I'd push it by driving four hours around dinnertime to gain an entirely free beach day. With two days, I'd spend one enjoying side trips to Cape Sagres and Lagos, and another just lingering in Salema. The only other Algarve stop to consider is Tavira. (If you're visiting in winter, Tavira—which is lively year-round—makes a better stop than tiny Salema, which slows down.)

Getting around the Algarve

Trains and buses connect the main towns along the south coast (skimpy service on weekends). Buses take you west from Lagos, where trains don't go. The freeway crossing the Algarve from Lagos to the Spanish border (and on to Sevilla, Spain) makes driving quick and easy. (See "Route Tips for Drivers in the Algarve," at the end of this chapter.)

Salema

One bit of old Algarve magic still glitters quietly in the sun—Salema. It's at the end of a small road just off the main drag between the big city of Lagos and the rugged southwest tip of Europe, Cape Sagres.

Quietly discovered by British and German tourists, this simple fishing village has three streets, many restaurants, a few hotels, time-share condos up the road, a couple of shipwreck bars, English and German menus, a classic beach with a new, paved promenade, and endless sun.

Salema Area

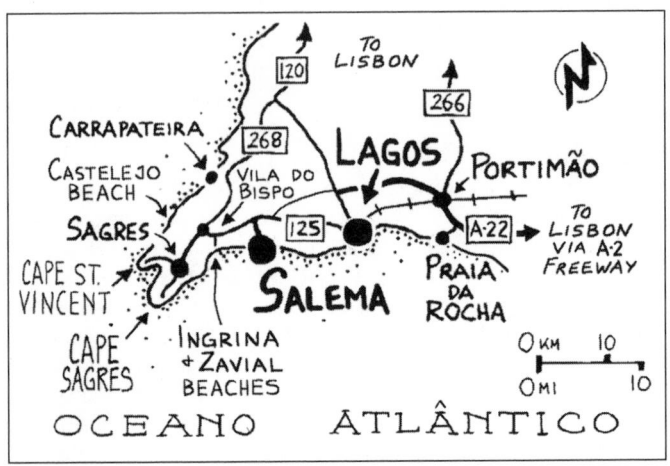

ORIENTATION

Tourist Information

Salema lacks an official TI, but the **Tutti Service** travel agency (see "Helpful Hints," below) and people in the bars, restaurants, and pensions have heard all the questions and are happy to provide answers. To study ahead, see www.salema.info.

Arrival in Salema

By Train and Bus: To get to Salema, you'll arrive first at Lagos (with the closest train station), the Algarve's transportation hub. From there, buses go nearly hourly between Lagos and Sagres (30-min ride, 10 miles, last bus departs Lagos around 20:30, fewer buses on weekends). Catch the bus at either the Lagos bus station (see "Lagos," later in this chapter) or at one of the stops along the waterfront of the historic town. About half the buses go right into the village of Salema. The others (marked *cruzt* in the schedule) drop you at the top of the road (that must be *cruzt*) into Salema (bus continues to Figueira). From here it's a 20-minute walk downhill into the village.

By Car: If you're coming from Spain on the freeway, exit at the second Lagos exit (marked Lagos Oeste/Vila do Bispo) and follow signs to Sagres/Vila do Bispo. Turn off at the sign for Salema. Parking is free and easy on the street (beware of the *No Parking* signs near the bus stop). If you want to stop in Lagos before continuing to Salema, take the first exit (Lagos Este). Leave Lagos via the street Avenida dos Descobrimentos and follow signs to Sagres/Vila do Bispo.

By Taxi: A cab from Lagos to Salema takes 20 minutes and costs about €18 (metered, but ask for an estimate first).

Helpful Hints

Money: Salema has an ATM at the entrance of the Atlântico Restaurante (see "Eating," page 123), but it wouldn't hurt to bring along a few extra euros just in case. Not all Salema restaurants accept credit cards, and there is no backup in case of an ATM malfunction.

Internet Access: You can get online at Tutti Service (see below) and at A Aventura Bar (see "Self-Guided Tour," below). Pensión Mare has good Web access, but only for guests (see "Sleeping," page 121).

Travel Agency: Tutti Service posts bus and train schedules; rents cars (€45/day or less), mopeds, and mountain bikes; books hotels and flights (such as cheap stand-bys to Germany and Britain); offers three-day to one-week condo rentals in Salema; arranges excursions; has Internet access and broadband phone service; and has free tourist maps of Lagos and the Algarve (normally open Mon–Fri 9:30–19:00, Sat 10:00–14:00, some Sun in summer, Oct–May closed at lunch, in tiny strip mall across from Hotel Residencial Salema, tel. 282-695-855, fax 282-695-920, tuttiservice@mail .telepac.pt, Andrea speaks English).

Taxi: Your hotel can arrange a taxi, or you can call Jose direct at mobile 919-385-139 or 919-422-061. Jose and his wife Isabel have two cars and are at your service: €18 to Lagos bus station or €30 for a quick 75-minute scenic tour of Cape Sagres/Cape St. Vincent, with short stops and a commentary (can also wait in Sagres for €7/hr). Isabel speaks fluent English and is a tour guide. This can be a great value when two couples team up to share the excursion. For €250, you could even taxi to Lisbon, Évora, or Sevilla. You'll see Jose at the taxi stall in the center parking lot.

SELF-GUIDED TOUR

Welcome to Salema

Salema has a split personality: The whitewashed old town is for locals and the other half was built for tourists. Locals and tourists pursue a policy of peaceful coexistence. Tourists laze in the sun while locals grab the shade.

Town Square Market Action: Salema's flatbed truck market rolls in weekday mornings—one truck each for fish, fruit, and vegetables, and a five-and-dime truck for clothing and other odds and ends. The tooting horn of the fish truck wakes you at 8:00. The bakery trailer sells delightful fresh bread and "store-bought" sweet rolls each morning (about 8:00–11:00). And weekday afternoons around 14:00 the red mobile post office stops by (unless its funding is cut by the government).

Fishing Scene: Salema is still a fishing village—but just barely. While the fishermen's hut no longer hosts a fish auction, you'll still see the old-timers enjoying its shade, oblivious to the tourists, mending their nets and reminiscing about the old days when life was "only fish and hunger." In the calm of summer, boats are left out on buoys. In the winter, the community-subsidized tractor earns its keep by hauling the boats ashore. (In pre-tractor days, such boat-hauling was a 10-person chore.)

Octopus is the main catch. The pottery jars stacked everywhere are octopus traps. Unwritten tradition allocates different chunks of undersea territory to each Salema family. The traps are tied about 15 feet apart in long lines and dropped offshore. Octopi, thinking these would make a cozy place to set an ambush, climb in and get ambushed. When the fishermen hoist them in, they hang on—unaware they've made their final mistake. The fisherman maces them out of their pot with a squirt of bleach. The octopus flops angrily into the boat bound for the market and, who knows... maybe onto your dinner plate.

Beach Scene: Suntanners enjoy the beach May through September. (I once got a sunburn in early May.) Knowing their tourist-based economy sits on a foundation of sand, locals hope and pray that sand returns after being washed away each winter. Some winters leave the beach just a pile of rocks.

Beach towns must provide public showers and toilets. The Atlântico Restaurante and Salema's Balneario Municipal (daily 14:00–19:00 in summer, showers-€1) each rent beach items (lounges-€3/day, bamboo sun shades-€2.50). The fountain in front of the Balneario Municipal is a reminder of the old days. When water to the village was cut off, this was always open. Locals claim the beach is safe for swimming, but the water is rarely really warm.

Salema

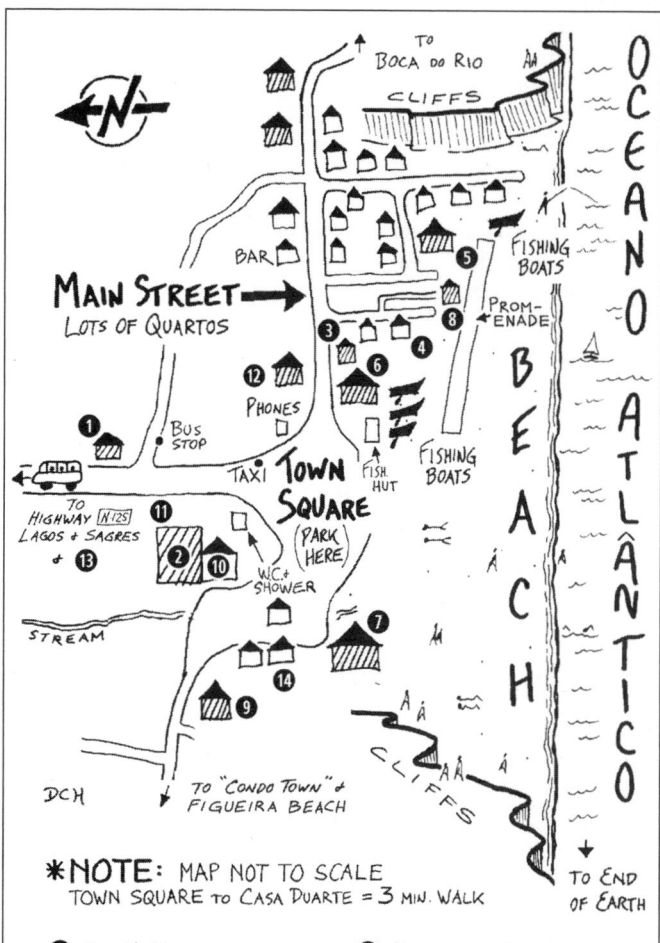

✳NOTE: MAP NOT TO SCALE
TOWN SQUARE TO CASA DUARTE = 3 MIN. WALK

1. Pensión Mare
2. Hotel Residencial Salema
3. Ribeiro Rooms
4. Acacio Rooms
5. Casa Duarte
6. Boia Bar & Rest.
7. Atlântico Restaurant
8. Mira Mar Restaurant
9. Restaurante Lourenço
10. Carapau Frances
11. Rest. Pizzeria O Barco
12. Salema Market
13. To Vila Velha Rest. & Castelejo Rest.
14. Tutti Service Travel Agency

A pre-breakfast stroll eastward is a pristine way to greet the new day. On the west end of the beach, you can climb over the rocks past tiny tide pools to the secluded Figueira Beach. (But be aware of when high tide comes in, or your route back will have to be overland.) While the old days of black widows chasing topless Nordic women off the beach are gone, nudism is still risqué today. If you go topless, do so with discretion. Over the rocks and beyond the view of prying eyes, Germans grin and bare it.

Community Development: The whole peninsula (west of Lagos) has been declared a natural park, and further development close to the beach is forbidden. Salema will live with past mistakes, such as the huge hotel in the town center that pulled some mysterious strings to go two stories over code. Up the street is a sprawling community of Club Med–type vacationers who rarely leave their air-conditioned bars and swimming pools. Across the highway a mile or two inland is an even bigger golfing resort (worth exploring by car) with a spa, pool, and tennis courts. The ramshackle old village of Salema is becoming less and less ramshackle as it's gradually bought up by northern Europeans for vacation or retirement homes.

Salema after Dark: Salema has several late-night bars, each worth a visit. Consider a Salema pub crawl to sample the local drinks. *Armarguinha* (ar-mar-GWEEN-yah) is a sweet, likeable almond liqueur. *Licor beirão* (LIK-kor bay-ROW; row rhymes with cow) is Portuguese amaretto, a "double distillation of diverse plants and aromatic seeds in accordance with a secret old formula." *Caipirinha* (kay-peer-EEN-yah), tasty and powerful, is made of fermented Brazilian sugarcane with lime, brown sugar, and crushed ice. And *moscatel* is the local sweet dessert wine.

Guillerme Duarte's **Atabua Bar** is the liveliest, offering patrons its famous sangria. Just up the street, at **A Aventura Bar,** Bertrand offers a pleasant atmosphere for sipping drinks (the *caipirinha* is good) and sending e-mail. And, up the hill (next to Lourenço's restaurant), the on-again-off-again **Carioca Bar** is a more bohemian-style hangout. For a late dessert or a sangria on the beach, drop by **Mira Mar.** Or just grab a bench on the promenade and ponder the moon and the waves.

SIGHTS

Coastal Boat Tours—Local English-speaking guide Sebastián offers a two-hour scenic cruise along the coast. He gives a light commentary on the geology and the plant and bird life as he motors halfway to Cape Sagres and back. Trips include nipping into some cool blue natural caves. Morning trips are best for bird-watching (herring gulls, falcons). Kicking back and watching the cliffs glide by, I felt like I was scanning a super-relaxing gallery of natural art. Consider being dropped at (nude) Figueira Beach just before returning to Salema (it's a 50-min walk home to Salema— bring shoes, a picnic, and extra water). Remember, some of these beaches only exist when the tide is low (check tides in the fishing hut on Salema's beach). Easygoing and gentle Sebastián charges little more than what it costs to run his small boat (€20 per person, daily mid-June–mid-Sept 10:30 and 13:30, 2–5 passengers, bring sweater, camera, and sunscreen, tel. 282-695-458, mobile 963-441-753, ask for Sebastián at fishermen's hut or book his tour through Pensión Mare or Tutti Service).

SLEEPING

Salema is crowded July through mid-September. August is horribly crowded. Prices jump up in July and August. The place is partially closed down in winter.

For maximum comfort there's no need to look beyond Pensión Mare. There's a basic and utilitarian high-rise hotel in the center of town. But for economy and experience, stay in a *quarto* (room), most of which are along the main road that parallels the waterfront. Fisher folk happily rent out rooms in their homes, most of which have separate private entrances.

Quartos don't serve breakfast, and breakfast at hotels isn't served until 8:30 (that's about when the bread guy arrives at Salema). Early birds can enjoy coffee and pastries from 7:30 on at Solmar Café next to the Tutti Service travel agency, opposite Hotel Residencial Salema.

Pension and Hotel

$$ Pensión Mare, a blue-and-white building looking over the village above the main road into town, is the best normal hotel value in Salema. An easygoing Brit named John runs this place, offering seven comfortable rooms (Sb-€38–50, Db-€55–65, Tb-€70–80, includes a wonderful breakfast) and three fully-equipped apartments (Db-€50–75, breakfast not available) in a tidy paradise (10 percent discount with this book and cash through 2006 if arranged discreetly and in advance, free Internet access, guests-only laundry service €5 per kilo—about 2 pounds, Praia de Salema, tel. 282-695-165, fax 282-695-846; the excellent Web site www.algarve .co.uk has a virtual tour of every room and some good Salema information). John will hold a room with a phone call and a credit card number.

$$ Hotel Residencial Salema, the oversized hotel towering crudely above everything else in town, is a good value if you want a basic, comfortable room handy to the beach. Its 32 red-tiled rooms

Sleep Code

(€1 = about $1.20, country code: 351)
 S = Single, **D** = Double/Twin, **T** = Triple, **Q** = Quad, **b** = bathroom, **s** = shower only. When a price range is given, the lowest is the winter rate and the highest is the peak-season summer rate. Credit cards are accepted only at Pensión Mare and Hotel Residencial Salema. English is spoken unless otherwise noted.

To help you easily sort through these listings, I've divided the rooms into three categories, based on the price for a standard double room with bath:

$$$ **Higher Priced**—Most rooms €80 or more.
  $$ **Moderately Priced**—Most rooms between €50–80.
   $ **Lower Priced**—Most rooms €50 or less.

all have air-conditioning, balconies, and partial views (Sb-€50–75; Db-€55 in April–May & Oct, €67 June and Sept, €85 July–Aug; 10 percent discount through 2006 with this book, includes breakfast, elevator, rents cars and mopeds, closed Nov–March, tel. 282-695-328, fax 282-695-329, www.hotelsalema.com, hotel.salema@clix.pt).

Quartos and Camping

Quartos abound along the residential street (running left from the village center as you face the beach). Ask one of the locals at the waterfront or check at the Boia Bar or Salema Market. Prices vary with the season, plumbing, and view, but if you're only staying one night, you're bad news. Doubles cost about €25–45 (forget breakfast and credit cards). Many places offer beachfront views. It's worth paying extra for rooms *com vista* (with a view). Some apartments are bright and sprawling, while some rooms are dark and musty. *Quartos'* landladies generally speak only a little English, but they're used to dealing with visitors. Many will clean your
laundry for about €3 or so. If you're settling in for a while or are on a tight budget, park your bags and partner at a beachside bar and survey several places. Except for August weekends, there are always rooms available for those dropping in. Especially outside of July and August, prices can be soft.

$ Maria Helena and Jorge Ribeiro, a helpful young couple, rent two small, simple doubles (S or D-€30 all year, one has a tiny view) and a charming tree-house-type suite with a kitchen, a view terrace, and a view toilet for Db-€40–50 (Rua dos Pescadores 83, tel. 282-695-289, mobile 967-183-328).

$ The **Acacio family** rents a humble ground-floor double (D-€25–30) and a fine upstairs apartment with kitchenette, balcony over the beach, and a great ocean view for up to five people (Db-€45, Tb-€50, Qb-€70, on "*quartos* street" at #91, tel. 282-695-473, Silvina doesn't speak English). She pouts if you're staying only one night.

$ **Casa Duarte** has four pleasant rooms (3 with views), a communal kitchenette, and two terraces (D-€25–35, €5 extra for 1-night stays, tel. 282-695-206 or their English-speaking daughter Cristina at tel. 282-695-307; or contact son Romeu, who owns the Salema Market). From "*quartos* street," turn right at Clube Recreativo and then left on the paved path. Duarte's is #7, the first building on the right.

Campers who don't underestimate the high tides sleep free and easy on the **beach** (public showers available in the town center) or at a well-run **campground** with bungalows a half-mile inland, back toward the main road.

EATING

Fresh seafood, eternally. The local specialty is *cataplanas*—fish, tomatoes, potatoes, onions, and whatever else is available—big

enough for two and cooked long in a traditional copper pot (somewhere between a pressure cooker and a steamer). Also look for grilled golden bream *(dourada grelhada)* and giant prawns *(camarões)*.

Salema has six or eight places all serving fine €10 meals. Happily, those that face the beach (the first 3 listed below) are the most fun and have the best service, food, and atmosphere. For a memorable last course at any of these places, consider taking your dessert wine *(moscatel)*, Brazilian sugarcane liquor *(caipirinha)*, or coffee to the beach for some stardust.

The **Boia Bar and Restaurant,** at the base of the residential street, has a classy beachfront setting, noteworthy service by a friendly gang, and a knack for doing whitefish just right (always with free seconds on good orange and green vegetables). Their vegetarian lasagna and salads are popular, as is their €7 bacon-and-eggs breakfast (daily 9:30–22:00, tel. 282-695-382).

The **Atlântico**—noisy, big, busy, and right on the beach—originated as a temporary beach restaurant and now enjoys a prime spot in a brand-new building. It has long dominated the Salema beach scene and is known for tasty fish, its wonderful beach-side terrace, and friendly service (daily 12:00–24:00, serving until 22:00, also rents lounge chairs and bamboo sun shades, ATM outside, tel. 282-695-142).

The intimate **Mira Mar,** farther up the residential street, is a last vestige of old Salema (unlike the Boia and Atlantico, which were both funky beachfront eateries until major renovations in 2004). Florentine and Dieter offer a more creative menu for those venturing away from seafood. Their €6.50 tapas plate—a hearty array of cold meats, veggies, and munchies—can make a meal and their *caldeirada* is a delightful Portuguese fish-and-vegetables stew, like *cataplanas* without the copper pot (Mon–Sat 12:00–24:00, closed Sun, cash only).

Restaurante Lourenço, a block up the hill, has no ambience or view but offers good-value meals, has a local clientele, and is *the* place for *cataplanas* (€20 for 2 people). Paulo serves while his mother, Aldina, cooks (daily 8:00–24:00, cash only; from Hotel Residencial Salema cross bridge, restaurant is a half-block uphill on your left; tel. 282-698-622).

Need a break from fish?

At **Carapau Frances,** in the town square, Gabrielle and Spiros, a Greek/French couple, serve good Greek and Italian food, including salads, vegetarian options, and cheap pizzas (Fri–Wed breakfast from 9:00, lunch from 12:00 and dinner from 18:00, closed Thu, cash only).

Restaurante Pizzeria O Barco offers more creative cooking, including Vietnamese and "the best pepper steak in town." While it has a Greek Isle atmosphere, it's not on the beach (daily 12:00–24:00, indoor/outdoor seating, live music on Saturday evenings, tel. 282-695-149).

Romeu's **Salema Market** has all the fixings for a great picnic (fresh fruits, veggies, bread, sheep's cheese, sausage, and *vinho verde*—new wine, a Portuguese specialty with a refreshing taste) to take with you to a secluded beach or Cape Sagres. Helpful Romeu (pronounced Romeo) also changes money and gives travel and *quartos* advice (July–Sept daily 8:00–20:00, Oct–June daily 8:00–13:00 & 15:00–20:00, on the "*quartos* street"). Another good grocery store, **Alisuper,** is in the tiny strip mall across from Hotel Residencial Salema.

Drivers who want a classy meal outside of town should consider the elegant **Vila Velha Restaurante** in Sagres or the **Castelejo Restaurante** at dreamy Praia do Castelejo (both listed on page 128).

Cape Sagres

In the days before Columbus, this rugged southwestern tip of Portugal was the spot closest to the edge of the Earth (flat, in those days). Prince Henry the Navigator, determined to broaden Europe's horizons and spread Catholicism, sent sailors ever further into the unknown.

His navigators' school was here, where shipwrecked and frustrated explorers were carefully debriefed as they washed ashore.

ORIENTATION

Portugal's "end of the road" is two distinct capes. Windy **Cabo St. Vincent** is actually the most southwestern tip. It has a desolate lighthouse that marks what was referred to even in prehistoric times as "the end of the world" (open to the public daily 10:00–17:00). Snoop around, peek over the far edge, and ask the attendant to spin the light for you. Outside the lighthouse, salt-of-the-earth merchants sell figs, seaworthy sweaters (€25 average), and "the Letzte Bratwurst vor Amerika" (last hotdog before America). **Cape Sagres,** with its old fort and Henry the Navigator lore, is the more historic cape of the two (€3, old church, temporary art exhibits, and dramatic views). At either cape, look for daredevil windsurfers and fishermen casting off the cliffs.

Lashed tightly to the wind-swept landscape is the salty **town of Sagres,** above a harbor of fishing boats. Sagres is a popular gathering place for the backpacking crowd, with plenty of private rooms in the center and a relaxing beach and bar scene.

Tourist Information: The TI is on the main street, Rua Comandante Matoso (Tue–Sat 9:30–13:00 & 14:00–17:30, closed Sun–Mon, tel. 282-624-873).

SIGHTS

Near Sagres

Sagres Fort and Navigators' School—The former "end of the world" is a craggy, wind-swept, wedge-shaped point that juts into the Atlantic (short drive or 15-min walk from Sagres). In 1420, Prince Henry the Navigator used church funds to establish a school here for navigators. Today, little remains of Henry's school, except the site of buildings replaced by later (sometimes new) structures. An 18th-century fortress, built on the school's original battlements, dominates the entrance to the point.

1. Plaque inside Entrance: After entering through the 18th-century battlements, find the carved stone plaque that honors Henry. The carved ship in the plaque is a caravel, one of the small, light craft that was constantly being reinvented by Sagres' shipbuilding grad students. The astrolabe, a compact instrument that uses the stars for navigation, emphasizes Henry's role in the exploration process.

2. Wind-Compass: Sagres' most impressive sight—a circle on the ground, 100 feet across and outlined by round pebbles—is

a mystery. Some think it was a large wind-compass *(rosa-dos-ventos)*. A flag flying from the center could immediately announce the wind's direction. Others speculate it's a large sundial. A pole in the center pointing toward the North Star (at a 37-degree angle, Sagres' latitude) would cast a shadow on the dial showing the time of day.

3. Remains of the School: The row of buildings beyond the wind-compass is where the school once was. The **tower-cistern** (abutting the end of the modern Exhibition Centre) is part of the original dorms. The small, whitewashed, 16th-century **Church of Our Lady of Grace** replaced Henry's church. The former Governor's House is now the restaurant/gift shop complex. Attached to the gift shop is a **wind-break wall** that dates from Henry's time but is largely rebuilt.

The Sagres school taught map-making, ship-building, sailing, astronomy, and mathematics (for navigating), plus botany, zoology, anthropology, languages, and salesmanship for mingling with the locals. The school welcomed Italians, Scandinavians, and Germans and included Christians, Muslims, and Jews. Captured Africans gave guest lectures.

Besides being a school, Sagres was Mission Control for the explorers. Returning sailors brought spices, gold, diamonds, silk, and ivory, plus new animals, plants, peoples, customs, communicable diseases, and knowledge of the routes that were added to the maps. Henry ordered every sailor to keep a travel journal that could be studied. Ship designs were analyzed and tweaked, resulting in the square-sailed, ocean-going caravels that replaced the earlier coast-hugging versions.

It's said that Ferdinand Magellan (circumnavigator), Vasco da Gama (sea route to India), Pedro Cabral (Brazil), and Bartolomeu Dias (Africa-rounder) all studied at Sagres (after Henry's time, though). In May 1476 the young Italian Christopher Columbus washed ashore here after being shipwrecked by pirates. He went on to study and sail with the Portuguese (and marry a Portuguese woman) before beginning his American voyage.

4. The Point: Beyond the buildings, the granite point itself is wind-swept, eroded, and largely barren, except for hardy, coarse vegetation admired by botanists. Walk on level paths around the edge of the bluff (a 40-min round-trip walk), where locals cast lines and tourists squint into the wind. You'll get great seascape views of Cape St. Vincent with its modern lighthouse on the site of an old convent. At the far end of the Sagres bluff are a naval radio station, a natural cave, and a promontory called "Prince Henry's Chair."

Sit on the point and gaze across the "Sea of Darkness," where monsters roam. Long before Henry's time, Romans considered it the edge of the world, dubbing it Promontorium Sacrum—Sacred ("Sagres") Promontory. Pilgrims who came to visit this awe-inducing place were prohibited to spend the night here—it was for the gods alone.

In Portugal's seafaring lore, capes, promontories, and land's ends are metaphors for the edge of the old, and the start of the unknown voyage. Sagres is the greatest of these.

Beaches—Many beaches are tucked away on the drive between Salema and Cape Sagres. Most of them require a short walk after you stop along N-125. In some cases, you leave your car on access roads or cross private property to reach the beaches—be considerate. In Salema, ask at Pensión Mare or the Tutti Service travel agency for directions to beaches before you head to Sagres. Furnas beach is fully accessible by car. You can access Ingrina and  Zavial beaches by turning south in the village of Raposeira. Many beaches have bars (the one at Ingrina beach is famous for their prawns—*piri-piri*).

The best secluded beach in the region is **Praia do Castelejo,** just north of Cape Sagres (from the town of Vila do Bispo, drive inland and follow the signs for 15 min). If you have a car and didn't grow up in Fiji, this really is worth the drive. Overlooking the deserted beach is **Castelejo Restaurante,** which specializes in *cataplanas,* the hearty local seafood stew (daily 12:00–22:00,

Prince Henry the Navigator
(1394–1460)

No swashbuckling sailor, Henry was a quiet scholar, organizer, religious man, and the brains behind Portugal's daring sea voyages. The middle child of King John I of Portugal and Queen Philippa of England, he was one of what was dubbed "The Marvelous Generation" *(Ínclita Geração)* that drove the Age of Discovery. While his brothers and nephews became Portugal's kings, he worked behind the scenes.

At age 21, he planned the logistics for the large-scale ship invasion of the Muslim city of Ceuta (1415), on the north coast of Morocco, taking the city and winning knightly honors. Awed by the wealth of the city—a terminus of the caravan route—and intrigued by the high-quality maps they found there, Henry decided to organize expeditions to explore the Muslim world. He hoped to spread Christianity, contain Islam, tap Muslim wealth, and find Prester John's legendary Christian kingdom, said to exist somewhere in Africa or Asia.

As head of the Order of Christ—a powerful brotherhood of soldier-monks—Grand Master Henry used their money to found a maritime school at Sagres. While Henry stayed home to update maps, debrief returning sailors, order supplies, and sign paychecks, brave seamen traveled off under Henry's strict orders not to return until they'd explored what was known as the "Sea of Darkness."

They discovered the Madeira Islands (1420), which Henry

7.5 miles from Salema at Praia do Castelejo, tel. 282-639-777). While beaches between Salema and Sagres offer more of a seaside landscape, beaches north of São Vicente are more rugged and wild since they're exposed to ocean wind and weather. If there's no sand in Castelejo when you visit, blame it on nature and enjoy the rock formations instead.

SLEEPING AND EATING

For a touch of local elegance in Sagres, pop into the lavish, waterfront **Pousada do Infante** (Db-€110–165, tel. 218-442-001, fax 218-442-085, www.pousadas.pt, info@pousadas.pt). The classy *pousada* (historic inn) is a reasonable splurge with a magnificent setting. At breakfast, you can sip coffee and enjoy the buffet while gazing out to sea.

Vila Velha Restaurante, another splurge, offers wonderfully unforgettable meals (Tue–Sun 18:30–22:00, closed Mon, reservations smart, near *pousada*, tel. 282-624-788).

planted with vineyards, and the Azores (1427), which Henry colonized with criminals. But the next expeditions returned empty-handed, having run into a barrier—a psychological one. Cape Bojador (at the southwest corner of modern Morocco), with its reefs and currents, was seen as the end of the world. Beyond that, sea serpents roamed, while the hot equatorial sun melted ships, made the sea boil, and turned white men black.

Henry ordered scared, superstitious sailors to press on. After 14 unsuccessful voyages, Gil Eanes' crew returned (1437), unharmed and still white, with new knowledge that could be added to corporate Portugal's map library.

Henry himself gained a reputation as an intelligent, devout, non-materialistic, celibate monk who humbled himself by wearing horsehair underwear. In 1437, Henry faced a personal tragedy. His planned invasion of Tangier failed miserably, and his beloved little brother Fernão was captured. As ransom, the Muslims demanded that Portugal return Ceuta. Henry (and others) refused, Fernão died in captivity, and Henry was devastated.

In later years, he spent less time at court in Lisbon, and more in desolate Sagres, where he died in 1460. (He's buried in Batalha; see page 166.) Henry died before finding a sea route to Asia and just before his voyages really started paying off commercially. A generation later, Vasco da Gama would sail to India, capping Henry's explorations and kicking off Portugal's golden age.

TRANSPORTATION CONNECTIONS

From Salema, Sagres is a 20-minute drive or hitch, a half-hour bus trip (nearly hourly trips from Salema, check return times), or a taxi ride (€30 for a 75-min round-trip, plus €7/hr for waiting time in Sagres).

Lagos

Lagos, with a beach-party old town and a jet-ski marina, is as enjoyable as a big-city resort can be. This major town on the west end of the Algarve was the capital of the Algarve in the 13th and 14th centuries. The first great Portuguese maritime expeditions embarked from here, and the first African slave market in Europe was held here. Though not advertised by the local TI, the slave market does appear on the TI's town map and currently operates as an art gallery (look for small *Galeria Mercado de Escravos* sign).

ORIENTATION

The old town, defined by its medieval walls, stretches between Praça Gil Eanes and the fort. It's a whitewashed jumble of pedestrian streets, bars, funky craft shops, outdoor restaurants, mod fountains and sculptures, and sunburned tourists. Search out the sea-creature designs laid in the pavement—some of them will probably be on your plate at dinner. The beaches with the exotic rock formations—of postcard fame—begin just past the fort with easy access via hiking trails.

Tourist Information

The Câmara Municipal TI is downtown at Largo Marquês de Pombal (daily 10:00–18:00, July–Aug until 20:00). Another TI is a bleak six-minute walk from the bus station, oddly marooned on a traffic roundabout at the entrance to town (May–Sept Tue–Thu 9:30–19:00, Fri–Mon 9:30–13:00 & 14:00–17:30, Oct–April 9:30–13:00 & 14:00–17:30, behind bus station, take Rua Vasco da Gama to the right, and continue straight, on roundabout across from boat-shaped fountain en route to Portimão, tel. 282-763-031).

Arrival in Lagos

The train and bus stations are a five-minute walk apart, separated by the marina and pedestrian bridge over a river. Neither the bus station nor the train station has luggage storage.

If you are coming from Spain on the A22 freeway, exit at Lagos Este and follow signs to *centro*.

SIGHTS

Coastal Boat Tours—Along the harborfront, you'll be hustled to take a sightseeing cruise. Old fishermen ("who know the nickname of each rock along the coast") sit at anchor under umbrellas while their salespeople on the promenade hawk 45-minute exotic rock and cave tours for €10.

More serious maritime adventures are sold (April–Oct) by a string of established companies with offices just over the marina bridge. **Bom Dia** offers three different tours by sailboat: a two-hour €15 grotto tour (with a chance to swim), a half-day €37 BBQ cruise (basically a grotto tour with a meal), and a full-day (10:00–17:00) €65 round-trip to Sagres (cash only, in marina at Lagos 10, WC on board, smart to reserve at least a day ahead in Aug,

Lagos

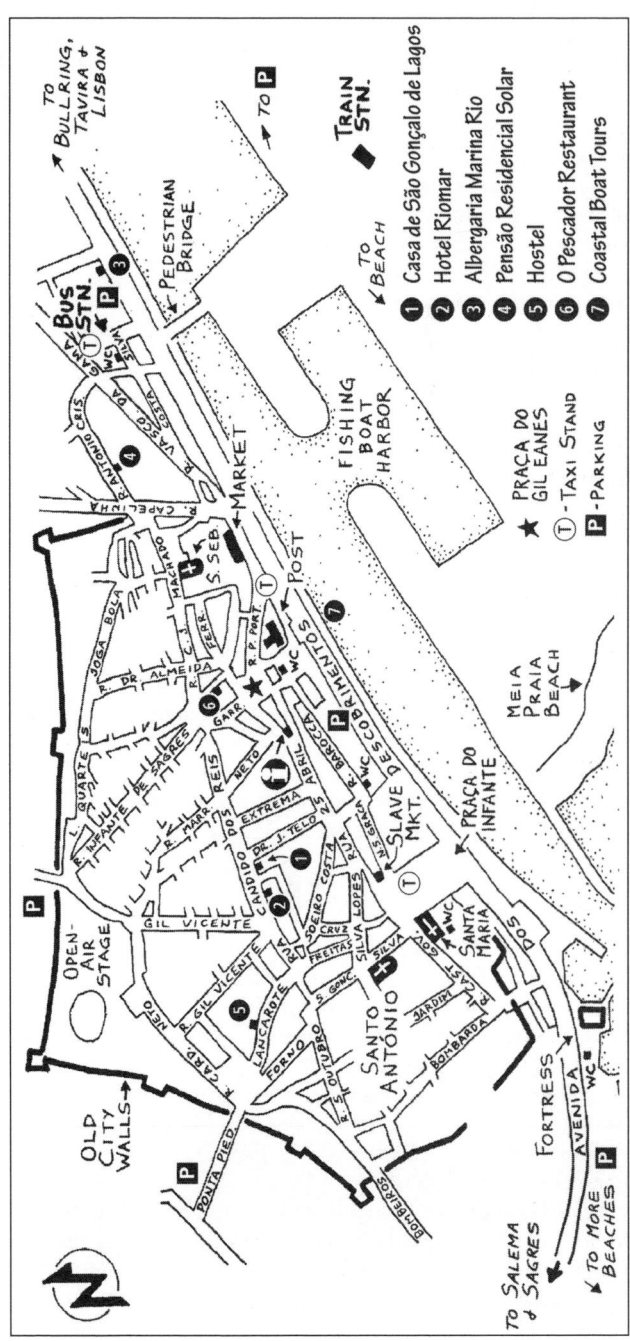

TO BULLRING, TAVIRA + LISBON

TO P

TRAIN STN.

① Casa de São Gonçalo de Lagos
② Hotel Riomar
③ Albergaria Marina Rio
④ Pensão Residencial Solar
⑤ Hostel
⑥ O Pescador Restaurant
⑦ Coastal Boat Tours

PEDESTRIAN BRIDGE

TO BEACH

BUS STN.

FISHING BOAT HARBOR

MARKET

★ — PRAÇA DO GIL EANES
① - TAXI STAND
P - PARKING

S. SEB.

POST

MEIA PRAIA BEACH

JOGA BOLA

DR. ALMEIDA

L. QUARTEIS

INFANTE DE SAGRES

REIS

NETO

BARROCCA

SLAVE DESCOBRIMENTOS

SLAVE MKT.

PRAÇA DO INFANTE

EXTREMA

DR. J. TELO

GIL VICENTE

CRUZ

FREITAS

SILVA

SILVA

SANTA MARIA

CARD. NETO

GIL VICENTE

LANCAROTE

FORNO

R. OUTUBRO

JARDIM

SANTO ANTÓNIO

OPEN-AIR STAGE

BOMBARDA

OLD CITY WALLS

PONTA PIED.

FORTRESS

AVENIDA

TO SALEMA & SAGRES

TO MORE BEACHES

N

tel. 282-764-670 or mobile 917-810-761, www.bomdia.info). Bom Dia, with partner **Algarve Dolphins,** is also in the dolphin-spotting game. Speedy boats whisk you through the waves in search of flippered friends (€30, 90 min, hourly departures, same contact info as above). **Dolphin Seafari** offers 90-minute dolphin-watching cruises (nearly all trips have dolphin sightings) and 45-minute speedboat tours just for fun (5/day in summer, cash only, big and sturdy inflatable lifeboat used for both trips, tel. 282-799-209 or mobile 919-359-359).

▲**Church of Santo António**—Rebuilt in part after the 1755 earthquake, this is considered one of the best Baroque churches in Portugal and is dedicated to the patron saint of the military, António. The church (free entry but rarely open) and adjoining regional archaeological and ethnology museum are worth a look (€2, Tue–Sun 9:30–12:30 & 14:00–17:00, closed Mon).

Bullfight—Lagos has a small, just-for-tourists bullfight in its dinky ring from June through September on most Saturdays at 18:30. Seats are a steep €20, but the 90-minute show is a thriller. Matadors face three bulls with covered horns. While the earlier portion on horseback is elegant, it gets rowdier later in the show, when a gang of guys pile on the bull while someone grabs the beast's tail and "water-skis" along behind. The event is accompanied by a three-person orchestra. Remember that the Portuguese, with few exceptions, have toned down the fights and do not kill the bull during the show—they do it later (see also "Portuguese Bullfight" on page 88).

Signs all along this touristy coastline advertise bullfights *(Stierkampf)* in German to attract tourists.

SLEEPING

(€1.20 = about $1, country code: 351)
When a price range is given, the lowest is the winter rate and the highest is the August rate. Lagos is enjoyable for a resort its size, but I must remind you that Salema is a village paradise and is only a 20-minute taxi ride (€18, metered, but ask for estimate first) or half-hour bus ride away. If you missed the last bus to Salema (leaves Lagos around 20:30), Albergaria Marina Rio and Pensão Residencial Solar are both within 100 yards of the bus station. Everyone speaks English.

$$ Casa de São Gonçalo de Lagos, a beautifully decorated 18th-century home with a garden, lovely tile work, parquet floors, and elegant furnishings, is a fine value. While the downstairs rooms are relatively plain, upstairs you'll find a plush Old World lounge, a dreamy garden, and 13 classy old rooms with all the comforts (Sb-€40–70, Db-€50–90, Tb-€70–125, depending on room and season, includes breakfast, closed Nov–March, cash or AmEx card only, Rua Candido dos Reis 73, on a pedestrian street 2 blocks off Praça Luis de Camões, a square that's a block behind the main square, tel. 282-762-171, fax 282-763-927).

$$ Hotel Riomar, next door, is a new, blocky, and tour-friendly place providing 42 rooms and more comfort than character for a decent price (Db-€45–60, Tb-€65–85, Qb-€85–100, includes breakfast, cash or AmEx card only, air-con, elevator, rooms on back lack street noise, Rua Candido dos Reis 83, tel. 282-770-130, fax 282-763-927).

$$ The big, slick **Albergaria Marina Rio** faces the marina and the busy main street immediately in front of the bus station. Its modern, 36 air-conditioned rooms come with all the amenities but not-so-smiley service. Marina views come with noise; quieter rooms are in the back. All rooms have twin beds (Sb-€42–93, Db-€44–95, extra bed-€14–29, includes breakfast and tax, small rooftop pool and terrace, elevator, Internet access, laundry service, Avenida dos Descobrimentos-Apartado 388, tel. 282-780-830, fax 282-780-839, www.marinario.com).

$$ Pensão Residencial Solar rents 29 very basic rooms (Sb-€25–45, Db-€35–70, includes breakfast and a fan, cheaper D-€20–40 rooms in annex up the hill and in *quartos* in the center, elevator, Rua António Crisogno dos Santos 60, tel. 282-762-477, fax 282-761-784).

$ The Club Med–like **youth hostel** is a lively, social, cushy, hammocks-in-the-courtyard experience (dorm bed in quad-€10–15, five Db-€28–45, breakfast-€1, kitchen facilities, Internet access, priority given to hostel members, non-members of any age are welcome, Rua Lançarote de Freitas 50, tel. 282-761-970, fax 282-769-684, lagos@movijovem.pt).

EATING

You'll find a variety of lively choices for dinner branching out in all directions from Praça Gil Eanes. Most of them offer a similar sampling of grilled fish with plenty of vegetables, but other options range from Italian to Indian. Home-style cooking is better closer to the market. One good choice is **O Pescador,** popular with both locals and tourists. In a simple, bright, paper-napkin atmosphere, they serve good *picanha* (Brazilian flank steak) and grilled fish (daily 12:00–22:00, Rua Gil Eanes 6–10, tel. 282-767-028).

TRANSPORTATION CONNECTIONS

From Lagos by Train and Bus to: Lisbon (5 trains/day, 5 hrs, transfer in Tunes; 8 buses/day, 4.5 hrs, likely transfer in Albufeira; €15 for bus or train), **Évora** (2 buses, at 7:00 and 15:00, 6 hrs, €14; 2 trains, at 8:20 and 17:15, 6–7 hrs, with 2 transfers, €14), **Tavira** (11 trains/day, 3 hrs; 6 buses/day, 1.5 hrs, transfer in Faro). Train info: tel. 808-208-208, bus info: tel. 289-899-700.

Connecting Lagos and Sevilla, Spain, by Bus: There are two buses per day in each direction year-round (€17, about 7 hrs from Lagos bus station to Sevilla's Plaza de Armas bus station, buy ticket a day or two in advance May–Oct). Ask the TI or a local travel agency for the latest bus schedule. This is the 2005 schedule: Lagos 6:30 to Sevilla 13:00; Lagos 13:45 to Sevilla 20:15; Sevilla 7:30 to Lagos 12:00; Sevilla 16:30 to Lagos 21:00. Note that Spanish time is one hour later than Portuguese time. Although you can get off (or on, if there's space) in Tavira, you'll pay the full price from Lagos to Sevilla for your trip.

From Lagos to Salema: Take a bus (nearly hourly, fewer on weekends, 30 min) or a taxi (€18); see "Arrival in Salema" on page 116 for details. In Lagos, to get to the bus station from the train station (ignore the "*quartos* women" who tell you Salema is 40 miles away), walk straight out of the train station, go right around the big fish warehouse, cross the pedestrian bridge and then the main boulevard, and walk straight into the white-and-yellow EVA bus station (tel. 282-762-944, www.eva-bus.com). Before heading to Salema, pick up return bus schedules and train schedules for your next destination (though as a fallback, Tutti Service travel agency in Salema has posted schedules).

Tavira

Straddling a river, with a lively park, chatty locals, and boats that share its waterfront center, Tavira is a low-rise, easygoing alternative to the other more aggressive Algarve resorts. It's your best

eastern Algarve stop. Because Tavira has good connections by bus and train (it's on the trans-Algarve train line, with nearly hourly departures both east and west), many travelers find the town more accessible than Salema. And, if you're driving from Sevilla to Salema, it's the perfect midway stop on the four-hour trip (just 2 miles off the freeway).

You'll see many churches and fine bits of Renaissance architecture sprinkled throughout the town. These clues are evidence that 500 years ago Tavira was the largest town on the Algarve (with 1,500 dwellings according to a 1530 census) and an important base for Portuguese adventurers in Africa. The silting up of its harbor, a plague, the 1755 earthquake, and the shifting away of its once-lucrative tuna industry left Tavira in a long decline. Today the town has a wistful charm and lives off its tourists.

ORIENTATION

Tavira straddles the Rio Gilão two miles from the Atlantic. Everything of sightseeing and transportation importance is on the south bank. A clump of historic sights—the ruined castle and main church—fills its tiny fortified hill and tangled Moorish lanes. But today, the action is outside the old fortifications along the riverside Praça da República and the adjacent shady, fountain- and bench-filled park. The old market hall is beyond the park. And beyond that is the boat to the beach island. The old pedestrian-only "Roman Bridge" leads from Praça da República to the north bank (with 2 recommended hotels and most of the evening and restaurant action).

Tourist Information
The TI is up the cobbled steps from the inland end of Praça da República (Tue–Thu 9:30–19:00, Fri–Mon until 17:30, closed during lunch and on Sun off-season, Rua Galeria 9, tel. 281-322-511). The TI's free leaflet describes a dozen churches with enthusiasm. But for most tourists, the town's sights can all be seen quickly (see "Welcome to Tavira" walk, below).

Arrival in Tavira
The train station is a 10-minute walk from the town center *(centro)*. To get to the center, leave the station in the direction of the blue *Turismo* sign, and follow this road downhill to the river and Praça da República. The riverside bus station is three blocks from the town center; simply follow the river into town. Drivers can park conveniently riverside on the main square *(zona pago*, €0.40/hr) for up to four hours.

Helpful Hints
Internet Access: Café Anazu has a gang of computers available daily from 10:30–24:00 (just over the bridge at Rua Pessoa 11). There are a few free terminals at the City Hall.

Bike Rental: You can rent bikes at **Sport Nautica** (just down from Café Anazu, Rua Pessoa 26, tel. 281-324-943).

Tavira

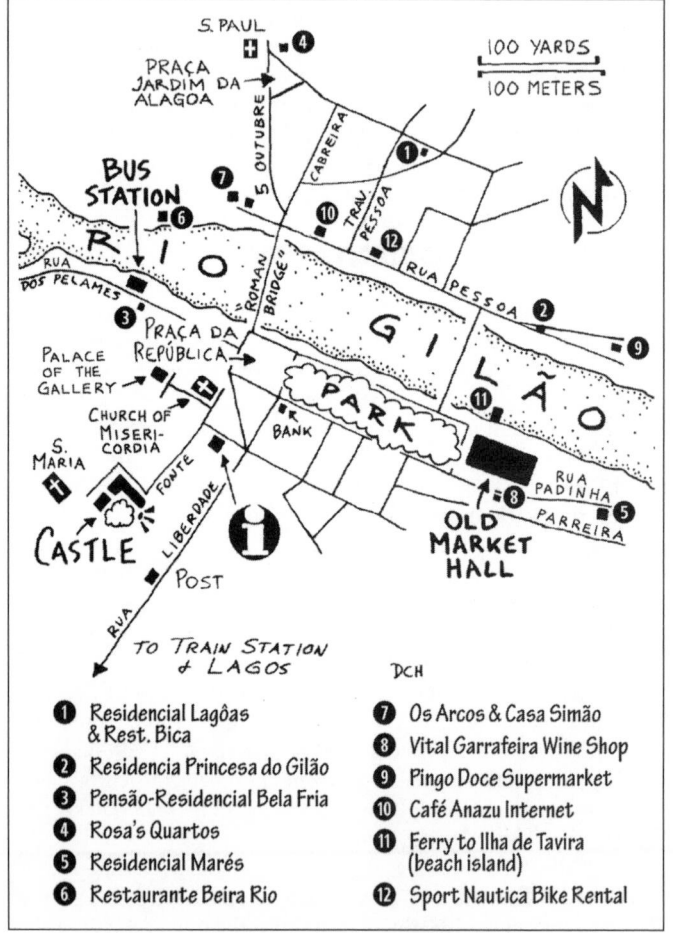

S. PAUL

PRAÇA
JARDIM DA
ALAGOA

100 YARDS
100 METERS

BUS
STATION

RIO

RUA
DOS PELAMES

PALACE
OF THE
GALLERY

CHURCH OF
MISERI-
CORDIA

S.
MARIA

CASTLE

Post

PRAÇA DA
REPÚBLICA

GILÃO

PARK

BANK

FONTE

LIBERDADE

RUA

TO TRAIN STATION
& LAGOS

OLD
MARKET
HALL

RUA
PADINHA

PARREIRA

DCH

RUA PESSOA

S OUTUBRE

CABREIRA

TRAV
PESSOA

ROMAN
BRIDGE

N

❶ Residencial Lagôas
  & Rest. Bica
❷ Residencia Princesa do Gilão
❸ Pensão-Residencial Bela Fria
❹ Rosa's Quartos
❺ Residencial Marés
❻ Restaurante Beira Rio

❼ Os Arcos & Casa Simão
❽ Vital Garrafeira Wine Shop
❾ Pingo Doce Supermarket
❿ Café Anazu Internet
⓫ Ferry to Ilha de Tavira
  (beach island)
⓬ Sport Nautica Bike Rental

SELF-GUIDED WALK

Welcome to Tavira Walk

This quick walk, rated ▲, starts at the TI (just uphill from the
town square) and covers everything of importance.

1. Old Town Gate: Only this unimpressive gate (just below
the TI) survives from Tavira's 16th-century walls. Check out the
crown and spheres—meant to remind visitors that they are in the
kingdom of Portugal—and the holes for bars that once locked
the door.

2. Church of Misericorda: At the top of the lane (above the
TI), the Church of Misericorda faced the city gate. Its facade,

dating from 1541, is considered the best Renaissance facade in the Algarve. Inside, you'll see a multitude of blue-and-white tile panels that show you how to lead a good Christian life. Meanwhile, a zealous attendant will make sure you don't take any photos inside (Mon–Fri 9:30–12:30, closed Sat–Sun).

3. Palace of the Gallery: From the church, hike left up the stepped lane to the Palace of the Gallery. This 17th-century Baroque palace, nearly the town's highest point, is nicknamed "Tavira's Acropolis." It's the biggest private mansion in town, but houses a smaller exhibition center on contemporary art that's open to the public.

4. Castle Garden: Climb left to the big Church of Santa Maria. On your left is a hunk of castle with a door leading to a garden (free, 8:00–17:00). The base of the castle wall is supposedly Neolithic, while later inhabitants—the Phoenicians in 8th century B.C., the Moors in eighth century A.D., and the Portuguese in the 13th century—added their own layers to the structure. The castle grounds are now a fragrant garden, offering a fine city view. Overlooking the city, notice Tavira's unique "treasury" rooftops—a little roof for each room of a building. This is likely inspired by visions brought home from Asia by local explorers.

5. Church of Santa Maria: Once a mosque, this church was transformed in the 13th century. Inside, the second chapel on the left is the only part that survived the 1755 earthquake. The third chapel has fine pink columns. The marble is actually painted wood as there was no marble in the Algarve and no money to import it.

The church's museum (crude but beautiful art in 2 rooms) and bell tower (peer past the bells to enjoy a commanding city view with surviving bits of town wall and coastline nearby) each cost €1. There's a WC at the base of the bell tower.

6. Roman Bridge: Leave the church, walk straight through a small garden down to the street, and make a left on Rua da Liberdade. Reach the riverfront, and find the pedestrian bridge on your left. The "Roman Bridge" may not be Roman, but it was here when the Moors came. The current structure is from 1657, with parts rebuilt after a 1989 flood. The more functional bridge on your right was designed to be temporary, until the Roman Bridge was fixed. But they decided it (rather than the Roman Bridge) was better for car traffic, and since 1989, the old bridge has been pedestrian-only.

7. The Riverside Park and Old Market Hall: This is where old folks gossip and children play. Walk past the bandstand and more "treasury roofs" (on the right) to the old market hall. A few black-and-white photos show how, in the 1990s, this was a noisy, colorful fish and produce market. Today it's for cafés and shops.

Beyond the market hall are a few fishing boats. Local fishermen are weathering tough times as the "natural park" classification of the coastal areas makes aggressive netting illegal, and Spanish fishermen are selling their catch very cheap.

SIGHTS

▲**Ilha de Tavira**—Tavira's great beach island is a hit for travelers. Ilha de Tavira is a long, almost treeless sandbar with a campground, several restaurants, and a sprawling beach. A summer-only boat takes bathers painlessly from downtown Tavira to the island (€1 round-trip, July–mid-Sept about hourly from 8:00–20:00, timetable at TI, departs from dock next to former market hall). It's an enjoyable ride even if you just go round-trip without getting out. Or you can bus, taxi, ride a rental bike, or bake during a shadeless 1.25-mile walk out of town to Quatro Aguas, where the five-minute ferry shuttles sunbathers to Ilha de Tavira (€1.50, ferry runs constantly with demand all year, last trip near midnight in high season to accommodate diners).

Near Tavira
▲**Barril Beach**—This fine beach resort is 2.5 miles from Tavira. Walk, rent a bike, or take a city bus to Pedras del Rei and then catch the little train (usually runs year-round) or walk 10 minutes through Ria Formosa National Park to the resort. Get details at the TI.

Cacela Velha—Just a couple miles east of Tavira (half-mile off the main road), this tiny village sits happily ignored on a hill with its fort, church, one restaurant, a few *quartos,* and a beach with the open sea just over the sandbar, a short row across its lagoon. The restaurant serves a sausage-and-cheese specialty fried at your table. If you're driving, swing by, if only to enjoy the coastal view and to imagine how nice the Algarve would be if people like you and me had never discovered it.

SLEEPING

(€1 = about $1.20, country code: 351)
Everyone speaks English unless otherwise noted. Prices usually shoot up in August.

$$ Residencial Marés, on the busy side of the river amid all the strolling and café ambience, has 25 good rooms, a restaurant, and a rooftop terrace. Some rooms on the second floor have balconies overlooking the river (Sb-€30–50, no singles in Aug; Db-€55, €70 in July and Sept, €85 in Aug; extra bed-€10, includes breakfast, air-con; Rua José Pires Padinha, on the TI side of the river just beyond old market hall; tel. 281-325-815, fax 281-325-819, maresresidencial@mail.telepac.pt).

$ Residencial Lagôas is spotless, homey, and a block off the river. Friendly Maria offers a rooftop patio with a view made for wine and candles, a communal refrigerator, and laundry washboard privileges (S-€20, D-€30, Db-€40, Tb-€50, no gouging in July and Aug, cheaper off-season, no breakfast, cash only, Rua Almirante Candido dos Reis 24, tel. 281-322-252, easy phone reservations). Cross the Roman Bridge from Praça da República, follow the middle fork on the other side, and turn right where it ends.

$ Residencia Princesa do Gilão, modern and hotelesque, offers 22 bright rooms. Choose between riverfront or quiet rooms on the back with a terrace (prices vary with the month, Sb-€40–60, Db-€50–70, Tb-€60–80, Qb-€65–85, includes breakfast, cash only, Rua Borda de Agua de Aguiar 10, cross Roman bridge and turn right along river, tel. & fax 281-325-171).

$ Pensão-Residencial Bela Fria is a basic eight-room place with a low-energy management. Its simple air-conditioned rooms are quiet, modern, and comfortable (Sb-€30, €50 July–Aug; Db-€40–50, €60 July–Aug; includes breakfast, Rua dos Pelames 1, directly across from bus station, tel. & fax 281-325-375).

$ For quiet, spacious, comfort, **Rosa's Quartos** are worth the communication struggles. Rosa rents 14 big, gleaming, marble-paved rooms on a quiet alley. Request her best rooms, which are in a separate building across the alley in back (D-€30, Db-€35, T-€45, Tb-€50, €5 more in Aug, cash only, over bridge and through Jardim da Alagoa square to Rua da Porta Nova 4, immediately across from St. Paul's church, unmarked door, tel. 281-321-547, friendly Rosa doesn't speak English).

EATING

Tavira is filled with reasonable restaurants. Lively, top-end places face the riverbank just beyond the old market hall. A few blocks inland, hole-in-the-wall places offer more fish per dollar. After dinner, take a stroll along the fish-filled river, with a pause on the Roman Bridge or in the park (if there's any action in the bandstand).

To find three good riverside eateries, cross the Roman Bridge, turn left, go upstream through the tunnel, and you'll see the rickety tables. **Restaurante Beira Rio** has great fish and an extensive menu (€10 meals, nightly 18:00–22:30, tel. 281-323-165). The neighboring **Os Arcos** and **Restaurante Casa Simão** are simpler, with cheap and tasty grilled fish.

For seafood, I enjoyed the inexpensive and relaxed **Restaurante Bica,** below the recommended Residencial Lagôas (see "Sleeping," above).

Vital Garrafeira offers snacks and light meals but it's mainly about port. It has an excellent, well-priced selection of port, plus higher-end Portuguese wines that are difficult to find elsewhere (daily 8:00–13:00 & 14:30–19:00, Rua José Padinha 66, tel. 281-322-482).

Picnics: Forage at the popular **Pingo Doce** supermarket chain, just across the river (daily 8:00–20:00).

TRANSPORTATION CONNECTIONS

From Tavira to: Lisbon (train or bus works fine: 5 trains/day, 5 hrs; 11 buses/day, 4.25 hrs), **Lagos** (train is better: 11 trains/day, change in Faro, 2–3 hrs). Train info: tel. 808-208-208, bus info: tel. 281-322-546.

Route Tips for Drivers in the Algarve

Lisbon to Salema (185 miles, 3.5 hrs): Following the blue *Sul Ponte* signs, drive south over Lisbon's 25th of April Bridge. A short detour just over the bridge takes you to the giant concrete statue of Cristo Rei (Christ in Majesty). Continue south by freeway until you hit the coast and follow signs west to Lagos. Take the Lagos Oeste/Vila do Bispo exit and follow signs to Vila do Bispo and Sagres. If you pay attention, you'll see the turn-off for Salema before Vila do Bispo. A modern freeway, less traffic, and the glory of waking up on the Algarve make doing this drive in the evening after a full day in Lisbon a reasonable option.

Algarve to Sevilla (175 miles, 3 hrs): Drive east along the Algarve. It's a 1.5 hour-drive from Salema to Tavira. Some hills are crowned by rotting windmills and others by mobile-phone towers. To visit Lagos, park along the waterfront by the fort and the Mobil gas station. From Lagos, hit the freeway (A22, direction: Lisboa/Faro, then *Espanha*) to Tavira. Leaving Tavira, follow the signs to *Espanha*. You'll cross over the bridge into Spain (where it's 1 hour later) and glide effortlessly (90 min by freeway) into Sevilla.

ÉVORA

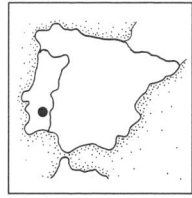

Deep in the heart of Portugal, in the barren, arid plains of the southern province of Alentejo, historic Évora (EH-voh-rah) has been a cultural oasis for 2,000 years. With an untouched provincial atmosphere, fascinating whitewashed old town, museums, a cathedral, a chapel of bones, and even a Roman temple, Évora (pop. 50,000) stands proudly amid groves of cork and olive trees.

Planning Your Time

With frequent bus connections (20/day, 2 hrs) to Lisbon, Évora makes a decent day trip from Portugal's capital city. You can stop by for an overnight stay en route to or from the Algarve, five hours away (1 bus and 3 trains a day). Drivers can sandwich Évora between Lisbon and the Algarve, exploring dusty droves of olive groves and scruffy seas of peeled cork trees along the way. Take the freeway from the Algarve to Beja and the nearly-as-fast highway from Beja to Évora. A super freeway zips you from Évora to Lisbon in 90 minutes.

With a day in Évora, take the "Welcome to Évora" walk outlined below, have a quick lunch, see the remaining sights, and enjoy a leisurely, top-notch dinner. After dinner, stroll the back streets and ponder life, like the retired men on the squares.

ORIENTATION

Évora's old town, contained within a medieval wall, is surrounded by the sprawling newer part of town. The major sights—the Roman Temple of Diana and early Gothic cathedral—crowd close together at the old town's highest point. A subtle yet still-powerful

Évora

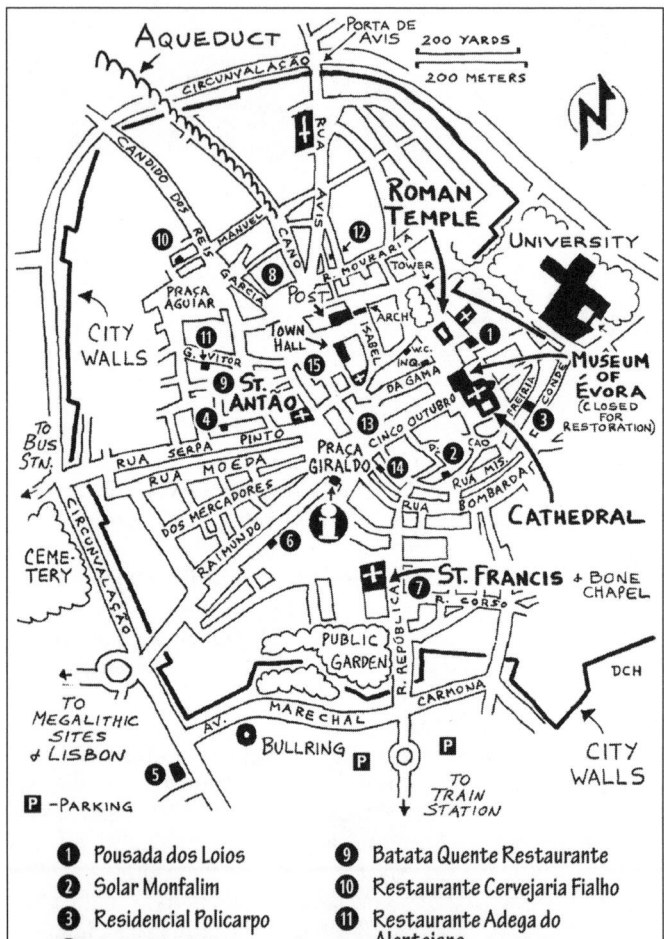

1. Pousada dos Loios
2. Solar Monfalim
3. Residencial Policarpo
4. Hotel Santa Clara
5. Hotel Ibis
6. Casa Palma Quartos
7. Produce Market
8. Rest. Cervejaria "1/4 Para As 9"
9. Batata Quente Restaurante
10. Restaurante Cervejaria Fialho
11. Restaurante Adega do Alentejano
12. Taberna Tipica Quarta-Feira
13. Mr. Pickwick's Restaurante
14. Policarpo City Tours
15. Praça de Sertorio

Alentejo Region

Southeastern Portugal is very sunny and very dry. The rolling, empty plains of the Alentejo (ah-len-TAY-zhoo) are dotted with large orchards and estates, Stone Age monoliths, Roman aqueducts, Moorish-looking whitewashed villages, and medieval Christian castles.

During the Christian reconquest of the country, Alentejo was the war zone. Christian conquerors turned huge tracts of recaptured land over to the care of soldier-monks of various religious-military orders, like the Knights Templar and the Order of Christ (which Prince Henry the Navigator once headed). Évora was governed by the House of Avis, which produced the kings of Portugal's Age of Discovery.

Despite its royal past, the Alentejo (the land "beyond the River Tejo," from the Latin *alem Tejo*) is an unpretentious land of farmers. Having been irrigated since Roman and Moorish times, the region is a major producer of wheat, cattle, wine... and trees. You'll see cork trees (green leaves, knotted trunks, red under-bark of recently-harvested trunks), oak (native to the country, once used to build explorers' caravels), olives (dusty green-silver leaves, major export crop), and eucalyptus (tall, cough-drop-smelling trees imported from Australia, grown for pulp).

Today the Alentejo region is known for being extraordinarily traditional, even considered backward by snooty Lisboans. The people of Alentejo are the butt of jokes. It's said you'll see them riding motorcycles in pajamas...so they can better lay into the corners. Many Portuguese call porno flicks "Alentejo karate." When I met a sad old guy from Alentejo, I asked him what was wrong; he explained that he was on the verge of teaching his burro how to live without food...but it died. In traditional Alentejo homes there's always a chair next to the bed, so they can sit down to rest after they get up.

charm is contained within the medieval walls. Find it by losing yourself in the quiet lanes of Évora's far corners.

Tourist Information

Pick up a free map at the TI on the main square at Praça do Giraldo 73 (daily April–Oct 9:00–19:00, Nov–March 9:00–18:00, tel. 266-730-032). The TI offers an excellent, 90-minute, €12 **city walk** every morning at 10:00 (just show up, minimum 2 people, tel. 963-702-392). This is a great opportunity to connect with a local and enliven your visit. Policarpo City Tours also offers guided city walks as well as bus tours (see page 153).

Arrival in Évora

The bus station is on Avenida São Sebastião. To reach the center from the station, it's either a short taxi ride (€4) or a 10-minute walk (exit station right, and continue straight all the way into town, passing through the city walls at the halfway point). The train station is on Avenida Dr. Barahona. From the train station to the center, it's a taxi ride (€5) or 25-minute walk up Avenida Dr. Barahona, continuing straight—on Rua da República—after you enter the city walls.

Drivers will find Évora's old town frustrating with all its tiny one-way streets. Use one of many free parking lots circling the town just outside the walls; most hotels are only a short walk away.

Helpful Hints

Internet Access: The big place in town is **Cybercenter,** with 20 computers and lots of local kids playing games (just downhill from main square at Rua dos Mercadores 42). The town hall on Praça de Sertorio has six free computers, though there's usually a wait.

Taxis: Cabs are helpful in this small but confusing town. They're parked on the main square (€3.50 minimum).

Shuttle Bus: The blue line on the streets marks the route of the "Linha Azul" (Blue Line), a shuttle bus that circles through the town, offering tired locals a convenient ride and tourists easy transport to and from the parking lots outside the walls. Hop on for a city joyride (they stop for anyone who waves, €0.50).

SELF-GUIDED WALK

Welcome to Évora

Évora's walled city is small. These sights are all within a five-minute walk of the main square, Praça do Giraldo (PRA-suh doo zhee-RAHL-doo). The walk takes about an hour, plus time visiting sights. If it's a hot day, go early in the morning or late in the afternoon (the cathedral closes at 17:00).

Since becoming a world heritage city (1986), the city has strictly preserved the old center, allowing no buildings over two stories tall. It works hard to be people-friendly and inviting. The charming colors you see are traditional in Alentejo: Yellow trim kept away evil spirits and

blue actually does keep away flies. Monster garbage cans hide under elegant smaller ones; at night trucks lift entire hunks of sidewalk to empty them. Jacaranda trees—imported from Brazil 200 years ago—provide shade through the summer and purple flowers in spring.

Évora was once a Roman town (2nd century B.C. to 4th century A.D.), important because of its wealth of wheat and silver, and its location on a trade route to Rome. We'll see Roman sights, though most of Évora's Roman past is buried under the houses and hotels of today (often uncovered by accident when plumbing work needs to be done in basements). The town fell under Moorish rule from the 8th to the 12th centuries. Around 1000, Muslim nobles divided the caliphate up into small city-states (like Lisbon), with Évora as this region's capital. And during its glory years (15th–16th centuries), Évora was favored by Portuguese kings, even serving as the home of King John III (1502–1557, Manuel I's son who presided over Portugal's peak of power...and its first decline). From Romans to Moors to Portuguese kings, this little town has a big history.

The Main Square: Start at Praça do Giraldo, Évora's main square. It was named after Giraldo the Fearless, the Christian knight who led a surprise attack and retook Évora from the Moors in 1165. As thanks, Giraldo was made governor of the town and the symbol of the city (Évora's coat of arms is a knight on a horse; see it crowning the lampposts). On this square, all that's left of several centuries of Moorish rule is their artistry, evidenced by the wrought-iron balconies of the buildings that ring the square (and the occasional distinctive Mudejar "keyhole" window found throughout the town).

Until the 16th century, the area behind the TI was the Jewish Quarter. Because Christians figured the Bible forbade the charging of interest, Jews did the moneylending. Hence the names of the streets such as Rua Moeda (road of money) and Rua de Mercadores (road of merchants).

The Roman triumphal arch that used to stand on this square was demolished in the 16th century to make way for the Church of Santo Antão (at the end of the square). In front of the church is a 16th-century fountain—once an important water source for the town (it marks the end of the aqueduct) and now a popular hangout for young and old.

The Portuguese King John III lived in Évora for 30 years in the 16th century. The TI is inside the palace where the king's guests used to stay. Others weren't treated as royally. A fervent

Welcome to Évora

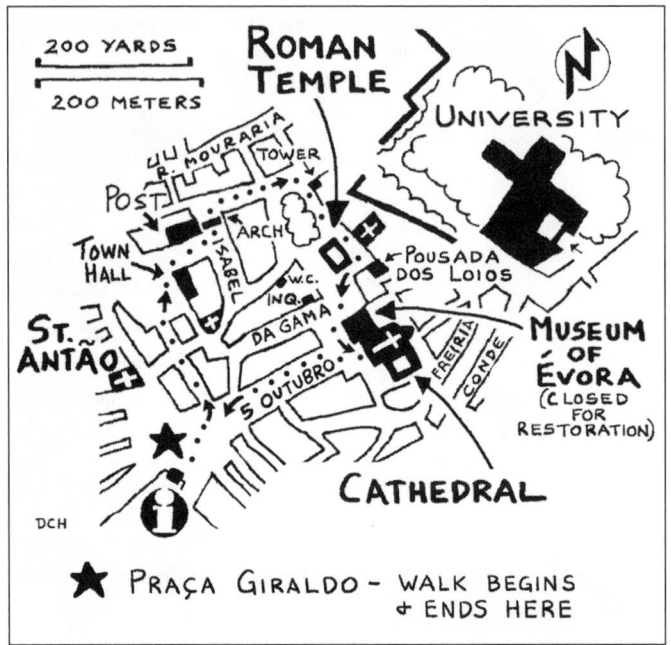

200 YARDS
200 METERS

ROMAN TEMPLE

UNIVERSITY

R. MOURARIA
POST
TOWER
ARCH
ISABEL
TOWN HALL
W.C.
INQ.
DA GAMA
ST. ANTÃO
5 OUTUBRO
POUSADA DOS LOIOS
FREIRIA
CONDE
MUSEUM OF ÉVORA
(CLOSED FOR RESTORATION)
CATHEDRAL
DCH

★ PRAÇA GIRALDO – WALK BEGINS & ENDS HERE

proponent of the Inquisition, King John sanctioned the deaths of hundreds of people who were burned as heretics on this square. On Tuesday mornings, the square is a traditional cattle-and-produce market with ranchers and farmers gathering (without their goods) to make deals—a medieval stock exchange based on trust. Notice the C.M.E. board (opposite the TI, near the start of Rua 5 de Outubro) where people gather to see who has died recently.

From the Main Square to the Roman Sights and Cathedral: Leave the square on Rua 5 de Outubro (opposite the TI office). The name of the road celebrates October 5, 1910, when Portugal shook off royal rule and became a republic. This little street has been a main shopping street since Roman times (we'll return to it later). Take the first left (at Mr. Pickwick's Restaurante) on Alcárcova de Cima, which in Arabic means "the place with water." A few steps farther on, you'll see a portion of a Roman wall built into the buildings on your right. After this, a series of modern windows show more of this wall, which used to surround what is now the inner core of the town. Below the last window, you can actually see the red paint of a Roman villa built over by the wall. (The wall that presently encircles Évora is 14th-century, fortified in the 17th century during Portugal's fight for independence from Spain.)

Walk straight, sniffing the wonderful scent of pastries coming from the kitchen of Café Arcada (we'll visit the café at the end of this walk), and cross the intersection to the blunt, granite, columned end of a 16th-century **aqueduct.** Continue straight on Travessa de Sertorio. The abnormally high sidewalk to your left is another part of the aqueduct.

Keep going straight. Within a block you'll reach a square, Praça de Sertorio. The tallest white building on the square is the **town hall.** Go inside (Mon–Fri 9:00–17:30, closed Sat–Sun, 6 computers with free Internet access). In the dark corner on the right is a view of a Roman bath that was uncovered during some building repair. To the right of this overlook is more of the ongoing excavation.

Exit the town hall to the right and take an immediate right around the town hall building. But look up to see a church built into a Roman tower (once part of the Roman wall you saw earlier) and, farther on, the arcaded post office *(correios)*.

Walk alongside the post office and take the first left, on Rua de Dona Isabel. You'll immediately see a **Roman arch**—Porta de Dona Isabel, once a main gate in the Roman wall. Below are some of the original Roman pavement stones (they're large and irregular in size and placement).

When you pass under the Roman wall, you're entering a neighborhood called Mouraria (for the Moors). After Giraldo the Fearless retook Évora, the Moors were still allowed to live in the area, but on the other side of this gate, beyond the city walls. They were safe here for centuries...until the Inquisition expelled them in the 16th century.

Turn right, walking along the road to a patch of grass showing Évora's coat of arms: Giraldo on horseback. Turn right at the tower, called the Five Corners (Cinco Esquinas) for its five sides, and walk a block up Rua A. F. Simoes to Évora's sight-packed square. Here, at the town's high point (1,000 feet above sea level), you'll see the Roman temple, fancy Pousada dos Loios, a public garden, and the dressy Jardim do Paço restaurant, known for its beautiful garden setting, pricey food, and summer evening concerts.

The **Pousada dos Loios,** once a 15th-century monastery, is now a luxurious hotel with small rooms (blame the monks). To the left of the *pousada,* stairs lead down to a church—Igreja dos Loios dos Duques de Cadaval—with an impressive gold altarpiece. This is the lavish mausoleum chapel of the noble Cadavals (still a big-time family). You'll walk upon Cadaval tombstones throughout your visit while taped Gregorian chants add to the ambience. Look for the two small trapdoors in the floor that flank the aisle, midway up the church. One opens up to a well (imagine the thoughts going through a bad boy's mind while sitting on this pew during a long service); the other reveals an ossuary stacked with bones.

The tile-work around the altar is 17th-century—mere decoration with traditional yellow patterns. Along the nave the tiles are 18th-century, with scenes to tell Bible stories. This coincided with the popularity of tapestries in France and Belgium that had the same teaching purpose. The grilled windows allowed cloistered monks to attend the Mass. The room to the right of the altar contains rare Muslim tile work, ancient weaponry, and religious art, including a cleverly painted Crucifixion (Cadaval church—€3, no need to purchase €5 combo-ticket for palace, no photos—strictly enforced—Tue–Sun 10:00–12:30 & 14:00–18:00, closed Mon).

The **Roman temple,** with its 14 Corinthian columns, was once part of the Roman forum and the main square in the first century A.D. Today the town's open-air concerts and events are staged here, against an evocative temple backdrop. It's beautifully floodlit at night. While known as the Temple of Diana, it was more likely dedicated to the emperor.

The Roman forum sprawled where the **Museum of Évora** stands today (closed indefinitely for restoration; part of the collection may be on display at Santa Clara Church, near recommended Hotel Santa Clara). In fact, an excavated section of the forum is in the courtyard of the museum, surrounded by a delightful mix of Roman finds, medieval statuary, and 16th-century Portuguese and Flemish paintings.

Across the square from the museum is a white building, now used by the university, but notorious as being the **tribunal of the Inquisition** (no need to enter). Here thousands of innocent people, many of them Moors and Jews, were tried and found guilty. After being condemned, the prisoners were taken in procession through the streets to be burned on the main square. In front of this building is a granite sculpture of a coffin with a body inside—a memorial to those who were killed.

The little street to the left of the Inquisition headquarters is **Rua de Vasco da Gama.** Globetrotting da Gama lived on this street after he discovered the water route to India in 1498. (His house, not open to the public, is 30 yards down the street at the smudged number #15 on your right.) Backtrack and turn right for the cathedral.

The **cathedral,** behind the museum, was built after Giraldo's conquest—on the site of the mosque. (For more on the cathedral, see "Sights," below.) The first cardinal of this church was Dom Henrique, who founded the town's university in 1559. Later

Dom Henrique became King Henrique after his great-nephew, the young King Sebastian, died in North Africa in a disastrous attempt to (get this) chase the Moors out of Africa. Henrique, who ruled only two years before he died, left no direct descendants (he was a cardinal and therefore supposedly chaste). The throne of Portugal passed to his cousin, King Philip II of Spain, starting a bleak 60-year period of Spanish rule (1580–1640) and the beginning of Évora's decline.

From the Cathedral back to the Main Square: Head downhill on the little street opposite the cathedral's entrance. It's the shopping street, Rua 5 de Outubro, which connects Évora's main sights with its main square. The street is lined with products of the Alentejo region: cork (even used as postcards), tile, leather, ironwork, and Arraiolos rugs (made with a distinctive weave in the nearby town of the same name).

On the shopping street, after you pass the intersection with Rua de Burgos, look left to see a blue **shrine** protruding from the wall of a building. The town built it as thanks to God for sparing it from the 1755 earthquake that devastated much of Lisbon. Ahead of you is the main square. The Chapel of Bones and town market are just a few blocks away on your left. But first, stop by Café Arcada, under the arcade next to the church. Considered the best pastry shop in town, it serves good coffee and the local specialty: fresh, sweet cheese tarts (*queijada*, kay-ZHAH-duh).

SIGHTS

Évora

▲▲Cathedral—Portugal has three archbishops, and one resides here in Évora. This important cathedral (of Santa Maria de Évora), built in the late 12th century, is a transitional mix of Romanesque and Gothic. The tower to the right is Romanesque (more stocky and fortress-like), and the tower to the left is Gothic (lighter, more windows). As usual, this was built upon a mosque (after the *Reconquista* succeeded here), and that mosque was built upon a Christian Visigothic chapel (religious and military tit-for-tat is nothing new).

Inside the cathedral, midway down the nave on the left, is a 15th-century painted-marble statue of a pregnant Mary. It's thought that the first priests, hoping to make converts out of Celtic pagans who worshipped mother goddesses, felt they'd have more success if they kept the focus on fertility. Throughout Alentejo, there's a deeply felt affinity for this ready-to-produce-a-savior Mary. Loved ones pray here for blessings during difficult deliveries. Across the aisle, a more realistic Renaissance Gabriel, added a century later, comes to tell Mary her baby won't be just any child. The 16th-century pipe organ still works. The 18th-century high altar is neoclassical. The muscular Jesus—though carved in wood—matches the marble all around.

The church admission alone costs €1, the church and cloister together are €1.50, and the church, cloister, and museum combo is €3, (church open daily July–Aug 9:00–17;00, Sept–June 9:00–12:00 & 14:00–17:00, last entry 30 min before closing, audioguide not very useful, no photos, WC under cloister entry). Each corner of the **cloister** bears a carving of one of the four evangelists. In the corner, a spiral stairway leads to the "roof," providing a close-up view of the cathedral's fine lantern tower and fortress-like crenellations and grand views of the Alentejo plains. This "fortress of God" design was typical of Portuguese Romanesque. Back on ground level, a simple chapel niche (on opposite corner from cloister entry) has a child-sized statue of another pregnant Virgin Mary (midway up wall on right) and the sarcophagi of four recent archbishops.

The **museum** is worth visiting. Center-stage in the first room is an intricate 14th-century, French-made, puzzle-like ivory statue of Mary (Virgem do Paraíso). Her "insides" open up to reveal the major events in her life. A photo below shows Mary folded up and ready to travel. Next, a long room lined with crude 15th-century Alentejo paintings has an extremely dramatic Rococo crucifix and the sacred treasures of this richest church in Alentejo. In the last room, a glass case displays a sparkling reliquary, containing pieces of the supposed True Cross (in a cross-shape), heavily laden with more than a thousand true gems, rotating to show off every facet.

The sunlit **choir** (late 15th to early 16th century) overlooks the cathedral. Its oak stalls are carved with scenes of daily life (hunting boars, harvesting, and rounding up farm animals). The huge contraption in the middle is a music stand. Notice the wide edge on the ends of the seats. Even the older clerics were expected to stand up for much of the service. But when the seat is flipped up, the edge becomes a ledge, making it possible for clerics to sit while they respectfully "stood."

▲▲▲Church of St. Francis and the Chapel of Bones—To get to the church from the main square, take the road to the left of the

imposing Bank of Portugal. At the end of the arcade, turn right on Rua da República. You'll see the church just ahead.

Imagine the church in its original, pure style—simple as St. Francis would want it. It's wide—just a nave lined by chapels. In the 18th century it became popular for wealthy

families to buy fancy chapels, resulting in today's gold-leaf hodge-podge. The huge Baroque chapel to the left of the altar is over the top, with St. Francis and Claire, his partner in Christ-like simplicity, surrounded by anything but poverty. It's slathered in gold leaf from Brazil. The fine 18th-century tiles tell stories of St. Francis' life.

The entrance to the **bone chapel** (Capela dos Ossos) is outside, to the right of the church entrance. The intentionally thought-provoking message above the chapel reads: "We bones in here wait for yours to join us" (€1, additional €0.25 to take photos, daily 9:00–13:00 & 14:30–18:00, Sept–May until 17:30). Inside the macabre chapel, bones line the walls and 5,000 skulls stare blankly at you from walls and arches. They were unearthed from various Évora churchyards. This was the work of three monks who were concerned about the way society was going and thought this would provide Évora, a town noted for its wealth in the early 1600s, with a helpful place to meditate on the transience of material things in the undeniable presence of death. The bones of the three Franciscan monks who founded the church in the 13th century are in the small white coffin by the altar.

After reflecting on mortality, pop into the **market** (immediately in front of the church entrance), busiest in the morning and on Saturday (closed Mon). Wander around. It's a great slice-of-life look at this community. People are proud of their produce. *"Posso provar?"* (POH-soo proo-VAHR) means "Can I try a little?" *Provar* some cheese and stock up for a picnic.

Now take a refreshing break in the **public gardens** (Jardim Publico, to the left as you exit church, at the bottom of Praça 1 de Maio). Just inside the gate, Vasco da Gama looks with excitement as he discovers a little kiosk café nearby selling sandwiches, freshly-baked goodies, and drinks. For a fine little lunch, try an *empada de galinha* (tiny chicken pastry) and a local specialty, *queijada* (sweet cheese tart). The gardens, bigger than they look, contain an overly restored hunk of the 16th-century Royal Palace (right of entry gate). Behind the palace, look over the stone balustrade to see a kids' playground and playfields. Life goes on—make no bones about it.

▲**University**—Originally known as the College of the Holy Spirit, this was established as a Jesuit university in 1559 by Dom Henrique, the cathedral's first archbishop (1512–1580). He was John III's brother, and later became a cardinal, grand inquisitor, and Portugal's king. Two hundred years later, Marquês de Pombal (see sidebar, page 62), the powerful minister of King José I, decided that the Jesuits had become too rich, too political, and—as the sole teachers of society—too closed to modern thinking. He abolished the Jesuit society in 1759 and confiscated their wealth. The university was closed until 1973 when it reopened as a secular school. Injecting 8,000 students into this town of 50,000 people (with 14,000 inside the walls) brought Évora a new vitality...and discos. Unlike the American-style campus, the colleges are scattered throughout the town.

The main entrance of the university is the old courtyard on the ground level (downhill from the original Jesuit chapel). Enter the inner courtyard (free Mon–Sat mornings, €1.50 on Sat 15:00–18:00 and Sun 10:00–14:00 & 15:00–18:00, tel. 266-740-800). While it's fun to visit when classes are in session, on Sunday all the rooms—while empty—are wide open for visitors. Attractive blue-and-white azulejo tiles (the biggest and best-preserved collection south of Lisbon) ring the walls and the classrooms (which line the courtyard arcades), with the theme of the original class portrayed in the tiles. Poke or peek into a classroom to see the now-ignored pulpit. Originally, Jesuit priests were the teachers and information coming from a pulpit was not to be questioned.

On Sundays you can enter the room directly across the courtyard from the entrance. Here major university events are held under the watchful eyes of Cardinal Henrique (the painting to the left) and young King Sebastian (to the right).

The university shop to the right of this room gives you a great look at the tiles. In the 16th century this was a classroom for students of astronomy—note the spheres and navigational instruments mingled with cupids and pastoral scenes. Imagine the class back then. Having few books, if any, the students (males only) took notes as the professor taught in Latin from the lectern in the back.

The cafeteria (off 2nd smaller courtyard behind the main one) thrives with students and offers super-cheap meals (Mon–Fri 8:30–18:00, closed Sat–Sun, WC).

Near Évora

Megalithic Sights—Near Évora, you'll find stony sights, including menhirs (standing stones, near Guadalupe and elsewhere); dolmens (rock tombs at Anta do Zambujeiro and Anta Capela de São Brissos); cromlechs (rocks in formation à la Stonehenge, at Cromeleque dos Almendres; see below); and a cave with prehistoric paintings (Gruta do Escoural, closed Mon). Depending on how much you want to see, you can do a 15- to 45-mile loop from Évora by **bus** (see below) or by **car** (list of rental-car agencies available at Évora's TI).

Policarpo's City Tour offers bus tours of the megaliths (€25 with live guide—4-person minimum, €20 without guide—2-person minimum, cash only, 3 hrs, offered daily depending on demand, book 2 days in advance in summer, Rua 5 de Outubro 63, tel. 266-746-970, www.incoming-alentejo.com, info@incoming-alentejo.com). Policarpo also offers other tours, including an €18 walking tour of Évora and a pricier Alentejo wine-tasting trip.

Cromeleque dos Almendres—This 4,000-year-old Portuguese Stonehenge stands in the midst of cork trees down a dirt road that's a five-mile (20 min) drive west of Évora (take main highway to Lisbon in the direction of Guadalupe, follow clear signposts to stones). Those in a hurry should skip the first signposted site (a lone 10-foot menhir) and continue to the second—95 rounded granite stones erected in the shape of an oval that likely served as a ritual gathering spot for Stone Age sun-worshippers. A posted description (in English) at the site tells more.

Bullfighting—Bullfights are rare in Évora, but nearby towns advertise fights on Saturday and Sunday through the season (roughly Easter–Sept, details from TI). Notice women are on the program now (perhaps to give a tired sport a little kick).

SLEEPING

$$$ Pousada dos Loios, once a 15th-century monastery, is now a classy, luxury hotel renting 30 well-appointed cells. While the rooms are small, the place sprawls with many fine public spaces, courtyards, and a small swimming pool (Db-€210, less Nov–March, air-con, free parking, Convento dos Loios, across from Roman temple, reserve with Central Booking Office at tel. 218-442-001,

Sleep Code

(€1 = about $1.20, country code: 351)
S = Single, **D** = Double/Twin, **T** = Triple, **Q** = Quad, **b** = bathroom, **s** = shower only. Unless otherwise noted, credit cards are accepted, English is spoken, and breakfast is included.

To help you easily sort through these listings, I've divided the rooms into three categories, based on the price for a standard double room with bath:

$$$ **Higher Priced**—Most rooms €100 or more.
$$ **Moderately Priced**—Most rooms between €50–100.
$ **Lower Priced**—Most rooms €50 or less.

fax 218-442-085, www.pousadas.pt, info@pousadas.pt).

$$ Solar Monfalim, a 16th-century noble house, seems unchanged from when it received its first hotel guests in 1892. This elegant hacienda-type place, with homey lounges and a Valium ambience, rents 26 rooms in a central and quiet location (Sb-€70, Db-€85, Tb-€112, air-con, pleasant breakfast room with balcony, parking-€3, Largo da Misericordia 1, tel. 266-750-000, fax 266-742-367, www.monfalimtur.pt, reservas@monfalimtur.pt).

$$ Residencial Policarpo, filling another 16th-century nobleman's mansion, also has a homey feel, with 20 simple rooms tucked around a courtyard. Joaquim, Michele, and David Policarpo carry on the family tradition of good hospitality (S-€30, Sb-€50, D-€35, Db-€55, Tb-€70, €5 less March–May and Oct, €10 less Nov–Feb, cash only, double-paned windows, air-con in rooms with bathroom, terrace, fireplace, easy parking, 2 entrances: Rua da Freiria de Baixo 16 and Rua Conde da Serra, near university, tel. & fax 266-702-424, www.pensaopolicarpo.com).

$$ Hotel Santa Clara, renting 41 comfortable rooms on a quiet side street, is a solid, professional, tour-friendly place with no character but a good location and price (Sb-€63, Db-€75, air-con, Travessa do Milheira 19; from Praça do Giraldo, take Rua Pinta Serpa downhill, then right on Milheira; coming from the bus station, turn left on Milheira after you enter city wall, tel. 266-704-141, fax 266-706-544, www.hotelsantaclara.pt, hotelsantaclara@mail.telepac.pt).

$$ Hotel Ibis, a cheap chain hotel, has 87 identical, Motel 6–type rooms a 15-minute walk from the center, just outside the city walls. Simple to find and offering easy parking, it's a cinch for drivers—but staying here is like eating at McDonald's in Paris (Sb/Db-€59, €47 in Oct–July, breakfast-€5, one child under 12 sleeps free, air-con, elevator, parking, Quinta da Tapada, tel. 266-760-700, fax 266-760-799, www.ibishotel.com).

$ Casa Palma Quartos is a charming and homey little place where Senhora Palma, who doesn't speak English, rents eight squeaky-clean rooms on a quiet street three blocks below the main square (Ss-€20, Ds-€25, Db-€30, cash only, Rua Bernardo Matos 29-A, tel. 266-703-560).

EATING

Restaurante Cervejaria 1/4 Para As 9 ("quarter to nine") is steamy with local families chowing down on favorites such as *arroz de tamboril* (a rice and seafood stew) and *açorda de marisco* (a spicy soup with clams, mixed seafood, and bread spiced with Alentejano herbs). They have an excellent wine list but I like to let the waiter recommend something good (€15 meals, daily 12:00–16:00 &

Versatile Cork

The cork extracted from the bottle of wine you're having with dinner is probably more local than the wine. The Alentejo region is known for producing cork. From the center of a baseball to a gasket on the space shuttle, from bulletin boards to coasters, cork is a remarkable substance, spongy and pliable but resistant to water.

Cork—used mainly for bottle stoppers—comes from the bark of the cork oak *(Quercus suber)*, a 30-foot tree with a sprawling canopy and knotty trunk that grows well in dry heat and sandy soil. After 25 years, a tree is mature enough for harvest. The outer bark is stripped from the trunk, leaving a "wound" of red-colored "blushing" inner bark. It takes nine years for the bark to grow back, then it can be harvested again—a cork tree keeps producing for more than 100 years. After harvesting, the bark is boiled to soften it up, then flattened. Machines cut the cork into the desired shape, or punch out bottle stoppers. These are then polished, producing wonderful, tasteless, odorless seals for wine bottles.

Portugal produces more than half the world's supply of cork (with Spain making much of the rest). These days, many wine stoppers are made from composite or artificial sources, which raises a debate among connoisseurs and perhaps threatens Portugal's cork industry. But even with the rise of plastic "corks," the cork business remains strong thanks to its insulation and acoustic uses.

19:00–23:00, some outdoor seating, Rua Pedro Simões 9, tel. 266-706-774).

Adega do Alentejano is like an above-ground wine cellar. Locals choose from cheap (€8/plate) traditional dishes, including tasty pork options. The menu is scrawled on chalkboards at the entrance and throughout the restaurant. Go early, as the place can fill up. If you didn't try *ginjinha* in Lisbon or Óbidos, finish your meal with a glass of the house-made cherry liqueur (Mon–Sat 12:00–15:00 & 19:00–22:00, closed Sun, cash only, Rua Gabriel Victor do Monte Pereira 21-A, from main square go alongside church on Rua João de Deus, then take 3rd left and keep walking, tel. 266-744-447, Nuno).

Taberna Tipica Quarta-Feira is a rustic eight-table tavern, festooned with patriotic Portuguese decor, where Ze Dias and his family proudly and expertly serve country cooking, including rabbit and partridge in season (€20 menu comes with a fine wine, Mon–Sat 12:00–15:00 & 19:30–22:00, closed Sun, hidden on a narrow street just north off Rua da Mouraria at Rua do Inverno 16, tel. 266-707-530).

Batata Quente Restaurante ("hot potato") has a more flamboyant menu than most, with traditional and creative dishes and lots of vegetables (€12 meals, Tue–Sun 12:00–16:00 & 19:00–22:30, closed Mon, air-con, near the center at Largo Santa Catarina 25, tel. 266-741-161).

Restaurante Cervejaria Fialho is a famous place where white-coated waiters feed Alentejo cuisine to Bogart-like locals. With €25 meals, it's expensive, but this is arguably the best food in town (Tue–Sun 12:00–24:00, closed Mon, arrive before 20:00 or make a reservation, air-con, Travessa das Mascarenhas 14, from main square go right alongside church—Rua João de Deus—for a 5-min walk, take 1st left after public square with theater, tel. 266-703-079).

Mr. Pickwick's Restaurante, with a few fun outdoor tables and a sedate interior, is just a block up Rua 5 de Outubro from the main square (serving traditional—in spite of the name—€8 plates with veggies and salad, lunch from noon, dinner from 19:00, closed Sun, Alcárcova de Cima 3, tel. 266-706-999).

TRANSPORTATION CONNECTIONS

From Évora to: Lisbon (by bus: 20/day, 2 hrs; by train: 2/day, 2.5–3.5 hrs, stops at Lisbon's Oriente Station), **Lagos** (by bus: 1/day, 5 hrs, transfer in Albufeira; by train: 2/day, 5.5 hrs with transfers at Funcheira and Tunes), **Coimbra** (6 buses/day, only 1 direct, 4.5 hrs), **Madrid** (4 buses/day, 7.5–10 hrs, book Spain tickets at Anibal Tours in Hotel da Cartuxa or at Eurolines office on 2nd floor of bus station; the 7.5-hr bus is overnight), **Sevilla** (2 buses/day on Sat, 1/day on Mon, Fri, and Sun only, 7.5 hrs). Bus info (no English spoken): tel. 266-769-410.

NAZARÉ
and NEARBY

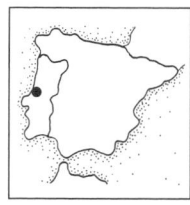

Nazaré, an Atlantic-coast fishing-town-turned-resort, is black-shawl traditional and beach-friendly. Several other worthy sights are within easy day-trip distance of Nazaré. You can drop by the Batalha Monastery, the patriotic pride and architectural joy of Portugal. If the spirit moves you, the pilgrimage site at Fátima is nearby. Alcobaça has Portugal's largest church (and saddest romance). And Portugal's incredibly cute walled town of Óbidos is just down the road.

Planning Your Time

While the far north of Portugal has considerable charm, those with limited time can enjoy maximum travel thrills here. This is an ideal stop if you're interested in a small-town side trip north from Lisbon or coming in from Salamanca or Madrid, Spain.

On a two-week trip through Portugal, Nazaré merits a day. There's another day's worth of sightseeing in Batalha, Alcobaça, and Fátima. See Óbidos on the way to or from Nazaré.

Nazaré

I got hooked on Nazaré back when colorful fishing boats littered its long, sandy beach. Now the boats motor comfortably into a new harbor a 30-minute walk south of town, the beach is littered with frolicking families, and it seems most of Nazaré's 10,000 inhabitants are in the tourist trade. But I still like the place.

You'll be greeted by the energetic applause of the surf, widows with rooms to rent, and big plates of steamed shrimp. Relax in the

Nazaré Fashions:
Seven Petticoats and Black Widows

Nazaré is famous for its women who wear skirts with seven petticoats. While this is mostly just a creation for the tourists, there is some basis of truth to the tradition. In the old days, women would sit on the beach waiting for their fishermen to sail home. To keep warm during a cold sea wind and stay modestly covered, they'd wear several petticoats in order to fold layers over their heads, backs, and legs. Even today, older and more traditional women wear short skirts made bulky by several—but not seven—petticoats. The ensemble is completed with a head scarf, chunky gold earrings, and house slippers.

You'll see some women wearing black, a sign of mourning. Traditionally, if your spouse died you wore black for the rest of your life. This tradition is still observed, although in the last generation, widows began remarrying.

Portuguese sun in a land of cork groves, eucalyptus trees, ladies in seven petticoats, and men who stow cigarettes and fishhooks in their stocking caps.

Even with its summer crowds, Nazaré is a fun stop that offers a surprisingly good look at old Portugal. Somehow the traditions

survive, and the locals are able to go about their black-shawl ways. Wander the back streets for a fine look at Portuguese family-in-the-street life. Laundry flaps in the wind, kids play soccer, and fish sizzle over tiny curbside hibachis. Squadrons of sun-dried and salted fish are crucified on nets pulled tightly around wooden frames and left under the midday sun. Locals claim they are delightful—but I don't know. Off-season Nazaré is almost empty of tourists—inexpensive, colorful, and relaxed, with enough salty fishing-village atmosphere to make you pucker.

Nazaré doesn't have any blockbuster sights. The beach, tasty seafood, and the funicular ride up to Sítio for a great coastal view are the bright lights of my lazy Nazaré memories.

Plan some beach time here. Sharing a bottle of chilled *vinho verde* (young white wine, a specialty of Portugal) on the beach at sundown is a good way to wrap up the day.

Nazaré

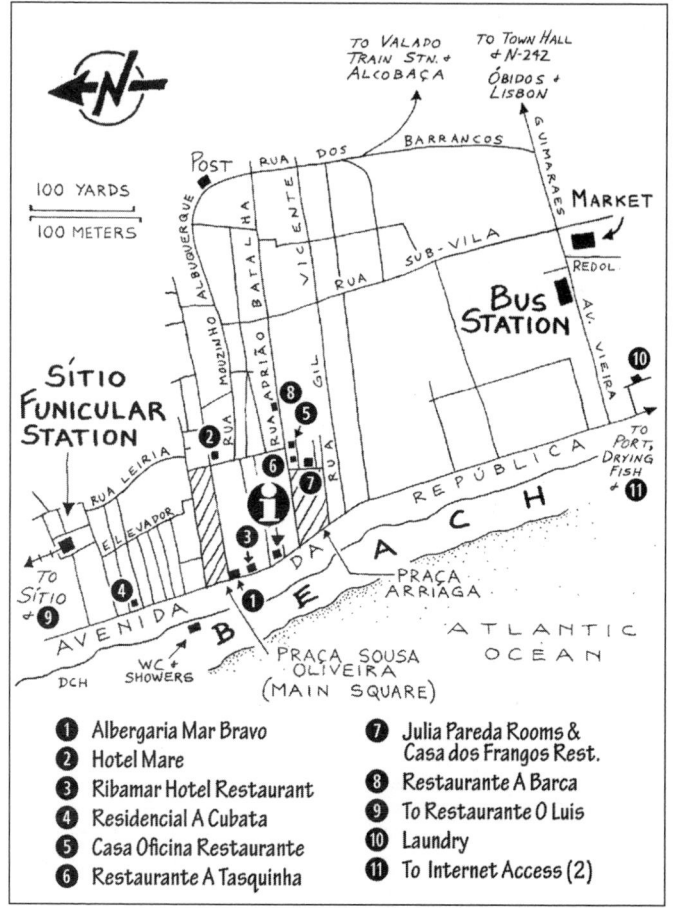

① Albergaria Mar Bravo
② Hotel Mare
③ Ribamar Hotel Restaurant
④ Residencial A Cubata
⑤ Casa Oficina Restaurante
⑥ Restaurante A Tasquinha
⑦ Julia Pareda Rooms & Casa dos Frangos Rest.
⑧ Restaurante A Barca
⑨ To Restaurante O Luis
⑩ Laundry
⑪ To Internet Access (2)

ORIENTATION

Nazaré faces its long beach, stretching north from the new harbor to the hill-capping old town of Sítio. Survey the town from Avenida da República, which lines the waterfront (leaving the bus station, turn right and walk a block to the waterfront). Scan the cliffs. The funicular climbs to Sítio (the hilltop part of town, €0.75). Also to your right, look at the road kinking toward the sea. The building (on the kink) with the yellow balconies is the Ribamar Hotel, next to the TI. Just beyond the Ribamar you'll find the main square (Praça Sousa Oliveira, with banks and ATMs) and most of my hotel listings.

Sítio feels like a totally separate village sitting quietly atop its cliff. Its people don't fish; they farm. Take the frequent funicular up for the spectacular view.

Tourist Information: The TI faces the beach south of the main square (daily July–Aug 9:00–21:00, Sept–June 9:00–13:00 & 14:30–19:00, tel. 262-561-194). Ask about summer activities and bullfights in Sítio.

Helpful Hints

Markets: A **flea market** pops up near Nazaré's town hall every Friday (9:00–13:00, at the inland end of the street the bus station is on) and the colorful **town market** bustles with fresh fish, produce, and caged rabbits in the morning (daily 8:00–13:00, Oct–May closed Mon, green building kitty-corner from bus station just behind taxi stand).

Internet Access: Café.com offers the fastest connection in town (daily 9:30–24:00, 6 computers, in Edificio Atlântico on Avenida da República), but the Cultural Center Library offers 30 minutes free (Mon–Fri 9:30–13:00 & 14:00–19:00, Sat 15:00–19:00, closed Sun, on main road along beach to harbor).

Laundry: At Lavanderia Nazaré, close to the bus station, Lucia will wash, dry, and fold your laundry for pick up the next day (€4/kg—about 2 lbs, Mon–Sat 9:00–13:00 & 15:00–19:00, closed Sun, Rua Branco Martins 17, tel. 262-552-761).

SIGHTS AND ACTIVITIES

The Beach—It's the domain of the beach tents—a tradition in Portugal. In Nazaré, the tents are run as a cooperative by the old women you'll see sitting in the shade ready to collect €6 or more a day. In the evening, piped music is played on the beach. The beach is groomed and guarded. Flags indicate danger level: red (no one in the water), yellow (wading is safe), green (no problem).

If you see a mass of children parading through town down to the beach, they're likely from a huge dorm in town that provides poorer kids from this part of the country with a summer break.

Boats used to line the beach in summer and fill the squares in winter, but when the harbor was built in 1986, that's where the boats ended up.

Funicular to Sítio—Nazaré's funicular was built in 1889—the same year as the Eiffel Tower—by the same disciple of Eiffel who built the much-loved elevator in Lisbon. The equipment and stations, however, have been modernized. Ride up the lift (follow signs to *ascensor*); it goes every 15 minutes (€0.75 each way, first run at 7:00, July–Aug every 5 min until 22:30 then every half-hour until 2:00 in the morning, Sept–June on the quarter-hour until

21:30 then every half-hour until 24:00, WCs at each station). Walk to the staggering Nazaré viewpoint behind the station at the top, then the main viewpoint past the many vendors at the promontory (wave to America).

Visit the small chapel dedicated to Our Lady of Nazaré. The story is depicted on tiles throughout the town. Dom Fuas, a local noble, was hunting deer and became so absorbed in the chase that he didn't realize he was about to go over the cliff. The Virgin Mary appeared suddenly and stopped him, saving his life. The unfortunate deer didn't see Mary in time.

Activities at Sítio—Sítio stages Portuguese-style **bullfights** on Saturday nights in summer (July–mid-Aug, tickets from €10 at kiosk in Praça Sousa Oliveira). Sítio's **NorParque** is a family-friendly **water park** with a pool, slides, and Jacuzzi (€10 for adults, €8 for kids ages 6–11, less after 14:00, June–mid-Sept 10:30–19:00, closed mid-Sept–May, opening may be delayed until July depending on weather, confirm hours at TI, watch for free shuttle bus parked on the main drag).

For **panoramic views** over the north beach *(praia norte)*, stroll toward the Farol lighthouse (10-min walk from Sítio's main square); **Restaurante Arimar,** on the left along the way, is a good place to take in the sunset with drinks or dinner (avoid windy days).

SLEEPING

You should have no problem finding a room, except in August, when the crowds, temperatures, and prices are all at their highest. You'll find plenty of hustlers meeting each bus and Valado train and waiting along the promenade. Even the normal hotels get into the act during the off-season. I've never arrived in town without a welcoming committee inviting me to sleep in their *quartos* (rooms in private homes).

I list a price range for each hotel: The lowest is for winter (roughly Jan–March), the sky-highest for mid-July through August. The rest of the year (approximately April–mid-July and Sept–Dec) expect to pay about midrange. You will save serious money if you arrive with no reservations and bargain, even at hotels.

Sleep Code

(€1 = about $1.20, country code: 351)
S = Single, **D** = Double/Twin, **T** = Triple, **Q** = Quad, **b** = bathroom, **s** = shower only. Unless otherwise noted, you can assume credit cards are accepted; breakfast is included at hotels but not *quartos;* and English is spoken.

To help you easily sort through these listings, I've divided the rooms into three categories, based on the price for a standard double room with bath during high season (April–Sept). The rest of the year it's 10–20 percent less:

$$$ **Higher Priced**—Most rooms €80 or more.
$$ **Moderately Priced**—Most rooms between €50–80.
$ **Lower Priced**—Most rooms €50 or less.

Hotels

$$$ Albergaria Mar Bravo is on the main square and the waterfront. Its 16 comfy rooms are great—modern, bright, fresh, and with balconies, eight of them with views (Sb-€50–90, Db-€50–120, prices vary depending on view and month, view breakfast room, free valet parking, air-con, elevator, attached restaurant serves seafood, Praça Sousa Oliveira 71-A, tel. 262-569-160, fax 262-569-169, www.marbravo.com, mar_bravo@clix.pt).

$$$ Hotel Mare, just off the Praça Sousa Oliveira, is a big, modern, American-style hotel with 36 rooms, some tour groups, and a rooftop terrace (Sb-€47–85, Db-€53–105, Tb-€57–118, all with air-con and balconies, double-paned windows, elevator, free parking lot, Rua Mouzinho de Albuquerque 8, tel. 262-561-122, fax 262-561-750, hotel.mare@mail.telepac.pt).

$$$ Residencial A Cubata, a friendly place on the waterfront on the north end, has 22 small, comfortable rooms and older bathrooms (Sb-€50–90, Db-€60–130, depends on view and season, noisy bar below though they've added soundproofing, Avenida da República 6, tel. 262-561-700, fax 262-561-706). For a peaceful night, forgo the private balcony, take a back room (saving some money), and enjoy the communal beachfront balcony.

$$ Ribamar Hotel Restaurant has a prime location on the waterfront, with an Old World, hotelesque atmosphere, including 25 rooms with dark wood and four-poster beds (Sb-€25–55, Db-€30–89, prices flexible, 4 rooms with balconies, good attached restaurant downstairs; parking-€5/day, €10 in Aug; Rua Gomes Freire 9, tel. 262-551-158, fax 262-562-224, ribamarnazare@mail.telepac.pt). Look for the yellow awnings and balconies.

Quartos

I list no dumpy hotels or cheap pensions because the best budget option is *quartos*. Like nowhere else in Iberia, locals renting spare rooms clamor for your business in Nazaré. Except perhaps for weekends in August, you can stumble into town any day and find countless women hanging out on the street (especially around the bus station) with fine modern rooms to rent. I promise. The TI's partial list of *quartos* totals 200. If you need a cheap room, they've got it. Their rooms are generally better than hotel rooms—for half the cost. Your room is likely to be large and homey, with old-time-elegant furnishings (with no plumbing but plenty of facilities down the hall) and in a quiet neighborhood, six short blocks off the beachfront action. I'd come into town and have fun looking at several places. Hem and haw and the price goes down.

$ Nazaré Amada rents seven fine rooms (average price for Db-€40, €30 Oct–June, Rua Adrião Batalha, garage, tel. 262-552-206, mobile 962-579-371).

$ Julia Pareda, who used to live in Canada, rents five nice rooms with private baths in a central location. Ask for an ocean view (average price for Db-€30-50, slightly more in Aug, on Praça Dr. Manuel Arriaga next to Casa dos Frangos and above café, tel. 262-553-516, mobile 967-468-011).

EATING

Nazaré is a fishing town, so don't order *hamburguesas*. Fresh seafood is tasty all over town, more expensive (but affordable) along the waterfront, and cheaper further inland. Waiters will sometimes bring you food (such as olives or bread) that you didn't order. Just push it away or you'll pay for it. Double-check your bill to make sure you're not being charged for something you didn't eat.

In this fishing village even the snacks come from the sea. *Percebes* are local boiled barnacles, sold as munchies in bars and on the street. Merchants are happy to demonstrate how to eat them and let you sample one for free (say *"Posso provar?"*). They're great with beer in the bars.

Try Portugal's light, young wine, *vinho verde;* with its champagne-like taste, it's perfect with shellfish. *Amêndoa amarga* is the local amaretto. For a tasty pastry, try a *pastel de feijão* (fay-ZHOW) from any café. This small tart with a puff-pastry shell has a filling similar to pecan pie, but it's actually made of white beans.

Popular **Restaurante A Tasquinha** dishes up authentic Portuguese cuisine with a cozy, picnic-bench ambience. Friendly, hardworking Carlos and his family serve their fish with a special sauce. He'll come to your table to personally check on your meal (Tue–Sun 12:00–15:00 & 19:00–22:30, closed Mon, Rua Adrião Batalha 54, tel. 262-551-945).

The family-run **Casa Oficina** serves home-style seafood dishes, not fancy but hearty, in a friendly setting that makes you feel like you're eating at someone's kitchen table. Sit with the locals, talk about what's on TV, and draw your home state on the paper tablecloth (daily 12:00–15:00 & 19:00–22:00, if it's quiet at night it may be closed, Rua das Flores 33, off Praça Dr. Manuel Arriaga; facing the restaurant Casa dos Frangos, take street immediately left, tel. 262-083-703).

Mom-and-pop **A Barca** bursts with yellow decor and tasty *sardinhas grelhadas* (grilled sardines). It's these kind of cozy, local spots that take the touristy edge off Nazaré (daily 12:00–15:00 & 19:00–22:00, Rua Adrião Batalha 75).

Chicken addicts can get roasted chickens to go at **Casa dos Frangos** (€6 chickens, daily 9:30–13:00 & 15:30–20:30, Praça Dr. Manuel Arriaga 20), while picnic gatherers can head for the covered *mercado* across from the bus station (daily 8:00–12:00, closed Mon Oct–May).

Restaurante O Luis in Sítio serves excellent seafood and local cuisine to an enthusiastic crowd in a cheery atmosphere. While few tourists go here, friendly waiters make you feel welcome (€10 dinners, Fri–Wed 12:00–24:00, closed Thu, air-con, Rua Dos Tanques 7, tel. 262-551-826). This place is worth the trouble if you want to eat well: Ride the funicular up to Sítio and exit right; take the steps down to the main drag; turn right on the main drag and walk to the bullring; take the street downhill left of the bullring; and then walk five minutes to Praça de Touros.

TRANSPORTATION CONNECTIONS

Nazaré's bus station is in the center, on Avenida Vieira Guimarães, a block inland from the waterfront. The nearest train station is at Valado (3 miles toward Alcobaça, connected by semi-regular €1.25 buses and reasonable, easy-to-share €8 taxis). To avoid this train-station headache, consider using buses instead of trains. For example, if you're heading to Lisbon, the direct bus is better, because taking the train requires getting from Nazaré to Valado's station to catch the train, then transferring in Cacém. Both the train and the bus end up at Lisbon's Sete Rios Station on the outskirts of the city, a Metro or taxi ride away from your hotel. (Note, however, when Lisbon's very central Rossio Station reopens, the train from Nazaré will stop there, equalizing the hassle factor between train and bus).

From Nazaré/Valado by Train to: Coimbra (6/day, 3.5 hrs, change at Bifurcação de Lares; see bus info below), **Lisbon** (3/day, change at Cacém, 2–3 hrs). Train info: tel. 808-208-208.

Nazaré and Nearby

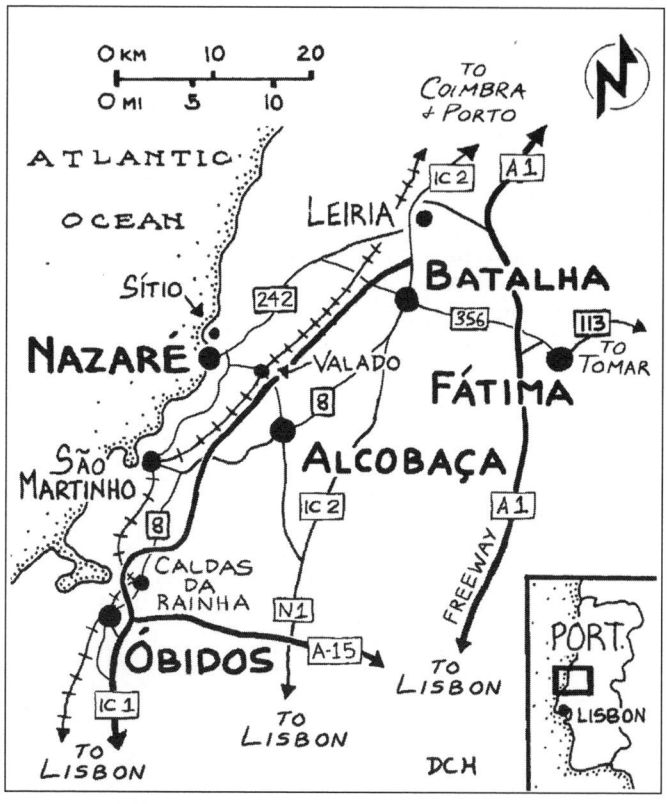

Nazaré by Bus to: Alcobaça (stopping at Valado, 12/day, 20 min), **Batalha** (6/day, 1 hr, some change at São Jorge), **Óbidos** (5/day, 1 hr; bus is better than train, most transfer in Caldas da Rainha), **Fátima** (3/day, 90 min), **Coimbra** (5/day, 2 hrs; bus is better than train, transfer in Leiria), **Lisbon** (10/day, 2hrs). Buses are scarce on Sunday. Bus info: tel. 707-223-344.

Day-Tripping from Nazaré to Alcobaça, Batalha, Fátima, or Óbidos: Traveling by bus you can see both Alcobaça and Batalha in one day (but not on Sun, when bus service is sparse). Alcobaça is easy to visit on the way to or from Batalha (and both are connected by bus with Óbidos). Ask at the bus station or TI for schedule information and be flexible. Fátima has the fewest connections and is farthest away. Without a car, for most, Fátima is not worth the trouble, but if you're heading by bus to Coimbra, you can go via Fátima. A taxi from Nazaré to Alcobaça costs about €10; agree on the price before leaving town.

Batalha

On August 14, 1385, two armies faced off on the rolling plains of Batalha to decide Portugal's future—independence or rule by Spanish kings? King John I of Portugal ordered his 7,000 men to block the road to Lisbon. The Spanish Castilian king, with 32,000 soldiers and 16 modern cannons, ordered his men to hold their fire. But when the Portuguese knights dismounted from their horses to form a defensive line, some hotheaded Spaniards—enraged by such a display of unsportsmanlike conduct by supposedly chivalrous knights—attacked.

Shoop! From the side came 400 arrows from English archers fighting for Portugal. The confused Castilians sounded the retreat, and the Portuguese chased them, literally, all the way back to Castile. A mere half hour (and several hundred deaths) after it began, the Battle ("Batalha") of Aljubarrota was won. (Spaniards say they were defeated by the plague.) King John I claimed the Portuguese crown and thanked the Virgin Mary with a new church and monastery.

The only reason to stop in the town of Batalha is to see its great monastery, considered Portugal's finest architectural achievement and a symbol of its national pride. Unfortunately, the highway runs directly in front of the monastery, but at least there's no missing it from the road.

Tourist Information: The TI, behind the monastery, has free maps and information on buses (daily May–Sept 10:00–13:00 & 15:00–19:00, Oct–April 10:00–13:00 & 14:00–18:00, Praça Mouzinho de Albuquerque, tel. 244-765-180). Batalha's market day is Monday morning (market is 200 yards behind monastery).

Arrival in Batalha: If you take the bus to Batalha, you'll be dropped off within a block of the monastery and TI. There's no official luggage storage, but you can leave luggage at the TI or monastery's ticket desk while you tour the cloisters. If you're driving, follow the signs to Batalha and park free opposite the church.

SIGHTS

Monastery of Santa María
Here's a self-guided tour of the town's most important sight (€4.50, daily April–Sept 9:00–18:00, Oct–March 9:00–17:00, free on Sun until 14:00, tel. 244-765-497).

Exterior (1388–1533): The Church of Our Lady of Victory (c.1388–1550) is a lacy, late-Gothic (pointed-arch) structure decorated with lacy Gothic tracery—stained-glass windows, gargoyles, railings, and Flamboyant pinnacles representing the

flickering flames of the
Holy Spirit. (Inside, we'll
see even more elaborate
Manueline-style orna-
mentation added a century
later.) The church's limestone has mellowed over
time into a warm, rosy,
golden color.

The equestrian statue outside the church is of Nuno Alvares
Pereira, who commanded the Portuguese in the battle and mas-
terminded the victory over Spain. Before entering the church,
study the carving on the west portal. Notice the two ranks of figures in the main arch over the entrance: first rank—angels with
their modesty wings; second rank—the angel band with different
instruments including a hillbilly washboard. Flanking the door are
two small coats of arms: Portugal's on the right and the House of
Lancaster's on the left (a reminder of Portugal's indebtedness to
England for its victory). On your way in, buy your €3 ticket for the
Royal Cloisters so you won't have to backtrack later.

Church Interior: The tall pillars leading your eye up to the
"praying hands" of pointed arches, the warm light from stained-
glass windows, the air of sober simplicity—this is classic Gothic,
from Europe's Age of Faith. The church's lack of ornamentation
reflects the vision of the project's first architect, Afonso Domingues
(worked 1388–1402). The first chapel on the right is the...

Founders' Chapel (Capela do Fundador): Center-stage is
the double sarcophagus (that's English style) of King John I and
his English Queen Philippa. The tomb statues lie together on their
backs, holding hands for eternity. This husband-and-wife team
ushered in Portugal's two centuries of greatness.

John I (born 1357, ruled 1385–1433), the bastard son of King
Pedro I (see "Alcobaça," page 174), repelled the Spanish invaders,
claimed the throne, consolidated his power by confiscating enemies' land to reward his friends, gave Lisbon's craftsmen a voice
in government, and launched Portugal's expansion overseas. His
five-decade reign benefited Portugal greatly. John's motto, "*Por
bem*" ("For good") is carved on his tomb. He established the House
of Avis (see the coat of arms carved in the tomb) that would rule
Portugal through the Golden Age. John's descendants (through
both the Avis and Bragança lines) would rule Portugal until the
last king in 1910.

John, indebted to English soldiers for their help in the
battle, signed the friendship Treaty of Windsor with England
(1386). To seal the deal, he was requested to marry Philippa of
Lancaster, the granddaughter of England's king. You can see

Batalha's Monastery of Santa Maria

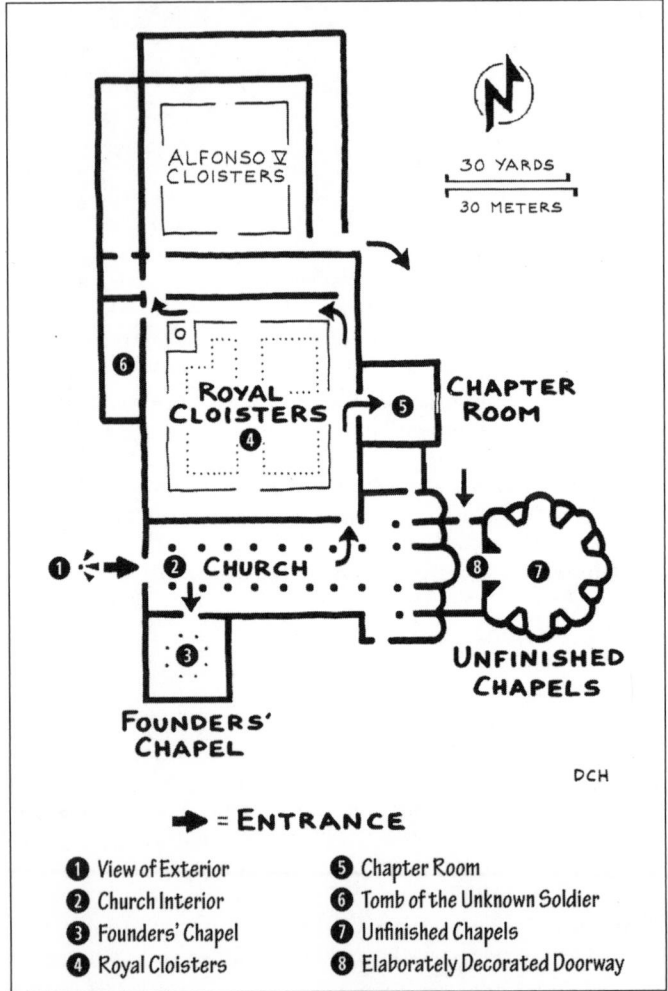

ALFONSO V CLOISTERS

30 YARDS
30 METERS

6 ROYAL CLOISTERS **4**

CHAPTER ROOM **5**

1 → **2** CHURCH **8** **7**

3

UNFINISHED CHAPELS

FOUNDERS' CHAPEL

DCH

➡️ = ENTRANCE

1 View of Exterior
2 Church Interior
3 Founders' Chapel
4 Royal Cloisters
5 Chapter Room
6 Tomb of the Unknown Soldier
7 Unfinished Chapels
8 Elaborately Decorated Doorway

their respective coats of arms carved at the head of the tomb.

Philippa (c. 1360–1415)—intelligent, educated, and moral—had already been rejected in marriage by two kings. John also was reluctant, reminding the English of his vow of celibacy as Grand Master of the Order of the Cross. He retreated to a monastery (with his mistress) before finally agreeing to marry Philippa (1387).

Philippa won John's admiration by overseeing domestic policy, boosting trade with England, reconciling Christians and Jews, and spearheading the invasion of Ceuta (1415) that launched the Age of Discovery.

At home she used her wide knowledge (trained personally by Geoffrey Chaucer and John Wycliffe) to inspire her children to greatness. She banished John's mistress to a distant convent but raised their children almost as her own, thus sparking the rise of the Bragança line that would compete for the throne.

John and Philippa produced a slew of talented sons, some of whom rest in **tombs** nearby. These are the golden youth of the Age of Discovery that the Portuguese poet Luis de Camões dubbed the "Marvelous Generation" *(Ínclita Geração).*

Henrique (wearing a church for a hat and a metal wreath in front) is Prince Henry the Navigator (1394–1460). When Philippa was on her deathbed with the plague, she summoned her son Henry to her side and made him swear he would dedicate his life to finding the legendary kingdom of Prester John—sending Henry on his own journey to explore the unknown. (Read more about Henry on page 128.)

Fernão, Henry's kid brother, attacked the Muslims at Tangier (1437) and was captured. When his family refused to pay the ransom (which would have meant returning the city of Ceuta), he died in captivity. Son Pedro, a voracious traveler and student of history, ruled Portugal as regent while his six-year-old nephew Afonso grew to manhood (heir Afonso's father, Duarte—John and Philippa's eldest—died of the plague after ruling for only 5 years; see "Unfinished Chapels," page 171).

The Founders Chapel is a square room with an octagonal dome. Gaze up (like John and Philippa) at the ceiling, an eight-pointed star of crisscrossing, pointed arches—a masterpiece of the Flamboyant Gothic style—that glow with light from stained glass. The central keystone (with John's coat of arms) holds all the arches-within-arches in place. Remember this finished chapel—a lantern roof atop tombs in an octagonal space—when you visit the Unfinished Chapels later. From the church, you enter the adjoining...

Royal Cloisters (Claustro Real): Architecturally, this open courtyard (show your ticket to enter) exemplifies Batalha's essence: Gothic construction from c. 1400 (the pointed arches surrounding the courtyard) filled in with Manueline decoration from c. 1500

(show your ticket to enter). The tracery in the arch features the cross of the Order of Christ (headed at one time by Prince Henry the Navigator) and armillary spheres—skeletal "globes" that showed what was then considered the center of the universe. The tracery is supported by delicate columns with shells, pearls, and coils of rope, plus artichokes

Portugal's House of Avis and its Coat of Arms

Seen on monuments at Belém, Batalha, Sagres, and even on the modern Portuguese flag, the Avis Coat of Arms is a symbol of the glorious Age of Discovery, when Portugal was ruled by kings of the Avis family.

In the center of the shield are five smaller shields, arranged in the form of a cross. (One theory goes that, after several generations of battle, the family shield—passed down from father to son—got beaten up, and the cross ripped apart into five pieces, held there by nails—the dots on the coat of arms.) Around the border are castles, representing Muslim cities conquered by Portugal's Christian kings. (Some versions have fleur-de-lis and personal emblems of successive kings.)

Some Important House of Avis Kings

Pedro I (ruled 1357–1367)—Buried with his beloved Inês de Castro at Alcobaça.

John I (r. 1385–1433)—Pedro's bastard son, he protected Portugal from a Spanish takeover and launched overseas expansion.

Manuel I (r. 1495–1521)—Ruler when all the overseas expansion began to pay off financially. He built the Monastery of Jerónimos at Belém, decorated in the ornamental style that bears his name.

John III (r. 1521–1557)—Ruler during Portugal's peak of power...and start of decline.

Sebastian (r. 1557–1578)—When Sebastian was lost in battle, the nation lost its way, leading to takeover by Spain.

and lotus flowers from the recently-explored Orient.

Picture Dominican monks in white robes, blue capes, and tonsured haircuts (shaved crown) meditating as they slowly circled this garden courtyard. They'd stop to wash their hands at the washbasin (*lavabo*, in the northwest corner, with a great view back at the church) before stepping into the adjoining refectory (dining hall) for a meal. Continue around to the...

Chapter Room: The self-supporting, star-vaulted ceiling spans 60 feet, an engineering tour-de-force by Master Huguet, a foreigner who became chief architect in 1402. Huguet brought Flamboyant Gothic decoration to the church's sober style. The ceiling was considered so dangerous to build (it collapsed twice) that only prisoners condemned to death were allowed to work on it. Today unknowing tourists are allowed to wander under it. Huguet supposedly silenced skeptics by personally spending the night in this room. (It even survived the 1755 earthquake.) Besides this ceiling, Huguet did the

Founder's Chapel and the Unfinished Chapels.

Portugal's Tomb of the Unknown Soldier sits under a mutilated crucifix called *Christ of the Trenches*—which accompanied Portuguese soldiers into battle on the WWI western front. The three small soldiers under the flame—which burns Portuguese olive oil—are dressed to represent the three most valiant chapters in Portuguese military history: fighting Moors in the 12th century, Spaniards in the 14th century, and Germans in the 20th century.

Follow the signs to the gift shop *(loja)* and walk into the next cloister. It's not nearly as interesting, so follow the signs to a square outside the church (WCs are to the left). Head right, to the...

Unfinished Chapels (Capelas Imperfeitas): The Unfinished Chapels are called by that name because, well, that's not a Gothic sunroof overhead. This chapel behind the main altar was intended as an octagonal room with seven niches for tombs, topped with a rotunda ceiling (similar to the Founders' Chapel). But only the walls, support pillars for the ceiling, and a double tomb were completed.

King Duarte and his wife Leonor lie hand-in-hand on their backs, watching the clouds pass by, blissfully unaware of the work left undone. Duarte (1391–1438), the oldest of John and Philippa's sons, was the golden boy of the charmed family. He wrote a how-to book on courtly manners. When, at age 42, he became king (1433), he called a *cortes* (parliament) to enact much-needed legal reforms. He financed and encouraged his brother Prince Henry's initial overseas explorations. And he began work on these chapels, hoping to make a glorious family burial place. But Duarte died young of the plague, leaving behind an unfinished chapel, a stunned nation, and his six-year-old son, Afonso, as the new king.

Leonor became the regent while Afonso grew up, but she proved unpopular as a ruler, being both Spanish and female. Duarte's brother Pedro then ruled as regent before being banished by rivals.

In 1509, Duarte's grandson, King Manuel I, added the **elaborately decorated doorway** (by Mateus Fernandes), a masterpiece of the Manueline style. The series of ever-larger arches that frame the door are carved in stone so detailed that they look like stucco. See carved coils of rope with knots, some snails along the bottom, artichokes (used to fend off scurvy), corn (from American discoveries), and Indian-inspired motifs (from the land of pepper). Contrast the doorway's Manueline ornamentation with the Renaissance simplicity of the upper-floor balcony, done in 1533.

Manuel abandoned the chapel after Vasco da Gama's triumphant return from India, channeling Portugal's money and energy instead to building a monument to the Age of Discovery launched by the Avis family—the Jerónimos Monastery in Belém (where he's buried).

TRANSPORTATION CONNECTIONS

From Batalha by Bus to: Nazaré (8/day, 1 hr), **Alcobaça** (8/day, 30 min), **Fátima** (4/day, 30 min), and **Lisbon** (5/day, 2 hrs). Expect fewer buses on weekends.

By Car: Batalha is an easy 10-mile drive from Fátima. You'll see signs from each site to the other.

Fátima

On May 13, 1917, three children were tending sheep when the sky lit up and a woman—Mary, the mother of Christ, "a lady brighter than the sun"—appeared standing in an oak tree. (It's the tree to the left of the large basilica.) In the midst of bloody World War I, she brought a message that peace was coming. World War I raged on, so on the 13th day of each of the next five months, Mary dropped in again to call for peace and to repeat three messages. Word spread, bringing many curious pilgrims. The three kids—Lucia, Francisco, and Jacinta—were grilled mercilessly by authorities trying to debunk their preposterous visions, but the children remained convinced of what they'd seen. (In 1930, the Vatican recognized the Virgin of Fátima as legit.)

Finally, on October 13, 70,000 people assembled near the oak tree. They were drenched in a rainstorm when suddenly, the sun came out, grew blindingly bright, danced around the sky (writing "God's fiery signature"), then plunged to the earth. When the crowd came to its senses, the sun was shining and the rain had dried.

Today, tens of thousands of believers come to rejoice in this modern miracle, most of them during the months of May to October. Fátima, Lourdes (in France), and Medjugorje (in Bosnia-Herzegovina) are the three big Mary sights in Europe.

ORIENTATION

Fátima welcomes guests. Surrounding the square are a variety of hotels, restaurants, and tacky souvenir stands. Apart from the 12th and 13th of most months, cheap hotel rooms abound.

Tourist Information: The TI is near the basilica (daily April–Sept 10:00–13:00 & 15:00–19:00, Oct–March 10:00–13:00 & 14:00–18:00, Avenida José Alves Correia da Silva, tel. 249-531-139).

Mary's Three Messages

1. Peace is coming. (World War I is ending. Later, during World War II, Salazar justified keeping Portugal neutral by saying it was in accordance with Mary's wishes for peace.)
2. Russia will reject God and communism will rise, bringing a second great war.
3. Someone will try to kill the pope. (This third secret was kept a secret for decades, supposedly lying in a sealed envelope in the Vatican. In 1981, Pope John Paul II was shot, inspiring him to visit Fátima in 2000, meet the surviving visionary, beatify the two who had died, and publicly reveal this long-hidden third secret.)

SIGHTS

Basilica—The huge neoclassical basilica (1928–1953), with its 200-foot tower and crystal cross-shaped beacon on top, could accommodate nearly half the population of Lisbon (300,000 people). Inside are paintings depicting the vision, and the tombs of two of the children who saw the vision. Both died shortly after the visions in the worldwide flu epidemic. The third, Lucia (the only one with whom Mary actually conversed), is still alive at 97, a Carmelite nun living near Coimbra. (Dress modestly to enter the church.)

Chapel of Apparitions—This marks the spot of the oak tree where Mary appeared to the three kids (located outside the church, beneath a canopy). Services take place daily 7:30–21:30 in a variety of languages; check the posted schedule for English.

Pilgrimage—On the 13th of the month, May to October, and on August 19, up to 100,000 pilgrims—some shuffling on their knees—traverse the mega-huge, park-lined esplanade (more than 160,000 square feet) leading to the church. Evening torchlit processions occur on two nights (usually the 12th and 13th). In 1967, on the 50th anniversary of the Vatican's acknowledging the miracle, 1.5 million pilgrims—including the pope—gathered here.

Museums—Visitors may want to check out two "museums" in town. The **Museo de Cera de Fátima** is a series of rooms telling the story of Fátima's visitation one scene at a time

with wax figures (€4.50, daily April–Oct 9:00–18:30, Nov–March 10:00–17:00, English leaflet describes each vignette). The **Museu-Vivo Aparições,** a low-tech sound and light show, tells the same story (€2.50, daily April–Oct 9:00–19:00, Nov–March 9:00–18:00, worthless without English soundtrack playing—ask). While the wax museum is better, both exhibits are pretty cheesy for those who are not inclined to take Fátima seriously.

TRANSPORTATION CONNECTIONS

From Fátima by Bus to: Batalha (3/day, 30 min), **Coimbra** (8/day, 1 hr), **Nazaré** (4/day, 80 min), and **Lisbon** (15/day, 1.5–2.5 hrs, depending on route); service drops on Sunday. Note that the stop closest to the basilica is listed on bus schedules as Cova de Iria, *not* Fátima.

Alcobaça

This pleasant little town is famous for its church, one of the most interesting in Portugal. I find Alcobaça a better stop than Batalha.

Tourist Information: The English-speaking TI is across the square from the church (daily May–Sept 10:00–13:00 & 15:00–19:00, Oct–April closes at 18:00, Praça 25 de Abril, tel. 262-582-377).

Arrival in Alcobaça: If you arrive by bus, it's a five-minute walk to the town center and monastery. Exit right from the station (on Avenida Manuel da Silva Carolino), walk a half block uphill, take the first right, and continue straight (on Rua Dom Pedro V). Hang a left just after passing a small plaza and you are in the main square.

If arriving by car, follow the *Mosteiro* sign at the roundabout (parking available in front of monastery, €0.10/30 min).

SIGHTS

▲▲Cistercian Monastery of Santa Maria—This abbey church, despite its fully Baroque facade, represents the best Gothic building in Portugal. It's also the country's largest church, and a clean and bright break from the heavier Iberian norm. Afonso Henriques began construction in 1178 after taking the nearby town of Santarém from the Moors. It became one of the most powerful abbeys of the Cistercian Order and a cultural center of 13th-century Portugal. This simple abbey is designed to be filled with hard work, prayer, and total silence. The abbey and cloisters cost €4.50 (daily April–Sept 9:00–19:00, Oct–March 9:00–17:00, tel. 262-505-128).

Nave and Tombs of Dom Pedro and Inês: A long and narrow nave leads to a pair of finely carved Gothic tombs (from 1360). These are of Portugal's most tragic romantic couple, Dom Pedro (King Peter I, 1320–1367, on the right) and Dona Inês de Castro (c. 1323–1355, on the left). They rest feet-to-feet in each transept so that on Judgment Day they'll rise and immediately see each other again. Pedro, heir to the Portuguese throne, was in love with the Spanish aristocrat Inês (see sidebar, page 176).

Notice the carvings on the tomb. Like religious alarm clocks, the attending angels are poised to wake the couple on Judgment Day. Pedro will lie here (as inscribed on the tomb) *"Até ao fim do mundo"*—until the end of the world, when he and Inês are reunited. The "Wheel of Life" below the finely-combed head of Pedro shows scenes from his life with Inês.

Elsewhere on the coffin are scenes from the life of St. Bartholomew—being skinned alive. Pedro's tomb is supported by lions, a symbol of royalty. Inês' tomb is supported by the lowly scum who murdered her...one holding a monkey, a symbol of evil. Study the relief at the feet of Inês: Heaven, the dragon mouth of Hell, and jack-in-the-box coffins on Judgment Day. Although Napoleon's troops vandalized the tombs, the story of Pedro and Inês endures *até ao fim do mundo*.

More Tombs and Relics in the Sacristy: To the right of the king's tomb, step into the neo-Gothic Hall of Tombs for more deceased royalty. Behind the High Altar is the sacristy. The room is indefinitely closed for maintenance, but look at the fine Manueline door. In the rear of the nave (where you entered), find the...

Hall of Kings: This hall—where you pay to enter—features statues of most of Portugal's kings, along with 18th-century tiled walls telling the story of the 12th-century conquest of the Moors and the building of the monastery. The sculpture facing the entrance features Afonso Henriques, first king of Portugal and

Pedro and Inês

Twenty-year-old Prince Pedro met 17-year-old Inês at Pedro's wedding to Inês' cousin Constance. The politically motivated marriage was arranged by Pedro's father, the king. Pedro dutifully fathered his son, the future king Fernando, with Constance in Lisbon, while seeing Inês on the side in Coimbra. When Constance died, Pedro settled in with Inês. Concerned about Spanish influence, Pedro's father, Afonso IV, forbade their marriage. You guessed it—they were married secretly, and the couple had four children. When King Afonso, fearing rivals to his ("legitimate") grandson's kingship, had Inês murdered, Prince Pedro went ballistic. He staged an armed uprising (1355) against his father, only settled after much bloodshed.

Once he was crowned King Pedro I the Just (1357), the much-embellished legend begins. He summoned his enemies, exhumed Inês' body, dressed it in a bridal gown, and put it on the throne, making the murderers kneel and kiss its putrid rotting hand. (The legend continues...) Pedro then executed her two murderers—personally—by ripping out their hearts, eating them, and washing them down, it is said, with a fine *vinho verde*. Now that's *amore*.

founder of this monastery, being crowned by Pope Innocent III and St. Bernard.

Cloisters: Cistercian monks built the abbey in 40 years, starting in 1178. They inhabited it until 1834 (when the Portuguese king disbanded all monasteries). The monks spent most of their lives in silence and were allowed to speak only when given permission by the abbot. To enjoy this cloister like the monks did: Meditate, pray, exercise, and connect with nature. As you multitask, circle counterclockwise until you reach the fountain—where the monks washed up before eating. In the cloisters, the fountain marks the entry to the...

Refectory or Dining Hall: Imagine the hall filled with monks eating in silence as one reads from the Bible atop the "Readers' Pulpit." Food was prepared next door.

Kitchen: The 18th-century kitchen's giant three-part oven could roast seven oxen simultaneously. The industrious monks rerouted part of the River Alcoa to bring in running water. And how about those hard surfaces?

Dormitory: Take the stairs up to the bare dormitory, from which you can see the transept of the church where Inês is buried. Pedro is in the distance, too. On this floor there is also a terrace onto the adjacent cloister and a stairway to the upper cloister with views to the abbey.

▲**Mercado Municipal**—An Old World version of Safeway is housed happily here under huge steel-and-fiberglass arches.

Inside the covered market, black-clad, dried-apple-faced women choose fish, uncaged and feisty chickens, ducks, and rabbits from their respective death rows. Wander among figs, melons, bushels of grain, and nuts (Mon–Sat 9:00–13:00, closed Sun, best on Mon). It's a five-minute walk from the TI or bus station; ask a local, *"Mercado municipal?"* There's also a flea market in town on Mondays by the Alcoa River.

▲▲**National Museum of Wine (Museu Nacional do Vinho)**— This museum, a half-mile outside Alcobaça (on the road to Batalha and Leiria, right-hand side), offers a fascinating look at the wine of Portugal (€1.50, Mon–Fri 9:00–12:30 & 14:00–17:30, closed Sat–Sun, tel. 262-582-222, www.ivv.min-agricultura.pt; your car is safer parked inside the gate). Run by a local cooperative winery, the museum teaches you more than you need to know about Portuguese wine in a series of rooms that used to house fermenting vats. With some luck you can get a tour—much more hands-on than French winery tours—through the actual winery.

TRANSPORTATION CONNECTIONS

From Alcobaça by Bus to: Lisbon (6/day, 2 hrs), **Nazaré** (1/day, 20 min), **Batalha** (9/day, 30 min), **Fátima** (5/day, 60 min, more frequent with transfer in Batalha). Bus frequency drops on Sunday. A taxi to the Nazaré/Valado train station costs about €7; to Nazaré, up to €10. Bus info: tel. 808-200-370.

Óbidos

Postcard perfect, Óbidos (OH-bee-doosh) sits atop a hill, its 14th-century wall (45 feet tall) corralling a bouquet of narrow lanes and flower-bedecked whitewashed houses. Óbidos is ideal for photographers who want to make Portugal look prettier than it is.

Óbidos

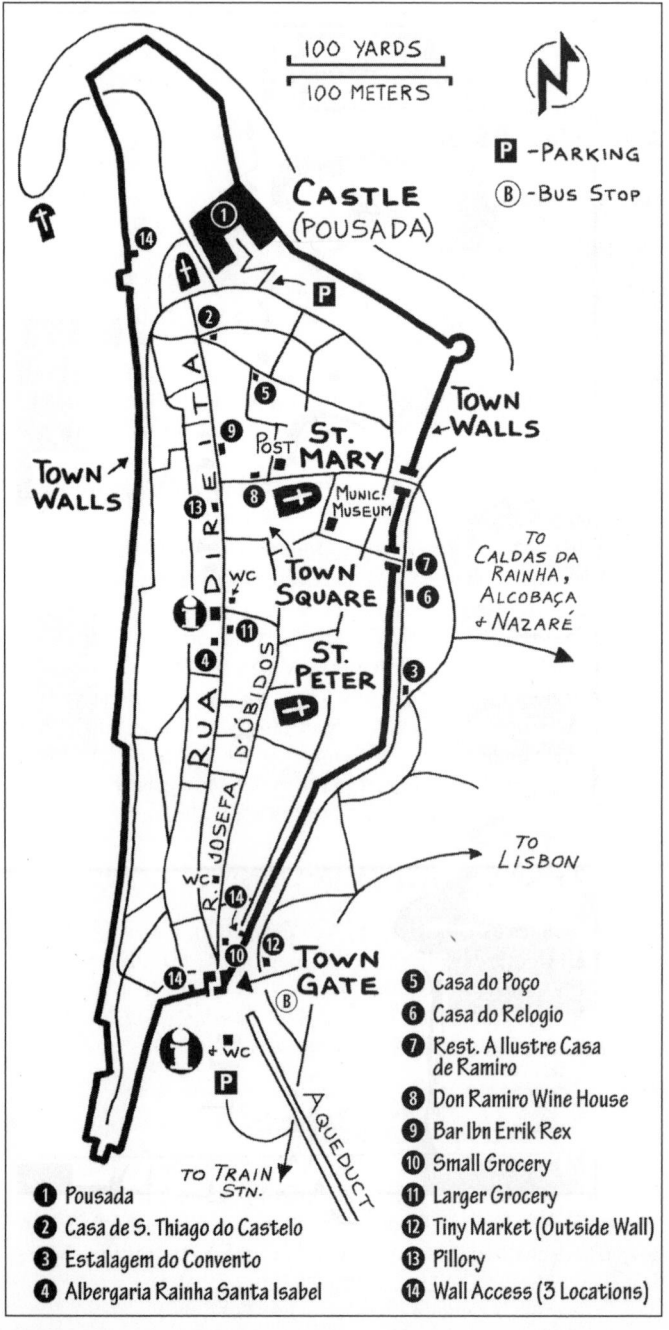

100 YARDS

100 METERS

P — PARKING
B — BUS STOP

CASTLE (POUSADA)

TOWN WALLS

TOWN WALLS

POST

ST. MARY

MUNIC! MUSEUM

TO CALDAS DA RAINHA, ALCOBAÇA & NAZARÉ

TOWN SQUARE

WC

ST. PETER

RUA DIREITA

R. JOSEFA D'ÓBIDOS

TO LISBON

WC

TOWN GATE

B

AQUEDUCT

TO TRAIN STN.

1 Pousada
2 Casa de S. Thiago do Castelo
3 Estalagem do Convento
4 Albergaria Rainha Santa Isabel
5 Casa do Poço
6 Casa do Relogio
7 Rest. A Ilustre Casa de Ramiro
8 Don Ramiro Wine House
9 Bar Ibn Errik Rex
10 Small Grocery
11 Larger Grocery
12 Tiny Market (Outside Wall)
13 Pillory
14 Wall Access (3 Locations)

Founded by Celts (c. 300 B.C.), then ruled by Romans, Visigoths, and Moors, Óbidos was unique as Portugal's "wedding city." In 1282, when King Dinis brought his new bride Isabel here, she liked the town so much he gave it to her (whatta guy). Later kings carried on the tradition—the perfect gift for a king to give to a queen who has everything. (Beats a toaster.) Today this medieval walled town is popular for lowly commoners' weddings. Preserved in its entirety as a national monument, it survives on tourism. Every summer morning at 9:30, the tour groups flush into town. Óbidos is especially crowded in August but it's worth a quick visit. Ideally, arrive late one day and leave early the next and enjoy the town as you would a beautiful painted tile. Or arrive mid-day and play Rowdy Yates with the *Rawhide* crush of tour groups.

Tourist Information: The TI is at Óbidos' main pay parking lot (€0.50/hour, TI open daily 9:30–18:00, shorter hours off-season, detailed audioguide-€5/2hrs, tel. 262-959-231). Another TI is on the main drag, Rua Direita.

Arrival in Óbidos: Ideally, take a bus to Óbidos and leave by either bus or train. If you arrive at the train station, you're faced with a 20-minute uphill hike into town. The bus drops you off and leaves from a stop that's much closer (upon arrival, go up the steps and through the archway on the right). Because there's no bus station and the train station is unstaffed, there's no official place to store luggage in town.

If you arrive by car, don't drive into tiny, cobbled Óbidos. Ample tourist parking is provided outside of town; another lot is by the castle/*pousada* (free, follow Pousada/Estalagem road, clean public WC as you walk into town). If you are staying inside the city walls, you need to walk to your hotel to get a magnetic card that will allow you in with your car.

SELF-GUIDED WALK

Welcome to Óbidos

Main Gate: Enter through the main gate in Óbidos' 14th-century wall. Stop to gaze up at the scenes related to the town's history—depicting centuries of battles and religion in blue-and-white tiles.

Like Dorothy entering a medieval Oz, you're confronted by two wonderful cobbled lanes. The top lane is the town's main drag, littered with tourists shopping and leading straight through Óbidos to its castle (ahead you can see its square tower, where this walk finishes).

Walk the Wall: After entering the old town through the main gate, notice the steep stairs (to your left) accessing the scenic-if-treacherous sentry path along the wall (other access points are near the castle/*pousada,* and uphill from the main church). You'll get views of the city and surrounding countryside from the 40-foot-high walls. The west (uphill) wall is best, letting you look over the town's white buildings with red roofs and blue or yellow trim. You can gaze at the Atlantic, six miles away. Until the 1100s, when the bay silted up, the ocean was half as far away, making this a hilltop citadel guarding a natural port. The aqueduct is from the 16th century.

• *Bypass the wall walk for now and head into town. Follow...*

Rua Josefa d'Óbidos: Continue straight along this less-traveled lower brick lane and notice the whitewash that keeps things cool; the bright blue-and-yellow trims, traditionally designed to define property lines; and the potted geraniums, which bloom most of the year, survive the summer sun well, and keep mosquitoes away. The Church of St. Peter has a fine, newly restored, Baroque altar covered with Brazilian gold leaf. After peeking in, exit the church and climb uphill to the main tourist drag.

• *Then turn right on...*

Rua Direita: Walking toward the castle on this main shopping drag, you'll pass typical shops and a public WC before reaching the...

Town Square: The lone column at the side of the road is the 16th-century pillory. Local bad boys were tied to this to endure whatever punishment was deemed appropriate. Studying it closely, you will notice Queen Leonor's crown circling the entire pillory. Now look even closer on the side facing the castle. The carved hanging shrimp net represents how fishermen found the body of 16-year-old Afonso, son of Manuel I and Leonor, in the Tejo River after a tragic and mysterious death. The net eventually became part of the queen's coat-of-arms. The huge pots you see once held olive oil instead of flowers. The small Municipal Museum, across the square, is not worth the €1.50 unless you enjoy stairs, religious art, and Portuguese inscriptions. But at the bottom of the square do enter the...

Church of St. Mary of Óbidos: Grab a seat on a front pew, surrounded by classic 17th-century tiles (church open daily). Notice the fine painted-wood ceiling over each of the three naves. To the left of the altar is a niche with a delicate Portuguese Renaissance tomb, featuring a pietà carved out of local limestone. On the right are three paintings, including *The Mystical Marriage of St. Catherine*, by Óbidos' most famous artist, the nun Josefa d'Óbidos (1634–1684). Return to the main shopping drag, and turn right for the...

Final Stretch to the Castle: On the left, pop into the **Don Ramiro Wine House**. This welcoming showcase for regional products—wine, cheese, and meat—serves your choice of wine by the half-bottle, and, if you'd like a light meal, a sampler plate of meats and cheese. Its atmospheric setting is dominated by a big, old grape press (open daily 8:30–20:00, on the main drag). Across the street, **Bar Ibn Errik Rex** is the most characteristic (and touristy) of several Óbidos *ginjinha* bars. Óbidos is famous for this much-loved Portuguese cherry liqueur, but you'll pay €2.50 a glass here and only €1 a shot in Lisbon (see description on page 64).

• *The main drag dead-ends at the top of town and the...*

Pousada: This former castle is now a fancy hotel (9 rooms, Db-€165–215, tel. 262-955-080, fax 262-959-148, guest@pousadas.pt).

On January 11, 1148, Afonso Henriques (Portugal's first king) led a two-pronged attack to liberate the town from the Moors. Afonso attacked the main gate at the other end of town (where tourists enter), while the Moorish ruler huddled here in his castle. Meanwhile, a band of Afonso's men snuck up the steep hillside behind the castle disguised as cherry trees. The doomed Moor ignored his daughter when she turned from the window and asked him, "Daddy, do trees walk?"

A lane to the left leads to the stairs accessing the town wall. But go uphill to the right, following the *pousada* signs to the terrace with the telescope for a city view. After savoring the view, go back to the bottom of the *pousada* and enter the archway to your right. Walk for one minute until you see the city wall. Turn around for a spectacular view of the castle—it's yours for the taking.

• *You can return to your starting point three ways: hiking along the upper town wall, exploring photogenic side lanes, or shopping and drinking your way back down the main drag.*

SIGHTS

Near Óbidos

Caldas da Rainha—A 10-minute drive or taxi ride from Óbidos, Caldas da Rainha is famous for its therapeutic springs, which have attracted royalty for rheumatism cures and aristocrats who wanted to make the scene. A venerable hospital now sits upon the source of those curative waters. The charming old center is more workaday than Óbidos, as mono-block development has swamped the suburbs. But the town is still filled with unexpected surprises. Stroll the lovely public gardens near the hospital, uncover the hidden meanings of the various stenciled graffiti, and gaze at a multitude of Art Deco buildings. Caldas da Rainha provides a good glimpse of everyday Portugal with the charm punched up just a notch. Ideally, drop by any morning (except Mon), when its farmers' market fills Praça da República with fruits, veggies, nuts, flowers, and lots of busy locals.

SLEEPING

(€1 = about $1.20, country code: 351)
To enjoy Óbidos without tourists, spend the night. Here are reasonable values in this overpriced toy of a town.

$$$ Casa de S. Thiago do Castelo, a fancy and characteristic little guesthouse at the base of the *pousada*/castle, rents eight elegantly appointed rooms around a chirpy *Better Homes and Tiles* patio. Lower levels offer three different salons to relax in, including one with a classy billiards table (Sb-€65, Db-€80 April–Oct, free parking, Largo de S. Thiago, tel. & fax 262-959-587, Helena).

$$$ Estalagem do Convento was built to house monks but they never showed up. Now it welcomes guests with solemn charm. The restaurant is somewhat pricey, but worth the splurge for the ambience. Consider eating here even if you don't stay the night (Sb-€77, Db-€89, suites-€105–119, extra bed-€18, air-con, outside wall with easy parking, Rua D. João d'Ornelas, tel. 262-959-216, fax 262-959-159, www.estalagemdoconvento.com, estconventhotel@mail.telepac.pt).

$$ Albergaria Rainha Santa Isabel is a hotelesque place marked by flags on the main drag in the center of the old town. If you're driving and feeling bold, call first to let them know you're approaching, stop long enough to drop your bags and get a parking permit, and drive on to the town square to park (Sb-€53–66, Db-€60–73, depending on room, higher in Aug, 3rd person-€18 extra, air-con, elevator, on the main 1-lane drag, Rua Direita, tel. 262-959-323, fax 262-959-115, www.arsio.com).

$ Casa do Poço, with four dim, basic rooms around a bright folksy courtyard, is just one of many homes renting rooms in the old center (Sb-€40–45, Db-€45–60, Travessa da Mouraria, follow main street to Casa de S. Thiago do Castelo then go downhill to the right, tel. 262-959-358, fax 262-959-282).

$ Casa do Relogio is a rustic eight-room place at the downhill end of town, just outside the wall. It's friendly and easy-going, providing no-stress parking and great comfort for the price (Sb-€40–45, Db-€45–58, Tb-€80 in peak of summer, Rua da Graça 12, tel. & fax 262-959-282, casa.relogio@clix.pt, Sarah).

EATING

Óbidos is tough on the average tourist's budget. Consider a picnic (see below) or one of the many cafés that offer cheap, basic meals.

Restaurante A Ilustre Casa de Ramiro is a big place 50 yards downhill from (and outside of) one of the town's east gates. It's dressy and characteristic but touristy, with a four-language menu

(€20 dinners, Fri–Wed 12:30–15:00 & 19:30–22:30, closed Thu, Rua Porta do Vale, tel. 262-959-194).

Picnics: Pick up your picnic at the small grocery store just inside the main gate (on the lower brick road), the larger grocery in the center on Rua Direita, or the tiny market just outside the town wall.

TRANSPORTATION CONNECTIONS

From Óbidos to: Nazaré (4 buses/day, 1 hr, most transfer in Caldas da Rainha), **Lisbon** (5 buses/day, 75 min; 8 trains/day, 2.25 hrs, transfer in Cacém), **Alcobaça** (6 buses/day, 1.5 hrs), **Batalha** (4 buses/day, 2 hrs). Far fewer buses run on weekends.

By Car to Lisbon: From Óbidos, the tollway zips you directly into Lisbon (€7).

COIMBRA

The college town of Coimbra (3 hours north of Lisbon by train, bus, or car) is Portugal's Oxford and the country's easiest-to-enjoy city.

Don't be fooled by the drab suburbs. Portugal's most important city for 200 years, Coimbra (koh-EEM-brah) remains second only to Lisbon culturally and historically. It served as Portugal's leading city while the Moors controlled Lisbon. Landlocked Coimbra was surpassed by the ports of Lisbon and Porto only as Portugal's maritime fortunes rose. Today, Coimbra is Portugal's third-largest city (pop. 150,000) and home to its oldest and most prestigious university (founded 1290). When school is in session, Coimbra bustles. During school holidays, it's sleepy. Any time of year, explore the great Arab-flavored old town—a maze of people, narrow streets, and tiny *tascas* (restaurants with just a few tables).

Planning Your Time

On a two-week swing through Portugal, give Coimbra a day. Browse through its historic university, fortress-like cathedral, and lively old town. If you're driving from central Spain, Coimbra makes a good first stop in Portugal.

ORIENTATION

Coimbra is a mini-Lisbon—everything good about urban Portugal without the intensity of a big city. I couldn't design a more delightful city for a visit. Most visitors skip Coimbra's modern center (with Portugal's biggest shopping mall, opened in 2005), and stick to the charming old town. There's a village-like feeling in the winding

Coimbra

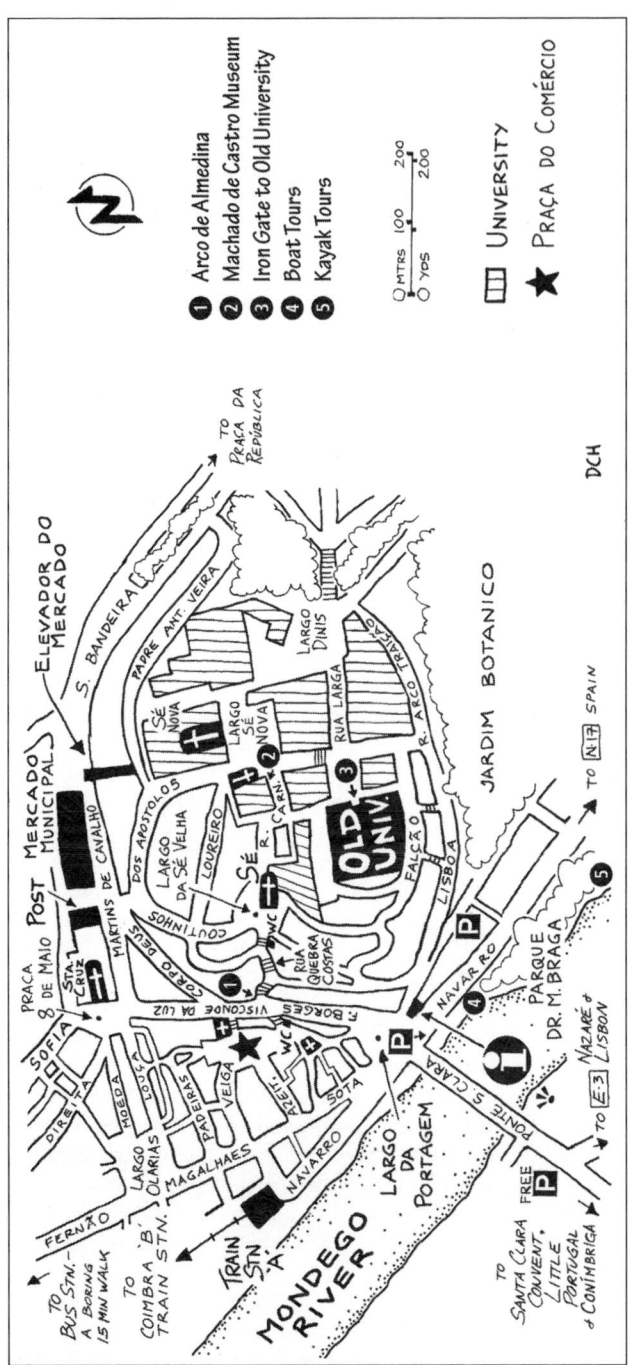

1 Arco de Almedina
2 Machado de Castro Museum
3 Iron Gate to Old University
4 Boat Tours
5 Kayak Tours

☐ UNIVERSITY

★ PRAÇA DO COMÉRCIO

MTRS 100 200
YDS 200

DCH

streets set on the side of the hill.
The high point is the old university. From there, little lanes mean-
der down like a Moroccan medina
to the main pedestrian street. This
street (named Visconde da Luz at
one end, then becoming Rua de
Ferreira Borges) runs from the
Praça 8 de Maio to the Mondego
River, dividing the old town into
upper (Alta) and lower (Baixa) parts.

From Largo da Portagem (the main square by the river),
everything is within an easy walk. The old town spreads out like
an amphitheater—timeworn houses, shops, and stairways all lead
up to the university. The best views are looking up from the far
end of Santa Clara Bridge and looking down from the observation
deck of the university. The TI and plenty of good budget rooms are
within several blocks of the train station.

Tourist Information

Pick up a free, info-packed map and the monthly cultural calendar at the helpful, English-speaking TI at Largo da Portagem
(May–Sept Mon–Fri 9:00–19:00, Sat–Sun 10:00–13:00 & 14:30–
17:30; Oct–April Mon–Fri 9:30–13:00 & 14:00–17:30, Sat–Sun
10:00–13:00 & 14:30-17:30; entrance on Avenida Navarro, tel. 239-
488-120, www.turismo-centro.pt, rtc-coimbra@turismo-centro
.pt). You can get bus schedules printed out for you, and find information on sights in central Portugal here.

Two more TIs are near the university: on Largo Dinis (Mon–
Fri 9:00–18:00, Sat–Sun 9:00–12:30 & 14:00–17:30, tel. 239-832-
591) and on Praça da República (Mon–Fri 10:00–18:30, closed
Sat–Sun, tel. 239-833-202). Yet another TI is at the town market
hall, Mercado Municipal (Mon–Sat 9:00–18:00, closed Sun, tel.
239-834-038).

Arrival in Coimbra

By Train: There are two main Coimbra train stations, A and B.
Major trains (e.g., from Lisbon and Salamanca) stop only at B
(think Big). From there, you can take a five-minute shuttle train
to the very-central Station A (free with the ticket that got you to
Station B). To find out exactly which train to take to get from B
to A, ask *"Comboio* (kom-BOY-oo) *para Coimbra?"* Some local
trains (e.g., to Nazaré and Porto) stop at both stations. Station B
has an ATM in one of its outside walls, opposite the *informações*
office. Taxis wait across the tracks (figure about €4 to Station A or
your hotel). Station A has a helpful, English-speaking *informações*

office, tucked away in a waiting room to the left of the main entrance, where you can get train schedules (daily 9:00–12:00 & 13:00–18:00 with occasional weekend closures, tel. 808-208-208). In Coimbra, the only place to buy train tickets and make train reservations (even for trips to Spain) is in Station A, at the ticket office next to the first-class waiting room.

By Bus: The bus station, on Avenida Fernão de Magalhães (tel. 239-855-270), has two ATMs (1 inside, 1 outside) and, across from the *informações* office and to the right, a baggage check that looks like a mailroom (€1 per bag, daily 8:00–18:30). The station is a boring but easy 15-minute walk from the center; exit the bus station to the right and follow the busy street into town. You can also catch a bus (#29 or #35) or take a taxi (€4).

If you're walking to the bus station to leave Coimbra, take Avenida Fernão de Magalhães past its intersection with Cabral and look to the left—the Neptuno café marks the station's subtle entrance. For bus schedules, don't go to the bus station—the TI prints timetables.

By Car: From Lisbon, it's an easy, two-hour straight shot on the slick Auto-Estrada A1 (€11 toll). You'll pass convenient exits for Fátima and the Roman ruins of Conímbriga along the way. Leave the freeway on the easy-to-miss first Coimbra exit, then follow the *Centro* signs. Two and a half miles after leaving the freeway, you'll cross the Mondego River. Take Avenida Fernão de Magalhães directly into town. Most hotels are near the train station (Station A) and the Santa Clara Bridge. If you arrive from north Portugal or central Spain, follow signs for *Centro/Largo da Portagem.*

The large, free lot immediately across the river is your handiest bet for free parking (you may need to wait for a spot to open up). You can also look for free parking along the streets over the river, but these aren't as safe as a lot. In town, you'll find big, convenient, clearly marked pay garages. Many hotels also have information on parking.

Helpful Hints

Money: ATMs and banks (Mon–Fri 8:30–15:00, closed Sat–Sun) are plentiful.

Internet Access: Internet Coimbra Câmara Municipal has eight computers and offers free access for a half hour. Because it's city-funded and free, you need to reserve a time slot in advance—drop by and show your passport to sign up (Mon–Fri 10:00–20:00, Sat–Sun 10:00–22:00; coming from the pedestrian street, it's past Praça 8 de Maio on your left at #38). For a standard Internet café, hike 10 minutes out of the old town from Praça 8 de Maio up Rua Olímpio Nicolau to the slick, modern **Spacenet** (€1/30 min, Mon–Sat 10:00–24:00, Sun

14:00–24:00, Avenida Sá da Bandeira 67, tel. 239-836-844).

Car Rental: Avis has a tiny office in Station A (Mon–Fri 8:30–12:30 & 15:00–19:00, closed Sat–Sun, tel. & fax 239-834-786), and Hertz is near the bus station at Rua Padre Estevão Cabral (tel. 239-834-750).

Bus Tickets: The **Abreu travel agency** sells domestic bus tickets as well as international tickets to Salamanca, Spain (€27) and beyond (Mon–Fri 9:00–12:30 & 14:30–18:30, plus May–Sept Sat 9:00–12:30, closed Sun, Rua da Sota 2, leaving Station A it's 100 yards immediately to your left, tel. 239-855-520).

Local Guides: While the city doesn't offer walking tours, the TI has a list of private guides, such as Maria Jose Fernandes (mobile 934-093-542, mariajf@portugalmail.pt) and Cristina Bessa (tel. 239-835-428, ffbessa@mail.telepac.pt). Local guides charge €85 for a half-day tour.

Getting Around Coimbra

If you're arriving by train at Station B, you'll need to take the free shuttle train to Station A (see "Arrival in Coimbra," above), which is within about a 10-minute walk of everything I've listed.

While most visitors do the entire city on foot, taxis are cheap (around €3–4 for a short ride) and a good option.

The cute little electric minibus (nicknamed *pantufinhas*, or "grandma's slipper") is silent and easy—designed to get old ladies up and down the steep hills of the old town. It makes a continuous 20-minute loop through the lower old town (Baixa) and around the upper old town (Alta), passing through Largo da Portagem, Praça 8 de Maio, and by the old cathedral. There are no regular stops—you just wave it down and tell the driver when you want off. Bus #34 and trolley #1 go from the old town to the university.

Local buses are expensive (€1.40, better value 3-ride pass-€1.60, 11-ride pass-€5.30, no time limit, sharable, ticket also valid for Coimbra's Elevador do Mercado to top of town).

SELF-GUIDED WALK

Welcome to Coimbra's Old Town

Coimbra is fun on foot, especially along its straight (formerly Roman), pedestrian-only main drag. Follow this quickie tour, which includes an elevator ride that transports you to the top of the hill.

• *Start your walk at the...*

Santa Clara Bridge: This has been a key bridge over the Mondego

---

Coimbra in History

1064   Coimbra is liberated from the Moors.

1135   Portugal's first king, Afonso Henriques, makes Coimbra his capital.

1211   Portugal's first parliament of nobles *(cortes)* convenes at Coimbra.

1256   Lisbon replaces Coimbra as Portugal's capital.

1290   The university is founded under "the poet king," Dinis (ruled 1279–1325). Originally in Lisbon, it moved to Coimbra in 1308.

1537   The university, after moving back to Lisbon, finally settles permanently in Coimbra under Jesuit administration.

1810   Napoleon's French troops sack Coimbra, then England's Duke of Wellington drives them out.

1928   António Salazar, a professor of political economy at Coimbra, becomes minister of finance, soon to be dictator.

River since Roman times. For centuries, it had a tollgate *(portagem)*. Cross the bridge for a fine Coimbra view.

• *At the end of the bridge on the Coimbra side is...*

Largo da Portagem: This square is a great place for a coffee or a pastry. Try Pastelaria Briosa (best pastries) or Café Montanha (with a big brass palm tree inside). The town's two special treats are *pastel de Santa Clara* (pastry made with almonds and marmalade) and *pastel de Tentúgal* (made with eggs, cream, and powdered sugar, €0.80 each). In the center of the square is a statue of the prime minister who, in 1834, shut down the city's convents and monasteries and earned the nickname "friar killer."

• *Stroll down the pedestrian street (Rua Ferreira Borges). After a 200-yard-long gauntlet of clothing stores, take the stairs (down 3 steps to your left) leading to a terrace overlooking the square below (pay public WC, sanitários, in the stairwell).*

Praça do Comércio: This pleasant square is shaped like a Roman chariot racecourse—and likely was one 2,000 years ago. In the Middle Ages, they used this place for bullfights. Beyond Praça do Comércio stretches the heart of the old town. Look at your map. The circular street pattern outlines the wall used by Romans, Visigoths, Moors, and Christians to protect Coimbra. Historically, the rich could afford to live within the protective city walls (the Alta, or high town). Even today, the Baixa, or low town, remains a poorer section, with haggard women rolling wheeled shopping bags, children running barefoot, and men lounging on the square like it's their life's calling. But it's a fine area to walk around during the day.

• *Return to the pedestrian street.*

Across the street from the overlook is the Edificio Chiado (part of Museu Municipal, with free local art exhibits). A few yards farther along (on your right), steps lead up through an ancient arched gateway—**Arco de Almedina**—into the old city and to the old cathedral and university. Later, we'll finish this walk by going downhill through this arch, after visiting the university.

Farther along the pedestrian drag, stop at the picturesque corner just beyond the cafés (where the building comes to a triangular corner). The steep road climbs into Coimbra's historic ghetto (no Jewish community remains) and the wonderful **A Capella** fado nightclub (see "Sights and Activities," page 193).

As you stroll along, you'll know it's graduation time if graduation photos are displayed in photographers' windows. Check out the students decked out in their traditional university capes (displaying rips on the hem—left side for family, right side for friends, backside for girlfriends) and color-coded sashes (yellow for medicine, red for law, and so on).

• *The pedestrian street ends at Praça 8 de Maio with the...*

Church of Santa Cruz: Soak in this church's impressive facade. Notice the subtle wires on the statuary—they're electrified to keep pigeons from dumping their corrosive loads on the tender limestone. Inside, the church is lavishly decorated with 18th-century tiles that tell the stories of the discovery of the Holy Cross (on left) and the life of St. Augustine (on right; the church is of the Augustinian order). The pulpit is considered one of the finest pieces of Renaissance work in Portugal.

Step behind the altar for a close-up look at two fine, 16th-century tombs. On the left lies the first Portuguese king, Afonso Henriques (1095–1185). Afonso "The Conqueror" reclaimed most of Portugal from the Moors, declared himself king, got the pope to approve the title, and settled down in his chosen capital—Coimbra. There, his wife gave birth to young Sancho, who later became king. Sancho I (1154–1211, tomb on right) was known as "The Populator." He saw the destruction that war had brought to the country and set about rebuilding and repopulating, inviting northern-European Crusaders (such as the Templar Knights) to occupy southern Portugal. In the 16th century, while on a pilgrimage to Santiago de Compostela, the great King Manuel I dropped by this church and was underwhelmed by the two kings' original tombs. He commissioned these beautifully carved replacements—much more fit for kings. Study the intimate faces. Notice how the kings seem only to be resting. (To make themselves more comfortable, they've "hung" their helmets and arm-guards just behind them.) For €2.50 you can explore the sacristy (entrance to right of main altar) and see the treasures of the church, pass through the impressive chapter room into a fine Manueline "cloister of silence," and check out the slick new art gallery filling the monks' former dining hall (daily 9:00–12:00 & 14:00–17:45).

People (and pigeons) survey the Praça 8 de Maio scene from the terrace of the recommended **Café Santa Cruz** (to the right of church, see "Eating," page 205). Built as a church but abandoned with the dissolution of the monasteries in 1834, this was the 19th-century haunt of local intellectuals. The altar is now used for lectures, poetry readings, small concerts, and art exhibits (the women's room is in a confessional).

• *Continue past the church and the city hall (Câmara Municipal, make an appointment here for free Internet access, see "Helpful Hints," above) to the noisy street. Turn right and go a block to find a park with a fountain (once a monastery cloister and Renaissance garden) and the cheap, handy Self-Service Restaurant Jardim da Manga (see "Eating," page 205). Keep going uphill along the busy Rua Olímpio Nicolau di Fernandes past the big post office to the...*

Mercado Municipal: This modern covered market is fun to explore and great for gathering picnic supplies (Mon–Sat 8:00–14:00, closed Sun). It's new, clean, and hygienic, but maintains the colorful appeal of an old farmer's market. See the "salt of the earth" in the faces of the women selling produce (their men are off in the fields...or the bars). For a sandwich and glass of wine for less than €2, head to the Bar do Mercado Requinte at the end of the ground floor. Check out the photos of the old market on the wall, and then go upstairs to the meat. Follow your nose to the far end, with all the fresh fish and dried cod. The Portuguese are the world's biggest cod eaters, but because cod is no longer found in nearby waters, the local favorite is imported from Norway. To the Portuguese, cod tastes much better dried and salted *(bacalhau)* than fresh.

• *From the fish hall, swim outside and find the sleek city elevator.*

Elevador do Mercado: Take the elevator to the top of the hill (€1.40/trip if you pay elevator operator, €1.60/3 trips or €5.30/11 trips if you buy tickets in store next door—marked *loja*—or at most kiosks; no time limit, sharable, also valid for buses; elevator runs Mon–Sat 7:30–23:30, Sun 9:00–23:30). Don't insert your ticket in the machine until the elevator operator is there. The lift whisks you up the long, steep hill (stop midway to transfer to funicular, no need to validate ticket again), offering commanding views of

Coimbra en route. At the top, exit to the right and head uphill, following signs to *Universidade*. Fifty yards up the cobbled lane, at the first intersection and crest of the hill, you'll find a local fraternity house called Real República Corsários das Ilhas (literally "Royal Commune of the Pirates of the Islands"). Notice the prominent graffiti on the wall that links McDonald's and the G8 (group of the 8 most powerful countries) with the skull and crossbones. These small university frat houses, called *repúblicas*, are communes that traditionally housed about a dozen students from the same region or provincial town. While some are highly cultured, the rowdier ones are often decorated with plunder from their pranks—stolen traffic signs and so on—giving rise to the local saying, "At night, many things happen in Coimbra."

• *Walk on past the* **Machado de Castro Museum** *(on right, described in "Sights," page 197, may be closed for restoration in 2006) to the big, fascist-designed university square (Praça da Porta Férrea). The Iron Gate entry to the old university is on your right.*

University: Explore the university (described in "Sights and Activities," below), then continue this town walk.

• *Leave the university—with your back to the Iron Gate, turn left, and take the steps down into the old town (following the steep lanes toward the old cathedral).*

As you wander, notice the white-paper diamonds in the windows—they mean "student room available for rent." Continuing on, you'll come to the old cathedral (Sé Velha, described below). Facing the cathedral is the recommended **Restaurante Trovador,** offering fado performances nearly every night (see "Eating," page 204; reservations essential for fado). The colorful little **Café Sé Velha,** on the corner immediately below the cathedral, is tiled with fine, traditional scenes from Coimbra. From there, a blue line on the cobbles marks the route of the electric minibus service (see "Getting Around Coimbra," page 188). Take the steep stairway leading down to the Rua Quebra Costas, the "Street of Broken Ribs." At one time, this lane had no steps and literally *was* the street of broken ribs. During a strong rain, this becomes a river. On your left at #50, find the photo shop that depicts traditional student life. The lane's many shops show off the fine, local, blue-and-white ceramic work called *faiança*. If you can't make it to Morocco, this dense jungle of shops and markets may be your next-best bet.

• *Rua Quebra Costas ends at...*

Arco de Almedina: This is the arch (literally named "gate to the medina") we saw earlier from the pedestrian street Rua Ferreira Borges. Part of the old town wall, the arch is a double gate with a 90-degree kink in the middle for easier defense. Looking back and up, notice the two square holes in the ceiling, through which boiling oil would be poured, turning attacking Moors into fritters. The holes are rudely nicknamed *mata-cães*—dog killers. Passing through the second arch, you'll end up unscathed on the pedestrian street.

SIGHTS AND ACTIVITIES

Coimbra's Old University

This venerable 700-year-old university, founded in 1290, was modeled after Bologna's university (Europe's 1st, A.D. 1139). Rated

▲▲▲, It's a stately, three-winged former royal palace (from when Coimbra was the capital), beautifully situated overlooking the city. At first, law, medicine, grammar, and logic were taught. Then, with the rise of seafaring in Portugal, astronomy and geometry were added. While Lisbon's university is much larger, Coimbra's university (with 25,000 students) is still the country's most respected. For visitors, the university marks the top of the old town. While most of it is fascist-era sprawl, the old core of the university (the palace section, with its fancy ceremonial halls, library, chapel, and main courtyard) makes for an interesting visit.

Cost and Hours: A combo-ticket for the two university sights that cost money to see—the Grand Hall and King John's Library—is €4 (otherwise €2.50 for the library alone, daily April–Oct 9:00–19:20, Nov–March 10:00–17:20, ticket office closes 20 min before sights). You'll get an entry time for the library (see "King John's Library," page 196).

Getting There: To get to the university, consider taking the elevator from the Mercado Municipal to the top of the hill (see "Welcome to Coimbra's Old Town" walk, page 188), or take a taxi to the Iron Gate, then sightsee Coimbra downhill.

Iron Gate—Find the gate to the old university (on Praça da Porta Férrea). Before entering, stand with your back to the gate (and the old university) and look across the stark, modern square at the fascist architecture of the new university. In what's considered one of the worst cultural crimes in Portuguese history, the dictator António Salazar tore down half the old town of Coimbra to build these university halls. Salazar, proud that Portugal was the last European power to hang onto its global empire, wanted a fittingly monumental university here. After all, Salazar—along with virtually everyone of political importance in Portugal—was educated at Coimbra, where he studied law and then became an economics

professor. If these bold buildings are reminiscent of Mussolini's
E.U.R. in Rome, perhaps it's because they were built in part by
Italian architects for Portugal's little Mussolini.

OK, now turn and walk through the Iron Gate. Traditionally,
freshmen—proudly wearing their black capes for the first time—
pass through the Iron Gate to enroll. And also traditionally, to get
out they had to pass through an Iron Gate gauntlet of butt kicks
from upperclassmen. Walk into the...

Old University Courtyard—The university's most important
sights all face this square: the Grand Hall (up the grand stairway on
the right between you and the clock tower), St. Michael's Chapel

Coimbra's Old University

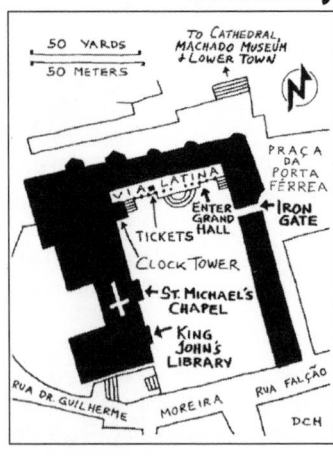

(straight ahead, through the
door, then to the left), and
King John's Library (across
the square, furthest door on
left, flanked by columns).

The statue in the square
is of King John III. While the
university was established in
1290, it went back and forth
between Lisbon and Coimbra
(back then, university students were adults, privileged,
and a pain to have in your
town). In 1537, John III finally
established the school permanently in Coimbra (away from
Lisbon). Standing like a good
humanist (posing much like
his contemporary, England's
Renaissance King Henry VIII), John modernized Portugal's education system Renaissance-style. But he also made the university
the center of Portugal's Inquisition.

Survey the square with your back to the gate. The dreaded
sound of the clock tower's bell—named the "baby goat" for its nag-
ging—calls students to class. On several occasions, the clapper has
been stolen. No bell...no class. No class...big party. A larger bell
(the "big goat") rings only on grand and formal occasions.

The arcaded passageway (upstairs) between the Iron Gate
and the clock tower is called Via Latina, from the days when only
Latin was allowed in this part of the university. Purchase your
ticket at the end of Via Latina, immediately under the tower. See
the following sights in any order you like. Note that regardless of
the admission time you're given to see the library, they may agree
to let you in early.

The Grand Hall (Sala dos Capelos)—Enter from the middle of Via Latina, climb the tiled stairway, and show your ticket (ask the ticket-taker if the *varanda* viewpoint is open; see next paragraph).

The Grand Hall is the site of the university's major academic ceremonies, such as exams and graduations. Tourists look down from balconies above the room. It was originally the throne room of the royal palace. Today, the rector's light-green chair sits throne-like in front. During ceremonies, students in their formal attire fill the benches, and teachers sit along the perimeter, as gloomy portraits of Portuguese kings watch from above. Since there is no clapping during these formal rituals, a brass band (on the wooden platform in the back) punctuates the ceremonies with solemn music.

View Catwalk (Varanda): Continue around the Grand Hall, past an ornately decorated former royal stateroom (now a place where oral exams are taken) and out onto the narrow observation deck for the best possible views of Coimbra. The viewpoint will likely be open, but may be closed if the weather's bad or there aren't sufficient staff to monitor the "only 10 people on the balcony at a time" rule. Ask the ticket-taker, *"A varanda está aberta?"*—"Is the veranda open?" Request the key by making a hand sign for "key" or saying *"chave"* (SHAH-veh).

From the viewpoint, scan the old town from right to left. Remember, before Salazar's extension of the university, this old town surrounded the university. The Baroque facade breaking the horizon is the "new" cathedral—from the 16th century. Below that, with the fine arcade, is the Machado de Castro Museum, housed in the former bishop's palace and located atop a Roman site (see below). And below that, like an armadillo, sits the old cathedral.

If you see any noisily painted yellow and blue windows, they mark a *república* frat house. Travelers during November and May might see parades of rowdy students in funny costumes, draped in signs, dragging tin cans—all part of the traditional initiation rites marking the beginning and end of the school year. This is when new students receive—and graduating students burn—the small, colored ribbons of their chosen major. Look beyond the houses to the Mondego River, the lengthiest entirely Portuguese river. Over the bridge is the 17th-century Santa Clara Convent—at 590 feet, the longest building in Coimbra.

St. Michael's Chapel—This chapel is behind the 16th-century Manueline facade (enter through door to the right of facade—once inside, push door on the left marked *capela*, free admission). The architecture of the church interior is Manueline—notice the golden "rope" trimming the arch before the altar. The decor is from a later time. The altar is 17th-century Mannerist, with steps unique to Portugal (and her South American colonies), symbolizing the steps the faithful take on their journey to heaven. The 2,100-pipe, 18th-century, German-built organ is notable for its horizontal "trumpet" pipes. Found only in Iberia, these help the organist perform the allegorical fight between good and evil—with the horizontal pipes trumpeting the arrival of the good guys. The box seats for the royal family are above the loft in the rear. Students and alums enjoy the privilege of having their weddings here.

The **Museum of Sacred Art,** further down the corridor, may still be closed for renovation in 2006. When it reopens, a painting of John the Baptist will again point the way to art that nuns and priests find fascinating. The museum was created in 1910 to keep the art in Coimbra when the new republic wanted to move it all to Lisbon. (Also in the corridor, you'll find WCs and a cheap, student-filled café with a lovely view of the river from the terrace.)

▲**King John's Library**—One of Europe's best-surviving Baroque libraries, this grand building displays 30,000 books in 18th-

century splendor. The zealous doorkeeper locks the door at every opportunity to keep out humidity. Buzz (on left) to get into this temple of thinking. While ticket-sellers are quick to issue entry times requiring a long wait, you're likely to get in early if you humbly ask the attendant if you can enter now.

Once you've received permission to enter, you might still have to wait outside a while, as other groups finish their 10-minute visits (followed by a 10-min closure to control humidity level). Inside, at the "high altar," stands the library's founder, the Divine Monarch John V. The reading tables, inlaid with exotic South American woods (and ornamented with silver ink wells), and the precious wood shelves (with clever hide-away staircases) are reminders that Portugal's wealth was great—and imported. Built Baroque, the interior is all wood. Even the "marble" on the arches of triumph that divide the library into rooms is just painted wood. (Real marble would add to the humidity.) The library's resident bats are well cared for and appreciated—they eat insects, providing a chemical-free way of protecting the books, and alert the guard to changing weather with their "eee-eee" cry. Look for the trompe l'oeil Baroque tricks on the painted ceiling. Gold leaf (from Brazil) is everywhere, and the Chinese themes are pleasantly reminiscent of Portugal's once vast empire. The books, all dating from before 1755, are in Latin, Greek, or Hebrew. Imagine being a student in Coimbra centuries ago, when this temple of learning stored the world's knowledge like a vast filing cabinet. As you leave, watch how the doorman uses the giant key as a hefty doorknob.

In Coimbra

Machado de Castro Museum—The museum may still be closed for restoration in 2006, but check at the TI or the sight to be sure. Housed in the old bishop's palace, it contains ceramics, 14th- to 16th-century religious sculpture (mostly taken from the dissolved monasteries), and a Roman excavation site. Upstairs, look for the impressive, 14th-century *Cristo Negro* carved in wood. Until a decade ago, when this statue was cleaned (and the black—from candle soot—came off), it was considered to be a portrait of a black Christ. Before you return downstairs, enjoy the views from the top-floor arcade.

The Roman building, with a basement crisscrossed with empty tunnels, provided a level foundation for an ancient Roman forum that stood where the museum does today. At the entrance, read the Latin-inscribed Roman stone: bottom line—"Aeminiens," referring to the people who lived in Roman Coimbra, then called Aeminium; fifth line—the fourth-century emperor of the day, "Constantio"; and the second line—a reference perhaps to an early alliance of barbarian tribes from the North Atlantic. Notice the few economical "plug-on" Roman busts—from the days when they'd keep the bodies, but change the heads each time a new emperor took power. The museum sometimes houses art exhibitions here in the Roman tunnels or on the ground floor (if not closed, then likely open Tue–Sun 9:30–12:30 & 14:00–17:30, closed Mon). Visit this before or after the old university, since both are at roughly the same altitude.

Old Cathedral (Sé Velha)—Same old story: Christians push out Moors (1064), tear down their mosque, and build a church. The Arabic script on a few of the stones indicates that rubble from the mosque was used in the construction. The facade of the main entrance, with its horseshoe-like arches, even feels Arabic. Notice the crenellations along the roof of this fortress-like Romanesque church; the Moors, though booted out, were still considered a risk. If this reminds you of Lisbon's cathedral, it should...it was designed by the same French architect.

The giant holy-water font shells are a 19th-century gift from Ceylon (now Sri Lanka), and the walls are lined with 16th-century tiles from Sevilla, Spain. The three front altars are each worth a look. The main altar is a fine example of Gothic styling.

The 16th-century chapel to the right contains one of the best Renaissance altars in the country. The apostles all look to Jesus as he talks, while musical angels flank the holy host. To the left of the High Altar, the Chapel of St. Peter shows Peter being crucified upside down. The fine points of the carving were destroyed by Napoleon's soldiers.

On the right just before the transept is a murky painting of Queen Isabel (Saint Elizabeth) with a skirt full of roses. This 13th-century Hungarian princess—with family ties to Portugal—is a local favorite with a sweet legend. Against the wishes of the king, she always gave bread to the poor. One day, when he came home early from a trip, she was busy doling out bread from her skirt. She pulled the material up to hide the bread. When the king asked her what was inside (suspecting bread for the poor), the queen—unable to lie—lowered the material and, miraculously, the bread had turned to roses. For this astonishing act, she was canonized as a saint in 1625.

The peaceful cloister (entrance near back of church) is the oldest Gothic cloister in Portugal. Well-maintained, though its walls are decaying, the courtyard offers a fine, framed view of the cathedral's dome. A tomb from 1064 in the cloister belongs to Coimbra's first Christian, post-Reconquista governor (church is free, cloisters cost €1; church open Mon–Thu 10:00–18:00, Fri 10:00–12:00, Sat 10:00–15:00, cloister closes from 13:00–14:00, closed Sun; the public is welcome to come to Mass, ask TI for schedule, WCs on your right inside cloister).

▲**Fado**—Portugal's unique, mournful traditional music, fado, is generally performed by women. But in Coimbra, men sing the fado. Roving bands of male students—similar to the Tuna bands in Spain's Salamanca—serenade around town for tips and the hearts of women. During the tourist season, you'll find sit-down fado nightly at Restaurante Trovador and Fado Diligencia (see "Eating," page 204), the A Capella piano bar (see next paragraph), and in the streets—the mayor organizes Thursday street concerts through the summer. The Galeria Almedina, under the Arco de Almedina, also puts on free, authentic fado shows (Sat in June–Aug, ask at TI for details).

A Capella, on the hill above the Church of Santa Cruz, is a tiny chapel that's been turned into a piano bar. While they often play jazz in the winter, it's all fado in the summer (nightly after 22:00). Come for the fado, the very cool scene, and the snacks and drinks (no cover but €5 minimum, reservations smart, at the triangular corner midway down the main drag, climb the steep Rua do Corpo de Deus 300 yards until you see the old chapel on your left, tel. 914-657-717).

Parque Dr. Manuel Braga—Coimbra's new, inviting riverside park sprawls upstream from the Santa Clara Bridge. You'll find boat tours, the recommended Italian restaurant Restaurante Itália and Irish pub Mondego (see "Eating," page 205), a strip of trendy evening spots, and the Portuguese Pavilion from the recent Hannover Expo (2000 World's Fair in Hannover, Germany).

Little Portugal (Portugal dos Pequenitos)—This is a children's (or tourist's) look at the great buildings and monuments of Portugal and its former empire in miniature, scattered through a park a couple of blocks south of town, straight across the Santa Clara Bridge. If you've been through some of Portugal already, it's fun to try and identify the buildings you've already seen, and look at what's to come (€5 for gardens and monuments, €6 for gardens plus maritime and clothing museums, daily March–May 10:00–19:00, June–mid-Sept 9:00–20:00, mid-Sept–Feb 10:00–17:00, last entry 30 min before closing).

Kayaks, Cruises, and Adventure Sports—O Pioneiro do Mondego buses you from Coimbra to Penacova (15 miles away), from where you **kayak** down the Mondego River for about four hours back into Coimbra (€20, 10 percent discount through 2006 with this book, daily June–Sept, 1- and 2-person kayaks available, book by phone, meet at park near TI, tel. 239-478-385 to reserve, Derek speaks English). Most people stop to swim or picnic on the way back, so it often turns into an all-day journey. For the first 12.5 miles, you'll go easily with the flow, but you'll get your exercise paddling the remaining stretch. To avoid the workout (and the more boring part of the Mondego River), ask to be picked up 2.5 miles before Coimbra, at Portela do Mondego, where the river's current slows down.

If you'd rather let someone else do the work, Basófias boats **cruise** up and down the river daily except Monday (€5, departs from dock across from TI at 15:00, 16:00, and 17:00, plus 2 more in summer, schedule posted at dock, 55 min, tel. 239-912-444).

Capitão Dureza, in the nearby town Foz da Figueira, specializes in **adventure sports**—at your own risk: rappelling, rafting, and canyoning (pick-up and drop-off in Coimbra, book by tel. & fax 233-427-772).

Near Coimbra

▲**Conímbriga Roman Ruins**—Portugal's best Roman site is impressive...unless you've been to Rome. What remains of the city is divided in two, in part because its inhabitants tore down buildings to throw up a quick defensive wall against an expected barbarian attack. Today, this wall cuts crudely through the site.

Purchase your tickets inside the main building, then enter the ruins before visiting the museum. Helpful arrows guide your

way through the site. The mansion under the protective modern
roofing is the grand finale, so
explore the remnants of the town
first. Remains of different houses
and shopping arcades begin the
visit, most with wonderful mosaics intact. Note how the columns
are made of preformed wedges.
After you see the public baths,
walk around...

The Wall: This immense structure was built in haste for protection, and it shows. Invasions from the north took place after
the Roman empire lost influence in this area, around A.D. 465. A
Christian Germanic tribe conquered the city and built a basilica at
the end of this wall.

Continuing along the wall, you will see parts of a house
belonging to a local landowner. Walk through the fields to the
rest of the site. Other houses and public baths are out there, even
though they are poorly signposted. On your way, you will see the
sparse ruins of the old forum. Backtrack to pass under the aqueduct and go around it (note the fallen stones which supported the
structure) to reach the site's most important find (under a protective roof). The **House of the Fountains** is an entire dwelling, with
most of its rooms and mosaics intact. Don't spend €0.50 on the
lazy fountain show (wait for one of the school groups to do it for
you), but enjoy the stories in the mosaics. Simple portraits, horses,
and numerous hunting scenes illustrate the daily routine in this
town during Roman times.

The Museum: Now return to the delightful museum that
highlights discoveries from decades of excavation. The room to
the right of the ticket counter describes daily life in Conímbriga,
displaying coins, dinnerware, and even grooming utensils (find the
spoon-shaped ear cleaners), all with good English descriptions.
The opposite room contains a miniature replica of the forum, along
with fine mosaics and a few tombstones. The best mosaic is of the
mythological, bull-headed Minotaur—follow the maze from the
center until you are safely out. The museum's café is an excellent
spot to have lunch before catching the return bus to Coimbra (€7
meals, same hours as museum). Or bring a picnic lunch and eat in
the gardens (€3, site open daily mid-March–mid-Sept 9:00–20:00,
mid-Sept–mid-March 9:00–18:00, museum opens an hour later,
closed Mon, www.conimbriga.pt).

Getting There: The ruins are nine miles southwest of
Coimbra on the road to Lisbon. On weekdays, two buses leave for
the ruins each morning across from Coimbra's Station A (€1.60,

Mon–Fri 9:05 and 9:35, Sat–Sun 9:35 only, AVIC bus stop is on the riverside opposite the station, 30-min trip). The return bus leaves from Conímbriga's parking lot (Mon–Sat 13:00 and 18:00, Sun 18:00 only). Two different companies serve the route: Joalto and AVIC. Confirm the destination by asking, *"Vai para Conímbriga?"* Otherwise, you could end up on one of the frequent buses to Condeixa (runs twice hourly) that stops a mile short of the ruins. Drivers should cross the Santa Clara Bridge and go uphill, following signs to Condeixa. Continue straight through town, and you will see brown signs guiding you to the ruins. Consider driving to Conímbriga on your way to or from Coimbra on Auto-Estrada A1; the freeway exit is clearly marked.

SLEEPING

These listings are an easy walk from the central Station A and Santa Clara Bridge. For the cheapest rooms, simply walk a block from Station A into the old town and choose one of countless *dormidas* (cheap pensions). River views come with traffic noise.

$$$ Hotel Astória gives you the thrill of staying in the city's finest old hotel (Sb-€89, Db-€105, extra bed-€30, includes breakfast, 10 percent discount in 2006 by showing this book at check-in, air-con, elevator—Coimbra's first, fine Art Deco lounges, ask hotel about parking or try public parking opposite hotel-€3/4 hrs, central as can be at Avenida Navarro 21, tel. 239-853-020, fax 239-822-057, www.almeidahotels.com, astoria@almeidahotels.com). Rooms with river views don't cost extra but come with some street noise. I prefer the quieter city-view rooms on the back.

$$ Hotel Bragança's dark lobby leads to 83 clean, comfortable, but sometimes smoky rooms, with modern bathrooms (Sb with

Sleep Code

(€1 = about $1.20, country code: 351)
S = Single, **D** = Double/Twin, **T** = Triple, **Q** = Quad, **b** = bathroom, **s** = shower only. Unless indicated otherwise, you can assume credit cards are accepted and English is spoken.

To help you easily sort through these listings, I've divided the rooms into three categories, based on the price for a standard double room with bath during high season (April–Sept). The rest of the year, it's 10 to 20 percent less.

$$$ Higher Priced—Most rooms €80 or more.
$$ Moderately Priced—Most rooms between €50–80.
$ Lower Priced—Most rooms €50 or less.

Coimbra Hotels and Restaurants

1. Hotel Astória
2. Hotel Bragança
3. Res. Moderna & Res. Domus
4. Ibis Hotel
5. Pensão Santa Cruz
6. Residencial Larbelo
7. Residência Coimbra
8. To Pousada de Juventude
9. Restaurante Trovador
10. Fado Diligencia
11. Adega Paço do Conde
12. Self-Service Rest. Jardim da Manga
13. Café Santa Cruz
14. Restaurante O Serenata
15. Restaurante Zé Manel
16. Restaurante Praça Velha
17. Casa Bizarro
18. Restaurante Itália
19. A Capella Fado Bar
20. Mondego Irish Pub & Other Eateries
21. Internet Coimbra Câmara Municipal
22. Spacenet Internet Café

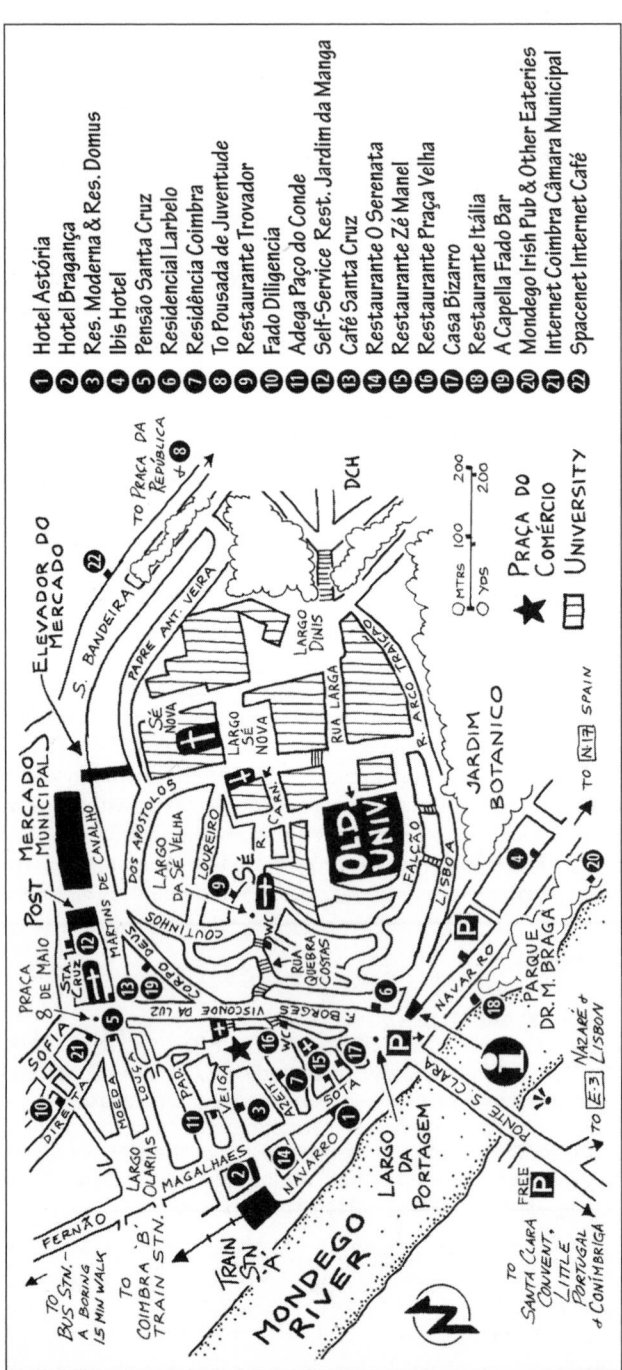

shower-€35, Sb with tub-€53, smaller Db with shower-€58, larger Db with tub-€68, Tb with tub-€85, Qb-€100, 10 percent discount with this book in 2006, includes breakfast, air-con, elevator, free parking in small lot if space available, Largo das Ameias 10, next to Station A, tel. 239-822-171, fax 239-836-135, hbraganza@mail .telepac.pt).

$ Residência Coimbra provides top hotel quality in a 10-year-old building for pension prices. Its 15 fine, air-conditioned rooms are buried in the old town on a quiet pedestrian lane, yet it's only 250 yards from Station A (Db-€45, 10 percent discount with this book in 2006, includes breakfast, all rooms have double beds, Rua das Azeiteiras 55, tel. 239-837-996, fax 239-838-124, Jose).

$ Residencial Moderna hides 17 delightful little rooms overlooking a pedestrian street. The six top-floor rooms come with parquet floors and a balcony—request *"com varanda"* (Sb-€20–30, Db-€45–50, prices soft off-season, breakfast free with this book in 2006, cash only, air-con, free parking nearby daily 20:00–8:00, Rua Adelino Veiga 49, 2nd floor, a block from Station A, tel. 239-825-413, fax 239-829-508, r.moderna@mail.pt, Fernandes family).

$ Residência Domus, across the street from the similar Residencial Moderna, rents 20 decent rooms in a cozy atmosphere (Sb-€25–28; Db-€25–30, Db with air-con-€35–40, double beds cheaper than twins; Tb-€45, 10 percent discount with this book in 2006, includes breakfast, Rua Adelino Veiga 62, tel. 239-828-584, fax 239-838-818, residencialdomus@sapo.pt, Sr. Santos).

$ Ibis Hotel, a modern high-rise, has 110 orderly little rooms that come with all the comforts. Well-located on a riverside park, this impersonal though reliable chain hotel is three blocks past the Santa Clara Bridge and the old town (Sb/Db-€50, breakfast-€5, 2 smoke-free floors, elevator, easy €3.50/day parking in basement, Avenida Emídio Navarro 70, tel. 239-852-130, fax 239-852-140, h1672@accor-hotels.com).

$ Pensão Santa Cruz overlooks the charming and traffic-free square called Praça 8 de Maio at the end of the pedestrian mall. It's a bright, homey place with 14 simple rooms that Vincent van Gogh would have enjoyed painting. You'll find lots of stairs, dim lights, and rickety balconies worth requesting (D-€15–23, Db-€25–30, most expensive June–Aug, prices are soft so ask for relief if you need it, cash only, Praça 8 de Maio 21, 3rd floor, tel. & fax 239-826-197, www.pensaosantacruz.com, mail@pensaosantacruz .com, Walter, Anna, and Oswald).

$ Residencial Larbelo, with Old World character, mixes frumpiness and former elegance. The old-fashioned staircase, classic breakfast room, and gentle, non-English-speaking management take you to another age (17 rooms, Sb-€25, Db-€40, Tb-€50, cheaper Oct–May, breakfast-€2.50, air-con, in front of the Santa

Clara Bridge at Largo da Portagem 33, tel. 239-829-092, fax 239-829-094).

$ Pousada de Juventude, the youth hostel, is on the other side of town in the student area past Praça da República. It's friendly, clean, and well-run, but is no cheaper than a simple *pensão* (€10.50 for members mid-June–mid-Sept, €8.50 off-season, 4- to 6-bed rooms, closed daily 12:00–18:00, Rua António Henriques Seco 14, coimbra@movijovem.pt, tel. 239-822-955).

EATING

Leitão (suckling pig), *cabrito* (baby male goat), and *chanfana* (goat cooked in wine) are specialties of this hilly Beira region. *Bairrada* and rich, red *Dão* wines, along with *Serra* cheeses, are produced in this area. The local pastries are *pastel de Santa Clara* (made with almonds and marmalade) and *pastel de Tentúgal* (flaky puff pastry filled with a sweet eggy mixture and dusted with powdered sugar).

Eating with Fado

Restaurante Trovador, while a bit touristy, serves good food in a classic and comfortable setting, with entertaining dinner fado performances nearly nightly in summer from 21:00 (Fri–Sat only off-season). It's *the* place for an old-town splurge (daily menu–€15–20, Mon–Sat 12:00–15:00 & 19:30–22:30, closed Sun, facing the old cathedral on Largo de Sé Velha 15, reservations essential to eat with the music—ask for a seat with a music view, tel. 239-825-475).

Fado Diligencia is a good spot for a fado sing-along in a warm, relaxed atmosphere, with or without dinner. They even know a few Beatles tunes, so request your favorite and take center stage if you're feeling bold. Food and drinks are reasonable, with a €5 minimum (€15 dinners, shows daily 22:30–2:00, Rua Nova 30; from Praça 8 de Maio, take Rua Sofia to your 2nd left, Diligencia is 2 blocks up on your right; tel. 239-827-667).

Eating without Fado

Adega Paço do Conde knows how to grill. Choose your seafood or meat selection from the display case as you enter. They'll pop it on the grill, serve it up, and then you can grab your table. Students, solo travelers, families, and pigeons like this homey place (€6 meals, Mon–Sat 11:00–22:00, closed Sun, Rua Paço do Conde 1; from Praça do Comércio, take the last left—Adelino Veiga, opposite the church, and walk 2 blocks to small square—Largo Paço do Conde; tel. 239-825-605, Alfredo).

Self-Service Restaurant Jardim da Manga is handy for a quick, easy, and cheap meal with locals. Sit indoors or outdoors next to a cool and peaceful fountain. Just slide a tray down the counter and pick what you like (€7 meals, Sun–Fri 12:00–14:30 & 19:00–22:00, closed Sat, in Jardim da Manga, behind Church of Santa Cruz, tel. 239-829-156).

Café Santa Cruz, next to the Church of Santa Cruz, is Old World elegant, with great coffee, simple toasted sandwiches, and outdoor tables offering great people-watching over Praça 8 de Maio (open daily).

Restaurante O Serenata is country-kitchen-cozy and fun, serving simple €7 meals (Mon–Sat 12:00–15:00 & 19:00–22:30, closed Sun, between train station and Largo da Portagem at Largo da Sota 6, tel. 239-826-729).

Restaurante Zé Manel is tiny, rustic, and authentically local. Judging from the walls—caked with notes from happy eaters—and the line of people waiting for a table, this place is a popular favorite. They serve about 20 local dishes (€8/1 meal, €14/2 meals, Mon–Sat 12:00–15:00 & 19:30–22:00, closed Sun, no reservations, arrive early or wait; unsigned restaurant is 20 yards directly behind Hotel Astória at Beco do Forno 12, tel. 239-823-790).

Restaurante Praça Velha is one of a few basic eateries—with waiters who aren't above conning tourists—serving acceptable meals on the wonderfully atmospheric square, Praça do Comércio (daily 8:00–24:00, Praça do Comércio 72).

Casa Bizarro is a small, white-tablecloth hole-in-the-wall serving up tasty Portuguese food at a good price (Sun–Fri 12:00–15:00 & 18:00–22:00, Sat 12:00–15:00, 30 yards behind Hotel Astória at Rua Sargento Mor 44).

Trendy Eating on the Riverside: Literally hanging over the river, modern **Restaurante Itália**—at Parque Dr. Manuel Braga, opposite the TI—serves good Italian food (€8 pizza and pastas, €10–12 meals, daily 12:00–24:00, reservations smart, riverside tables limited to parties of 4 in busy times, tel. 239-838-863). A small strip of hip restaurants opened nearby in 2005, all with modern indoor or breezy riverside seating. The **Mondego Irish Pub** serves hamburgers, steaks, and Irish beer with live music—generally Irish—most nights (daily from noon until after midnight, tel. 239-837-092).

Picnics: Shop at the colorful, covered market Mercado Municipal, behind the Church of Santa Cruz (see "Mercado Municipal," page 191; Mon–Sat 8:00–14:00, closed Sun) or at hole-in-the-wall *mini-mercados* in the side streets. The well-maintained gardens along the river across from the TI are picnic-pleasant.

TRANSPORTATION CONNECTIONS

From Coimbra by Bus to: Alcobaça (3/day, 90 min), **Batalha** (4/day with transfer in Leiria, 75 min), **Fátima** (9/day, 1 hr), **Nazaré** (6/day, 1.75 hrs), **Lisbon** (15/day, 2.5 hrs), **Évora** (4/day, 4.25 hrs), **Porto** (17/day, 1.5 hrs). Bus info: tel. 239-855-270. Frequency drops on weekends, especially Sunday.

By Train to: Nazaré/Valado (6/day, 3.5 hours, transfer in Bifurcação de Lares; the bus is a better option—see above—because Nazaré/Valado train station is 3 miles away from Nazaré), **Porto** (18/day, 1 hr on fast train, 2 hrs on slow train, most trains end at Porto's central São Bento Station), **Lisbon** (hrly, 2 hrs; for Lisbon center, get off at Santa Apolónia Station; for Lisbon airport, hop off at Oriente Station and take the bus to airport; all Coimbra/Porto trains stop at both stations 9 min apart). Train info: tel. 808-208-208, www.cp.pt.

To Salamanca, Spain: One **train** per day departs at 18:30 and drops you in Salamanca at 1:00 in the morning (5.5 hrs, note that Spanish time is 1 hour later). The far better option is the direct **bus** (€27, departs daily at 9:45, arrives at 17:00 in Salamanca, then continues on to Madrid, arriving at 20:00); to guarantee a place, book a couple of days in advance. You can confirm schedules and buy your bus ticket by phone or in person at the Abreu travel agency in Coimbra (see "Helpful Hints," page 188) more easily than at Coimbra's bus station (Intercentro office, tel. 239-827-588, no English spoken).

PORTO

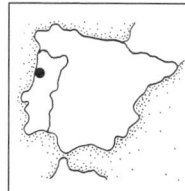

You can't get a complete picture of Portugal without a visit to Porto—the capital of the north, and the country's second city (with 265,000 residents and a metropolitan area sprawling to over a million). Porto is proud of the things that make it different, and fiercely clings to its long-standing rivalry with Lisbon...especially where soccer is concerned.

Porto is less polished than Lisbon, but it's also full of charm. Houses with red-tiled roofs tumble down the hills to the riverbank; prickly church towers dot the skyline; mosaic tiles line streets; and flat-bottomed boats called *rabelos* ply the lazy river.

The city's name comes from the Romans, who dubbed the port town Portus Cale. When Porto's Christians conquered the southern Moors in the Middle Ages, the city's name became the name of the whole country. The many British people who have shaped Porto have also dubbed it "Oporto" (literally "the port"), a corruption of the town's true name. While various guidebooks and postcards call it this, locals never do.

Porto's tourism slogan, "Authenti**city**," captures its gritty, warts-and-all character. The people of Porto claim they're working too hard to worry about being pretty; an oft-repeated saying is "Coimbra studies, Braga prays, Lisbon parties...and Porto works."

Straight-laced, nose-to-the-grindstone Porto has enjoyed something of a cultural renaissance in recent years. In 2001, it was designated as a European Capital of Culture. Two exciting showpieces of contemporary architecture have been built in the last five years: the Serralves Museum and the House of Music. European Union money has been pouring in, funding a revamping of the public transportation system and more. With this ongoing

Porto Overview

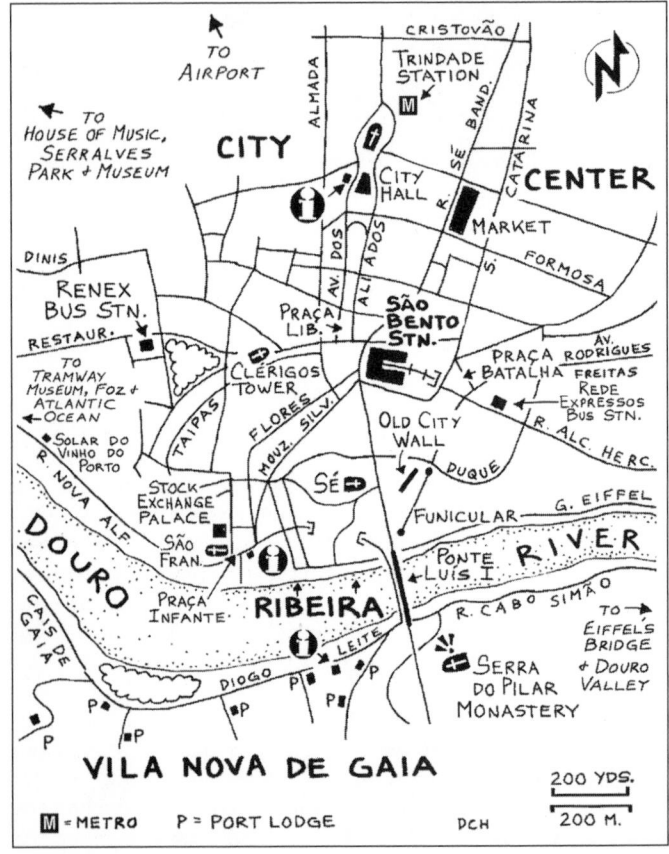

construction, Porto is ever-changing, often chaotic, and still well worth a visit. At a minimum, use it as a gateway to the stunning Douro Valley.

For visitors, Porto itself is interesting, offering two high-impact sightseeing thrills: the Old World, postcard-perfect ambience of the riverfront Ribeira district, and the opportunity to learn more about (and taste) the port wine that ages here. Porto also features other unexpected treats, including sumptuous Baroque churches and civic buildings, a bustling real-world market hall, and quirky but worthwhile museums.

Though the weather is always changing, it's usually marginal. You're likely to get sun and rain at the same time—when the locals exclaim, "The widow's going to remarry."

Planning Your Time

Porto offers one very busy day's worth of sightseeing (or better yet, 2 relaxed days). Begin your day by exploring the urban city center above the town (poke around the market hall and climb the Clérigos Tower for a visual orientation). Wander past the cathedral and clamber down one of the steep lanes to the Ribeira district for lunch. Spend 30 minutes each touring the breathtaking interiors of the Stock Exchange Palace and São Francisco Church. Then head across the river to tour a couple of port-wine lodges before returning to Ribeira for dinner. With a second day, slow down, taste more port, cruise the river, and add a visit to the Serralves Museum and Park.

Ideally, combine your visit to Porto with a trip up the Douro Valley (about 2 hrs away—see next chapter).

ORIENTATION

Porto (POR-too, as locals say) sprawls on the hilly north bank of the Douro River, near where the river meets the Atlantic Ocean. The tourist's Porto is compact, but confusing and steep—making distances seem longer. Get a good map and wear comfortable walking shoes (or just grab a taxi whenever you need a quick connection).

It helps to think of the tourist's Porto in two parts: The first is the **Ribeira** (ree-BAY-rah), right on the river, with a twisty street plan and oodles of ambience. Praça Infante Dom Henrique (Henry the Navigator Square), near the top of the Ribeira, has several intriguing sights, including the Stock Exchange Palace and São Francisco Church. From here, ramshackle old homes scramble steeply uphill toward the second part...

The modern **city center,** hovering above the Ribeira, surrounds the broad boulevard called Avenue of the Allies (Avenida dos Aliados). This area is the decaying urban heart of Porto, packed with office buildings and shoppers and peppered with hotels. You'll also find a smattering of squares, monuments, and sights (including the market hall and cathedral). At the top of the hill, the Clérigos Tower stands as the city's most recognizable landmark.

Across the river shine the neon signs of Porto's main tourist attraction, the port wine cellars *(caves do vinho do porto)* in **Vila Nova de Gaia,** technically another town.

The Douro is spanned by six bridges (2 steel, 4 concrete). The only one you're likely to cross is the monstrous steel **Ponte Dom Luís I** (cars and pedestrians use lower level; upper level for Metro trains only).

Visitors venturing farther out find Porto to be a city of contrasts. Its outskirts boast bright, spacious, prim residential neighborhoods, like those around **Serralves Museum and Park.**

Tourist Information

Porto has two TIs: in the **city center** across from City Hall (at the top of Avenida dos Aliados, Rua Clube dos Fenianos 25, tel. 223-393-472 or 223-293-470); and at the top of **Ribeira,** a block above the river, kitty-corner from the Stock Exchange Palace (Rua Infante Dom Henrique 63, tel. 222-009-770; both TIs open June–mid-Sept daily 9:00–19:00, mid-Sept–May Mon–Fri 9:00–17:30, Sat–Sun 9:30–16:30, www.portoturismo.pt).

Pick up the free, one-page city map with sights and hotels and the useful information pamphlet. They also sell reasonable museum booklets and city walk guides (€1–2), none of which is essential. The Porto Tour Pass, covering public transport plus minor discounts at sights, isn't a good value for most visitors. The free, quarterly *Agenda do Porto* guide lists cultural events in the city in Portuguese and English (www.agendadoporto.pt).

In the main TI on Avenida dos Aliados, you'll also find the helpful **transport office** (called Loja da Mobilidade). They can answer your questions about transportation to, within, or out of Porto; they can especially help you understand the bus-station mess (see "Arrival in Porto," below) and get a handle on the ever-changing local transit picture (toll-free tel. 800-220-905, www.cm-porto.pt).

Arrival in Porto

By Train: Porto has two train stations. Regional trains, including those serving the Douro Valley, use the very central **São Bento Station** (for a description of this beautifully decorated station, see "Sights—In the City Center," on page 218).

Trains coming from farther away, including Lisbon and Coimbra, arrive at the similarly manageable **Campanhã Station,** on the east edge of town. If your train stops at both stations, get off at São Bento (it's closer to hotels). If you have to get off at Campanhã, you have three options for getting into the center: Take a taxi to your hotel (figure €7 with luggage to most city-center accommodations); catch a train to the São Bento Station (6/hr, free on any ticket to Porto); or use the new Metro across the street (take it to the Trindade stop downtown).

By Bus: Confusingly, each of Porto's many bus companies operates its own garage, meaning there's no central bus station.

The transport desk in the main TI can clear up the confusion (see "Tourist Information," above). All of the garages are more or less in the city center. Here are a few of the more useful companies, with their addresses and telephone numbers: **Rede Expressos** (abbreviated RE, to Lisbon and Coimbra; Rua Alexandre Herculano, tel. 222-006-954, www.rede-expressos.pt); **RENEX** (to Lisbon; Campo Mártires da Pátria, tel. 222-003-395); **Rodonorte** (to Lisbon and Coimbra; Rua Ateneu Comercial do Porto, tel. 222-004-398, www.rodonorte.pt); and **Internorte** (to Spain, including Santiago de Compostela and Madrid; Praça da Galiza 96, tel. 226-052-420).

By Car: Porto is a headache by car. Stow it at your hotel or a nearby parking garage. Approaching from Lisbon and Coimbra on the A-1 expressway, pay a toll and then follow signs for Ponte da Arrábida. After crossing the bridge, take the first right and follow *centro* signs (or the little bull's-eyes) into downtown.

By Plane: Porto's airport is 11 miles north of the city center. Since it's international (with connections beyond Iberia), it's used by people throughout northern Portugal and Spain. The new Metro connects the airport to the center (Trindade stop). You can also take the STCP Aerobus (€4, every 30 min from 7:30–19:00, drops you right downtown at Avenida dos Aliados) or a taxi (figure €20). Airport info: tel. 229-432-400.

Helpful Hints
Closed Day: Virtually all Porto museums are closed on Monday.

Festivals: June 24th is St. João Day, Porto's big holiday, with a *rabelo* regatta and late-night partying.

Internet Access: OnWeb Cyber Bar is a handy, cheap Internet café with fast access and great ambience (Mon–Sat 10:00–2:00 in the morning, Sun 15:00–2:00 in the morning, a block below TI at Avenida dos Aliados 291).

Laundry: A convenient, full-service laundry hides almost underground at the west end of the Ribeira district (between São Francisco Church and the river on Rua da Reboleira). Drop off your laundry, pay €6 for the load, wander the Ribeira, and pick it up two hours later (Mon 8:30–13:00, Tue–Fri 8:30–19:30, Sat 8:30–19:00, closed Sun).

Best Views: There are fine views all along the Ribeira riverfront embankment, but they're even better from across the river in Vila Nova de Gaia (looking back toward Porto). You'll enjoy the views from the top of Clérigos Tower, from the terrace next to the cathedral, or from Mosteiro da Serra do Pilar (the monastery across the river, just above the big steel Ponte Dom Luís I bridge). But the best vantage point of all is from a boat in the river itself (see "Cruising the Douro," page 215).

Porto at a Glance

▲▲**Port Wine Lodges at Vila Nova de Gaia** Porto's single best activity: touring the cellars where its most famous product ages... and tasting some, too. **Hours:** Varies; generally daily, last tours at 18:00, some lodges closed Sat–Sun.

▲▲**Strolling the Ribeira Embankment** Exploring Porto's picturesque riverfront, with its arcades and colorful Old World homes. **Hours:** Always open.

▲**São Francisco Church** Gothic church dripping with Baroque gold. **Hours:** Daily March–Oct 9:00–18:00, Nov–Feb 9:00–17:00.

▲**Stock Exchange Palace** Astonishing monument to civic pride, with room after sumptuous room. **Hours:** By tour only, daily April–Oct 9:00–19:00, Nov–March 9:00–13:00 & 14:00–18:00.

▲**Cruising the Douro** Lazy one-hour cruises up and down the river offering the city's best views. **Hours:** Generally daily 10:00–20:00 in summer (until 17:00 off-season).

▲**Clérigos Church and Tower** Porto's towering landmark, with a 225-step climb to sweeping views over the urban sprawl. **Hours:** Daily April–Oct 9:30–13:00 & 14:30–19:00, Nov–March until 17:00.

▲**São Bento Train Station** Entry hall decorated with huge and impressive azulejo-tile murals. **Hours:** Always open.

Getting Around Porto

The city is currently engaged in what is supposedly Europe's biggest construction project—extending their tramlines and gradually building a new, mostly-above-ground Metro. (Smug Lisboners love to tease that only Porto would build an above-ground "underground.")

Porto's public transportation system can be confusing and is often changing, but here's what the picture *should* look like in 2006: The network includes buses, trams, the new Metro, and a funicular (see next page). **Buses** are handy for getting to the Serralves Museum and Park (#78), or to the port-wine lodges in Vila Nova de Gaia, across the river (#57 and #91). The only **tram** line of interest to a tourist is #1E, with a historic car that shudders along the river from the Ribeira, past several museums, to the Foz district (see "Tram to Foz" on page 216). **Metro** lines include Blue (connecting Campanhã Station to the center), Yellow (includes São Bento Station and Vila Nova de Gaia, across the river; likely not

▲**Market** Lively, old-fashioned produce and meat market...with old-fashioned sanitary conditions. **Hours:** Mon–Fri 8:30–17:00, Sat 8:30–13:00, closed Sun.

▲**Serralves Foundation Contemporary Art Museum and Park** Sprawling park with impressive museum, Art Deco mansion, and relaxing grounds. **Hours:** Museum open April–Sept Tue–Thu 10:00–19:00, Fri–Sat 10:00–22:00, Sun 10:00–20:00 (until 19:00 Oct–March), closed Mon; park and house open Tue–Sun 10:00–20:00 (open Sat–Sun until 19:00 Oct–March), closed Mon.

▲**Solar do Vinho do Porto** Classy, one-stop spot for port tastings. **Hours:** Mon–Sat 14:00–24:00, closed Sun.

Tramway Museum Collection tracing the history of electrical transport. **Hours:** Tue–Fri 9:30–12:30 & 14:30–18:00, Sat–Sun 15:00–19:00, closed Mon.

House of Henry the Navigator Birthplace of the explorer, with history exhibits. **Hours:** Tue–Sat 10:00–12:30 & 14:00–17:30, Sun 14:00–17:30, closed Mon.

Cathedral Monstrous church overlooking the town, with fine azulejo-decorated cloister and otherwise dull interior. **Hours:** Church open daily in summer 9:00–12:30 & 14:30–19:00, until 18:00 in winter; cloister open daily in summer 9:00–12:15 & 14:30–18:00, until 17:15 in winter, closed Sun morning.

complete in 2006), and Red (connecting the airport to the center and Campanhã Station, ready by 2006). All Metro lines converge at the Trindade stop, two blocks behind the city hall and Avenida dos Aliados.

Prices are confusing, since the bus and Metro systems don't entirely cooperate. Your fare depends on your mode of transportation and which "zones" you travel in. If you plan to use public transit for non-stop sightseeing, get the **Euro pass** (€4/1 day, €9/3 days), which covers all types of transportation in all zones.

While an **Andante** card gets you cheaper tickets on the Metro, trams, funiculars, and buses (buy for €0.50, recharge with more credit at TIP vending machines and kiosks), I'd keep it simple and just pay a premium by picking up single tickets (€1.30) from the driver as you board.

By Funicular: A handy funicular (Elevador dos Guindais) connects the Ribeira district (at the base of the Ponte Dom Luís I bridge) to the top of the steep hill above (at the remains of the city wall, down the Rua de Augusto Rosa from Praça da Batalha). If you're dining in the Ribeira, note that the funicular stops running at 20:00 (€1, every 10 min, daily 8:00–20:00).

By Taxi: Taxis are a good option in this hilly city. Most rides are fairly short and cost only around €3. For rides within the city limits, the meter should be on T1 during the day (€1.90 drop charge) and T2 at night (21:00–6:00, €2.25 drop charge). Each kilometer costs about €0.40. A luggage surcharge of €1.50 is legit. It's easy to find taxi stands, and you'll pay €0.75 more to call one (try Invicta, tel. 225-076-400).

TOURS

The city of Porto operates an ingenious, extremely useful agency called **Porto Tours** (daily April–Oct 9:00–19:00, Nov–March 9:00–17:30, in old medieval watchtower next to cathedral at Calçada Dom Pedro Pitões 15, tel. 222-000-073, www.portotours .com, portotours@mail.telepac.pt). This organization, which takes no commission and is not biased toward any particular company, will help you sort through all of the walking, bus, boat, and even helicopter tour options in Porto and up the Douro. They'll also confirm times, answer questions, and sell tickets for any of the following tours.

While there are no regularly scheduled English walking tours, Porto Tours can help you arrange for a private **local guide** (around €100/half-day). Maria Jose Aleixo is good (€85/half-day, tel. 962-700-156, aleixo19@sapo.pt).

In this steep, tiring city, a **bus tour** is worth considering. You have two options: a typical, stay-mainly-on-the-bus tour (€30, 3.5 hrs, live guide in 4 languages) and a hop-on, hop-off version (€13, 2-hr circuit with 9 stops, can hop off and catch a later bus, 1 bus/hr, daily 10:00–16:00). There's also a silly **tourist train** that includes a stop at a port-wine lodge across the river (€6, 75 min, 2/hr, leaves from in front of cathedral daily on the hour, 10:00–17:00 in high season, less frequently off-season, tel. 800-203-983). For bus tours of the town and side-trips to the Douro Valley and even Santiago, consider the strangely named "Rent A Cab" tour company (details at Porto Tours, www.rentacab.pt).

SIGHTS

Along the Riverfront

The riverfront Ribeira (ree-BAY-rah; literally, "riverbank") district is where it's at in Porto. It's the city's most scenic and touristy quarter, with the highest concentration of good restaurants (and postcard racks). I've listed these sights beginning in the Ribeira, then stretching west (toward the Foz district).

▲▲**Strolling the Ribeira Embankment and Cais e Praça da Ribeira (Square)**—This is Porto's best lazy-afternoon activity. As you stroll, imagine the busy port scene before the promenade

was reclaimed from the river—riverboats laden with cargo lashed to the embankment, off-loading their wine and produce into 14th-century cellars (still visible). The old arcades lining the Ribeira promenade are jammed with hole-in-the-wall restaurants (most not as "local" as they seem) and souvenir shops. Behind the arcades stand skinny, colorful houses draped with drying laundry fluttering like proud flags, while the locals who fly them stand on their little balconies, gossiping. Riverfront property taxes were based on frontage—promoting the construction of these narrow, deep, and undeniably picturesque buildings.

The Ribeira neighborhood looks up at the Ponte Dom Luís I bridge, rising 150 feet above the river. In the 1880s, Teofilo Seyfrig, a protégé of Gustave Eiffel, stretched this Eiffel Tower–sized, wrought-iron contraption across the 500-foot-wide Douro. Eiffel himself built a bridge in Porto, the Ponte Dona Maria Pia, a bit upstream.

While it offers few individual sights, the Ribeira is Porto's most enjoyable area for killing time and basking in Old World ambience. Shoppers eventually find **O Cântaro,** run by the English-speaking Oliveira family (Mon–Sat 9:00–19:00, closed Sun, a block back from embankment near the east end—toward the bridge—at Rua da Lada 50-56, tel. 223-320-670). Among the trinkets for sale are ceramics, hand-painted tiles, embroidery, and filigree. Ask them for a filigree-making demonstration to see tiny gold and silver wires twisted and soldered into intricate patterns.

▲**Cruising the Douro**—One-hour "Six Bridges" cruises, operated by several different companies, leave continually from the Ribeira riverfront. These relaxing excursions float up and down the river, offering a fine orientation and glimpses of all of Porto's bridges (including the majestic steel Ponte Dona Maria

Pia, right next to the new concrete Ponte de São João). The boats, which generally run daily 10:00–20:00 in summer (until 17:00 off-season), come in two types: smaller, traditional *rabelos* (€7.50) and bigger, modern cruise boats (€5–8). Each tour is essentially the same. Shop around a bit before committing to a boat (to avoid being over-charged).

Moored in Porto, and all along the Douro River, are the old-fashioned boats called *rabelos*. These were once the only way to transport the wine downriver to Porto. These boats, which look Oriental, have flat bottoms, a big square sail, and a very large rudder to help them navigate the rough, twisty course of the river. The region's famous port wine is produced about 60 miles up the river (see next chapter) and aged in lodges here.

▲**Solar do Vinho do Porto**—This port-wine-tasting facility, operated by the Port and Douro Wines Institute (which runs a similar place in Lisbon—see page 52), is Porto's finest spot for sampling a stunning array of ports. The price per taste or per bottle depends on the quality of the port, from €1 to a small fortune (light food, but no meals). If they call it "port," you'll find it here, in plush tasting rooms inhabiting an elegant old villa and river-view tables in the garden—delightful at sunset. While it's more fun to tour the cellars across the river, this is a handy one-stop opportunity to try several ports. And after 18:00, when all the lodges close, this stays open (Mon–Sat 14:00–24:00, closed Sun, Rua de Entre Quintas 220, tel. 226-094-749, www.ivp.pt). The villa shares a lush park with a domed sports hall, just up from the river beyond the Ribeira in the direction of Foz (see below). Take tram #1E from Ribeira, then hike uphill; or, from the city center, take bus #3 from Praça Liberdade (bottom of Avenida dos Aliados). Your best bet is to taxi to and from here, as this place is fairly far from anything else I've described in this chapter.

Tramway Museum (Museu do Carro Eléctrico)—If you like electric public transit, you'll love this clever place, which traces the history of Porto's trams from the horse-drawn versions (the first in Iberia) to today's super-modern and still-under-construction Metro (€3.50, Tue–Fri 9:30–12:30 & 14:30–18:00, Sat–Sun 15:00–19:00, closed Mon, Alameda Basílio Teles 51, take tram #1E from Ribeira—see below, tel. 226-158-185, http://museu-carro-electrico.stcp.pt).

Tram to Foz—Antique tram cars (line #1E) scenically rattle their way from the Ribeira district (in front of São Francisco Church, see below), along the Douro, to the Foz district (buy €1.30 ticket from driver, good

for 1 hr, or use Andante card or Euro pass, trip takes about 20 min, departures generally at top and bottom of each hour until around 21:00).

Foz do Douro (or simply "Foz") is one of Porto's trendiest, greenest, wealthiest, and most relaxing quarters, situated where the river meets the Atlantic. There's no real destination in Foz; simply wander through the park (Jardim do Passeio Alegre, with miniature golf, fancy old WC pavilion, and a nondescript café), hike up to the lighthouse, ponder the sea, watch fishermen mending their nets, smell the seaweed, and tram back.

Near Praça Infante Dom Henrique

These sights are on or near Praça Infante Dom Henrique (Henry the Navigator Square), a long block uphill from the Ribeira district.

▲**São Francisco Church**—This is Porto's only church in the Gothic style—complete with a rose window, stair-step buttresses, and a statue of St. Francis of Assisi on the front. Today it's a museum with three parts: a so-so collection of items from the church and monastery; the strange but boring catacombs *(ossário)* under the church, tightly packed with the bones of former parishioners (the bodies left under the wooden floor boards to rot and then transferred to the neat little niches in the walls); and, the unquestionable highlight, the extravagant Baroque interior, from the 17th and 18th centuries.

While ravaged by Napoleon and during Portugal's 19th-century civil war, the interior remains stunning, with lavish wood carvings slathered in some 900 pounds of gold. Wander down the main aisle like a bewildered 18th-century peasant. On the right, find the monks being beheaded by Moors. On the left, find the over-the-top Jesse's Tree (1718), a very literal interpretation of the family tree of Jesus, resting upon Mary—here, St. Mary of good voyages, the patron saint of navigators (€3 gets you into all 3 sections, daily March–Oct 9:00–18:00, Nov–Feb 9:00–17:00, Rua Infante Dom Henrique, tel. 222-062-100).

▲**Stock Exchange Palace (Palácio da Bolsa)**—This unassuming building is neither a stock exchange nor a palace, but a breathtaking monument to civic and commercial pride, with some of the most lavishly decorated rooms in Portugal.

The people of Porto have always taken pride in being hard workers. Commerce came to define Porto, as royalty or religion would define other cities (like Lisbon and Braga, respectively). The Commercial Association of Porto (Associação Comercial do Porto) even had its own system of courts and representative to the king. In 1832, the monastery of the São Francisco Church burned down, and the queen offered the property to the Commercial Association. They seized the opportunity to show off, crafting a building that would demonstrate the considerable skill of Porto's tradesmen.

You'll tour a dozen rooms. The place is rife with symbolism and intricate, time-consuming craftsmanship intended only to impress: the complex patterned floors, carefully pieced together with Brazilian and African wood (only from Portugal's colonies); an incredibly detailed inlaid table, created over three years using wood scraps from those same floors; a room that looks like it's made of finely carved woodwork and bronze—until you realize it's all painted plaster and gold leaf. Almost everything is original; little refurbishment has been needed.

The knock-your-socks-off finale is the sumptuous Arabian Room. This grand hall—inspired by Granada's Alhambra, and painstakingly decorated in Moorish style over 18 years with wood, plaster, and gold leaf—is an explosion of civic pride.

The "Palace" can only be visited on a guided tour. (The building still houses the offices of the Chamber of Commerce, and is often rented out for events.) Tours leave every 30 minutes in whatever language is necessary (often English, plus another language). You may have to wait up to 30 minutes for an English tour; it's easy to call ahead to set up an appointment (€5, daily April–Oct 9:00–19:00, Nov–March 9:00–13:00 & 14:00–18:00, in big building marked "Associação Comercial do Porto" on Rua Ferreira Borges, tel. 223-399-013, www.palaciodabolsa.pt).

House of Henry the Navigator (Casa do Infante)—Porto's favorite son was supposedly born in this mansion 600 years ago. While the current exhibits on Porto's medieval history are pretty worthless (hence the free admission), the museum plans to expand for 2006 (Tue–Sat 10:00–12:30 & 14:00–17:30, Sun 14:00–17:30, closed Mon, Rua da Alfândega 10, tel. 226-081-000). For more on Hank, see page 128.

In the City Center

There aren't many museums in the modern urban sector of Porto, but there are a handful of interesting squares, churches, and monuments. I've listed these sights in walking order—roughly from top to bottom, beginning at City Hall (near the TI) and working downhill toward the cathedral and then back around through the shopping district.

Avenue of the Allies (Avenida dos Aliados)—This is the main urban drag of Porto—named for the alliance created in 1387 when the Portuguese King John I married the English princess Philippa, establishing a long and happy trading partnership between the two nations. This strip is where the city goes to work. Lined with elaborate examples of various architectural eras (mostly Art Nouveau and Art Deco), it reminds me of Prague's

Wenceslas Square. It's watched over at the top by the huge city hall (Câmara Municipal). Behind that is the Trindade Church, and nearby you'll find the station (also called Trindade) where all of Porto's Metro lines converge.

At the bottom of the avenue is **Praça da Liberdade** (Liberty Square). Stand on the tiny island with the single yucca tree. A few steps in front of you is an equestrian statue of Dom Pedro—a hero in the 1832 Civil War who advocated for a limited, constitutional monarchy. Dom Pedro won...and he's holding the constitution to prove it.

Orient yourself with this spin tour, using an imaginary clock for a compass. Start by facing the horse. The city hall is at the top of the square. At about 1 o'clock (behind trees) is the "Imperial McDonald's," perhaps the fanciest in Europe (formerly the Imperial Café). Check it out and ponder the battle of cultural elegance against global economic efficiency. At 3 o'clock is the blue-tiled church of St. Ildefonso (up the hill, in the shopping district). At 4 o'clock (50 yards away) is the corner of the São Bento Train Station. And at 9 o'clock is Clérigos Church, with its famous view tower.

Clérigos Church and Tower (Igreja e Torre dos Clérigos)—This oval-shaped church with a disproportionately tall tower is the masterwork of Nicolau Nasoni, the man who chose to go for Baroque (see sidebar on next page).

The real attraction is climbing the tower—one of Porto's icons. Two hundred twenty-five steps take you 250 feet up to the top, where you'll be greeted by a jumble of tightly packed red roofs and commanding views over the city. Nasoni built the tower in six sections, each one more elaborate than the last, topped with a round dome and spiked with pinnacles. Imagine trying to climb this tower from the outside, then consider that a father-son duo did just that in 1917 (€1.50 daily April–Oct 9:30–13:00 & 14:30–19:00, Nov–March until 17:00, Rua São Filipe de Nery, tel. 222-001-729).

The little, frilly, white building across the square is worth a peek. **Lello & Irmão bookstore,** built in 1906, boasts a lacy exterior and a fancy Art Nouveau interior. It looks like wood, but it's

Nicolau Nasoni
(1661–1773)

In the 1720s—a boom time in Porto—the Italian Nasoni found work as a painter in Porto. His swirling, colorful paintings wowed Porto, and Nasoni got plenty of work. He married a Portuguese woman, had five kids, and made Porto his home. Soon he was employed as an architect, hiring skilled local artisans to turn his trademark cherubs, garlands, and cumulus clouds into granite, wood, and poured plaster. Even stark medieval churches had their facades topped with Baroque towers and their interiors paneled and spackled in billowy, gilded designs. Prolific to the max, Nasoni redid Porto in the Baroque style (much as Bernini did in Rome), creating palaces and churches throughout the area.

The Clérigos Church, which consumed three decades of his life (1731–1763), shows his flair for theatrics. He fit the structure into its hilltop location, putting the tower at the back on the highest ground, dramatically reinforcing its height. Nasoni worked in stages: first the church, then the Chapter House (residence for priests and monks), and topped it all off with the tower.

The church facade displays Nasoni's characteristic frills, garlands, and zigzags. Inside is an oval-shaped nave built out of granite and marble but covered with ornate carvings. See the high altar—a wedding-cake structure with Mary on top—and the tomb of Nasoni, who asked to be buried here.

mostly made of painted plaster with gold leaf. Follow the quaint tracks to the book trolley. Climb the sagging staircase to a cute tearoom (Rua das Carmelitas 144).

Backtrack, crossing Avenida dos Aliados, and continue on to the...

▲**São Bento Train Station (Estação São Bento)**—The main entry hall of this otherwise dull station features some of Portugal's finest azulejos. These vivid, decorative, hand-painted tiles show historical and folk scenes from the Douro region. Tiles on the left (when facing the tracks) show local forces preparing to reconquer the south of Portugal and add it to the kingdom. Tiles on the opposite wall (far right when looking at the tracks) show the 1387 wedding of Portugal's King John I and the English princess Philippa, which established the Portuguese-English alliance. (Notice the fine portrait of Philippa and the depiction of the cathedral as it looked in the 14th century.) Below is the immediate result of the marriage—their son, Prince Henry the Navigator, shown conquering Ceuta for Portugal in 1415. While humble Ceuta was just a small chip of Morocco (across from Gibraltar), it marked an important first step in the creation of a soon-to-be vast Portuguese empire. The track-side tiles celebrate the traditional economy, such as the transport of port wine. The multicolored tiles near the top trace the history of transportation, starting with Roman chariots (in the corner above Henry) and culminating in the arrival of the first train. Notice the words "Douro" and "Minho" near the ceiling. These are the major rivers in this part of Portugal and the key regions linked by these trains. Porto's favorite meeting point is right here, "under the clock."

To orient from the station, stand outside with your back to the main entrance. Over your right shoulder (2 blocks up the hill) is Praça da Batalha (Battle Square), the gateway to Porto's shopping district and old-fashioned market hall (see "Porto's Shopping Neighborhood," below). At your 2 o'clock is the bottom of Avenida dos Aliados. On the hill to your left is the cathedral. And the streets in front of you and to the left lead down to Ribeira.

Cathedral (Sé)—This hulking, fortress-like, 12th-century Romanesque cathedral—graced with an 18th-century Baroque remodel job—is gloomy and stark inside. While big and important, it's actually pretty dull. But the adjacent cloister and the main altarpiece make a visit worthwhile. The altarpiece sums up the exuberance of Porto in the 1720s, when the city was booming, the local bishop was temporarily away in Lisbon, and Italian Baroque was sweeping through town. On the

side walls flanking the altar are faded, fake-architecture paintings by Nicolau Nasoni (see sidebar, page 220), the Italian who came to Porto to paint the cathedral's sacristy and soon became Porto's most influential architect. See his grand staircase out in the cloister (and see his Clérigos Church, page 219).

The cloister's walls are decorated with elaborate azulejo tiles illustrating the amorous poetry of the Bible's Song of Songs. The €0.50 pamphlet is pretty skimpy, but the well-produced €5 English guidebook explains it all, including the text that inspired the azulejos (cathedral entry free, open daily in summer 9:00–12:30 & 14:30–19:00, until 18:00 in winter; cloister and sacristy cost

€2 to enter, daily in summer 9:00–12:15 & 14:30–18:00, until 17:15 in winter, closed Sun morning; Terreiro da Sé, tel. 222-059-028).

In the cathedral's small square, you'll find a fine view of the old town, a 20th-century column standing where the old pillory once doled out harsh justice, and the massive **Bishop's Palace,** still the home of the bishop and his offices. The immensity of this 18th-century building reflects the bishop's power in that era. It dominates the skyline of Porto. A surviving gate from Porto's two-mile-long wall, which protected the city in the 14th century, currently houses the **Porto Tours** office (an excellent resource for information on all kinds of activities in the city—see "Tours," page 214).

Facing the cathedral, walk around to the left to the statue of Vímara Peres, a Christian warrior who reconquered this region from the Moors in 868 (it was lost again within 2 generations and remained under Muslim control until the final reconquest in about 1100). From here, survey the city and find the church with the blue facade in the distance. The São Bento Train Station is just to its right, and the copper dome of the city hall breaks the skyline above it. Below you spreads the seedy district called "Sé" (meaning "his eminence," the bishop's honorific). This neighborhood, the oldest in town, is run-down and depopulating; the government is encouraging people to move in by luring them with economic incentives. The atmospheric streets beyond the medieval gate twist their way down into the Ribeira district.

A 300-yard walk up the street behind the cathedral (to the bottom of Rua da Augusto Rosa) takes you to the impressive last remains of the town wall (access from the leafy square for fine river views), and the top of the Funicular dos Guindais (which zips down to the Ribeira riverfront). Hike two blocks up Rua da Augusto Rosa to Praça da Batalha (described below) and the start of the shopping district.

Porto's Shopping Neighborhood

Porto's bustling, local-feeling shopping district is a wonderful place to people-watch. Most of the action is along Rua Santa Catarina, which runs roughly parallel to Avenida dos Aliados a few blocks east. Begin at Praça da Batalha (just up Rua 31 de Janeiro from São Bento Station), and follow this route to the Old World market hall.

Praça da Batalha (Battle Square)—This neglected square has a fine azulejo-tiled church, the Igreja de Santo Ildefonso (its blue tiles reminiscent of Moorish patios, depicting scenes from the life of the church's patron saint), the 19th-century National Theater (originally the Opera House), and the deserted but impressive Art Deco Cinema Batalha. This square, with its inviting benches, is where the old guys hang out. At the north end of the square, branching off to the left of the blue-tiled church, is...

▲**Rua Santa Catarina**—Porto's main shopping street is busy and (mostly) traffic-free by day, quiet by night. A stroll along here gives you a sense for today's Porto—as well as yesterday's, including the

venerable Art Nouveau Café Majestic, the circa-1900 hangout for the local intelligentsia. Step in. Porto's pet name for a little coffee is *cimbalino*—named for the traditional Italian espresso-making machines. Outside Café Majestic (on the nearby corner), the FNAC department store has an Art Deco glockenspiel performance (daily at 9:00, 12:00, 15:00, and 18:00) in which Henry the Navigator, St. John the Baptist—Porto's patron saint—and two poets (who look like Lincoln and Einstein) parade around.

The Rua Santa Catarina sidewalk is a good example of Calçada Portuguesa, Portugal's unique limestone and basalt mosaic work. It's handmade and high-maintenance...but apparently worth the effort and expense to locals. Notice all of the shoe stores. Along with wine, northern Portugal's industry is powered by textile and shoe factories.

If you head up the street two blocks and turn left on Rua Formosa (note the Pearl of the Market shop at #279, filled with traditional and edible souvenirs), you'll run into the...

▲**Market (Bolhão)**—Porto's vibrant, traditional market still thrives, despite competition from newer shopping malls. This is a great place to wander—especially in the morning—and take in the sights, sounds, and smells of real-world Porto (Mon–Fri 8:30–17:00, Sat 8:30–13:00, closed Sun).

As you enter, the butchers are to the left, the fishermen to the right, and produce and flowers dead ahead. Check out the butcher section, with half-pigs hanging from the ceiling, and display cases full of unusual specialties...such as *sangue cozido* (coagulated cow blood). Then wander through the seafood section. If it's springtime, you may see a favorite local delicacy pulled from the river: *lampreia* (eel). They say eels are so tasty because they dine on the flavorful garbage in the Douro. The market's old-fashioned sanitary conditions aren't quite up to European Union snuff, but the EU seems to look the other way.

Around the market are lively shops. At one corner is Casa

Horticula, with a wide variety of seeds. In bakery windows, the big, round, dark breads are called *broa*, made with corn and rye, and the breads with bits of sausage baked in are *folar*. The cheeses on display are either *ovelha* (sheep) or *cabra* (goat). *Bom-apetite!*

Port Wine Lodges in Vila Nova de Gaia

Just across the river from Porto, the town of Vila Nova de Gaia is where much of the world's port wine comes to mature. Port-wine grapes are grown, and a young port is produced, about 60 miles upstream, in the Douro Valley. Then, after sitting for a winter in silos, the wine is shipped here, to age for years in lodges on this cool, north-facing bank of the Douro. Eighteen companies run these lodges, holding down the

port fort and offering tours and tastings. For wine connoisseurs, touring a port-wine lodge *(cave do vinho do porto)* and sampling the product is a ▲▲ attraction. Like so many miniature "Hollywood" signs climbing the riverbank, you'll see the 18 different company names proudly marking their lodges in Vila Nova de Gaia.

Venturing into Vila Nova de Gaia is well worth the trip. But to taste port from all the lodges under one roof without leaving Porto, visit the Solar do Vinho do Porto (see page 216).

Orientation: Vila Nova de Gaia (or just "Gaia") is technically a separate town from Porto, even though it's just across the river and feels like part of the city. The town operates its own handy **TI** with information about the lodges (mid-June–mid-Sept daily 10:00–18:00, closed Sun off-season, on the riverbank near Sandeman lodge at Avenida Diogo Leite 242, tel. 223-703-735, www.cm-gaia.pt).

Getting to Vila Nova de Gaia: Simply walk (or catch a cab) from the Ribeira district across the big, steel Ponte Dom Luís I bridge. From the city center, take bus #32 from Avenida dos Aliados, or bus #57 or #91 from Praça Almeida Garrett (in front of São Bento Station). After crossing the bridge, the bus stops first at the Calem lodge, then near Sandeman and the TI.

Tours and Tastings: Port tasting is a subjective business, and no single lodge is necessarily the best. If you're a port enthusiast, you probably already have a favorite (or can quickly decide on one, with a little enjoyable research). Though more serious European visitors choose one lodge to visit, American tourists are known to hop between three or four in a single day...before stumbling back to their hotels. Allow 30 minutes per visit.

At any lodge, the procedure is about the same. Individual

travelers simply show up and ask for a tour, passing any wait time by learning about the port (via posted information or a video) or getting started on the tasting. Sometimes the tours and tastings are free; other times, there's a modest entry fee (which is refunded if you buy a bottle). Before you go (or while waiting for your tour), educate yourself by reading the "Port Wine Crash Course" sidebar, next

page; "Brits on the Douro," on page 244; and "Growing—and Stomping—Grapes in the Douro Valley," on page 244.

The highest-profile company, **Sandeman,** is sort of the Budweiser of port—a good first stop for novices. They were the first port producer to create a logo for their product, which you'll see everywhere: a mysterious man wearing a black cloak (representing a Portuguese student's cape) and a rakish *Shadow* hat (worn by Spanish horse-riders, symbolizing the sherry that Sandeman makes in Jerez). Sandeman provides the most corporate, mainstream, accessible experience for first-timers—with a short walk, a 10-minute video, and two tastes (€3, April–Oct daily 10:00–12:30 & 14:00–18:00, Nov–March daily 9:30–12:30 & 14:00–17:30, right on the riverfront at Largo Miguel Bombarda 3, tel. 223-740-533, www.sandeman.com). But if you're serious about port—or want to pretend to be—go elsewhere. Note that, because Sandeman and Ferriera (described below) are part of the same conglomerate, if you take one tour you get a half-price discount for the other.

For more discriminating tastes, try Taylor and Croft (now affiliated with each other). I toured the classy **Taylor** lodge—near the top of the hill, with stunning views back on Porto—and enjoyed it. After watching an informative video, I learned a little about the history of the company (which, like many port producers, began in the sheep business) and about the Douro Valley's unique microclimates (see next chapter). Then I saw the various sizes of wooden vats in which different kinds of ports are aged (free, Mon–Fri 10:00–18:00, also Sat in July–Aug, always closed Sun, high up but worth the hike at Rua do Choupelo 250, tel. 223-742-800, www.taylor.pt).

The **Croft** tour is similar, but you also get to see vintage port being aged in bottles, as well as a fun "library" of dusty old ports (the oldest is from 1834). You'll also learn how to properly open and present an old bottle of port. The trade-off: The views are not as good (free, daily 10:00–18:00, Largo Joaquim de Magalhães 23, tel. 223-742-800, www.croftport.com).

Port Wine Crash Course

Port is a medium-sweet wine (20 percent alcohol), usually taken as a *digestif* after dinner, sometimes with strong cheese to balance its powerful flavor. The wine is fortified with *aguardente* (grape brandy, more like grappa, sometimes called "grape essence") at a ratio of about 4:1. This brandy is also distilled from wine, so it blends nicely with the port. The introduction of brandy halts fermentation early, leaving more sugar in the port (standard wines ferment for 10–12 days; port for only 2–3 days). After the brandy is added, the wine ages in wood or in bottles, anywhere from two years to (for big spenders) over a century.

For most people, "port" means a tawny port aged 10 to 20 years—the most common type. But there are actually multiple varieties of port; the two general categories are wood ports (aged in wooden vats or barrels) and vintage ports (aged in bottles). Over 40 varieties of grapes, both red and white, can be used for port production.

The basics: **Ruby** is young (aged 3 years), red, and inexpensive, with a strong, straightforward port taste. Note that some ports are **white**—young and robust, but with white grapes (some white "ports" sold today are an attempt to approximate Spain's dry *fino* sherries, though they're sweeter).

Tawny, the wood port with a rusty color, is the most typical version—the one most Americans imagine when they think of port. It's older, lighter, mellower, and more complex than L.B.V. (see below). It's aged in smaller barrels, maximizing exposure to wood (and, therefore, oxygen)—which gives it a nuttier flavor than the more fruity, younger ports. Tawny port is aged 10, 20,

Other popular lodges include **Graham's** (gives a better sense of the variety, with tastings of older ports; free, May–Sept daily 9:30–18:00, Oct–April Mon–Fri 9:30–13:00 & 14:00–17:30, closed Sat–Sun, Rua Rei Ramiro, Quinta do Agro 514, tel. 223-776-330, www.grahams-port.com); and **Ferreira,** whose lodge comes with classical music—"to help age the wine" (smaller, less touristy, with an interesting tour and some fine museum artifacts; €2.50, daily 10:30–12:30 & 14:00–18:00, marked by its big sign at the end of the riverfront promenade at Avenida Ramos Pinto 70, tel. 223-746-107). For more ideas, ask the TIs in Porto or Nova Vila de Gaia, or just follow the signs.

30, or 40 years, but it's not all the same vintage; to enhance the complexity of the flavor, any tawny is a combination of several different ages. So a "30-year-old tawny" is predominantly 30 years old, but also has minor components that are 10 or 20 years old. Once blended, it takes about eight months for the various ports to "marry"—so, ideally, a tawny should have been bottled at least that long before you drink it.

Vintage port (if you can afford it) is a ruby. Rather than being a blend from many different years, it comes from a single harvest. Only wine from the very best years is selected to become vintage. After port ages for two or three years in wooden casks, it's tasted to determine whether it's worthy of the vintage label. (If not, they keep it in the wooden casks longer to become L.B.V.—see below.) If the port is good enough to be classified as vintage, it's bottled and aged another 10–30 years or more—the glass, rather than wood, makes the difference in the aging process. Sediment is common in the bottles, so it must be decanted. And if it's really old, the cork may deteriorate—so the top of the bottle is heated up with a pair of red-hot tongs, then cold water is poured over it to break it off cleanly.

Late Bottle Vintage (L.B.V.) was invented after World War II, when British wine lovers couldn't afford true vintage port. L.B.V. is a blend of wines from a single year, which age together in huge wooden vats for four to six years. The size of the vats means less exposure to wood, which makes it age more quickly, but without losing its fruitiness and color. After five years, it's bottled and sold (later than an actual vintage port—hence the name). This affordable alternative saved the port-wine industry.

Port's stodgy image makes it unpopular among young Portuguese. Many Americans consider port an acquired taste; for this reason, many port producers along the Douro also make a more straightforward red wine. But as I always say: "Any port in a storm..."

Away from the Center

▲**Serralves Foundation Contemporary Art Museum and Park (Fundação de Serralves)**—Porto's contemporary art museum, surrounding park, and unique Art Deco mansion are a ▲▲▲ half-day excursion for art lovers...and worthwhile for anyone looking for a lush green space to relax in (€2.50 for park only, €5 for museum and park; museum open Tue–Thu 10:00–19:00, Fri–Sat 10:00–22:00, Sun 10:00–20:00—until 19:00 Oct–March, closed Mon; park and house open Tue–Sun 10:00–20:00, open Sat–Sun until 19:00 Oct–March, closed Mon; tel. 808-200-543, www.serralves.pt). The complex is about 1.5 miles west of the center in a wealthy residential area at Rua Dom João de Castro 210, just south of the busy Avenida da Boavista. From the center, you can reach it most easily via bus #3, which you can catch at Praça Liberdade (bottom of Avenida dos Aliados; take it to Gomes Costa stop, then walk 1 block south to the museum). You can also take bus #78 to the Serralves stop (less convenient from downtown—the most central place to catch it is at the big Boavista Rotunda).

The complex—which claims to be the most-visited museum in all of Portugal—is managed by the Serralves Foundation. The Foundation was formed in 1989 with two goals: the advancement of contemporary art, and the appreciation of landscape and environment as an artistic concept. These goals, symbolized by the giant red hand shovel near the front gate, drive the layout of the complex: a gigantic contemporary art facility on the edge of a carefully planned park. The whole thing is based around the Art Deco mansion of a count who lived here in the 1930s. When the Foundation was formed, the government bought the house and surrounding land for them to encourage them to pursue their goals. A decade later, in 1999, the museum opened.

The **museum** presents temporary exhibits by Portuguese and global artists. The enormous, blocky, U-shaped building was designed by prominent Portuguese architect Álvaro Siza Vieira, who took much inspiration from the existing mansion. As in most important contemporary-art museums, its vast white exhibition spaces are modified to suit the art displayed (windows and walls continually disappear and reappear). The museum also contains an auditorium and a library. If you're making a day of it, consider the museum's **restaurant,** which serves cheap, good, cafeteria-style food for lunch, then goes upscale—with a stylish makeover in the late afternoon—to become a fancy, expensive dinner spot.

The **park** around the museum has been designed very carefully to compartmentalize each section; when you're in one part of the grounds, you can't see the rest. This is a very peaceful place to wander. Hiding in here somewhere are a pleasant rose garden, a tea house overlooking a former tennis court, a lake, a small farm with animals, a gardening school, and Casa de Serralves itself.

The **house (Casa de Serralves)** is, for many, the most interesting part of the whole experience: a huge, pink Art Deco mansion that looks like the home of a 1950s Hollywood celebrity. On two sides, long manicured hedges and fountains stretch to the horizon. Look for the private chapel in back—also pink Art Deco. You can usually go inside the house to check out the cavernous interior. As you step through the fancy gate inside the living room, remember that in the last century, someone actually lived here. Ponder how the design of this place is reflected in the museum. The best part is upstairs: the mirrored, pink-marbled bathroom, dramatically overlooking the grounds. (Casa de Serralves is included in park admission, same hours as park.)

House of Music (Casa da Música)—This landmark concert hall finally opened in 2005 after years of construction postponements. (It was supposed to be finished in 2001, when Porto was a European Capital of Culture—but, as with most new construction in Porto, delays ensued.) It was designed by Dutch architect Rem Koolhaas's OMA, the firm that also built Seattle's new Central Library (www.oma.nl). Contemporary-architecture fans will find it at the big Boavista Rotunda northwest of the center.

SLEEPING

There are lots of cheap sleeps in Porto—but none in the desirable Ribeira district (where prices are higher). I've listed the only two options in Ribeira, along with several fine places up above, in the city center. The cheaper the place, the greater the chance that English isn't spoken and the grottier the bathroom. You'll almost always have to climb a few stairs to get to the elevator (if they have one).

In the City Center

There are several cheap pensions lining the big Avenida dos Aliados, but they're generally a bad value (with old furnishings and lots of street noise). I've found better options nearby, generally within a few blocks of this main drag.

$$$ Quality Inn Praça da Batalha offers 113 predictable, business-class rooms near the São Bento Station. It shares a slightly seedy square with a beautiful azulejo church and the

---

Sleep Code

(€1 = about $1.20, country code: 351)

S = Single, **D** = Double/Twin, **T** = Triple, **Q** = Quad, **b** = bathroom, **s** = shower only. Unless otherwise noted, breakfast and taxes are included, credit cards are accepted, and English is spoken.

To help you easily sort through these listings, I've divided the rooms into three categories, based on the price for a standard double room with bath during high season:

$$$ **Higher Priced**—Most rooms €80 or more.
$$ **Moderately Priced**—Most rooms between €40–80.
$ **Lower Priced**—Most rooms €40 or less.

beginning of Porto's pedestrian shopping drag (rates fluctuate wildly: Sb-€50–100, Db-€50–100, but generally rates are more like Sb-€65, Db-€70–80; non-smoking rooms, air-con, elevator, Internet in lobby, Praça da Batalha 127, tel. 223-392-300, fax 222-006-009, www.choicehotelsportugal.com, quality.batalha @grupo-continental.com).

$$ Hotel Internacional fits 35 super-modern rooms into the heavy, granite-and-tile shell of an old monastery just two blocks off the Avenida dos Aliados. If you're looking for the formality of a hotel, modern comforts, and a good location at a reasonable price, this is unbeatable (Sb-€60–70, Db-€70–90, prices depend on day and season, air-con, elevator, Rua Do Almada 131, tel. 222-005-032, fax 222-009-063, www.hi-porto.com, info@hi-porto.com).

$$ Grande Hotel de Paris Residencial brags it was the first hotel in Porto with water in the rooms. Its 45 faded but fine rooms—all with antique furniture—are spread out over three interconnected buildings, each with a grand atrium and sloping floors. This proudly run place has big, classy public spaces (Sb-€34–46, standard Db-€42–50, bigger "classic" Db with views cost €2 more, highest prices are for Aug, extra bed-€16–20, 10 percent discount with this book in 2006 off-season, cash only, non-smoking rooms, elevator, Internet in lobby, relaxing garden, Rua da Fábrica 27-29, 1 block up from Avenida dos Aliados, tel. 222-073-140, fax 222-073-149, www.ghparis.pt, direccao@ghparis.pt, David).

$$ Pensão São Marino is a lesser-value pension with 14 simple rooms and a beautiful tiled entryway overlooking a charming, peaceful square (Sb-€35, Db-€40–45, Tb-€48–52, higher prices are for July–Aug, Praça Carlos Alberto 59, tel. 223-325-499, fax 222-054-380, info@residencialsmarino.com, no English spoken).

$$ Residencial O Escondidinho rents 23 smallish, spartan but solid rooms with modern bathrooms at reasonable rates (Sb-€30, Db-€45, includes breakfast, elevator, across from Pensão Residencial Belo Sonho at Rua Passos Manuel 135, tel. 222-004-079, fax 222-026-075, residencialescondidinho@aeiou.pt).

$ Pensão Duas Nações is a well-run place—as comfy as such a cheap place can be—with 20 colorful rooms and we-try-harder management. It overlooks a square straight up Rua Fábrica, a few blocks from Avenida dos Aliados. The "two nations" are Portugal and Brazil, still friends after all these years (S-€13, Sb-€20, D-€20–22, Db-€30, T-€30, Tb-€40, Q-€40, Qb-€48, cash only, no breakfast but adjacent to handy café, Internet in lobby, Praça Guilherme Gomes Fernandes 59, tel. & fax 222-081-616, www.duasnacoes.com.pt, duasnacoes@mail.telepac.pt).

$ Pensão Residencial Belo Sonho is well-maintained and family-run (no English spoken), just up the street from the Café Majestic and the main shopping drag, Rua Santa Catarina. Its

Central Porto Hotels and Restaurants

1. Quality Inn Praça da Batalha
2. Grande Hotel de Paris Res. & Hotel Internacional
3. Pensão São Marino
4. Pensão Duas Nações
5. Pensão Residencial Belo Sonho & Residencial O Escondidinho
6. "Imperial McDonald's"
7. Restaurante Regaleira
8. Restaurante Guarany
9. Restaurante Abadia
10. Confeitaria-Restaurante do Bolhão
11. Majestic Café
12. Coffee Shop
13. Internet Café
14. Lello & Irmão Bookstore

15 rooms are a good value (Sb-€15–25, Db-€25–35, Tb-€35–55, higher prices for June–Oct, cash only, Rua Passos Manuel 186, tel. 222-003-389, fax 222-012-850).

In the Ribeira

There are only a couple of hotels convenient to the Ribeira scene, and neither is a particularly good value. But...location, location, location.

$$$ Pestana Porto Hotel is a worthwhile splurge, with Porto's best location, right on the Douro in the heart of the Ribeira action. Its 48 slightly outmoded rooms occupy 11 old Ribeira buildings, now converted to plush accommodations and connected by glass walkways (standard Sb-€124, riverview Sb-€147, standard Db-€140, riverview Db-€163, extra bed-€47, Internet discounts often available, air-con, elevator, Praça de Ribeira 1, tel. 223-402-300, fax 223-402-400, www.pestana.com, pestana.porto@pestana.com).

Hotels and Restaurants in Porto's Ribeira District

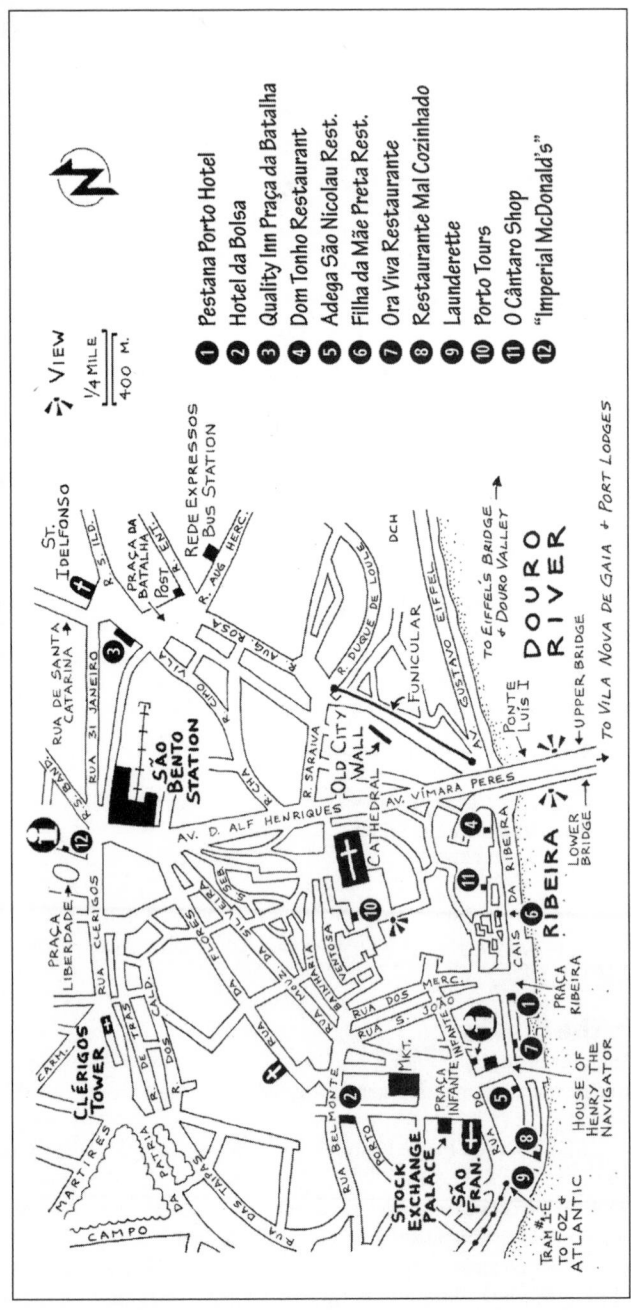

N↑ VIEW

¼ MILE
400 M.

1 Pestana Porto Hotel
2 Hotel da Bolsa
3 Quality Inn Praça da Batalha
4 Dom Tonho Restaurant
5 Adega São Nicolau Rest.
6 Filha da Mãe Preta Rest.
7 Ora Viva Restaurante
8 Restaurante Mal Cozinhado
9 Launderette
10 Porto Tours
11 O Cântaro Shop
12 "Imperial McDonald's"

\$\$ Hotel da Bolsa, a few blocks above the Ribeira scene, is plush and modern with more comfort than character. It has a great location and 36 decent rooms (Sb-€60–66, Db-€72–80, extra bed-€18–20, higher rates are for April–Oct, air-con, elevator, Rua Ferreira Borges 101, tel. 222-026-768, fax 222-058-888, www .hoteldabolsa.com, hoteldabolsa@mail.telepac.pt).

EATING

Porto is famous for its tripe. Legend has it that when Porto's favorite son, Prince Henry the Navigator, set out for his explorations, the city slaughtered all of its mature livestock to send along with his crew—keeping only the guts for themselves. While waiting for the next generation of animals to grow up, Porto's cooks devised many ingenious ways of preparing innards. The tradition stuck, and to this day, people from Porto are known as *tripeiros.* You'll most typically see it Porto-style *(tripas a moda do Porto)*: in a thick stew, with beans, sausage, chicken, and scant vegetables. The tripe itself doesn't have much taste—though I couldn't keep myself from thinking about digestive processes while I ate it.

For something easier to stomach, try *caldo verde*—a tasty soup made with potatoes and thinly chopped cabbage. For a quick meal, locals like a *Francesinha* (literally, "little French girl")—a sandwich with various meats, dripping with a seafood-base gravy.

Many restaurants save their patrons money by portioning their dishes for two people. Generally, if the menu has two price columns, the cheaper list is for small portions (plenty for 1) and the higher-priced list is for dishes that will easily feed two.

In the Ribeira

There's a wide range of dining options in the Ribeira, and they're all touristy. Strolling along the waterfront and following your nose is a good option. You can also try wandering the back lanes to find a spot that feels right—you'll be trading river views for lower prices and local color. If you're looking for specific guidance, here are some possibilities. The seafood's fresh, except on Mondays (since fishermen don't go out on Sundays).

Dom Tonho, atop the arcade near the bridge, is every local's top recommendation for a Ribeira splurge. The place is white-tablecloth classy, at once Old World and mod. The food—traditional Portuguese cuisine, with an emphasis on fresh fish—is only slightly more expensive than nearby tour-group alternatives (most main dishes €12–20, plus seafood splurges, proud wine list, indoor and outdoor seating, daily 12:30–15:00 & 19:30–23:00, Cais da Ribeira 13-15, tel. 222-004-307, www.dtonho.com). Its pricey but tempting appetizers are explained well on the menu.

Adega São Nicolau is a friendly, simple, hole-in-the-wall peeking out from an alley, featuring fresh traditional seafood dishes (most around €9, Mon–Sat 12:00–15:00 & 19:00–23:00, closed Sun, Rua São Nicolau 1, tel. 222-008-232).

Filha da Mãe Preta is a cut above the several interchangeable midrange places along the embankment. Sit outside, with Douro views, or in the azulejo-tiled interior (check out the big mural of Porto upstairs; most dishes €8–10, full courses splittable for 2, Mon–Sat 12:00–15:30, 18:00–22:30, closed Sun, Cais da Ribeira 40, tel. 222-055-515).

Ora Viva Restaurante is a humble but exuberantly decorated, long-and-skinny dining hall a block off the waterfront. The hardworking Pinto family specializes in traditional grilled meat and fish dishes. It's a little less touristy than the Ribeira norm, with locals, decent food, and good prices (€7 meals, on menu "1/2" means single portion, "1" means double portion; Rua Fonte Taurina 83, tel. 222-052-033). Antonio promises a free drink (before or after your dinner) if you set this book on the table.

If you need to satisfy your fado fix, there's a handful of options in Porto. **Restaurante Mal Cozinhado** (literally, "Poorly Cooked") features professional fado performers, expensive dishes (€15–20), and fancy drinks (€5–15). The food and drinks are overpriced, but consider them the entrance fee for the fado (open for dinner nightly at 20:30, music starts at 21:30 and ends at 1:00 in the morning; a couple of blocks up from the Douro at Rua do Outeirinho 11, tel. 222-081-319).

In the City Center

Restaurants are scattered all around the city center, but since this is a business district, many of them are lunch-only. The dining's more atmospheric in Ribeira, but these are convenient if you're staying in the center.

The famous "Imperial McDonald's," inhabiting the former Imperial Café at the bottom of Avenida dos Aliados, is actually the most elegant fast-food spot you'll ever find. From here, there are plenty of eateries nearby—walk around the block to the local bistro **Restaurante Regaleira** (open daily, Rua do Bonjardim 87, tel. 220-006-465) and several cheap and venerable diners. Across the boulevard and uphill a block is the classy **Restaurante Guarany** (open daily, Avenida dos Aliados 85, tel. 223-321-272).

Restaurante Abadia gives a warm welcome and has two floors of happy eaters—locals and tourists—dining on large portions of straightforward Portuguese cuisine. This place is a no-brainer for a fine, central meal. Split a huge half-portion of their Porto-style tripe with your travel partner, balanced with something a little more predictable (closed Sun, €7 half-portions and tasty omelets, €9–15 full-portion splittable main dishes; 100 yards in front of market hall entry—walk around the block to find it on side-street Rua do Ateneu Comercial do Porto #22–24, tel. 222-008-757).

Confeitaria-Restaurante do Bolhão, which faces the market-hall entrance, has been pleasing local shoppers since 1896. This bustling bakery/brasserie has enticing take-away items in front and an inviting old-time dining hall in the rear (the more elegant basement is less lively and soulful). You'll find fresh baked goods, omelets, and fish along with €4 soup and sandwich specials (daily 6:00–21:00, Rua Formosa 339, tel. 223-395-220).

The **Majestic Café** isn't just a coffee house—it's an institution. This elegant Art Nouveau café has been Porto's neighborhood living room for over a century. Today, it's a fine place for a coffee or a light—and expensive—lunch (Mon–Sat 9:30–24:00, closed Sun, Rua Santa Catarina 112, tel. 222-003-887).

The hip, modern **coffee shop** at Rua de Passos Manuel 63 has American-style coffee drinks, ice-cream concoctions, good soups, and €3 toasted sandwiches. It's popular with young people, and convenient for a caffeine jolt or a quick, central meal (Mon–Sat 7:30–20:00, closed Sun, 50 yards down from Café Majestic at Rua de Passos Manuel 63).

TRANSPORTATION CONNECTIONS

Trains

Regional trains use the more central São Bento Station; long-distance trains use the Campanhã Station on the east edge of town. The two stations are connected by frequent trains (see "Arrival in Porto," page 210). All trains leaving São Bento also stop at Campanhã (the next station).

From Porto's São Bento Train Station to: Peso da Régua (10/day, 2–2.5 hrs), **Pinhão** (7/day, 2.5–3 hrs), slow regional train to **Coimbra** (hrly, 2.25 hrs).

From Campanhã Train Station: Fast Alfa Pendular and Intercity trains (both require reservation, buy at station) to **Coimbra** (almost hrly, 1.25 hrs) and **Lisbon** (almost hrly, 3.25 hrs; slow 4.5-hr regional train also available).

To reach **Santiago de Compostela, Spain,** you'll take a train bound for the Spanish port city of Vigo (1/day, 8:00 departure, 4.5 hrs; en route to Vigo, you may change at the border town of

Valença). Once in Spain, you can change to the Santiago-bound train in Vigo, but most conductors will encourage you instead to change trains before that, in the town of Redondela. This works fine, since Vigo is on a dead-end track, so that any train going to Vigo also goes through Redondela on the way. (In other words, if you change in Vigo instead of Redondela, you'll simply spend more time on the train and less time at the station.) Frustratingly, rail-information people in Porto generally can't tell you much about parts of the journey beyond the Spanish border. Consider instead a bus tour (see below).

Buses

Remember, each bus company has its own mini-station; there's no central bus terminus (for addresses and telephone numbers, see "Arrival in Porto," page 210). Various companies compete on the same route (for example, 4 companies go to Lisbon). Ask the transport office at the TI about the handiest bus for your itinerary (see "Tourist Information," page 210; toll-free tel. 800-220-905). Don't bother trying to get to the Douro Valley (Peso da Régua or Pinhão) by bus; it takes twice as long as the train.

From Porto by Bus to: Coimbra (operated by Rede Expressos, Rodonorte, and others; best is Rede Expressos—almost hrly, 1.5 hrs, more frequent early and late, sparse mid-afternoon), **Lisbon** (best via RENEX or Rede Expressos, at least hrly, 3 hrs), **Santiago de Compostela, Spain** (run by Internorte; 4/week in winter, 6/week in summer, 5.25 hrs).

Santiago Note: To get to Santiago de Compostela, consider taking an all-day guided bus tour from Porto. It takes 2 to 3 hours via the expressway. You can skip out on the return to Porto. For information on these tours, ask at the Porto Tours office (see page 214).

DOURO VALLEY

(Vale do Douro)

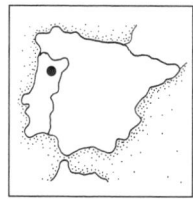

The best single activity in northern Portugal is exploring the scenic Douro Valley—the birthplace of port wine—with an otherworldly, ever-changing terrain sculpted by centuries of hardy farmers. The river's steep, craggy, twisting canyons have been laboriously terraced to make a horizontal home for grape vines and olive and almond trees. Unlike the Rhine, the Loire, and other great European rivers, the Douro was never a strategic military location. So, rather than fortresses and palaces, you'll see farms, villages...and endless, tidy rows of rock terraces, which took no less work—and are no less impressive—than those castles and châteaux. Locals brag, "God made the earth, but man made the Douro."

The Douro (DOH-roo) River begins as a trickle in Spain (where it's called Duero), runs west for 550 miles (350 miles of which is in Portugal), and spills into the Atlantic at Porto. The name likely means "river of gold" (though some trace it to a Celtic word for water), perhaps because of the way the sun shines on the water, or the golden-brown silt it carries after a heavy rain.

In the 17th century, British traders developed a taste for the wines from the Douro region. "Op-port-unity" knocked in 1756, when the Marquês de Pombal demarcated the region—establishing it as the only place that port wine could be produced. To this day, port remains the top industry—and tourist draw—of the Douro Valley. The 50-mile stretch on either side of Pinhão is home to some 4,000 vintners and scores of *quintas*—vineyards that produce port (and often table wine and olive oil). While many *quintas* are private, others offer tours and tastings, and some have accommodations as well.

The Douro hillsides change colors throughout the year—dusty

brown in winter, scrubby green in summer, and glowing gold in fall. The 5,000-foot-high Marão Mountain cradles the region, protecting it from the ocean air and creating a microclimate. The temperature varies from snowy in the winter to arid and 100°F degrees in the summer—perfect for growing grapes. Much of the Douro's dramatic ambience was changed in the 1970s, when a series of dams were built for hydroelectric power, taming the formerly raging river into the meandering stream seen today.

But while the scenery and the port are sublime, the towns along the Douro (Peso da Régua and Pinhão) are fairly dull. If you've got wheels, consider staying at one of the many *quintas* that offer accommodations—ranging from simple rooms on family farms to one of the most breathtaking *pousadas* in Portugal. To many, the Douro Valley will feel low-energy and underwhelming (especially outside of September's harvest time, when it's quiet), but it does have the world's best port and a unique—if subtle—charm.

Planning Your Time

This area merits two days (including travel time to and from Porto, with an overnight along the river). Port-wine enthusiasts may well want more time. If you want only a glimpse, the Douro as a day trip from Porto is doable, either on your own (about 2 hrs by car or 2–3 hours by train each way) or with a package tour (see below). I find the city of Porto more interesting and would favor it over the Douro Valley when allocating limited vacation time.

Note that since Porto is a business-oriented city, its hotels are often cheaper on weekends. In contrast, the Douro Valley—since it's primarily a tourist zone—is more crowded (and often more expensive) on weekends. Ideally, visit Porto on the weekend and the Douro during the week.

Drivers should make a beeline for this best part of the Douro Valley (see next section), and explore at will. Without a car, you're limited as to where you can stay and which *quintas* you can tour— but you still have enough options to make the trip worthwhile. To maximize sightseeing thrills, take the slow boat cruise from Porto to Peso da Régua. Visit the sights in Régua, then settle in for the night (or, if you're staying in Pinhão, take the train or boat there). In the morning, hike to Quinta de la Rosa (near Pinhão) for the 11:00 tour and tasting. When you've had enough of the wine and rugged scenery, head back to Porto via train.

Douro Valley

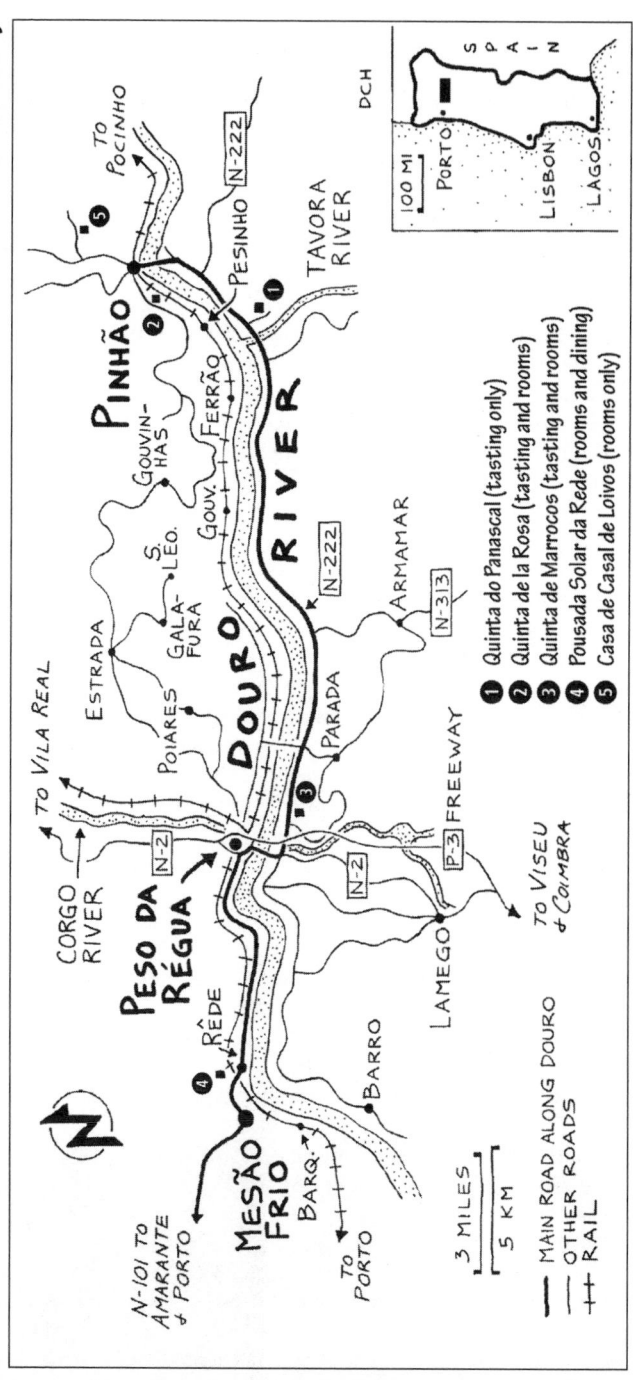

1 Quinta do Panascal (tasting only)
2 Quinta de la Rosa (tasting and rooms)
3 Quinta de Marrocos (tasting and rooms)
4 Pousada Solar da Rede (rooms and dining)
5 Casa de Casal de Loivos (rooms only)

— MAIN ROAD ALONG DOURO
--- OTHER ROADS
+++ RAIL

ORIENTATION

The Douro runs for 350 miles through the northern Portuguese heartland. The most interesting segment—and the heart of the port wine–growing region—is easily the 17-mile stretch between Peso da Régua and Pinhão.

Coming from Porto, you'll see that the first 55 miles of the Douro are pretty and lush. When you reach the town of **Mesão Frio,** the terrain becomes far more arid and dramatic. The prized demarcated port wine-growing region of the Douro technically begins here and stretches all the way to the Spanish border.

Peso da Régua, about seven miles beyond Mesão Frio, is the biggest town of the region and a handy home base. Seventeen miles beyond Peso da Régua is smaller **Pinhão.** Each town has a big, fancy hotel and one or two cheap *residencial*s, with a *quinta* nearby. Peso da Régua benefits from more striking scenery, but feels urban and functional; Pinhão enjoys more of a small-town ambience and has better accommodations. Neither is worth going out of your way to visit.

The Douro Azul company has something of a monopoly in the region, operating the biggest tour boats as well as running several of the accommodations (including Vintage House Hotel in Pinhão and the Solar da Rede *pousada* near Peso da Régua).

I've described the most enjoyable and accessible stretch of the Douro, but there's lots more—vineyards stretch all the way to Spain. The train goes as far as Pocinho. Just south of Pocinho, Vila Nova de Foz Côa sits between the Douro and a fine "archaeological park" with cave paintings.

A big part of your Douro experience will be determined by where you choose to sleep. The only memorable place is the classic Vintage House Hotel in Pinhão. Both the Quinta de la Rosa and Quinta de Marrocos offer you a homey farm experience. And the Pousada Solar da Rede is a royal countryside retreat. Each is described below.

Getting Around the Douro Valley

By Boat: Lazy cruise boats float up and down the Douro between Porto, Peso da Régua, and Pinhão. (The feisty Douro was tamed in the 1980s by a series of 5 dams with locks, including the highest one in Europe, the Barragem do Carrapatelo—which inches boats up and down, like a giant elevator, over 140 feet.)

The boat trip takes about seven hours from Porto to the heart of the Douro, and comes with a lunch and passage through two locks (and, for the longer trips, a 3rd lock between Peso da Régua and Pinhão). If you've got the time and don't have a car, this is a slow but scenic way to enjoy the Douro Valley.

Various companies do the trip; generally, several different boats go daily April through November (only Sat–Sun in March, no boats Dec–Feb). Figure €70–90 to Régua or Pinhão; seniors should ask about discounts, especially on weekdays. Most travelers take a train or bus back to Porto from Régua in the same

day as part of a package deal. But if you want to spend the night on the Douro, it's easy to catch a train back on your own (or buy a 2-day package, which includes lodging).

The largest company, **Douro Azul,** has big boats that are popular with tour groups. It's often a bit more expensive, but the service is professional and the food is good. They also offer various package itineraries that include overnights at fancy hotels and *pousadas* (tel. 223-402-515, www.douroazul.com).

Some travelers prefer smaller companies, which can cost a little less and offer a more personal experience. Your best bet is to comparison-shop the options for the day you want to cruise with the excellent **Porto Tours** office in Porto. Since it's run by the city, this agency offers unbiased advice and charges no commission (daily April–Oct 9:00–19:00, Nov–March 9:00–17:30, in old medieval watchtower next to cathedral at Calçada Dom Pedro Pitões 15, tel. 222-000-073, www.portotours.com, portotours@mail.telepac.pt).

By Train: A regional train connects Porto's São Bento Station with Peso da Régua (10/day, 2–2.5 hrs); it usually continues another 30 minutes to Pinhão (7/day). There's also a historic steam train that choo-choos you between Douro towns on Saturdays (April–Oct, Régua to Pinhão costs €10, 40 min, other towns also possible; run by Douro Azul, see contact info above).

By Car: The region is easy by car. From Porto, zip on the A4 expressway to Amarante, then N101 through the mountains to Mesão Frio (total trip to Régua around 2 hrs). Once in the heart of the Douro, the riverside road follows the north bank from Mesão Frio to Régua. From there, you'll cross to the south bank (on the middle of the 3 bridges) to continue on N222 into the valley to Pinhão (where you'll cross back to reach the town). The 17-mile stretch of river covered in this chapter is about a 30-minute drive—everything I've mentioned is no more than a few minutes' side-trip from the river.

When passing through Amarante, it's an easy and logical pit-stop to detour into the town center to check out the old Roman bridge and impressive church and convent of São Gonçalo.

If you're driving from Coimbra to the Douro Valley, you'll save time and mileage by coming directly through the mountains (via Viseu and Lamego), rather than taking the expressway up the coast to Porto and then over.

TOURS

Quintas Tours and Tastings

The main attraction of the Douro Valley is touring the *quintas,* the farms that produce port and table wines. It's an informal scene and easy for drivers; simply pull into any *quinta* listed here (or any marked *rota do vinho do Porto*), and ask for a quick tour and a taste. Even if they have a specific time for tours (listed below where applicable), you can often get a shorter, less formal tour at other times. Ideally, call ahead and ask when you should show up.

Each *quinta* (KEEN-tah) works differently; most tours and tastings are free. The tours of big companies' *quintas* are slick, but feel like stripped-down versions of the tours you'll do in the port wine lodges back in Porto (with the happy exception of Quinta do Panascal—see below). The smaller, independent *quintas* are more intimate, and offer a chance to meet the people who have devoted their lives to making the best wine they can.

At *quintas* operated by big companies, it's fine not to buy. But if a family-run place gives you an in-depth tour, it's polite to buy at least a token bottle.

These are the best *quinta* experiences on this stretch of the Douro. I've noted the best options for non-drivers.

▲▲**Quinta do Panascal**—This wonderful *quinta* produces Fonseca—a name familiar to port lovers for its high quality. It's the only *quinta* that allows you to roam on your own through the terraced vineyards. From the riverside road you'll side-trip up the valley of the Távora River. Venturing up the rough gravel road, you'll feel like you are discovering a special, hidden gem. Yet

upon arrival, you'll enjoy the slick efficiency of a corporate producer (Fonseca also owns Taylor and is a port-wine giant). Because of its delightfully remote location, and because it gets you out among the grapes, it's the best *quinta* tour on the Douro.

The tour is self-guided, so there's no wait once you arrive. You'll be given a 30-minute audioguide and set free to wander through the vineyards and take in the sweeping views (while listening to dry, humorless commentary about the history of port and of the company). Then you'll return to the lodge to watch a 10-minute video (which brings the otherwise still fields to life) while tasting two ports (free, daily 10:00–18:00 in summer, closed Sat–Sun Nov–March, tel. 254-732-321, www.fonseca.pt).

Getting There: This place is only accessible by car; it's well-marked off the Régua-Pinhão road (N222), up a thrilling little side road that follows the Távora River as it branches off from the Douro (closer to Pinhão).

▲**Quinta de la Rosa**—This family-run *quinta* is serious about its wine and eager to show it off on a free one-hour tour of the facil-

ity with a generous tasting (April–Oct 9:00–13:00 & 14:00–18:00). The real reason to stop here is to enjoy an in-depth, friendly tour with a finale of four tastings (€2.50, daily in summer at 11:00, call ahead off-season to arrange; 1 mile downstream from Pinhão, tel. 254-732-254, fax 254-732-346, www.quintadelarosa.com).

Getting There: This is perhaps the only family *quinta* that is close enough to a town that you can do it without a car (20-min hike from Pinhão). For directions and information on their accommodations, see "Sleeping—Near Pinhão," page 253.

Other Tours and Tastings—Many of the accommodations listed in this chapter also offer tours and tastings.

The finest ports—for serious wine-lovers—are at **Vintage House Hotel's** "Academia do Vinho" in Pinhão. They offer three types of "tutored tastings": port introduction (€15/person), port wine alternated with chocolate (€20/person), and vintage port in bottles so old they're opened with red-hot tongs (€25/person). The tastings are generally in the afternoon; call to check the schedule and reserve a spot (shop open daily 10:00–13:00 & 14:00–19:00, tel. 254-730-230, see page 252). They also offer three-hour classes on port appreciation (around €63/person, 4-person minimum; call for details). Since it's right in the center of Pinhão, this place is an easy choice for non-drivers.

At the other end of the spectrum is the loose, informal, family-run **Quinta de Marrocos** (see page 250), a great place to sample simple ports while chatting with the family that made them (daily, 9:00–18:00). You could hoof it here from Peso da Régua (across

Brits on the Douro: The History of Port

Port is actually a British phenomenon. Because Britain isn't suitable for growing grapes, its citizens traditionally imported wine from France. But during wars with France (17th and 18th centuries), Britain boycotted French wines, and looked elsewhere. They considered Portugal—but since it was farther away, wine often didn't survive the long sea journey to England.

The port-making process was supposedly invented accidentally by a pair of brothers who fortified the wine with grape brandy to maintain its quality during the long trip to England. The wine picked up the flavor of the oak, and the English grew to like the fortified taste and oaky flavor. Port production was perfected by the British in the succeeding centuries, and many ports carry British-sounding names (Taylor, Croft, Graham).

In 1703, the Methuen Treaty reduced taxation on Portuguese wines—making port even more popular. In 1756, Portugal's Marquês de Pombal demarcated the Douro region—the first such designation in Europe. From that point on, only true "port wine" came from this region, following specific regulations of production, just as the name "champagne" technically means wines from a specific region of France. Traditionally, farmers and landowners were Portuguese, while the British bought the wine from them, aged it in Porto, and handled the export business. But that arrangement changed in the late 19th century, when an infestation of an American insect called phylloxera (which

the river and about 1.5 miles upstream), but it's not as easy by foot as Quinta de la Rosa, above.

The **Solar da Rede** *pousada* runs a *quinta* with tastings, by the river between Peso da Régua and Mesão Frio (drivers only; see page 250). The refined **Solar do Vinho do Porto** (see page 248), in downtown Peso da Régua, is another fine tasting option, especially for those without a car.

Growing—and Stomping— Grapes in the Douro Valley

Port wine can technically only be grown in the Douro Valley, which is unique among European rivers. One glance at those endless neat rows of terraces—and the harsh, arid terrain that somehow produces something so flavorful—and visitors can't help but wonder: How do they do it?

Near Porto, the Douro has a continental climate, with moderate temperatures and a fair amount of precipitation. The vineyards you see along this stretch produce not port, but "green wine" (*vinho verde*—Portugal's refreshing and sprightly light white wine).

smuggled itself to the Old World in the humid climate of speedy steamboats) devastated the Portuguese—and European—wine industry.

In the Douro Valley, you'll see lasting evidence of the phyl-

loxera infestations in the "dead" terraces, overgrown with weeds and a smattering of olive trees. During the infestations, these particular terraces were treated with harsh chemicals that contaminated the soil, rendering it suitable only for growing olives, but not grapes. Other terraces were left untouched, as Portuguese vintners simply gave up. Unable to produce usable grapes for over a decade, they sold their land to British companies who were willing to wait until a solution could be found. It was, as phylloxera-resistant American root stock began to be used throughout Europe. Port production resumed, this time on British-owned land.

Today, Porto and the Douro Valley see many British tourists. Though it's largely undiscovered by Americans, this region is a real hotspot among wine-loving Brits.

About 55 miles inland, around Mesão Frio, chains of mountains stretch to the north and south. East of here, the climate changes dramatically, becoming Mediterranean: very hot and dry in summer, with heavy rainfall and extreme cold in winter.

The heart of the Douro is characterized by microclimates. A few miles can make a tremendous difference in terms of temperature, precipitation, humidity, and farming conditions. Even within the same vineyard, each parcel of land has its own characteristics. These subtle changes infuse the grapes with completely different aromas and flavors. Over the years, vintners have learned to micromanage their grapes, fine-tuning specific qualities to get the very best port for their conditions.

The terrain around the Douro is a combination of slate and granite, called schist *(xisto)*. Thanks to geological processes, the shale-like layers of soil are oriented vertically or at an angle, as opposed to being stacked on each other horizontally. This allows the winter rainfall to easily penetrate the earth, building up in underground reserves. The grapevines' roots plunge deep—up to 30 feet—in order to reach this water through the long, dry summer.

Douro vineyards are terraced, giving the valley an unusually dramatic look. Building and maintaining these terraces *(geios)* is

expensive, and grapes planted there must be cultivated by hand. More recently, some of the bigger companies have attempted different methods: using bulldozers to create larger terraces (called *patamares*) that can be worked by machines; or smoothing out the hillside and planting the vines in vertical rows. (Purists don't like these new methods, which also have their disadvantages—including fewer plants per parcel.) Within the demarcated region, farmers are not allowed to irrigate, except with special permission.

Because the crops here are worked mostly by hand, it can be hard to find good workers (especially for pruning, a delicate task requiring certain skills). Most young people from the Douro move to the cities on the coast. To encourage them to stay, the government offers subsidies and other incentives.

To make the finest port, many *quintas* along the Douro still stomp grapes by foot—not because of quaint tradition, but because it's the best way. Machines would break the grapes' seeds and stems, releasing a bitter flavor—but soft soles don't. During harvest time (late-Sept–early-Oct), the grapes are poured into big granite tubs called *lagares*. A team of two dozen stompers line up across from each other, put their arms on each other's shoulders, and march, military-style, to crush the grapes. The stomping can last three or four days, and generally devolves into a party atmosphere—with tourists sometimes paying to join in.

Port traditionally stays in the Douro Valley for one winter after it's made, as the cold temperatures encourage the wine and

Rabelo **Boats**

Up until the 1970s, when the Douro was tamed by dams, boats called *rabelos* navigated the treacherous waters, carrying port from the hillsides to the cellars of Porto. It was a three-day trip to cover the 50 to 100 miles. A crew of four loaded the barrels onto the small, 20-foot boats. For the downstream trip, the captain stood on a platform to spy rocks and shallows ahead,

using the long rudder to guide the flat-bottomed boat through whitewater and hairpin turns. It was dangerous work, and the river was once lined with shrines where superstitious sailors prayed.

At Vila Nova de Gaia, they unloaded their cargo—a mere eight barrels, typically—and headed back. For the slow trip upstream, the tall, square sail helped them ride the prevailing westerly winds. Otherwise, they were pulled by ropes up the worst stretches by men or oxen on towpaths that used to line the riverbank.

Nowadays, the Douro is quiet, port is shipped via tanker trucks, and the few remaining *rabelos* are docked by *quintas* for ambience and advertising.

brandy to marry. Then it's taken to Porto, where the more humid, mild climate is ideal for aging. For centuries, port could technically only be aged, marketed, and sold in Porto. But this was deregulated in 1987, and now any Douro *quinta* that offers tours sells its port directly to visitors.

The vineyards along the Douro are traditionally separated by olive trees, many of which produce fine olive oil. The farming demands of olives fit efficiently with those of grapes. There are also almond, orange, apple, and cherry trees, which locals use to make jam.

Peso da Régua

Peso da Régua (PAY-zoo dah RAY-gwah)—or simply "Régua," as it's called by locals—is the administrative capital of the Douro Valley. With 22,000 people, Régua actually feels urban, with modern five- and six-story apartment blocks and hotels that somehow seem out of place in these starkly beautiful surroundings. While the town itself isn't worth the trip, the views and access into the surrounding countryside make it worth considering as a home base—or at least a transportation hub.

ORIENTATION

Peso da Régua consists of basically two bustling streets that run parallel to the Douro. There are three bridges at the east (upriver) end of town.

Tourist Information: The town's **TI** is at the west (down-river) end of town (July–Sept daily 9:00–12:30 & 14:00–17:30, Oct–June Mon–Fri 9:00–12:30 & 14:00–17:30, closed Sat–Sun, Rua da Ferreirinha, tel. 254-312-846).

Arrival in Peso da Régua: The train station and two recommended hotels are at the edge of the center near the bridges, and the TI is at the west end of the center (downstream). The boat dock is more or less in the middle of town (disembark to the right, walk up the hill for train station and hotels; for the TI, disembark to the left, climb hill, swing right at fountain, and continue straight 3 blocks).

Tours: A cheesy **tourist train** meets arriving boats and does a one-hour circuit (€9, 2 stops: mountaintop viewpoint and wine cellar for tasting). There are also various informal **boat** trips to villages up and down the Douro (ask TI for details).

SIGHTS

Peso da Régua's sights are few, and most worthwhile for people without cars (who can't get into the countryside, where time is better spent). Downtown, you'll find **Casa do Douro,** the grand headquarters of the local port-wine industry (with pretty stained-glass windows inside).

▲**Douro Museum (Museu do Douro)**—This fine little museum traces the industry and culture of the Douro Valley, with a 3-D relief map of the region, stuffed specimens of local wildlife, models showing the construction of *rabelo* boats, and traditional costumes and musical instruments. You'll also see items relating to port production: tools, casks, barrels, decanters, port wine bottles and labels, and advertising posters (€1, Tue–Sun 10:00–18:00, closed Mon, tel. 254-324-320). At press time, the museum shared the old warehouse with the Solar do Vinho do Porto (at Rua da Alegria 39 in downtown Régua, see below), but it will likely move to a new location in town (and begin charging admission) in 2006—ask the TI or your hotel.

▲**Solar do Vinho do Porto**—This facility, run by the Port and Douro Wines Institute, offers tastings and information about the region's products. Atmospherically situated in a renovated old warehouse (Armazém, or Warehouse, #43), with comfy chairs, it's a handy place to sample a variety of ports (daily in summer 11:00–23:00; off-season Mon–Sat 11:00–20:00, closed Sun; right downtown at Rua da Alegria 39, tel. 254-320-960, www.ivp.pt). You'll pay €1–20 per glass; the menu has meats, cheeses, and other delicious, traditional port-tasting snacks.

Quinta de São Domingos—The *quinta,* on a hill just above Peso da Régua, produces port for the big company Castelinho. This is the region's giant, impersonal *quinta*—a standard stop for large tour groups. This corporate experience reminds me of some of the port wine lodges in Vila Nova de Gaia near Porto—not what you came all the way to the rustic Douro Valley for. The only thing good about it is its convenience for those without a car (free 10-min tour with a short movie and 2 tastes, daily 9:00–13:00 & 14:00–18:00, tel. 254-320-260). It's just above Régua at the train-station end of town (near the bridges); by foot, walk east (upriver) along the tracks, then cross the tracks through the hard-to-find gate (by the small pink building), and continue uphill to the *quinta* (about 15 min total).

SLEEPING AND EATING

You have two basic options for sleeping in the Douro Valley: stay in a boring hotel or *residencial* in one of the towns (most likely Peso da Régua or Pinhão), or sleep at a picturesque *quinta* or *pousada* in the countryside. The in-town hotels are handy for those using public transportation, but if you've got a car, the *quintas* offer a better value and a more memorable Douro experience. The fancier places serve meals and have half-board options.

The Douro is extremely crowded during the grape harvest in late September and early October, and good rooms are in short supply to begin with; if visiting during this time, book as far ahead as possible. Simpler places charge the same rates year-round; more expensive hotels charge more for weekends and during busy season (roughly May–Oct).

In Peso da Régua

You have two options, neither of which is traditional or charming: a tasteful, well-located hotel, and a cheap, basic *residencial*. If you have a car, get out of town!

$$ Hotel Régua Douro is the only classy option in town. With a top-floor panoramic breakfast room and 77 comfortable rooms—many of them with sweeping river views—it's a fine splurge (Sb-€42–80, Db-€66–100, higher prices are for July–Oct and Sat, riverview rooms are a good value at only €4 more than city-view rooms; air-con, elevator, expensive Internet in lobby,

Sleep Code

(€1 = about $1.20, country code: 351)
S = Single, **D** = Double/Twin, **T** = Triple, **Q** = Quad, **b** = bathroom, **s** = shower only. Unless otherwise noted, credit cards are accepted, English is spoken, and breakfast and tax are included.

To help you easily sort through these listings, I've divided the rooms into three categories, based on the price for a standard double room with bath during high season:

$$$ Higher Priced—Most rooms €100 or more.
$$ Moderately Priced—Most rooms between €50–100.
$ Lower Priced—Most rooms €50 or less.

Largo da Estação da C.P., tel. 254-320-700, fax 254-320-709, www .hotelreguadouro.pt, hotelreguadouro@mail.telepac.pt).

$ Pensão Residencial Império has a convenient, central location in a stark tower a block from the station and across the street from Hotel Régua Douro. Its 35 rooms are basic, musty, and surrounded by busy streets, but the price is right (Sb-€27, Db-€40, Tb-€55, air-con, Rua Vasques Osório 8, tel. 254-320-120, fax 254-321-457).

Near Peso da Régua

$$ Quinta de Marrocos is a wonderful option if you want to stay at a real-life family farm. The Sequeira family farmhouse operates a simple shop and a family vineyard making good ports and table wines. The four rooms include a rustic yet deluxe living room, where the port's always out. Staying here, with the four dogs and farm hands, is a fun, authentic experience. It's a rare opportunity to spend time with locals who really love what they do (Sb-€50, Db-€60, 10 percent discount with this book in 2006, on N222 across the river and about 1.5 miles upstream from Peso da Régua, tel. 254-313-012, fax 254-322-680, www.quintademarrocos.com, qmarrocos@hotmail.com, Rita and her mother, Maria Elisa). They also rent a private, two-bedroom, family-friendly house on their property (€100). For information on wine tastings, see page 243.

Between Rêde and Mesão Frio

In the countryside between these two river towns, about 15 minutes downriver from Peso da Régua, is a delightful, elegant *pousada* that captures the Douro spirit. More than simply a place to sleep and eat, **$$$ Pousada Solar da Rede** is a destination in itself. This

18th-century manor house, surrounded by vineyards and overlooking a particularly scenic stretch of the Douro, has been converted into a 12-room *pousada* with regal historic furnishings. Throughout the estate, accessed by cobbled paths through the terraced hillsides, are another 17 rooms in various smaller villas with charming country decor. This is a great spot if you're honeymooning—or want to pretend to be. Relax at the swimming pool, stroll through the manicured gardens, feel like a noble in the antique-ridden reading room, or hike up the mountain to a high-altitude picnic table—all with some of the Douro's best views (standard Db-€112–190, deluxe Db-€135–229, 2-story suite-€217–257, top prices are weekends April–Oct, lower prices are for during the week and Nov–March, air-con, tel. 254-890-130, fax 254-890-139, www.pousadas.pt, solar.da.rede@douroazul.com). When you reserve, tell them whether you want a room in the more formal manor house or one of the fun-loving villas (with generally better views).

Eating at Solar da Rede: Even if you're not sleeping here, the *pousada* is a fine destination for a fancy dinner—and a chance to wander the grounds and take in the vistas. You'll enjoy crisp but friendly service and fine Portuguese cuisine (main dishes €20–30, half-board for guests costs €26 without wine, open daily 12:30–15:00 & 19:30–22:00, reservations required for non-guests, same contact info as *pousada*). The *pousada* also operates its own *quinta*, with tastings closer to the river (€5 for 3 tastes, call *pousada* for details).

Getting There: Coming by car from Régua, follow the main road west (downstream) towards Mesão Frio; flags mark the road up to the *pousada* on your right after the village of Rêde. If you don't have wheels, the hotel offers a free shuttle service from the train station in Rêde (on the main Porto-Régua line; arrange in advance).

Pinhão

Pinhão (peen-YOW)—known locally as the "heart of the Douro"—feels like a real, workaday small town, where locals go on with their im-port-ant business, oblivious to the tourists streaming through their streets. The big white silos are where the wine spends its first winter awaiting shipment downstream to Porto.

ORIENTATION

Pinhão has virtually no sights, but makes for a handy home base. Even if you don't arrive by train, be sure to check out the **train station**—adorned with azulejo tiles illustrating the people and traditions of the countryside. A few accommodations in and

near Pinhão don't take credit cards; the lone **ATM** is in the BPI bank, on the left near the west end of town (toward Casal de Loivos).

Arrival in Pinhão: The town has a train station along the main road, and a boat landing down below on the river. The two *residencial*s are across the street from the station, and Vintage House Hotel is just upriver, next to the bridge. If arriving by **boat,** disembark to the right for the Vintage House; to reach the *residencial*s or the station, leave the boat to the left, then loop up and to the right, around the big concrete wine-storage vats.

Tours: You have various options for **boat trips** on the Douro. Vintage House Hotel organizes river trips on traditional *rabelo* boats for guests and non-guests (€15 for 90-min trip, May–Oct daily at 10:30 and 16:00, Nov–April daily 11:00 and 15:00, call to reserve, tel. 254-730-230). Or try the informal cruise, on a modern boat, offered by Praia Bar down by the dock (€8–15 depending on length, daily in summer, call or show up to ask about today's schedule, tel. 254-731-556).

SLEEPING

In Pinhão

Your in-town options are a plush splurge hotel or two humble *residencial*s. The *residencial*s are next door to each other, across from the train station. Both operate fine restaurants, and both have riverview rooms that cost no extra but come with some street noise; neither speaks English, but each one has an English-speaking son who is available only sometimes.

$$$ Vintage House Hotel is *the* place if you want to splurge on a fancy, formal hotel on the Douro (as opposed to a hillside *pousada* or manor house). The place is all class, with a wonderfully atmospheric bar (with tree-trunk rafters), a good restaurant with an over-the-top formal interior and riverside terrace outdoor seating, and a wine shop featuring expensive tastings for aficionados (see "*Quintas* Tours and Tastings," page 243). Each of its 43 rooms has a river view and a terrace or balcony, and elegant tile in the bathroom. The halls are lined with baskets of free local oranges and apples, as well as 19th-century photos of the Douro (Sb-€107–155, Db-€121–170, extra bed-€43-57, child's bed-€22–27, suites €140–298, higher prices are for May–Oct, air-con, elevator, between train station and bridge at Lugar da Ponte, tel. 254-730-230, fax 254-730-238, www.hotelvintagehouse.com, vintagehouse @hotelvintagehouse.com).

$ Residencial Douro offers 14 fresh rooms, many with cute riverview balconies (Sb-€30, €35 with breakfast, Db-€45, €50 with breakfast, cash only, air-con, Largo da Estação, tel. & fax 254-732-404, Oliveira family).

$ Residencial Ponto Grande has 17 comparable rooms with lower prices and older furnishings (Sb-€25, Db-€38, cash only, air-con, Rua António Manuel Saraiva 41, tel. 254-732-456, Vieira family).

Near Pinhão

$$ Quinta de la Rosa, a mile downstream of Pinhão, is a riverside winery offering six comfortable rooms with traditional country furnishings; all but one overlook the river (Db-€75, a bit less for 2 nights and off-season; extra bed-€20, Sb costs the same as Db in season, but only €60 off-season; optional €25/person half-board includes wine; tel. 254-732-254, fax 254-732-346, www.quintadelarosa .com, sophia@quintadelarosa.com). They also offer in-depth tours and wine tastings (see page 243).

Getting There: Drivers leave Pinhão to the west (downriver) and look for the *quinta* on the left. If walking: from the boat landing, cross the blue pedestrian bridge and continue 20 minutes (or take a €6 taxi from Pinhão station).

Above Pinhão, in Casal de Loivos

$$ Casa de Casal de Loivos hovers on a lofty perch above Pinhão, with perhaps the most dramatic views in all Douro Valley. The warm Sampayo family has converted a 17th-century manor house into a six-room hotel with quaintly rustic furnishings and commanding Douro vistas. The family brags that when the BBC filmed a show about the best views in the world, they set up their camera right here (Sb-€70, Db-€90, half-board-€23/person, cash only, swimming pool, closed Jan, tel. & fax 254-732-149, www .casadecasaldeloivos.com, casadecasaldeloivos@ip.pt).

Getting There: The house is in the village of Casal de Loivos, atop the mountain over Pinhão. Leaving Pinhão to the west (downriver), first follow signs for Alijó, then for Casal de Loivos, and wind your way up the mountain roads. Once in town, look for the poorly marked villa on your right; if you reach the overlook with the white railing, you've gone a block too far. If you don't have wheels, catch a taxi from Pinhão's train station (about €6).

APPENDIX

PORTUGUESE CAPSULE HISTORY

2000 B.C.–A.D. 500—Prehistory to Rome

Portugal's indigenous race, the "Lusiads," was a mix from many migrations and invasions—Neolothic stone builders (2000 B.C.), Phoenician traders (1200 B.C.), northern Celts (700 B.C.), Greek colonists (700 B.C.), and Carthaginian conquerors (500 B.C.).

By the time of Julius Caesar (50 B.C.), rebellious Lusitania (Portugal) was finally under Roman rule, with major cities at Olissipo (Lisbon), Portus Cale (Porto), and Ebora (Évora). The Romans brought laws, wine, the Latin language, and Christianity. When Rome's empire fell (A.D. 400), Portugal was saved from barbarian attacks by Christian, Germanic Visigoths ruling distantly from their capital in Toledo.

A.D. 711–1400—Muslims vs. Christians, and Nationhood

North African Muslims invaded the Iberian Peninsula, settling in southern Portugal. Christians retreated to the cold, mountainous north, with central Portugal as a buffer zone. For the next five centuries, the Moors made Iberia a beacon of enlightenment in Dark Age Europe, while Christians slowly drove them out, one territory at a time (Faro was the last Portuguese town to fall, in 1249). Afonso Henriques, a popular Christian noble who conquered much Muslim land, was proclaimed king of Portugal (1143), creating one of Europe's first modern nation states. John I solidified Portugal's nationhood by repelling a Spanish invasion (1385) and establishing his family (the House of Avis) as kings.

Famous Portuguese

Viriato (d. A.D. 139)—Legendary warrior who (unsuccessfully) resisted the Roman invasion.

Afonso Henriques (d. 1189)—Renowned Muslim-slayer and first king of a united, Christian nation.

Pedro I, the Just (1320–1367)—Father of John I, famous for his devotion to his murdered mistress, Inês de Castro.

John I (1358–1433)—Preserved independence from Spain, launched overseas expansion, fathered Prince Henry, established the House of Avis as the ruling family.

Manuel I, the Fortunate (r. 1495–1521)—Promoter of Vasco da Gama's explorations that made Portugal wealthy. Manueline, the decorative art style of that time, is named for him.

Vasco da Gama (1460–1524)—Discovered sea route to India, opening up Asia's wealth.

Pedro Cabral, Bartolomeu Dias, Ferdinand Magellan—Cabral discovered Brazil (1500), Dias rounded the tip of Africa (1488, paving the way for Vasco da Gama), and Magellan (sailing for Spain) led the first circumnavigation of the globe (1520).

Luis de Camões (1524?–1580)—Swashbuckling adventurer and poet who captured the heroism of Vasco da Gama in the epic poem, *The Lusiads*.

Marquês de Pombal (1699–1782)—Prime minister who tried to modernize backward Portugal and who rebuilt Lisbon after the 1755 quake.

António Salazar (1889–1970)—"Portugal's Franco," a dictator who led Portugal for four decades, slowly modernizing while preserving rule by the traditional upper classes.

1400–1600—The Age of Discovery

With royal backing, Portugal built a navy and began exploring the seas, motivated by profit and a desire to Christianize Muslim lands. When Vasco da Gama finally inched around the southern tip of Africa and found a sea route to India (1498), suddenly the wealth of all Asia was opened up. Through trade and conquest, tiny Portugal became one of Europe's wealthiest and most powerful nations, with colonies stretching from Brazil to Africa to India to China. Unfortunately, the easy money destroyed the traditional economy. When King Sebastian died, heirless, in a disastrous and draining defeat, Portugal was quickly invaded by Spain (1580).

1600–1900—Slow Fade

The "Spanish Captivity" (1580–1640) drained Portugal. With a false economy, a rigid class system, and the gradual loss of their profitable colonies, Portugal was no match for the rising powers of Spain, England, Holland, and France. The earthquake of 1755

Six Dates that Shaped Portugal

1498 Vasco da Gama sails Portugal into a century of wealth.

1755 An earthquake rocks Lisbon into poverty.

1822 Portugal loses Brazil as a colony.

1910 The monarchy is deposed and repressive military regimes rule.

1974 A left-wing revolution brings democracy.

1986 Portugal joins the European Community (the forerunner of the European Union), boosting the economy.

---

and Napoleon's invasions (1801–1810) were devastating. While the rest of Europe industrialized and democratized, Portugal lingered as an isolated, rural monarchy living off meager wealth from Brazilian gold and sugar.

1900s—The Military and Democracy

Republican rebels assassinated the king, but democracy was slow to establish itself in Portugal's near-medieval class system. A series of military-backed democracies culminated in four decades of António Salazar's "New State," a right-wing regime benefiting the traditional upper classes. Salazar's repressive tactics and unpopular wars abroad (trying to hang onto Portugal's colonial empire) sparked the Carnation Revolution of 1974. After some initial political and economic chaos, Portugal finally mastered democracy. The tourist industry and subsidies from the European Union have put Portugal on the road to prosperity.

Festivals and Public Holidays in 2006

Portugal erupts with fiestas and celebrations throughout the year. Semana Santa (Holy Week) fills the week before Easter with processions and festivities all over Iberia, but especially in Sevilla.

This is a partial list of holidays and festivals. For more information, contact the Portuguese National Tourist Office (listed in this book's introduction) and check these Web sites: www.whatsonwhen.com, www.holidayfestival.com, and www.festivals.com.

Jan 1	New Year's Day
Early Feb	Carnival (Mardi Gras)
April 9–16	Holy Week
April 16	Easter
April 25	Liberty Day (parades, fireworks)

2006

JANUARY
S	M	T	W	T	F	S
1	2	3	4	5	6	7
8	9	10	11	12	13	14
15	16	17	18	19	20	21
22	23	24	25	26	27	28
29	30	31				

FEBRUARY
S	M	T	W	T	F	S
			1	2	3	4
5	6	7	8	9	10	11
12	13	14	15	16	17	18
19	20	21	22	23	24	25
26	27	28				

MARCH
S	M	T	W	T	F	S
			1	2	3	4
5	6	7	8	9	10	11
12	13	14	15	16	17	18
19	20	21	22	23	24	25
26	27	28	29	30	31	

APRIL
S	M	T	W	T	F	S
						1
2	3	4	5	6	7	8
9	10	11	12	13	14	15
16	17	18	19	20	21	22
23/30	24	25	26	27	28	29

MAY
S	M	T	W	T	F	S
	1	2	3	4	5	6
7	8	9	10	11	12	13
14	15	16	17	18	19	20
21	22	23	24	25	26	27
28	29	30	31			

JUNE
S	M	T	W	T	F	S
				1	2	3
4	5	6	7	8	9	10
11	12	13	14	15	16	17
18	19	20	21	22	23	24
25	26	27	28	29	30	

JULY
S	M	T	W	T	F	S
						1
2	3	4	5	6	7	8
9	10	11	12	13	14	15
16	17	18	19	20	21	22
23/30	24/31	25	26	27	28	29

AUGUST
S	M	T	W	T	F	S
		1	2	3	4	5
6	7	8	9	10	11	12
13	14	15	16	17	18	19
20	21	22	23	24	25	26
27	28	29	30	31		

SEPTEMBER
S	M	T	W	T	F	S
					1	2
3	4	5	6	7	8	9
10	11	12	13	14	15	16
17	18	19	20	21	22	23
24	25	26	27	28	29	30

OCTOBER
S	M	T	W	T	F	S
1	2	3	4	5	6	7
8	9	10	11	12	13	14
15	16	17	18	19	20	21
22	23	24	25	26	27	28
29	30	31				

NOVEMBER
S	M	T	W	T	F	S
			1	2	3	4
5	6	7	8	9	10	11
12	13	14	15	16	17	18
19	20	21	22	23	24	25
26	27	28	29	30		

DECEMBER
S	M	T	W	T	F	S
					1	2
3	4	5	6	7	8	9
10	11	12	13	14	15	16
17	18	19	20	21	22	23
24/31	25	26	27	28	29	30

May–June	Algarve Music Festival, Algarve
May 1	Labor Day (closures)
May 13	Pilgrimage to Fátima
June	Lisbon's Festival, Lisbon
June 10	Portuguese National Day
June 13	St. Anthony's Day, Lisbon
June 13	Pilgrimage to Fátima
June 29	St. Peter's Day, Lisbon
July 13	Pilgrimage to Fátima
Aug 13	Pilgrimage to Fátima
Aug 15	Assumption (religious festival)
Aug 19	Pilgrimage to Fátima
Sept 13	Pilgrimage to Fátima
Mid-Sept	Our Lady of Nazaré Festival, Nazaré
Oct 5	Republic Day (businesses closed)
Oct 13	Pilgrimage to Fátima

Nov 1	All Saints' Day
Dec 1	Independence Restoration Day
Dec 8	Feast of the Immaculate Conception
Dec 25	Christmas
Dec 31	New Year's Eve

Let's Talk Telephones

This is a primer on telephoning in Europe. For specifics on Portugal, see "Telephones" in the Introduction.

Dialing Direct

Making Calls within a European Country: What you dial depends on the phone system of the country you're in. About half of all European countries use area codes; the other half uses a direct-dial system without area codes.

If you're calling within a country that uses a direct-dial system (Portugal, Spain, Belgium, the Czech Republic, France, Italy, Switzerland, Norway, and Denmark), dial the same number whether you're calling within the city or across the country.

In countries that use area codes (such as Austria, Britain, Finland, Germany, Ireland, the Netherlands, and Sweden), dial the local number when calling within a city, and add the area code if calling long-distance within the country. Example: The phone number of a hotel in Munich is 089/264-349. To call it in Munich, dial 264-349; to call it from Frankfurt, dial 089-264-349.

Making International Calls: Always start with the international access code (011 if calling from the U.S. or Canada, 00 from Europe), then dial the country code of the country you're calling (see list below).

What you dial next depends on the particular phone system of the country you're calling. If the country uses area codes, drop the initial zero of the area code, then dial the rest of the area code and the local number. Example: To call the Munich hotel from Portugal, dial 00, 49 (Germany's country code), then 89-264-349.

Countries that use direct-dial systems (no area codes) differ in how they're accessed internationally by phone. For instance, if you're making an international call to Portugal, Spain, Italy, the Czech Republic, Norway, or Denmark, simply dial the international access code, country code, and phone number. Example: The phone number of a hotel in Madrid is 915-212-900. To call it from Portugal, dial 00, 34 (Spain's country code), then 915-212-900. But if you're calling Belgium, France, or Switzerland, drop the initial zero of the phone number. Example: The phone number of a Paris hotel is 01 47 05 49 15. To call it from Portugal, dial 00, 33 (France's country code), then 1 47 05 49 15 (the phone number without the initial zero).

European Calling Chart

Just smile and dial, using this key:
AC = Area Code, LN = Local Number.

European Country	Calling long distance within ...	Calling from the U.S.A./ Canada to ...	Calling from a European country to ...
Austria	AC + LN	011 + 43 + AC (without the initial zero) + LN	00 + 43 + AC (without the initial zero) + LN
Belgium	LN	011 + 32 + LN (without initial zero)	00 + 32 + LN (without initial zero)
Britain	AC + LN	011 + 44 + AC (without initial zero) + LN	00 + 44 + AC (without initial zero) + LN
Croatia	AC + LN	011 + 385 + AC (without initial zero) + LN	00 + 385 + AC (without initial zero) + LN
Czech Republic	LN	011 + 420 + LN	00 + 420 + LN
Denmark	LN	011 + 45 + LN	00 + 45 + LN
Finland	AC + LN	011 + 358 + AC (without initial zero) + LN	00 + 358 + AC (without initial zero) + LN
France	LN	011 + 33 + LN (without initial zero)	00 + 33 + LN (without initial zero)
Germany	AC + LN	011 + 49 + AC (without initial zero) + LN	00 + 49 + AC (without initial zero) + LN
Greece	LN	011 + 30 + LN	00 + 30 + LN
Hungary	06 + AC + LN	011 + 36 + AC + LN	00 + 36 + AC + LN
Ireland	AC + LN	011 + 353 + AC (without initial zero) + LN	00 + 353 + AC (without initial zero) + LN
Italy	LN	011 + 39 + LN	00 + 39 + LN

European Country	Calling long distance within ...	Calling from the U.S.A./ Canada to ...	Calling from a European country to ...
Netherlands	AC + LN	011 + 31 + AC (without initial zero) + LN	00 + 31 + AC (without initial zero) + LN
Norway	LN	011 + 47 + LN	00 + 47 + LN
Poland	AC + LN	011 + 48 + AC (without initial zero) + LN	00 + 48 + AC (without initial zero) + LN
Portugal	LN	011 + 351 + LN	00 + 351 + LN
Slovakia	AC + LN	011 + 421 + AC (without initial zero) + LN	00 + 421 + AC (without initial zero) + LN
Slovenia	AC + LN	011 + 386 + AC (without initial zero) + LN	00 + 386 + AC (without initial zero) + LN
Spain	LN	011 + 34 + LN	00 + 34 + LN
Sweden	AC + LN	011 + 46 + AC (without initial zero) + LN	00 + 46 + AC (without initial zero) + LN
Switzerland	LN	011 + 41 + LN (without initial zero)	00 + 41 + LN (without initial zero)
Turkey	AC (if no initial zero is included, add one) + LN	011 + 90 + AC (without initial zero) + LN	00 + 90 + AC (without initial zero) + LN

- The instructions above apply whether you're calling a fixed phone or mobile phone.
- The international access codes (the first numbers you dial when making an international call) are 011 if you're calling from the U.S.A./Canada, or 00 if you're calling from anywhere in Europe.
- To call the U.S.A. or Canada from Europe, dial 00, then 1 (the country code for the U.S.A. and Canada), then the area code and number. In short, 00 + 1 + AC + LN = Hi, Mom!

Country Codes

After you dial the international access code (00 if you're calling from Europe, 011 if you're calling from America or Canada), dial the code of the country you're calling.

Austria—43	France—33	Poland—48
Belgium—32	Germany—49	Portugal—351
Britain—44	Gibraltar—350	Slovakia—421
Canada—1	Greece—30	Slovenia—386
Croatia—385	Ireland—353	Spain—34
Czech Rep.—420	Italy—39	Sweden—46
Denmark—45	Morocco—212	Switzerland—41
Estonia—372	Netherlands—31	Turkey—90
Finland—358	Norway—47	U.S.A.—1

Directory Assistance

In Portugal, dial 118 for local numbers and 177 for international numbers.

U.S. Embassy

In Lisbon: Avenida das Forças Armadas, tel. 217-273-300, www.american-embassy.pt

Numbers and Stumblers

- Europeans write a few of their numbers differently than we do. 1 = 1 , 4 = 4, 7 = 7. Learn the difference or miss your train.
- In Europe, dates appear as day/month/year, so Christmas is 25/12/06.
- Commas are decimal points and decimals commas. A dollar and a half is 1,50, and there are 5.280 feet in a mile.
- When pointing, use your whole hand, palm down.
- When counting with fingers, start with your thumb. If you hold up your first finger to request one item, you'll probably get two.
- What Americans call the second floor of a building is the first floor in Europe.
- Europeans keep the left "lane" open for passing on escalators and moving sidewalks. Keep to the right.

Metric Conversion (approximate)

1 inch = 25 millimeters	32 degrees F = 0 degrees C
1 foot = 0.3 meter	82 degrees F = about 28 degrees C
1 yard = 0.9 meter	1 ounce = 28 grams
1 mile = 1.6 kilometers	1 kilogram = 2.2 pounds

1 centimeter = 0.4 inch   1 quart = 0.95 liter
1 meter = 39.4 inches   1 square yard = 0.8 square meter
1 kilometer = .62 mile   1 acre = 0.4 hectare

Climate Chart

First line, average daily low; second line, average daily high; third line, days of no rain.

	J	F	M	A	M	J	J	A	S	O	N	D
Lisbon												
	46°	47°	50°	53°	55°	60°	63°	63°	62°	58°	52°	47°
	57°	59°	63°	67°	71°	77°	81°	82°	79°	72°	63°	58°
	16	16	17	20	21	25	29	29	24	22	17	16
Faro (Algarve)												
	48°	49°	52°	55°	58°	64°	67°	68°	65°	60°	55°	50°
	60°	61°	64°	67°	71°	77°	83°	83°	78°	72°	66°	61°
	22	21	21	24	27	29	31	31	29	25	22	22

Temperature Conversion: Fahrenheit and Celsius

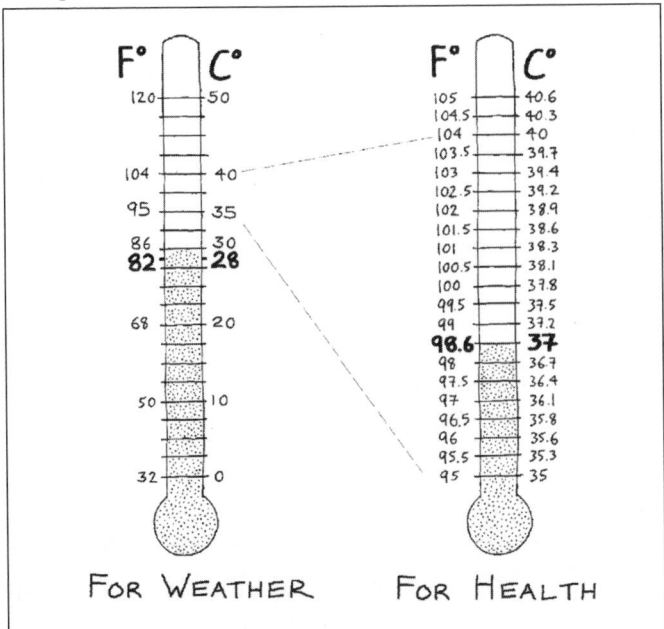

Europe takes its temperature using the Celsius scale, while we opt for Fahrenheit. For weather, remember that 28°C is 82°F—perfect. For health, 37°C is just right.

Making Your Hotel Reservation

Most hotel managers know basic "hotel English." Faxing or e-mailing are the preferred methods for reserving a room. They're more accurate than telephoning and much faster than writing a letter. Use this handy form for your fax or find it online at www.ricksteves.com/reservation. Photocopy and fax away.

One-Page Fax

To: _____ @ _____
        hotel   *fax*

From: _____@ _____
         name   *fax*

Today's date: _____ / _____ / _____
              day   *month*   *year*

Dear Hotel _____ ,
Please make this reservation for me:

Name: _____

Total # of people:_____ # of rooms: _____ # of nights: _____

Arriving: _____ /_____ /_____   My time of arrival (24-hr clock): _____
          day *month* *year*   (I will telephone if I will be late)

Departing: ____ /____/_____
           day *month* *year*

Room(s): Single _____Double ___Twin _____Triple ____ Quad_____

With: Toilet _____ Shower_____Bath _____ Sink only _____

Special needs: View___ Quiet ___ Cheapest ___ Ground Floor ___

Please fax, mail, or e-mail confirmation of my reservation, along with the type of room reserved and the price. Please also inform me of your cancellation policy. After I hear from you, I will quickly send my credit-card information as a deposit to hold the room. Thank you.

_____
Signature

_____
Name

_____
Address

_____
City   *State*   *Zip Code*   *Country*

_____
E-mail Address

Portuguese Survival Phrases

In the phonetics, nasalized vowels are indicated by an underlined **n** or **w**. As you say the vowel, let its sound come through your nose as well as your mouth.

Good day.	Bom dia.	boh<u>n</u> **dee**-ah
Do you speak English?	Fala inglês?	**fah**-lah een-**glaysh**
Yes. / No.	Sim. / Não.	seeng / no<u>w</u>
I (don't) understand.	(Não) compreendo.	(no<u>w</u>) koh<u>n</u>-pree-**ayn**-doo
Please.	Por favor.	poor fah-**vor**
Thank you. (said by male)	Obrigado.	oh-bree-**gah**-doo
Thank you. (said by female)	Obrigada.	oh-bree-**gah**-dah
I'm sorry.	Desculpe.	dish-**kool**-peh
Excuse me (to pass).	Com licença.	koh<u>n</u> li-**sehn**-sah
(No) problem.	(Não) há problema.	(no<u>w</u>) ah proo-**blay**-mah
Good.	Bom.	boh<u>n</u>
Goodbye.	Adeus.	ah-**deh**-oosh
one / two	um / dois	oo<u>n</u> / doysh
three / four	três / quarto	traysh / **kwah**-troo
five / six	cinco / seis	**seeng**-koo / saysh
seven / eight	sete / oito	**seh**-teh / **oy**-too
nine / ten	nove / dez	**naw**-veh / dehsh
How much is it?	Quanto é?	**kwahn**-too eh
Write it?	Escreva?	ish-**kray**-vah
Is it free?	É gratis?	eh **grah**-teesh
Is it included?	Está incluido?	ish-**tah** een-kloo-**ee**-doo
Where can I find / buy...?	Onde posso encontrar / comprar...?	**ohn**-deh paw-soo ayn-kohn-**trar** / kohn-**prar**
I'd like / We'd like...	Gostaria / Gostaríamos...	goosh-tah-**ree**-ah / goosh-tah-**ree**-ah-moosh
...a room.	...um quarto.	oo<u>n</u> **kwar**-too
...a ticket to ___.	...um bilhete para ___.	oo<u>n</u> beel-**yeh**-teh **pah**-rah
Is it possible?	É possível?	eh poo-**see**-vehl
Where is...?	Onde é que é...?	**ohn**-deh eh keh eh
...the train station	...a estação de comboio	ah ish-tah-**sow** deh koh<u>n</u>-**boy**-yoo
...the bus station	...a terminal de autocarros	ah tehr-mee-**nahl** deh ow-too-**kah**-roosh
...the tourist information office	...a informação turistica	ah een-for-mah-**sow** too-reesh-tee-kah
...the toilet	...a casa de banho	ah **kah**-zah deh **bahn**-yoo
men	homens	**aw**-may<u>n</u>sh
women	mulheres	mool-**yeh**-rish
left / right	esquerda / direita	ish-**kehr**-dah / dee-**ray**-tah
straight	em frente	ayn **frayn**-teh
What time does this open / close?	A que horas é que abre / fecha?	ah keh **aw**-rahsh eh keh **ah**-breh / **feh**-shah
At what time?	A que horas?	ah keh **aw**-rahsh
Just a moment.	Um momento.	oo<u>n</u> moo-**mayn**-too
now / soon / later	agora / em breve / mais tarde	ah-**goh**-rah / ayn **bray**-veh / maish **tar**-deh
today / tomorrow	hoje / amanhã	**oh**-zheh / ah-ming-**yah**

In the Restaurant

I'd like / We'd like...	Gostaria / Gostaríamos...	goosh-tah-**ree**-ah / goosh-tah-**ree**-ah-moosh
...to reserve...	...de reservar...	deh reh-zehr-**var**
...a table for one / two.	...uma mesa para uma / duas.	**oo**-mah **may**-zah **pah**-rah **oo**-mah / **doo**-ahsh
Non-smoking.	Não fumar.	now foo-**mar**
Is this table free?	Esta mesa está livre?	ehsh-tah meh-zah ish-**tah** lee-vreh
The menu (in English), please.	A ementa (em inglês), por favor.	ah eh-**mayn**-tah (ayn een-**glaysh**) poor fah-**vor**
service (not) included	serviço (não) incluído	sehr-**vee**-soo (now) een-kloo-**ee**-doo
cover charge	tixa aplicada	**tī**-shah ah-plee-**kah**-dah
to go	para fora	**pah**-rah **foh**-rah
with / without	com / sem	kohn / sayn
and / or	e / ou	ee / oh
specialty of the house	especialidade da casa	ish-peh-see-ah-lee-**dah**-deh dah **kah**-zah
half portion	meia dose	**may**-ah **doh**-zeh
daily special	prato do dia	**prah**-too doo **dee**-ah
tourist menu	ementa turistica	eh-**mayn**-tah too-**reesh**-tee-kah
appetizers	entradas	ayn-**trah**-dahsh
bread	pão	pow
cheese	queijo	**kay**-zhoo
sandwich	sandes	**sahn**-desh
soup	sopa	**soh**-pah
salad	salada	sah-**lah**-dah
meat	carne	**kar**-neh
poultry	aves	**ah**-vish
fish	peixe	**pay**-shee
seafood	marisco	mah-**reesh**-koo
fruit	fruta	**froo**-tah
vegetables	legumes	lay-**goo**-mish
dessert	sobremesa	soo-breh-**may**-zah
tap water	água da torneira	**ah**-gwah dah tor-**nay**-rah
mineral water	água mineral	**ah**-gwah mee-neh-**rahl**
milk	leite	**lay**-teh
(orange) juice	sumo (de laranja)	**soo**-moo (deh lah-**rahn**-zhah)
coffee	café	kah-**feh**
tea	chá	shah
wine	vinho	**veen**-yoo
red / white	tinto / branco	**teen**-too / **brang**-koo
glass / bottle	copo / garrafa	**koh**-poo / gah-**rah**-fah
beer	cerveja	sehr-**vay**-zhah
Cheers!	Saúde!	sah-**oo**-deh
More. / Another.	Mais. / Outro.	maish / **oh**-troo
The same.	O mesmo.	oo **mehsh**-moo
Bill, please.	Conta, por favor.	**kohn**-tah poor fah-**vor**
tip	gorjeta	gor-**zheh**-tah
Delicious!	Delicioso!	deh-lee-see-**oh**-zoo

For hundreds more pages of survival phrases for your trip to Portugal, check out *Rick Steves' Portuguese Phrase Book.*

INDEX

Accommodations: *See Pousadas;* Sleeping; *and specific destinations*

Afonso Henriques: 59, 174–176, 181, 190, 255, 256

Age of Discovery (1400-1600): 9, 35, 83, 143, 170, 256; Maritime Museum (Belém), 57, 81; Monument to the Discoveries (Belém), 57, 81–84

Airfares: 3

Airports: Lisbon, 42, 44, 100; Porto, 211

Alcobaça: 174–177

Alentejo: 141–156; about, 143. *See also* Évora

Alfama, the (Lisbon): 41, 58–61; eating, 94–96; fado, 88; map, 59; market, 45, 58, 85; tours, 48–50; walking tour, 58–61

Algarve, the: 113–140; map, 114; transportation, 115

Amarante: 241–242

American Express: 13; Lisbon, 45

Anta Capela de São Brissos: 152

Anta do Zambujeiro: 152

Anthony, Saint: 61, 65

Apartment rentals: 26

Aquarium, in Lisbon: 72

Archaeological sites: 152–153. *See also* Romans, ancient

Architecture: Manueline, 76. *See also* Churches and cathedrals; Monasteries; *and specific buildings*

Arco de Almedina (Coimbra): 190, 192–193

Armazéns do Chiado (Lisbon): 56–57, 86, 98

Art museums: Decorative Arts Museum (Lisbon), 56, 60; Machado de Castro Museum (Coimbra), 197; Museu de Arte Popular (Belém), 57, 85; Museum of Sacred Art (Coimbra), 196; Museu Nacional de Arte Antiga (Lisbon), 56, 69–70; Museu Nacional do Azulejo (Lisbon), 56, 70; Serralves Foundation (Porto), 213, 227–229; Sintra Museum of Modern Art, 109

ATM machines: 12–14; Lisbon, 45. *See also specific destinations*

Avenida da Liberdade (Lisbon): 65–66; eating, 99; sleeping, 93–94

Avenida dos Aliados (Porto): 218–219

Avis Coat of Arms: 170

Azulejos: 68, 85, 107, 152, 251; Museu Nacional do Azulejo (Lisbon), 56, 70; Porto Cathedral, 213, 221–222; São Bento Station (Porto), 210, 212, 220–221, 235

Back Door travel philosophy: 33

Bairro Alto (Lisbon): 41, 51–58; eating, 96–97; fado, 87–88; map, 53; walking tour, 51–58

Baixa (Lisbon): 41, 62–65; nightlife, 86–87

Banks: 12–14; Lisbon, 45

Barril Beach: 138

Batalha: 166–172

Beaches: Barril Beach, 138; Cabo da Roca, 112; Cacela Velha, 138; Cape Sagres, 127–128; Cascais, 112; Estoril, 112; Figueira Beach, 121; Lagos, 130; Nazaré, 157, 159, 160; nudist, 120, 121; Praia Adraga, 112; Sagres, 125; Salema, 118, 120, 123; Tavira, 138

Belém: 41, 73–85; eating, 75; ferries, 75–76; information, 42, 75; map, 74; sights, 57, 76–85; sleeping, 94; transportation, 73, 75

Belém Tower: 57, 84–85; eating, 75

Berardo Collection (Sintra): 109

Bica funicular (Lisbon): 48, 49

Biking: Lisbon, 72; Tavira, 135

Birdwatching: 120–121

Bishop's Palace (Porto): 222

Boat cruises: Coimbra, 199; Douro River, 240–241, 252; Porto, 212, 215–216; Lagos, 130, 132; Lisbon, 51; Salema, 120–121

Bone Chapel (Évora): 150–151

Books, recommended: 9

Bookstores: Lisbon, 54, 55; Porto, 219–220

Bosch, Hieronymus: 69, 70

Brits on the Douro: 244–245

Budgeting: 3

Bullfights: Évora, 153; Lagos, 132; Lisbon, 88–89; Sítio, 161

Buses: 15, 17–18; map, 18; Alcobaça, 174, 177; the Algarve, 115; Batalha, 172; Coimbra, 187, 188, 206; Évora, 144, 156; Fátima, 174; Lagos, 130, 134; Lisbon, 43–44, 47, 50; Nazaré, 164–165; Óbidos, 179, 183; Porto, 210–211, 212, 236; Salema, 116; Sintra, 105

Business hours: 11

Cabo da Roca: 101, 112; tours, 102–103
Cabo St. Vincent: 125
Cabral, Pedro: 82, 83, 127, 256
Cabs: *See* Taxis
Cacela Velha: 138
Café A Brasileira (Lisbon): 51, 55
Cais do Sodré Station (Lisbon): 43, 103
Cais e Praça da Ribeira (Porto): 215
Caldas da Rainha: 181
Camões, Luis de: 79, 80, 112, 169, 256; memorial to (Belém), 79–80
Campanhã Station (Porto): 210, 235
Campgrounds: 26; Salema, 122–123; Tavira, 138
Campo de Santa Clara (Lisbon): 45, 58, 85
Canyoning: 199
Capela dos Ossos (Évora): 150–151
Cape Sagres: 125–129; boat tours, 120–121
Caravels: about, 81
Car rentals: 19–20; Coimbra, 188
Car travel: 15, 20–21; best two-week trip, 4–5; distance and time, 20; road signs, 19; the Algarve, 140; Coimbra, 187; Douro Valley, 241; Évora, 144; Lisbon, 44, 100; Óbidos, 179, 183; Porto, 211; Salema, 116; Sintra, 103, 105
Casa da Música (Porto): 229
Casa de S. Thiago do Castelo (Óbidos): 181, 182
Casa do Infante (Porto): 213, 218
Casal de Loivos: 253
Cascais: 112
Castelejo Restaurante: 124, 127–128
Castelo dos Mouros (Sintra): 109
Cathedrals: *See* Churches and cathedrals
Cell phones: 22
Cervejaria da Trindade (Lisbon): 54
Chapel of Bones (Évora): 150–151

Chiado (Lisbon): 51–58; map, 53; shopping, 56–57, 85–86; walking tour, 51–58
Christ of Majesty statue (Lisbon): 49, 73
Churches and cathedrals: Clérigos Church (Porto), 219, 220; Coimbra Old Cathedral, 197–198; Évora Cathedral, 148–150; Fátima, 172–173; Lisbon Cathedral, 57, 65; Misericorda (Tavira), 136–137; Our Lady of Grace (Sagres), 126; Porto Cathedral, 213, 221–222; St. Francis (Évora), 150–151; Santa Cruz (Coimbra), 190–191; Santa María (Tavira), 137; Santa María de Évora, 148–150; Santa María de Óbidos: 180; Santo António (Lagos), 132; Santo Ildefonso (Porto), 219, 222–223; São Domingos (Lisbon), 64; São Francisco (Porto), 212, 217; São Roque (Lisbon), 52, 54, 56. *See also* Monasteries
Clérigos Church and Tower (Porto): 219, 220
Climate: 5–6, 263
Coach Museum (Belém): 57, 76–77
Coimbra: 184–206; eating, 204–205; helpful hints, 187–188; information, 186; maps, 185, 202; planning tips, 184; sights, 188–201; sleeping, 201–204; transportation, 186–187, 188, 206; walking tour, 188–193
Coimbra Old Cathedral: 197–198
Coimbra's Old University: 192, 193–197; map, 194
Coin markets, in Lisbon: 85
Colombo Shopping Mall (Lisbon): 85–86
Columbus, Christopher: 81, 127
Conímbriga: 199–201
Convento da Madre de Deus (Lisbon): 56, 70
Convento do Carmo (Lisbon): 54–55
Cork: about, 155
Credit cards: 12; lost or stolen, 13
Cristo Rei (Lisbon): 49, 73
Cromeleque dos Almendres: 152–153
Cruises: *See* Boat cruises
Cuisine: *See* Eating; Food; Markets

Currency exchange: 12
Customs regulations: 14

Decorative Arts Museum (Lisbon): 56, 60
Dias, Bartolomeu: 79, 83, 127, 256
Dining: *See* Eating; *and specific destinations*
Discounts: 11; Lisbon, 42
Dolphin-watching cruises, in Lagos: 132
Don Ramiro Wine House (Óbidos): 180–181
Douro Azul: 240–241
Douro Museum (Peso da Régua): 248
Douro River: 209–210, 214–215, 237, 240; cruises, 212, 215–216, 240–241, 252
Douro Valley: 237–253; map, 239; planning tips, 238; port wine, 237, 244–247; *quintas*, 242–244; tours, 242–244, 248; transportation, 240–242
Drinks: 28, 30–31. *See also* Port wine; Wine and vineyards
Driving: *See* Car travel

Earthquake of 1755: 58, 63, 149, 256–257
Eating: 28–31; budgeting, 3; glossary of terms, 31, 266; tipping, 30; typical Portuguese foods, 29. *See also* Markets; *and specific destinations*
Economy: 37
Edifcio Chiado (Coimbra): 190
Edward VII Park (Lisbon): 49, 66
El Corte Inglés (Lisbon): 86
Electricity: 11
Elevador da Glória (Lisbon): 49, 52, 63
Elevador de Santa Justa (Lisbon): 49, 52, 57, 64–65
Elevador do Mercado (Coimbra): 191–192
Elevador dos Guindais (Porto): 213
E-mail: *See* Internet access
Embassy, in Lisbon: 262
Estoril: 112
Euro currency: 12
Évora: 141–156; eating, 154–156; information, 143; maps, 142, 146; planning tips, 141; sights,
144–153; sleeping, 153–154; transportation, 144, 156; walking tour, 144–149
Évora Cathedral: 148–150
Évora Museum: 148
Exchange rates: 12

Fado: about, 88; Coimbra, 198, 204; Lisbon, 87–88; House of Fado, 56, 61
Fátima: 172–174
Ferreira (Vila Nova de Gaia): 226
Ferries: Belém, 75–76; Ilha de Tavira, 138; Lisbon, 73
Festivals: 257–259
Figueira Beach: 121
Fishing: Nazaré, 157; Salema, 118
Flag: 37
Folk Art Museum (Belém): 57, 85
Fonseca: 242–243
Food: glossary of terms, 31, 266; typical Portuguese, 29. *See also* Eating; Markets; *and specific destinations*
Foz (Porto): 212, 216–217
Foz da Figueira: 199
Foz do Douro (Porto): 217
Fundação de Serralves (Porto): 213, 227–229
Fundação Ricardo do Espírito Santo Silva Museum (Lisbon): 56, 60
Funiculars: Coimbra, 191–192; Lisbon, 47; Porto, 213–214; Sítio, 159, 160–161
Furnas Beach: 127

Geography: 36
Ginjinha: 64, 155, 181
Golf, in Salema: 120
Government: 37
Grand Hall (Coimbra): 195
Gruta do Escoural: 152
Guidebooks: 8–9; Rick Steves', 7–8
Guitar Museum (Lisbon): 56, 61
Gulbenkian Museum (Lisbon): 56, 66–69, 86; map, 67

Henry the Navigator: 81–82, 125, 169, 220–221, 233; biographical sketch, 128–129; books about, 9; house of (Porto), 213, 218; school (Sagres), 125–127
Historic inns: *See* Pousadas
History: 255–257

Holidays: 257–259

Hotels: overview of, 24–27; reservations, 26–27; reservations form, 264. *See also specific destinations*

House of Fado and Portuguese Guitar (Lisbon): 56, 61

House of Henry the Navigator (Porto): 213, 218

House of Music (Porto): 229

Igreja e Torre dos Clérigos (Porto): 219, 220

Ilha de Tavira: 138

Information sources: 6–9. *See also specific destinations*

Ingrina Beach: 127

Internet access: 24; Coimbra, 187–188; Lisbon, 45; Porto, 211. *See also specific destinations*

Iron Gate (Coimbra): 193–194

Jerónimos Monastery (Belém): 57, 77–81

Jewish Quarter (Évora): 145–146

John (João) I: 106–107, 128, 166, 167–171, 194, 218, 220, 256

John (João) III: 145–146, 170, 194, 256

Kayaking: 199

King John's Library (Coimbra): 196–197

Koolhaas, Rem: 229

Lagos: 129–134; map, 131

Language: 11–12; basic survival phrases, 265; food terms, 31, 266

Largo da Portagem (Coimbra): 189

Largo das Portas do Sol (Lisbon): 51, 60

Largo de São Domingos (Lisbon): 64

Largo do Carmo (Lisbon): 54–55, 85

LisboaCard: 42, 47, 104–105

Lisbon: 36, 38–100; arrival in, 43–44; eating, 94–99; excursion areas, 101–112; helpful hints, 44–45; information, 42; layout of, 41–42; nightlife, 86–89; planning tips, 40–41; shopping, 85–86; sights, 51–85; sleeping, 90–94; tours, 48–51, 102–103; transportation, 42, 43–44, 46–47, 99–100; walking tours, 51–61

Lisbon Airport: 42, 44, 100

Lisbon Cathedral: 57, 65

Lisbon earthquake of 1755: 58, 63, 149

Lisbon Experience: 81

Little Portugal (Coimbra): 199

Lodging: *See Pousadas; Sleeping; and specific destinations*

Loios Pousada (Évora): 147–148, 153–154

Machado de Castro Museum (Coimbra): 197

Magellan, Ferdinand: 9, 82, 84, 127, 256

Mail: 24. *See also specific destinations*

Majestic Café (Porto): 223, 235

Manuel I (the Fortunate): 36, 38, 70, 76, 77, 79, 170, 171, 190–191, 256

Maps: about, 9–10. *See also specific destinations*

Marao Mountain: 238

Maritime Museum (Belém): 57, 81

Markets: Alcobaça, 177; Caldas da Rainha, 181; Coimbra, 191, 205; Évora, 146, 151; Lisbon, 45, 58, 85; Nazaré, 160; Porto, 223–224; Salema, 117–118, 124; Tavira, 135, 137

Megaliths: 152–153

Mesao Frio: 240

Metric system: 11, 262–263

Metro: Lisbon, 47; Porto, 212–213

Miradouro de Largo das Portas do Sol (Lisbon): 49

Miradouro de Santa Luzia (Lisbon): 60

Miradouro de São Jorge (Lisbon): 58

Miradouro de São Pedro Alcântara (Lisbon): 49, 51, 52

Misericorda Church (Tavira): 136–137

Mobile (cell) phones: 22

Monasteries: of Jerónimos (Belém), 57, 77–81; of Santa María (Alcobaça), 174–177; of Santa María (Batalha), 166–171; map, 168

Mondego River: 187, 188–189, 199

Money: 12–14; budgeting, 3; safety tips, 11, 13

Money-saving tips: *See Discounts*

Monserrate: 110

Monument to the Discoveries (Belém): 57, 81–84
Moors (Muslims): 181, 222, 255–256; the Algarve, 113, 137; Coimbra, 184, 189, 192–193; Évora, 145, 147, 148, 149; Lisbon, 49, 58–61, 65, 68; Sintra, 109
Museo de Cera de Fátima: 173–174
Museu de Arte Popular (Belém): 57, 85
Museu de Marinha (Belém): 57, 81
Museu do Carro Eléctrico (Porto): 213, 216
Museu do Douro (Peso da Régua): 248
Museu dos Coches (Belém): 57, 76–77
Museum of Ancient Art (Lisbon): 56, 69–70
Museum of Sacred Art (Coimbra): 196
Museu Nacional de Arte Antiga (Lisbon): 56, 69–70
Museu Nacional do Azulejo (Lisbon): 56, 70
Museu Nacional do Vinho (Alcobaça): 177
Museu-Vivo Aparições (Fátima): 174
Music: House of Music (Porto), 229. *See also* Fado

Nasoni, Nicolau: 219–220, 221
National Museum of Wine (Alcobaça): 177
National Palace (Sintra): 106–107
National Theater (Lisbon): 86–87
National Tile Museum (Lisbon): 56, 70
Navigators' School (Sagres): 125–127
Nazaré: 157–165; map, 159
Newspapers: 11
Nightlife: budgeting, 3; Lisbon, 86–89; Salema, 120. *See also* Fado
NorParque (Sítio): 163

Óbidos: 177–183; map, 178
Óbidos wall: 179–180
O Cântaro (Porto): 215
Oceanário (Lisbon): 72
Olisipónia (Lisbon): 59–60
Olive oil: 28, 171, 247
Orient Express: 50

Our Lady of Grace Church (Sagres): 126
Our Lady of Nazaré: 161

Padrao dos Descobrimentos (Belém): 57, 81–84
Palácio da Bolsa (Porto): 212, 217–218
Palácio de Pena (Sintra): 107–109
Palácio Nacional (Sintra): 106–107
Parque das Naçoes (Lisbon): 70, 72, 85
Parque Dr. Manuel Braga (Coimbra): 199, 205
Passports: 10
Pedro I (the Just): 167, 170, 175, 176, 177, 256
Penacova: 199
Pena Palace (Sintra): 107–109
Peso da Régua: 240, 247–251
Pessoa, Fernando: 55, 98
Pinhão: 240, 251–253
Pombal, Marquês de: 39, 49, 54–55, 62, 65, 66, 152, 237, 256
Ponte Dom Luís I (Porto): 210, 213, 215
Population: 36
Porto: 207–236; arrival in, 210–211; eating, 233–235; helpful hints, 211; information, 210; layout of, 209–210; planning tips, 209; shopping, 222–229; sights, 212–213, 214–229; sleeping, 229–233; tours, 214; transportation, 210–211, 212–214, 235–236
Porto Brandão: 75–76
Porto Cathedral: 213, 221–222
Porto Tours: 214, 222, 241
Portugal dos Pequenitos (Coimbra): 199
Portuguese Guitar Museum (Lisbon): 56, 61
Portuguese National Tourist Office: 6
Port wine: about, 31, 226–227, 244–245; Douro Valley, 237, 242–247; *quintas,* 242–244; Vila Nova de Gaia, 212, 224–227
Port Wine Institute: Lisbon, 52, 56; Peso da Régua, 244, 248–249; Porto, 213, 216, 224
Post offices: 24; Lisbon, 45. *See also specific destinations*
Pousadas: 26; Cape Sagres, 128;

Coimbra, 204; Évora, 147–148, 153–154; Óbidos, 181, 182; Solar da Rede, 244, 250–251
Praça da Batalha (Porto): 221, 222–223
Praça da Liberdade (Porto): 219–220
Praça do Comércio (Coimbra): 189–190
Praça do Comércio (Lisbon): 42, 65
Praça do Giraldo (Évora): 145–146, 149
Praça dos Restauradores (Lisbon): 41, 62–63; sleeping, 90–91
Praça Infante Dom Henrique (Porto): 209, 217–218
Praia Adraga: 112
Praia do Castelejo: 127–128

Quintas: 109–110, 242–244, 249, 253

Rabelos: 211, 215–216, 247, 248, 252
Rafting: 199
Railpasses: 10, 15, 16, 17
Rail travel: See Train travel
Raposeira: 127
Rappelling: 199
Reader feedback: 32
Reading, recommended: 9
Régua: 240, 247–251
Rental properties: 26
Restaurants: See Eating; and specific destinations
Ribeira (Porto): 209, 211, 214–217; eating, 233–234; information, 210; sleeping, 231, 233
Ribeira embankment (Porto): 212, 214–215
Romans, ancient: 127, 207, 242, 255; Coimbra, 197, 199–201; Évora, 141, 145–148; Lisbon, 65, 67; Tavira, 137
Rossio (Lisbon): 41, 52, 63–64; eating, 97–99; nightlife, 86–87; sleeping, 90–91, 93
Rossio Station (Lisbon): 43, 63
Royal Cloisters (Batalha): 169–170
Rua de Vasco da Gama (Évora): 148
Rua Garrett (Lisbon): 55–56
Rua Santa Catarina (Porto): 223; eating, 235

Safety tips: 11, 13
Sagres: 125–129
Sagres Fort: 125–127

St. Francis Church (Évora): 150–151
St. Michael's Chapel (Coimbra): 195–196
Salamanca (Spain): transportation, 206
Salazar, António de Oliveira: 36, 54, 71, 72, 193, 256, 257
Salema: 115–124; eating, 123–124; information, 116; maps, 116, 119; nightlife, 120; sights, 117–120; sleeping, 121–123; transportation, 116–117
Sandeman (Vila Nova de Gaia): 224, 225
San Pedro Park belvedere (Lisbon): 49, 51, 52
Santa Apolónia Station (Lisbon): 42, 43
Santa Clara Bridge (Coimbra): 188–189, 199
Santa Cruz Church (Coimbra): 190–191
Santa María Church (Tavira): 137
Santa María de Évora: 148–150
Santa María de Óbidos: 180
Santa María Monastery (Alcobaça): 174–177
Santa María Monastery (Batalha): 166–171; map, 168
Santiago de Compostela (Spain): transportation, 235–236
Santo António Church (Lagos): 132
Santo Ildefonso (Porto): 219, 222–223
São Bento Train Station (Porto): 210, 212, 220–221, 235
São Domingos Church (Lisbon): 64
São Francisco Church (Porto): 212, 217
São Gonçalo: 242
São Jorge Castle (Lisbon): 56, 58–59
São Roque Church (Lisbon): 52, 54, 56
Sé: See Churches and cathedrals
Seasons: 5–6
Serralves Foundation (Porto): 213, 227–229
Sevilla (Spain): transportation, 134
Shopping: budgeting, 3; hours, 11; Lisbon, 85–86; Porto, 222–229; VAT refunds, 14
Sightseeing: best two-week trip, 4–5; budgeting, 3; priorities, 4. See also specific sights and destinations

Sintra: 101–111; eating, 111; information, 104–105; map, 104; sights, 106–110; sleeping, 110–111; transportation, 101–103, 105–106, 111

Sintra Museum of Modern Art: 109

Sítio: 158–161; eating, 164

Skiing: 36

Sleep code: 25

Sleeping: 24–27; budgeting, 3; phones, 22, 23; reservations, 26–27; reservations form, 264. *See also* Pousadas; *and specific destinations*

Soccer: 37

Solar da Rede Pousada: 244, 250–251

Solar do Vinho do Porto: *See* Port Wine Institute

Stock Exchange Palace (Porto): 212, 217–218

Tagus River: *See* Tejo River

Tavira: 134–140; map, 136

Távora River: 243

Taxes: VAT refunds, 14

Taxis: 18; Évora, 144; Lisbon, 47–48; Porto, 214; Salema, 117; Sintra, 105; tipping, 30

Tejo River: 36, 38, 41; cruises, 51; ferries, 75

Telephones: 21–24, 259–262

Temptations of St. Anthony (Bosch): 70

Tennis: Salema, 120

Time zones: 10–11

Tipping: 30

Tomb of the Unknown Soldier (Batalha): 171

Torre dos Clérigos (Porto): 219, 220

Tourist information: 6–7. *See also specific destinations*

Tours: best two-week trip, 4–5; Cabo da Roca, 102–103; Douro Valley, 242–244, 248; Évora, 143; Lisbon, 48–51, 102–103; Porto, 214; Rick Steves', 10; Salema, 120–121

Toy Museum (Sintra): 110

Train travel: 15–17; best two-week trip, 4–5; map, 18; the Algarve, 115; Coimbra, 186–187, 206; Évora, 144, 156; Lagos, 130, 134; Lisbon, 43, 99–100; Nazaré, 164; Óbidos, 179; Porto, 210, 235–236; Salema, 116; Sintra, 101–102, 105, 111; Tavira, 135

Tramway Museum (Porto): 213, 216

Transportation: 15–21; budgeting, 3; map, 18. *See also* Boat cruises; Buses; Car travel; Train travel

Travel smarts: 6

Trolleys, in Lisbon: 48–50, 52

25th of April Bridge (Lisbon): 72–73, 86

University of Coimbra: 192, 193–197; map, 194

University of Évora: 151–152

Valado: 164–165

Vale do Douro: *See* Douro Valley

Vasco da Gama: 38, 70, 73, 80, 82, 127, 151, 256; books about, 9; tomb of (Belém), 79

Vasco da Gama Bridge (Lisbon): 51, 72

VAT refunds: 14

Vila do Bispo: 127

Vila Nova de Gaia: 209, 247; port wine lodges, 212, 224–227

Vintage House Hotel (Pinhão): 240, 243, 252–253

Virgin of Fátima: 172, 173–174

Viriato: 256

Viúva Lamego (Lisbon): 55, 85

Water park, in Sítio: 161

Weather: 5–6, 263

Wine and vineyards: 28, 30–31; Douro Valley, 242–247; Lisbon, 52; National Museum of Wine (Alcobaça), 177; Óbidos, 180–181. *See also* Port wine

Zavial Beach: 127

CREDITS

Researchers

To help update this book, Rick relied on the help of...

Robert Wright

Robert Wright was raised in Memphis, but now lives a bit farther south—Buenos Aires, Argentina. A long-time Iberophile and a guide for Rick Steves tours, Robert spends his free time searching for the best *cataplana* and *vinho verde* in Portugal.

Images

Lisbon: View from Largo Santa Luzia	Rick Steves
Sintra: National Palace	Robert Wright
The Algarve:	Rick Steves
Évora: Roman Temple	Rick Steves
Nazaré and Nearby:	Dave Hoerlein
Coimbra:	Rick Steves
Porto:	Cameron Hewitt
Douro Valley:	Rick Steves

Start your trip at
www.ricksteves.com

Rick Steves' website is packed with over 3,000 pages of timely travel information. It's also your gateway to getting FREE monthly travel news from Rick— and more!

Free Monthly European Travel News

Fresh articles on Europe's most interesting destinations and happenings. Rick will even send you an e-mail every month (often direct from Europe) with his latest discoveries!

Timely Travel Tips

Rick Steves' best money-and-stress-saving tips on trip planning, packing, transportation, hotels, health, safety, finances, hurdling the language barrier…and more.

Travelers' Graffiti Wall

Candid advice and opinions from thousands of travelers on everything listed above, plus whatever topics are hot at the moment (discount flights, packing tips, scams…you name it).

Rick's Annual Guide to European Railpasses

The clearest, most comprehensive guide to the confusing array of railpass options out there, and how to choo-choose the railpass that best fits your itinerary and budget. Then you can order your railpass (and get a bunch of great freebies) online from us!

Great Gear at the Rick Steves Travel Store

Enjoy bargains on Rick's guidebooks, planning maps and TV series DVDs— and on his custom-designed carry-on bags, wheeled bags, day bags and light-packing accessories.

Rick Steves Tours

Every year more than 6,000 lucky travelers explore Europe on a Rick Steves tour. Learn more about our 30 different one-to-three-week itineraries, read uncensored feedback from our tour alums, and sign up for your dream trip online!

Rick on Radio and TV

Read the scripts and run clips from public television's "Rick Steves' Europe" and public radio's "Travel with Rick Steves."

Respect for Your Privacy

Ordering online from us is secure. When you buy something from us, join a tour, or subscribe to Rick's free monthly travel news e-mails, we promise to never share your name, information, or e-mail address with anyone else. You won't be spammed!

Have fun raising your Travel I.Q. at
www.ricksteves.com

Travel smart...carry on!

The latest generation of Rick Steves' carry-on travel bags is easily the best—benefiting from two decades of on-the-road attention to what really matters: maximum quality and strength; practical, flexible features; and no unnecessary frills. You won't find a better value anywhere!

Convertible, expandable, and carry-on-size:
Rick Steves' Back Door Bag $99

This is the same bag that Rick Steves lives out of for three months every summer. It's made of rugged water-resistant 1000 denier Cordura nylon, and best of all, it converts easily from a smart-looking suitcase to a handy backpack with comfortably-curved shoulder straps and a padded waistbelt.

This roomy, versatile 9" x 21" x 14" bag has a large 2600 cubic-inch main compartment, plus three outside pockets (small, medium and huge) that are perfect for often-used items. And the cinch-tight compression straps will keep your load compact and close to your back—not sagging like a sack of potatoes.

Wishing you had even more room to bring home souvenirs? Pull open the full-perimeter expando-zipper and its capacity jumps from 2600 to 3000 cubic inches. When you want to use it as a suitcase or check it as luggage (required when "expanded"), the straps and belt hide away in a zippered compartment in the back.

Attention travelers under 5'4" tall: This bag also comes in an inch-shorter version, for a compact-friendlier fit between the waistbelt and shoulder straps.

Convenient, expandable, and carry-on-size:
Rick Steves' Wheeled Bag $129

At 9" x 21" x 14" our sturdy Rick Steves' Wheeled Bag is rucksack-soft in front, but the rest is lined with a hard ABS-lexan shell to give maximum protection to your belongings. We've spared no expense on moving parts, splurging on an extra-long button-release handle and big, tough inline skate wheels for easy rolling on rough surfaces.

Wishing you had even more room to bring home souvenirs? Pull open the full-perimeter expando-zipper and its capacity jumps from 2600 to 3000 cubic inches.

Rick Steves' Wheeled Bag has exactly the same three-outside-pocket configuration as our Back Door Bag, plus a handy "add-a-bag" strap and full lining.

Our Back Door Bags and Wheeled Bags come in black, navy, blue spruce, evergreen and merlot.

For great deals on a wide selection of travel goodies, begin your next trip at the Rick Steves Travel Store!

Visit the Rick Steves Travel Store at
www.ricksteves.com

Rick Steves

More *Savvy*. More *Surprising*. More *Fun*.

COUNTRY GUIDES 2006

England
France
Germany & Austria
Great Britain
Ireland
Italy
Portugal
Scandinavia
Spain
Switzerland

CITY GUIDES 2006

Amsterdam, Bruges & Brussels
Florence & Tuscany
London
Paris
Prague & The Czech Republic
Provence & The French Riviera
Rome
Venice

BEST OF GUIDES

Best of Eastern Europe
Best of Europe

As the #1 authority on European travel, Rick gives you inside information on what to visit, where to stay, and how to get there—economically and hassle-free.

www.ricksteves.com

PHRASE BOOKS & DICTIONARIES

French
French, Italian & German
German
Italian
Portuguese
Spanish

MORE EUROPE FROM RICK STEVES

Easy Access Europe
Europe 101
Europe Through the Back Door
Postcards from Europe

RICK STEVES' EUROPE DVDs

All 43 Shows 2000-2005
Britain
Eastern Europe
France & Benelux
Germany, The Swiss Alps & Travel Skills
Ireland
Italy
Spain & Portugal

PLANNING MAPS

Britain & Ireland
Europe
France
Germany, Austria & Switzerland
Italy
Spain & Portugal

For a complete listing of Rick Steves' books, see page 7.

Avalon Travel Publishing
1400 65th Street, Suite 250
Emeryville, CA 94608

AVALON
publishing group incorporated

Avalon Travel Publishing
An Imprint of Avalon Publishing Group, Inc.

Printed in the USA by Worzalla.
First printing October 2005.

Thanks to Cameron Hewitt for writing the original versions of the
Porto and Duoro Valley chapters.

Portions of this book were originally published in Rick Steves' Spain & Portugal © 2005,
2004, 2003, 2002, 2001, 2000, 1999, 1998, 1997, 1996 by Rick Steves.

For the latest on Rick Steves' lectures, guidebooks, tours, and public television series,
contact Europe Through the Back Door, Box 2009, Edmonds, WA 98020, tel. 425/771-
8303, fax 425/771-0833, www.ricksteves.com, rick@ricksteves.com.

ISBN(10): 1-56691-964-9
ISBN(13): 978-1-56691-964-7
ISSN 1551-837X

Europe Through the Back Door Managing Editor: Risa Laib
ETBD Editor: Kevin Yip
Avalon Travel Publishing Series Manager: Patrick Collins
Avalon Travel Publishing Project Editor: Madhu Prasher
Copy Editor: Chris Hayhurst
Indexer: Stephen Callahan
Production and Typesetting: Patrick David Barber, Holly McGuire
Research Assistance: Robert Wright
Cover Design: Kari Gim, Laura Mazer
Interior Design: Jane Musser, Laura Mazer, Amber Pirker
Maps and Graphics: David C. Hoerlein, Lauren Mills, Laura VanDeventer, Mike
   Morgenfeld
Front Matter Color Photos: © Julie R. Coen
Front Cover Images: front image, train station, Aveiro © Richard l'Anson/Lonely Planet
   Images; back image: Albufeira © Roberto Soncin Gerometta/Lonely Planet Images

Distributed to the book trade by Publishers Group West, Berkeley, California.